er,

le

itor: Russ Becker

980 by The Benjamin/Cummings Publishing
. Philippines copyright 1980 by The Benjamin/
blishing Company, Inc.

Congress Cataloging in Publication Data

la B
ement of word processing operations.

des index.
Word processing (Office practice)   2.   Office
hent.   I.   Title.
.2.C4   651.7   79–57476
-8053–1759–7

ghij-DO–83210

Benjamin/Cummings Publishing Company, Inc.
7 Sand Hill Road
lo Park, California 94025

Preface

Scope of the Text

As today's offices integrate modern technologies, the responsibilities and tasks performed by their personnel are undergoing extensive changes that require knowledgeable individuals to manage and direct operations and to supervise daily activities.

There is much discussion about merging office technologies—particularly data processing and word processing. Equipment and information processed in the one area frequently overlaps into the other. Regardless of the manner in which a firm organizes various office functions, the raison d'etre is that of *processing information*.

Today's office worker may begin a job in one function or department and depending upon that individual's desires, skills, and objectives, move into an entirely different position, performing tasks requiring new or different skills.

Office workers who are responsible for these changing technologies and operations need to understand and be able to apply management skills to these operations. This text introduces and analyzes the role of those who supervise and manage word processing operations as they fit into this information processing cycle. Its purpose is to instruct the student in each of the specific skills required of a word processing manager or supervisor.

Audience

Word processing and related office technologies offer ever-widening career opportunities for those who are willing to work to achieve the required management and supervisory skills. Those interested in pursuing these opportunities by developing word processing management and supervisory skills might be:

- Personnel already employed in word processing positions, such as managers, supervisors, coordinators, or secretaries.
- College students enrolled in business management, other business majors, or word processing courses.
- Personnel employed in managerial or supervisory positions in firms utilizing or considering the implementation of word processing.

Text Organization

The 19 chapters of the text have been organized in the following manner:

- Introduction.
- Part I: The Word Processing Manager's Roles.
- Part II: Feasibility Studies.
- Part III: Designing the Appropriate Word Processing System.
- Part IV: Implementing the Word Processing System.
- Part V: Implementation.

The first two parts explore the development of and the reasons for the technological changes occurring within offices, as well as the skills required to employ these new technologies. Part III, covering feasibility studies, explains how to collect and summarize data, analyze and design office systems, justify costs, and present the study findings to management.

Part IV discusses the preparations prior to implementing word processing. These include: developing the implementation schedule, structuring and designing the new system, planning personnel alignment, writing job descriptions, staffing, preparing the budget and facilities, writing procedures manuals, and establishing orientation and training programs.

Implementation of a word processing system, examined in Part V, consists of orienting and training users and operating personnel, directing daily operations, and managing the total system. Measurement and control play an important part in continuing operations, as well as encouraging personnel, both operating staff and users, to take advantage of the system's capabilities.

The growth of word processing—the expansion, the development of new systems, and the integration with other office technologies—is one of the most exciting aspects of the field. The challenge of using modern technology to make work more creative and to set achievable objectives offers organizations control over their operations in order to minimize costs while expanding their information processing capabilities. Even more exciting are the challenges word/information processing and modern technology integration offer to those who work in these systems—to direct and plan their own career objectives and to supervise and direct others to become more resourceful in their daily office work.

The text is supplemented by an instructor's resource guide that provides those who teach and direct the training with course outlines, tests, and supplementary information.

Acknowledgments

I would like to thank those who participated in the early reviews: Marcia Anderson, Ron Svedjan, Marybeth Boyle, Shirley Long, Randall Warner, and Mimi Will. In addition, advisors who greatly affected the final development of the text were Cliff Lindsey, Peter Yesne, George Zavidil, Shirley Waterhouse, and Doris Sadovoy. Those of us who have been involved in the development of this text firmly believe Marion Harper's statement, "To manage well is to manage the future. To manage the future is to manage information."

Aptos, California   *Paula B. Cecil*

Contents

Part II
FEASIBILITY STUDIES   37

Chapter 3
Planning the Survey   39

Chapter 4
Collecting and Summarizing Data   61

Chapter 5
An Example of a Feasibility Study—
The Middletown Bank   **97**

Part III
DESIGNING THE APPROPRIATE WORD PROCESSING
SYSTEM   119

Chapter 13
Writing Procedures 309

Chapter 14
Selling the Program—Orientation 325

Chapter 15
Developing Training Programs   **343**

Part V
IMPLEMENTATION   359

Chapter 16
Implementing the New System   **361**

Chapter 17
Managing Operations   **389**

"What is needed is the ability to perceive the crucial patterns among the various bits, pieces, and mountains of information, activities, and events ... the Management Point of View."

CHAPTER 1

Introduction

OVERVIEW

Modern technology offers ever increasing opportunities to automate office activities by means of microcomputers, solid-state electronics, and computerized office equipment. This equipment can increase office productivity with decreased human effort. However, there must be a system of procedures performed and managed by capable office personnel. To operate effectively, this system must be managed, directed, and controlled.

This chapter explains the skills required to manage word processing operations so that the system will achieve the desired objectives of the firm.

OBJECTIVES

After reading the introduction, you will have learned:

1. The background and concept of word processing.
2. The reasons people who are able to manage word processing are needed.
3. The principle of word processing and its implications.
4. The skills required to manage word processing.

BACKGROUND: THE TECHNOLOGICAL REVOLUTION

Exactly what is modern technology? Most of us think of computers, transistors, satellite communications, and today's tiny microscopic computer chips that make it pos-

Quote from Robert L. Katz, *Management of the Total Enterprise* (Englewood Cliffs, N.J.: Prentice-Hall, 1970), p. 9.

sible to use a hand-size calculator to balance our checking accounts or watch live on television the Olympic games being played on the other side of the world.

Beginning in the 1950s, modern technology has automated manufacturing to speed up production and lower costs, reduced the time required to transport goods and people across the world, increased the speed of communicating information from one location to another in microseconds, and increased the speed and amount of information processed by computers to meet whatever challenges mankind could design.

"The computer is today's version of the Old West's Colt .45. It's the great equalizer."[1] Thanks to modern technology, man has taken his first step on the moon; a heart patient can have open-heart surgery and proceed to live an ordinary life; machines can monitor body functions to locate problem areas; and a sports fan can sit comfortably at home and have a closer view of a football play than the fan seated in the stadium.

How has this technology affected modern business? Today's marketing representative can board an airplane; fly across the country; and remove a tiny card from a wallet and project it upon a screen to produce life-size images to illustrate equipment, plants and facilities, statistical tables, and flowcharts.

After witnessing an accident, a police officer may stop and dictate a report from an automobile by talking into a handheld dictation unit. Figure 1–1 shows a portable note taker being used to record a meeting. A service engineer may be servicing a customer when a buzzer sounds from a small device on his or her belt and a voice relays another service call message. The engineer may then step into a phone booth, insert a coin, and dictate information regarding the call just finished before moving to service the waiting customer. Upon returning to the office, a typed copy of the report may be waiting for signature.

A legal secretary may type a final page of a will for a waiting client by keyboarding onto a televisionlike screen while the other pages print out on a separate typewriter (see Figure 1–2). A technician may take a blueprint from a file and transmit a copy over the telephone in a matter of seconds from the originating office in Chicago to an office in Los Angeles.

These are but a few examples of modern technology in operation in today's offices.

CHANGES IN PEOPLE'S LIVES

"At home you will have an earth station on the roof for satellite communication with any other home earth station in the country. Your television set will contain a powerful computer that regulates your house's heating and cooling systems, notifies fire department or police in an emergency, does your taxes, and lets you beat it in a game of chess. Your telephone will be a data entry system

[1] John Fletcher, "The Next Computer Revolution," *Mainliner Magazine*, June 1978, pp. 33–38.

Norelco's pocket size portable Notetaker is useful in the boardroom and in a   **FIGURE 1-1**
private office, because a conference microphone provides an automatic recording
level which brings in every voice clear and sharp for exact transcription.
(Photo courtesy of Philips Business Systems, Inc.)

and calculator. Letters will be typed, orders will be placed, bills will be paid, and files will be searched all by computer."[2]

The above prediction is one of many being made these days to take place no later than the year 2000. Already people are experiencing changes in their private lives resulting from modern technology. One can cook a meal in a matter of minutes in a microwave oven directly from the freezer. Or one can play parlor tennis, polo, pong, and other sports matches on a home television set. It is possible to store a favorite television program on a cassette for later, more convenient viewing. And people can purchase their own small computers at retail outlets to take home and program for private use. All of these are not predictions: they are today's reality. How has this come about? Modern technology has entered our daily lives, both at home and at work.

[2] Ibid., pp. 33–38.

FIGURE 1-2   **The Redactor II features a high-speed printer and a full-page display on which characters are enlarged two-fold. The system can store up to 5000 characters per page. (Photo courtesy of Redactron, a Subsidiary of Burroughs.)**

The Changing Office

These are vastly changing times for those individuals who spend their working hours in offices. From the part-time worker, mail messenger, file clerk, secretary, administrator, department head to top management, office life is changing throughout the world.

Application of this modern technology to the office has been entitled **word processing**, a label created by International Business Machines Corporation in 1969 by a manager in Germany. Originally, the definition referred to originators who dictated over the telephone from different locations in a firm. Requests for repetitive standard letters that were stored on a magnetic tape were recorded over a dictation recorder and transcribed by a secretary, who recorded names and addresses onto another magnetic tape. The secretary then produced the form letters by merging the two tapes (the one containing the stored letter and the one containing the names and addresses) and automatically processing those words to produce an original letter to each person (see Figure 1-3). The secretary was processing the dictator's words to produce the desired document. This idea has expanded because the secretary was able to save a great deal of time by producing these letters much faster than anticipated.

No matter how many times or ways it is defined, word processing is extremely elusive and difficult to explain and understand. Some of the simpler early definitions include (a) communicating one's ideas to another, generally in typewritten form; (b) the process of transmitting one's ideas to the recipient; and (c) the combination of people, procedures, and equipment involved in transmitting ideas to another.

Why is word processing suddenly growing so large and so rapidly? Word processing is expected to expand for the same reason that data processing and factory automation have expanded: to increase productivity while containing or reducing costs.

IBM's MT/ST, which merges addresses on one tape with a letter contained   **FIGURE 1-3**
on the other to produce an original letter to each addressee.
(Photo courtesy of International Business Machines, Inc.)

Word processing is based upon the concept that offices can no longer afford to operate in their traditional manner, mainly because of the tremendous growth in paper volume and associated costs. Growth in worldwide government controls and demands for information have resulted in the need for more and more paper documents.

At the same time, costs of doing business have skyrocketed. What does it cost to operate a business today? One must first pay for the office space, the office furniture, and lighting and electricity. Salaries and wages with accompanying fringe benefits must be met each month. Many companies now offer not only medical insurance, but dental coverage as well. In addition, there are typewriters, calculators, computers and terminals, copiers, telephone equipment, and other equipment such as TWX, Telex, or other communicating/distributing equipment. And, of course, the office personnel must have such supplies as pencils, pens, printed forms, and a large supply of paper.

Whatever an organization needs in order to conduct its operations, one fact is undeniable: all aspects of operating an office today have experienced tremendous inflation, resulting in what may be a profit squeeze. This has forced many firms to take control of their operating costs and see where and how they can lower their internal office operating costs.

Today's businesses are looking at word processing as the solution to the problem. Modern technology in the office is applied to increase productivity of personnel while reducing costs, just as it has for manufacturing, engineering, and processing of data. Imagine the following dialogues taking place:

Arnold Morrison, executive for Mammoth Industries, a large international manufacturing firm, stated recently:

Morrison: Our firm has had three major openings that we have been unable to fill for two months. We have advertised in the newspaper, listed the openings with placement agencies, and informed our office equipment sales representatives that we were seeking personnel with the necessary experience and qualifications for these positions. We have had only a few responses, and none of them met our qualifications.

Response: Exactly what are these positions you can't fill?

Morrison: The most important is that of a Word Processing Manager, and the others are for a Correspondence Supervisor and an Administrative Supervisor. Can you suggest how we can locate qualified people to fill these jobs?

Debbi Lee, a student in business at a community college, is interviewing Audrey McDonald, Word Processing Manager for Mythical Enterprises, Inc.

Debbi: I would like to have a position such as yours. How did you become word processing manager for Mythical?

Audrey: I had been an executive secretary for Mythical for six years. Before that I had worked as an interviewer in the personnel department and for several other companies as a private and an administrative secretary. When Mythical decided to install a word processing system, they interviewed all interested and qualified secretaries in the company, and I was selected.

Debbi: How did you get your training?

Audrey: All of our first word processing equipment was purchased from Microcom Corporation, who sent me to their special supervision/management school in New York for two weeks. They also conducted an office analysis surveying our operations and suggested the most appropriate equipment, which was manufactured by them, of course. After I returned from school they assisted me in setting up our operating procedures and in training our personnel. I never could have done the job without their assistance.

Debbi: How could I prepare myself for such a job? I'm getting out of school at the end of the year. How could I obtain such a job if I had the training?

Audrey: My suggestion to you is to continue with school and learn all you can about word processing.

Debbi: What classes should I take?

Audrey: I understand that our community college teaches word processing concepts and automatic typing and is beginning to teach word processing management and supervision. I would definitely take those courses as well as other business courses such as machine transcription, business English, communications, even data processing. In addition, I would suggest working at least part time in a company with word processing operations.

Debbi: Do you like your job? Are you glad you made the change from being an executive secretary? I would think it would be much harder work with less freedom.

Audrey: I love my job and wouldn't change it for anything, unless it were to take on a higher level management position. I have learned so much and feel as if I still have more to learn. Several of my friends have been promoted from word processing manager to administrative managers in their companies. We have a very strong team spirit at Mythical, largely as a result of the fact that we in word processing serve so many different departments. The only reason I would leave my job would be if I had to move to another city, and then I would seek another job like the one I have.

Mammoth and Mythical may be fictional business firms, but the situations described are factual. More and more firms throughout private industry and government are implementing word processing on a large scale. In order to run these operations, they are discovering that their office personnel must learn new skills. At the same time, individuals seeking office jobs are discovering that they, too, need to learn new skills to obtain the top jobs in modern offices.

THE PRINCIPLE OF WORD PROCESSING

Do not think that word processing simply implies purchasing expensive automated equipment to increase personnel productivity and reduce office costs. Word processing equipment is much more expensive than regular typewriters and pencils and yellow pads of paper. It alone will not reduce rising office costs. Word processing means applying systems management principles and modern technology to the office. In this way, productivity can be increased, costs can be reduced, and organizational objectives can be met according to a specific office situation.

Word processing is a system (*system* most simply being defined as input, processing, and output), and a word processing system can be viewed in this manner. A broader view of a word processing system would include (a) automating office equipment, (b) training personnel in the required skills and working as a part of a team, (c) implementing efficient workflow procedures, and (d) managing (planning, organizing, directing, measuring, and controlling) the operations.

WORD PROCESSING IMPLICATIONS

Word processing, as originally conceived, implied the processing of a person's ideas (words) by dictating into recording machines which rapidly capture those ideas so that they can be typed efficiently by using automated typewriters. Today, because of the many equipment peripherals and capabilities being invented as a result of modern technology, word processing has expanded and may encompass many other operations.

DIFFERENT WORD PROCESSING STRUCTURES

For Mythical, word processing consists of the **centralization** of typing, including reports, proposals, charts, statistical information, and daily correspondence, which means a method of organizing which concentrates decision-making at the head of the group. **Correspondence secretaries** (sometimes called word processing specialists) produce this typing on word processing typewriters as shown in Figure 1-4. **Administra-**

FIGURE 1-4   Typed copy can be quickly edited and printed out error-free with the Xerox display
typing system with modular components that can be grouped into combinations
to fit most word processing requirements. The full-page unit in the foreground
can show 66 lines of text, each 102 characters wide. Its electronic control
allows the secretary to move the pointer in any direction on the screen.
The display typewriter in the background features a 24-character screen.
(Photo courtesy of Xerox Corporation.)

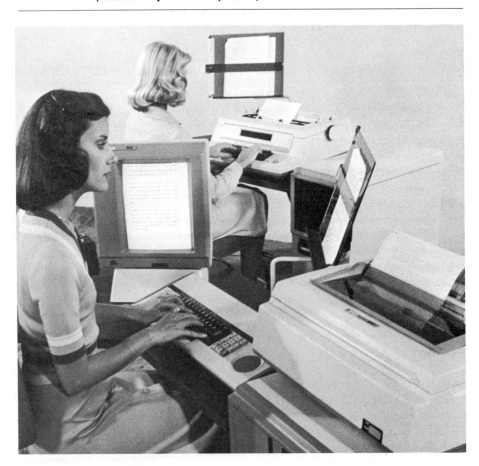

tive secretaries serve departments covering three floors in two buildings and handle projects and phones, process the mail, file, and make copies; some dictate over the telephone to the **correspondence center** (a group of secretaries who type documents).

At Mammoth, word processing consists of several specialized **work groups** located near the word originators (marketing staff, engineers, purchasing agents, accountants). One group consists of correspondence secretaries as illustrated in Figure 1–5, while the other group is made up of administrative secretaries. The correspondence secretaries perform all the typing functions; the others perform administrative functions and special projects for the executives and their staff.

Secretaries employed at Robbins, Logan, Garcia, & Cicero, a medium-size law firm in Cincinnati, Ohio, still work for the same attorneys as they did before implementing word processing. The difference is that each secretary has a word processing typewriter and dictation transcriber, allowing faster and easier transcription and production of documents.

Vicom Enterprises, an international organization, implemented word processing five years ago. Since that time, they have added many sophisticated elements to their

---

The work group pictured uses the Vydec dual-disk text editors and the autoprint   **FIGURE 1-5**
option on their printer. Autoprint allows operators to leave the Vydec units
unattended while it automatically types form letters with variable addresses and
text, prints and collates multipage documents, inserts standard headers and
footers, paginates, adjusts margins, and adds page numbers.
(Photo courtesy of Vydec, Inc.)

information processing system. Their word processing begins when originators dictate their documents over telephones to central recorders or into portable handheld dictation units. Word processing specialists next transcribe the dictation on word processing typewriters that record the information onto floppy disks. Some of the documents produced (after signature, which may follow several revision cycles on the word processors) are communicated into a central computer, while other documents are distributed to administrative secretaries. The secretaries then reproduce several copies on an office copier or have large volumes reproduced on an automated duplicator. A records processing specialist creates **microfiche** (filmed microimages) copies from documents transmitted to the computer and stores the microfiche in the central records processing department. Other documents recorded onto magnetic media are edited on a **CRT** (cathode ray tube) screen preparatory to printing final copy on phototypesetters. Some documents are distributed from the word processing recording by communicating directly to another such unit or through the company's TWX and Telex network to other company offices located in cities across the country.

Each of the above described organizations has a word processing system. Some have been installed longer than others; some have merged several operations along with the first dictate/produce phase of word processing. Many will be making more changes as their systems grow older and the people grow with them. Modern technology automatically creates new skills, and people need to learn those skills to coexist with modern technology.

No matter how you see it, word processing requires one basic fundamental: workers performing the work must have the knowledge, technical expertise, and the attitudes to make the application of modern science succeed in the office.

WHY WORD PROCESSING MANAGEMENT TRAINING IS NEEDED

As pointed out by Arnold Morrison and Audrey McDonald, more and more firms are implementing word processing systems. As a result, people with the ability to manage and implement word processing are needed to fill these requirements. It is up to the schools, colleges, and industry to provide this training to office and business workers and students preparing for modern office jobs. It is necessary through education to fill the gap that currently exists between unskilled people who are unable to obtain the positions they would like and firms that have the openings but are unable to fill them with trained personnel.

WHY FIRMS NEED GOOD WORD PROCESSING MANAGERS

Good management is the key to successfully developing a word processing system. Beginning and continuing success of word processing relies upon skillful management. A well-managed word processing system aims to solve a firm's paper-processing problems and meet predetermined objectives by using personnel productively while reducing or containing costs.

FUNCTIONS OF THE WORD PROCESSING MANAGER

Table 1–1 illustrates the following five basic functions of the management process:

1. Planning (what is to be accomplished)
2. Controlling (so that plans can be achieved or replanned)
3. Staffing (with personnel to do the work)
4. Organizing (activities to be performed)
5. Leading (to get the desired action or results by motivating, informing, coordinating, and supervising)

These five functions as they relate to managing word processing break down into 14 required skills. While identifying each of these skills, keep in mind that the most important element in business and management is the human element. It is the framework within which the system must work, and any formula for a word processing system operates through its people. No matter how small or how large the system, it depends upon the people to make it work.

SKILLS REQUIRED TO MANAGE WORD PROCESSING

The 14 specific skills required of the word processing manager or supervisor are the ability to:

1. Comprehend the management or supervisory role.
2. Conduct an orientation meeting to explain word processing.

The Five Basic Functions of the Word Processing Manager Broken Down into Basic Skills   TABLE 1-1

Planning	Comprehending the role
	Making a feasibility study
	Designing a new system and selecting equipment
	Keeping current
Controlling	Controlling and coordinating
	Measuring productivity
Staffing	Writing job descriptions and selecting and training personnel
Organizing	Summarizing current system
	Developing procedures for the system
	Developing training materials
Leading	Conducting orientation meeting prior to study
	Presenting survey results
	Guiding and developing personnel
	Communicating with management, users, and staff

3. Plan, organize, and conduct a feasibility study.
4. Summarize that system, designating the problem areas.
5. Design an improved system.
6. Present the results of the survey and proposed new system to top management and company personnel, including middle management, work originators, and staff.
7. Develop working procedures for the new system.
8. Develop training materials for company personnel, including management, work originators, and word processing personnel.
9. Design word processing job descriptions, then select and train operating and using personnel.
10. Control and coordinate operations.
11. Measure the system's productivity and ability to accomplish preset objectives with ongoing evaluations of operational status.
12. Guide, advise, and develop personnel and continually be aware of attitudes of workers who seek job satisfaction.
13. Coordinate and communicate with top management, intermediate management, and other departments, using personnel to get feedback and to keep up-to-date on fluctuations in workloads.
14. Keep current regarding new developments in technology and management.

This text mainly emphasizes the management and coordination of the major components of word processing systems: equipment, procedures, and personnel. From the original consideration of implementing word processing to continual monitoring and planning for future growth and change, this text is directed towards the problems faced by the person who is responsible for managing the situation.

SUMMARY

Modern technology in the form of computerized office equipment makes it possible for offices to increase their productivity just as computers have increased processing of data for scientific and business purposes. The application of this computerized technology to the office is termed word processing, since information in the office is processed in the form of words. By using word processing, firms can reduce their operating costs and use their personnel much more efficiently. This is important because of the necessity to lower or control the inflationary costs of internal operations.

In order for word processing to perform this function, it needs to be managed just as any other business operation. No matter how it is structured, whether centralized or decentralized, it needs to be managed by a person who has the necessary skills to make the system operate efficiently to meet the firm's word processing objectives.

Word processing is a fairly new field, and therefore few people have those skills necessary to manage its operations. The word processing manager needs to be able to apply the five management skills (planning, controlling, staffing, organizing, and leading) which encompass the following:

*   Comprehending the role of a manager.
*   Planning, organizing, and conducting a feasibility study.

- Conducting orientation meetings.
- Summarizing data from studies and designing improved systems.
- Presenting survey results and proposed new systems to management and other members of the firm.
- Developing procedures and training programs.
- Designing job descriptions and staffing personnel.
- Controlling, monitoring, and coordinating operations.
- Directing personnel.
- Coordinating and communicating with top management, other departments, users, and operating staff.

REVIEW QUESTIONS

1. Give four examples of the way modern technology has affected manufacturing, engineering, communications, and people's personal lives from the early 1950s to the present.
2. Give three reasons why office jobs are being changed as a result of modern technology.
3. Give three reasons why a firm might be unwise *not* to consider word processing.
4. What is meant by the principle of word processing? Explain it from the simple definition to a broader one. What does it mean to you?
5. Describe two kinds of word processing structures.
6. List three objectives that firms have in implementing word processing.
7. What is the most important element of word processing? Why?
8. List six skills needed to successfully manage word processing.

DISCUSSION QUESTIONS

1. Discuss the relationship between and implications of data and word processing.
2. Compare the ways in which a job as a secretary would differ in a firm with and without word processing.
3. Why would a person want to learn word processing skills?
4. Why would a firm decide to purchase word processing equipment? Discuss the impact this has upon the rest of the office.
5. Describe what you would expect to gain in your firm if you, as its president, decided to implement word processing.

PART I

THE WORD PROCESSING MANAGER'S ROLES

Since the importance of word processing to the organization has only recently been acknowledged (since the 1970s), the word processing manager is a fairly new member of the management team yet is expected to be an expert in the field of word processing.

This section discusses the role of the word processing manager, the skills and knowledge required to adequately fulfill this role, and the differences between managing and supervising word processing.

"A good manager is able to use people, things, and ideas effectively."

CHAPTER 2

Responsibilities of Word Processing Managers and Supervisors

OVERVIEW

Offices are places where people perform work, specifically paperwork, in order to accomplish jobs, which may be in the area of law, medicine, insurance, banking, education, government, or some other kind of business. Offices that implement word processing expect the word processing manager to manage the paperwork operations. What are the roles of the word processing manager in performing a job? How do they differ from those of a supervisor? This chapter explains the different roles a word processing manager plays while carrying out the duties of the job.

OBJECTIVES

After completing this chapter, you should be able to describe the responsibilities of a word processing manager or supervisor for:

1. Conducting a feasibility study.
2. Selecting equipment.
3. Planning the working environment.
4. Implementing control.
5. Directing operations.

6. Staffing.
7. Maintaining efficient operations, including measurement and control.
8. Keeping current and flexible.
9. Coordinating and reporting.
10. Communicating.

RESPONSIBILITIES OF THE WORD PROCESSING MANAGER

The role of the word processing manager is that of planner, administrator, and leader. The manager delegates the supervising and carrying out of daily operations to the person next in line, who, in the management of word processing, is usually the word processing supervisor. In those firms where there is no position bearing this title, such as in small companies or word processing operations, the person to whom these responsibilities are delegated might be the coordinator; lead secretary; or senior word processing, correspondence, or administrative secretary.

The word processing manager has the responsibility, authority, and accountability for being the ultimate word processing decision-maker. Just exactly what does this encompass?

Design

The word processing manager is accountable for the overall design of the word processing system, including the operating structure (whether it is centralized or decentralized), workflow, and working procedures.

Although the word processing manager may not actually design the system, the manager is the one who approves the system. An analyst or technician may have drawn up the office structure, designed the workflow, and planned the procedures; the word processing manager is accountable for them.

Equipment Selection

In most cases, the word processing manager relies upon the advice and technical expertise of word processing specialists and consultants in matching the firm's needs to the most appropriate equipment; however, the ultimate decision of equipment selection is made by the word processing manager.

The selection of word processing equipment usually starts with dictation equipment: individual desktop or portable units and telephone or wired systems, including message recorders which allow company personnel to phone in their dictation while away from the office. (See Figure 2-1.)

The most important equipment to be selected for the word processing operation is the production equipment: typewriters, memory or intelligent typewriters, stand-alone **text editors** (word processing typewriters that can add, delete, correct, and change format before automatic playout of finished documents), **shared-** (or distributed) **logic systems** (systems in which several keyboard terminals use the same memory

FIGURE 2-1

Transcriptionists at Mills Hospital in San Mateo, California, are using Sony transcribers. Each of the four Networks (Sony's computerized central dictating systems) seen in the background holds a 24-cassette front-loading tape carousel that accepts 18 hours of continuous dictation. (Photo courtesy of Sony Corporation, Business Products Division.)

and processing powers of one computer), or computer text-editing systems. Figure 2–2 shows an information processor.

Word processing typewriters are frequently called **word processors**, demonstrating their key role in the word processing cycle. Since IBM introduced the **MT/ST** (magnetic tape selectric typewriter) in 1964, the range in capabilities of word processing typing equipment has grown unbelievably, making the selection of the right word processing typing system for a firm exceptionally complex. IBM has held as high as 80 to 90 percent of this marketplace and is generally regarded as its leader. The number of other firms manufacturing and marketing word processing typing equipment grows daily, even though some of the early companies that competed with IBM are no longer around. The majority of large office equipment manufacturing firms have joined the

---

FIGURE 2-2   **This IBM information processor features a functional display, high-density diskette storage, 96-character multilingual keyboard, and a high-speed impact printer. (Photo courtesy of International Business Machines, Inc.)**

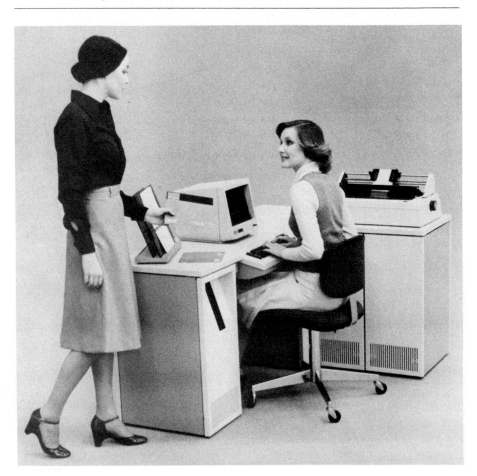

competition. Large firms offering a small or extensive selection of production equipment include Xerox, Lanier, Wang, 3M Company, Burroughs, NBI, Vydec, Raytheon, and Addressograph/Multigraph. Not only is the number of firms growing, but the families of word processing typing equipment are also growing. Very few vendors offer only one piece of equipment. For example, one company has a single standalone unit, two simplified versions of it at lower costs, and a small shared-logic system. When this system is not large enough to handle the number of keyboards required (or the expanded volume), the company offers a larger system which can consist of ten keyboards and several printers (see Figure 2-3).

The person responsible for selecting word processing equipment needs to have up-to-date knowledge, which requires considerable time and effort. The word processing manager also needs to devote time to perfecting other management skills important to the job. The word processing manager therefore is frequently wise to rely upon the advice and technical expertise of a consultant or equipment specialist while keeping aware of current equipment.

Other office equipment selected might include filing and storage media (particularly **microfilm** and **microfiche**), copying and duplicating machines, communications to other word processing typing equipment or computers or by means of **facsimiles**, TWX or Telex systems (many word processing typewriters can be read into TWX or Telex), optical character readers, and phototypesetting machines. Figure 2-4 shows a word processor producing communications by means of Telex.

Other Equipment and Supply Decisions

In addition to being accountable for the selection of the word processing equipment, the word processing manager is responsible for ensuring that adequate and appropriate supplies are ordered. This may include preprinted forms, **fan-folded** continuous paper

---

System 5, Wang's lowest priced CRT-based standalone text processor is available   FIGURE 2-3
in two models, which use totally compatible media—distinct advantages for those
who may expand their systems as their requirements grow.
(Photo courtesy of Wang Laboratories, Inc.)

FIGURE 2-4   The Telex tape option allows users of Vydec systems to communicate through the worldwide network of 250,000 teletypewriter terminals. Messages stored on Vydec disks can be punched onto paper tape for entry into domestic and international, switched, or private-wire teletypewriter services, eliminating time-consuming rekeying of text onto tape. (Photo courtesy of Vydec, Inc.)

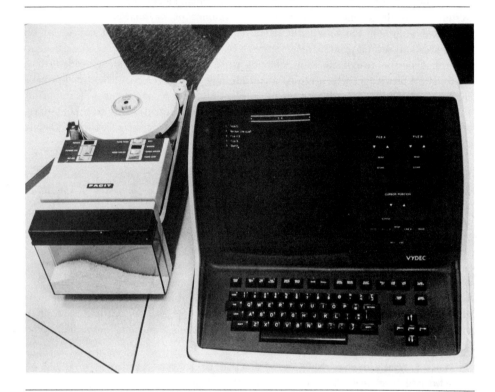

(paper supplied in flat, folded form) for the word processing typewriters, typing ribbons, selection of print styles, ample storage media for the equipment. The task might also include having a current reference library of dictionaries, suppliers, and word processing publications.

Working Environment

The word processing manager is responsible for ensuring that the selected location meets the physical requirements for the planned operations, allowing adequate space, convenience to users, and appropriate working conditions. Although the manager probably seeks the advice of consultants and experts, the responsibility rests on word processing management to make sure the working environment meets the standards and requirements necessary for a successful system. Elements to consider are layout, design, lighting, sound reduction, ventilation, carpeting, decorating, and convenient document pickup and delivery. Accessibility to the word processing staff by the users is important also. Although some word processing centers discourage the users (or principals) from visiting the center, the trend is to encourage communication between the originators and those who produce their work. Figure 2-5 demonstrates the benefits of a well-planned production area: visual and acoustical privacy and easily accessible components.

Implementation Control

The word processing manager is accountable for implementing and controlling the word processing system. This includes preparing, planning, launching, and directing word processing operations. Implementation activities include scheduling document production to meet deadline requirements, developing contingency plans for exceptions to the usual routines, and planning continuation programs for both operations and training.

Continuation operations means upgrading equipment to meet growth requirements, increase productivity, and adjust workflow procedures to meet changing situations. Continuation operations might also mean adding new departments or projects to the present production schedule.

Directing

The word processing manager sets the stage and is responsible for directing the policies and strategy of the word processing program. If the word processing system encompasses origination and production of documents, these operations are directed by the word processing manager. When operations such as communications and distribution are handled by word processing, the word processing manager is also accountable for setting these operational policies and for determining any necessary strategy.

Once the Word Processing Department handles another internal service operation such as filing and storage, the word processing manager becomes accountable for directing these services as well.

Herman Miller's Action Office open plan. (Photo courtesy of   **FIGURE 2-5**
Action Office System, Herman Miller, Inc.)

Staffing

It is up to the word processing manager to make the ultimate personnel decisions. This includes developing the specific word processing job descriptions, planning what tasks are to be performed, determining what skills are required, and analyzing the general picture of each word processing position. Sometimes the word processing manager may rely upon the advice from experts and word processing consultants in order to make these decisions.

The word processing manager is accountable for screening and selecting all word processing personnel and for conducting the internal training programs for managers, users or principals, and the word processing staff.

Efficient Operations

It is up to the word processing manager to set the efficiency standards for word processing and see that they are met. This includes selecting departments or document projects that word processing will serve, anticipating the daily volume and turnaround time, and planning the project scheduling.

Once the planned schedule is published, the word processing manager is accountable for maintaining feedback to determine how well the system is meeting its schedule and planned objectives.

Currency and Flexibility

A part of the maintenance of the system by the word processing manager requires measuring the results achieved against the objectives and making adjustments where necessary. A good manager is flexible in adjusting to emergency situations while meeting the daily planned turnaround time. This implies building a system of cooperation and understanding among the users so that they can adjust to being bumped when emergencies occur.

The word processing manager is expected to be aware of changing conditions or future expectations so that the word processing system can meet any situation.

Another important responsibility of the word processing manager is keeping up-to-date on a professional basis with other word processing activities. The word processing manager may be active in local professional organizations, subscribe to national word processing publications, and stay in touch with various vendors in order to keep current with changes occurring in techniques and technology. Being aware of ways in which word processing can expand its capabilities to benefit the organization and increase its efficiency is one of the word processing manager's major responsibilities.

In addition, the word processing manager needs to keep current in such areas as:

- New methods of organizing which may benefit the firm.
- Better training techniques and tools to improve job performance.
- New proven techniques of directing personnel in their work, including personnel communications and motivation.
- Improved, simplified, or more comprehensive methods of measuring and control-

ling the word processing production to meet established productivity and human behavior goals.
- Improved planning techniques to expand the capabilities of word processing.

Coordinating

The word processing manager is an important member of the management team, not of top management but of those departments responsible for maintaining the efficient internal operations of the organization. The word processing manager is therefore accountable for coordinating with other service department managers for the purpose of achieving organizational objectives. For instance, if the Word Processing Department produces typewritten documents which next are sent to the Duplication Department where large volumes of high-quality documents are produced on high-speed duplicators, the word processing manager must meet the Duplication Department's deadlines. In other words, the departments are working together to meet the organization's daily deadlines and turnaround requirements, which are delegated to the supervisor responsible for the continuing operation routine.

Reporting

In order for an organization to monitor its various operations, it must have an effective monitoring system. Word processing management is responsible for reporting to three levels: top management; peer management; and the working staff, which includes the supervisors and word processing operating personnel.

Because of its unique role in the internal operations of an organization, word processing is a key link. It is therefore important that the word processing manager set up and direct an effective communications network throughout the organization as well as within the word processing system.

Communications

The word processing manager is responsible for directing a system which will produce typewritten documents efficiently and effectively for the entire organization: top management, middle management, working staff, and those who create documents to be typewritten. It can therefore be extremely valuable to distribute communications frequently throughout the organization to advise everyone of the effectiveness of word processing for the company. Such communications would include news bulletins; status reports; and memos informing personnel of achievements, successes, outstanding performance, or unusual solutions to unique situations or problems. Good communication between word processing and its users can often mean the difference between failure or success of the system.

Communications Roles of Word Processing Managers

Word processing managers communicate not only with others within their organization but with their customers as well, i.e., with those whose work they produce. Therefore, active communication between the word processing manager and the customer is very important to the success of the firm.

The word processing manager needs to be a well-organized and businesslike professional. A manager who is disorganized and inefficient is not apt to convince customers to do business with his or her company. The manager needs to assume various roles to project a successful image.

Salesperson   One of the most important early roles of the word processing manager is selling prospective customers on word processing. To do this, the manager must be able to describe the system clearly, outline its advantages, and explain the benefits of using it. Presenting an active illustration can be most successful. For example, a lawyer who dictated a legal complaint which generally had to be revised was asked by the word processing manager to give that complaint to the word processing secretary for typing. After the attorney revised the first version, the secretary made the revisions and returned the document within a few minutes. The attorney was amazed. It had usually taken much longer to type the document, since the secretary formerly had to retype all the marked up pages, not just the changes. The lawyer expressed satisfaction by informing other attorneys of the time saved and helped the manager sell them on using word processing for their benefit.

Service Representative   Good marketing representatives will drop in on customers frequently to assure that they are satisfied with their products. They know they may not be in the market to buy, but.they service the account to promote goodwill. They know the value of goodwill. It is difficult to criticize someone who goes out of his or her way to perform whatever services are required. A word processing manager who makes it a point to drop in on customers (principals) to check with them to see if the work they receive is meeting their standards will be respected and accepted. Many managers have the principals take the work directly to the secretaries and have the secretaries deliver the work, primarily to achieve active open communication. In this way, the customer can build up confidence in the system and gently make suggestions which the secretary might not receive without this communication.

Periodic meetings of the word processing staff should provide opportunities for the secretaries to compare notes on customer reactions and comments so that everyone is aware of what is being said about the word processing system.

Listener   No matter how service-oriented the system may be, there will be times when customers express complaints. The word processing manager needs to listen to these complaints, respond appropriately, and establish policies when necessary. Most of all, the manager should set a positive tone rather than one that is argumentative or antagonistic.

Supplier of Information   Occasionally the customers have to be told that they are in error. The manager needs to guide the staff in resolving the problems caused by the principals by informing those in error of the right way to use the system. The operator might attach a production evaluation form to the document being returned to the originator. A check mark can indicate cases in which the secretary was slowed down by lack of instructions, poor instructions, or poor input. If recurring poor input causes problems, the supervisor should visit those principals who are chronic misusers of word processing and tactfully explain the problems and subsequent results.

Tour Guide   The manager is frequently visited by marketing representatives from word processing equipment and supply vendors, teachers and classes, and other who would like to see the firm's word processing system in action. Often these visits can interrupt the work of the manager and occasionally of the staff. Because these visits may be important to the manager and the firm, they should be handled professionally. Although it is necessary for the word processing manager to keep up-to-date with the industry, at the same time, work should not be interrupted. Arrangements should be made so that meetings take place at locations convenient for all and are scheduled to cause the least amount of interference with operations. Most supervisors schedule visits from other firms' representatives and teachers and classes at times when the work is slow or in a way in which they will not interfere with important work deadlines. Some supervisors do not allow many visitors because of the need for confidentiality or the possibility of interference with the work schedule.

Coordinator   As a member of the service management team, the word processing manager needs to develop a team relationship with the other service departments such as the print shop and the communications or mailroom. Scheduling needs to be arranged to coordinate with those departments in order to meet the firm's or principal's deadlines. When dealing with scheduling and the other departments, the manager should communicate well ahead of time so that the other manager is not presented with a last-minute deadline. Communicating should occur regularly, not just during problem situations.

WORD PROCESSING AS THE KEY TO A FIRM'S EFFECTIVE COMMUNICATIONS

Because word processing produces (and sometimes distributes) documents, executives, managers, staff, and other originators depend upon word processing as the key link in the firm's communications. Therefore, the word processing manager needs to continually seek methods to improve communications for the firm.

The word processing manager is responsible for the control of the word processing organization and thus is the key link in the word processing communications chain. Because the function of word processing is to produce documents for the unit or firm it supports, the manager handles the complete workflow from input to output of those documents. In this process, the manager directs the system of production, which includes analyzing work, striving to continue efficient production and reporting, and communicating the status of the production effort to users and to others to whom this is important.

Methods of Communicating

A person in a business organization needs to understand the language of the business in order to avoid mistakes, misunderstandings, wasted effort, and inefficiencies. Word processing managers are responsible for the communication devices used in their organization and for analyzing and improving those devices.

Communications may be spoken, written, or active. Face-to-face (or spoken) communication takes place when people are conversing with one another. Written communication is the most formal and carries the most impact, because it becomes one's official statement about a matter. Active communication, or the way people act, can be more important than the words people say.

Spoken   Spoken communication in organizations can occur during informational discussions, formal interviews and evaluations, staff meetings, and training sessions. Word processing managers use group spoken communications to develop team spirit, share ideas and suggestions, solve problems, and establish group identity. Formal spoken individual communications occur during evaluations and interviews, while informal ones may occur at any time. Telephone communications are very important and are frequently misunderstood. A good way to assure accurate telephone communication is for the listener to repeat the information received.

Written   Written communications in firms may include correspondence, schedules, reports, and bulletins. Reports are one of the most important in word processing, since management relies upon regular reports to make plans and decisions. Schedules are also very important, since the staff, users, and various departments depend upon the word processing schedules to know the status of their work. Schedules must be kept up-to-date by the word processing supervisor so that the work can be handled on time. News bulletins are another good written communications tool by which word processing can inform members of the firm what word processing is doing, how, and why. Other documents used by word processing for communication purposes are progress reports, minutes of meetings, agendas, evaluations, and summaries.

Written communications might also include publicity releases such as weekly status reports, schedule boards, memos, or announcements of special events, directives, and procedures forms and manuals. Communications between employees within an organization is of vital interest to the well being of the organization and its word processing.

The U.S. Air Force distributes monthly reports indicating the amount of work accomplished each month by word processing, the status of the workload (jobs on hand), overtime, machine down time, and comments from supervisors regarding special situations.

Other forms of written communications in firms are route sheets which follow a job from one department to another, visible card files to keep track of progress of jobs, dispatching or peg boards, load charts, and progress charts. Figure 2-6 is an example of a document used to communicate information.

Active   Word processing emphasizes team spirit and the ability to work happily with others. The overall attitude of an individual greatly influences a person's career

WORD PROCESSING JOB CONTROL DOCUMENT

No. **0156**

ORIGINAL MS COPY

Originator _____ Phone _____

Department _____

Title of Job _____ Hold Media Until _____

Date Submitted _____ Date Due _____

Instructions   No. **0156**

PAPER:	PITCH:	SPACING:	HARD COPY:
☐ Letterhead	☐ 10(pica)	☐ Single	☐ Draft
☐ Bond	☐ 12(elite)	☐ Double	☐ Final
☐ Other	☐ Proportional	☐ 1½	☐ Justify

PRODUCTION COUNT COPY

Special Instructions _____

_____

Variable Inserts

Name _____ Address _____

Variables 1. _____ 2. _____

3. _____ 4. _____

Signature _____ Copies to _____

Job Classification

GENERATION:	INPUT:	CATEGORY:
☐ Original	☐ Long hand	☐ Correspondence
☐ Revision	☐ Dictation	☐ Text
	☐ Hard copy	☐ Statistical
	☐ Edited copy	☐ Forms
		☐ Prerecorded

DOCUMENT CONTROL COPY

Typist Data   No. **0156**

Media No. _____ Reference No. _____

Margins _____ Tabs _____ Operator _____

Production Control Information

Time in _____ Time Out _____ No. Pages _____

Time Started _____ Time Completed _____ Total Processing Time _____ opportunities in the firm. It is therefore up to the word processing manager to encourage active communication in the word processing department. By conducting the department in a businesslike manner, the word processing manager sets the tone for the operating staff.

Positive communications with the three groups with whom the word processing manager communicates—management, clients, and staff—are important to the success of that manager and of word processing operations. Such communications may be one-on-one or group communications, such as informal get-togethers and planned meetings.

Formal group communications in which the word processing manager participates may be orienting, selling, or training. Orientation, training, and followup group communication sessions require careful planning and organizing to be effective. Preparing word processing group presentations is covered in Chapter 14.

Examples of active group communications might include attending meetings with other managers, management, and the staff. During meetings with other managers, word processing managers need to be actively interested and cooperative. This may help to convince those who are reluctant to accept word processing to become willing to give it a try and possibly to become supporters.

A word processing manager should project interest in the firm's well-being and a willingness to go more than half way in working with other departments and clients. At all times, the word processing manager should demonstrate professionalism, including such qualities as organization, confidence, and the ability to manage the job.

Communications Tips

It is important to remember to offer help and make suggestions, select the appropriate time to communicate, be prepared for impending emergencies, be tactful, and admit a mistake when you are wrong. By serving, the word processing manager establishes a feeling of cooperation and flexibility while at the same time managing a well-organized system of procedures and schedules. Other managers respect a manager in control but like to think that adjustments can be made to meet their emergency requirements, too.

Listening and informing helps the word processing manager respond to problems and complaints from clients and at the same time advise them how they can help improve the system.

Communications need to be maintained with visitors, including marketing representatives who frequently help the word processing manager maintain currency in the rapidly changing technology. Other visitors the manager needs to know how to handle are teachers and personnel from schools or other firms seeking to learn how their word processing works in their system. If these visits are important to the firm, they need to be scheduled so that they do not interfere with efficient operations. A word processing manager reflects attitudes externally as well and needs to be keenly aware of word processing's active communications with outsiders.

Internal communications with other service departments need to be developed and occur regularly, not just at deadline crunch times when the word processing manager needs them.

THE WORD PROCESSING MANAGER AND FEASIBILITY STUDIES

The early part of this chapter described the word processing manager as the person responsible for the decision-making of the word processing system, including selecting the design and equipment, writing job descriptions, hiring personnel, and managing all of the ingredients of a word processing system. In many cases, however, the analysis of the present system, generally described as a feasibility study, is not made by the word processing manager.

How a Firm Comes To Implement Word Processing

When organizations realize that they need and want to improve their present method of producing documents, or method of processing words, they usually consider word processing. This may be a result of competing with or observing that other firms performing the same kind of business have increased their personnel productivity and are able to process their work faster, at considerably lower costs, or with better quality or have solved problems similar to theirs through word processing. These firms want to know if the same results can be achieved by them. For example, many law firms were early users of word processing equipment, and some have well-organized and efficient word processing systems.

Word processing has become known as the modern method to conduct office operations, mainly because one firm learns from another how it has increased its efficiency or productivity by using word processing. The word spreads throughout that particular kind of business and among other business enterprises.

The same can be said for word processing in many large firms and industries. As an example, medical clinics and large hospitals have had medical transcription centers for years and have had to turn to dictation equipment to replace longhand in order to meet their critical deadlines. Another example is the insurance industry. (See Figure 2-7.) Because of the demand for more and more paperwork, the insurance business was a pioneer in word processing systems, mainly using correspondence centers to produce the high volume of necessary daily documents. Large manufacturing companies with engineering documents, marketing proposals, and heavy volumes of daily correspondence were also early implementers of word processing systems.

How a Firm Prepares for Word Processing

In many instances, a feasibility study was formerly made by an outside vendor to determine whether word processing would improve their operations. After the study was completed and the firm decided to implement the system, management (frequently with the advice of the vendor) selected an executive secretary or some other employee to become its word processing manager. That individual was expected to take over the system planned and designed by the vendor. In such cases, the word processing manager did not have the original responsibility for the system's design and

---

**FIGURE 2-7   The word processing supervisor at Blue Cross/Blue Shield of Oklahoma installed
a Sony network dictation system. (Photo courtesy of Business Products Division.)**

---

plan. But once someone was selected to take over the word processing manager's job, the responsibility to plan and design rested upon his or her shoulders.

Currently, the same situation may still apply: the word processing manager may not be the one to make the study, design the system, select the equipment, plan procedures, or perhaps even select the personnel. But once selected and placed in the position, the word processing manager is responsible for the success of the system.

In some cases, a firm may hire someone or promote someone from within the firm into that position and expect that person to do everything that has been prescribed in this chapter: design the new system, select equipment and personnel, plan the jobs and procedures, and prepare to run the system. Or the firm may select someone to be the project manager of the survey who will handle all the original planning and decision-making for the new system (if indeed there is to be a new system) and then choose someone else to be the word processing manager.

Other firms may hire outside consultants to make the feasibility study and design the new system, its jobs, and procedures. The system is then turned over to the person selected to be the word processing manager.

In conclusion, the word processing manager ultimately is responsible for the management of the system, whether or not that person was originally involved in the development of the word processing system. Frequently the word processing manager will then delegate to technical experts such functions as office analysis and work measurement. In other words, the technical expert on dictation equipment might recommend the most appropriate dictation system; the production equipment specialist might make that equipment recommendation, and so forth. The word processing manager will depend upon specialists for their expert advice in making the right decisions.

In analyzing volume and applications when preparing to expand word processing and add additional departments or projects, the word processing manager may not be the one to make the analyses. Rather, systems analysts may conduct the analysis, evaluate the results, and design the new system. The word processing manager then may act upon recommendations of the analyst to make decisions.

The next chapter describes how Middletown Bank decided who should investigate the feasibility of word processing and how they proceeded.

SUMMARY

The word processing manager plans, administers, and delegates the supervising of the operations to the supervisor or the person next in line in the organization.

The word processing manager is the ultimate decision-maker for the following tasks:

- Designing the word processing system.
- Selecting equipment, although this may be determined with the advice of internal specialists and technicians or outside consultants.
- Determining the working environment, including location, space, equipment, supplies, and lighting.
- Directing the overall planning and control from the overview to specific operating procedures.
- Directing the word processing program.
- Staffing the personnel (including the job structure plan), developing job descriptions, and selecting operating personnel and promoting their career development.
- Operating efficiently and meeting the objectives set by management and the design of the word processing system.
- Coordinating and communicating with the users, other service departments, management, and the operating staff.
- Keeping up-to-date with changing technologies and other influential factors in the field and maintaining flexibility in adapting to changing needs and environmental factors.
- Reporting to top management, middle management, users, other service departments, and to the operating staff.

These responsibilities of the word processing manager reflect the five activities of a manager: planning, controlling, organizing, staffing, and leading.

Communications between word processing and its users can mean the difference between the success or failure of the system. Therefore, the word processing manager's spoken, written, and active communications within the firm are exceedingly important.

The word processing manager needs to communicate a professional, objective demeanor, continually selling the benefits of word processing and serving the users as special customers. The word processing manager should be tactful and considerate toward word processing users and operating staff.

The word processing manager needs to develop effective written communications as well as demonstrate a professional demeanor during face-to-face and active communications. Written communications are important because they become one's statements of policy and procedures, as well as a means of informing others of the status of operations. Spoken and active communicating exchanges occur daily, and both affect and reflect the spirit and morale of the word processing staff in its role within the organization.

The word processing manager may not always be the person who conducts a firm's feasibility studies. A firm may hire outside analysts or consultants, use internal systems analysts, or use a word processing equipment vendor to perform its feasibility studies.

Frequently a firm may conduct a feasibility study and, after the new system has been designed, select the person to be the word processing manager. Sometimes the person selected for this position is presently an executive or administrative secretary or supervisor within the firm. Other times someone is hired from outside the firm.

Even though the word processing manager may not have conducted the feasibility study, he or she is responsible for the successful implementation of the system and its continuing operations.

REVIEW QUESTIONS

1. Name five examples of equipment the word processing manager might select.
2. What considerations might the word processing manager use to decide what would be the most appropriate environmental conditions for word processing operations?
3. What is the most important equipment selection to be made in word processing? Why is this most important?
4. What other kinds of equipment might be handled by word processing and therefore be the word processing manager's responsibility to select?
5. Name three implementation responsibilities of the word processing supervisor.
6. In what ways does the word processing manager become flexible?
7. Name one of the word processing manager's major responsibilities which reflects on the word processing system's capabilities. Why is this important to the success and growth of the system?
8. What are the reporting responsibilities of a word processing manager? How can they be carried out?
9. Name three reasons which might lead to a firm's investigating the feasibility of word processing.
10. Describe the ways the word processing manager is the key link in word processing communications.

DISCUSSION QUESTIONS

1. Discuss the word processing manager's role in the design of the system.
2. How does IBM's new equipment offering to the market influence and affect the word processing industry?

3. Discuss why being flexible is important.
4. Discuss what currency means to a word processing manager.
5. Discuss the steps a word processing manager takes to coordinate with other departments in the firm.
6. Discuss the value of written communications between a firm's word processing manager and its employees.
7. Compare the way that word processing studies were done in the past with the way they are being carried out by firms investigating word processing today.

CASES

Case 2-1   Technology Supply Company

Vision Products is a medium-size, high-technology company in Massachusetts which supplies products to its customers for use with its word processing and data processing systems. The president of Vision, Harrison Black, decided to hire an experienced word processing manager to implement a word processing system in the firm.

After interviewing applicants, President Black hired Jerome Edwards to manage word processing for the firm. Jerome had been supervising word processing in a large law firm for several years and was up for promotion when he decided to change jobs. Jerome has a master's degree in business administration and worked in the Personnel and Accounting Departments of a large steel company before taking the word processing supervisory position. His goal is to become the head of administrative operations for a medium-size or large firm, and he feels this is exactly the opportunity he is seeking.

Explain how Jerome should go about implementing word processing at Vision. President Black made it clear to Jerome that he has complete management backing and support to implement whatever system he feels most appropriate, including the structure, procedures, equipment, and personnel jobs and salaries.

Case 2-2   Electric Company

Fisher Electric Company in Durham, North Carolina, implemented a word processing center in 1974. Since that time, the original supervisor has left the firm and the new supervisor has been unsuccessful in meeting the word processing objectives and the needs of the users. Considerable attrition of word processing personnel resulted, as well as dissatisfaction among company personnel. Management therefore transferred the current supervisor to another position and hired a new supervisor from outside. The new supervisor, Helen Adams, has a background as an executive secretary, public relations staff assistant, and supervisor of a 10-person word processing center in another electric company where she had turned around negative attitudes and resistance into a very successful word processing operation.

Fisher management feels that Helen has the personality and aggressiveness required to make their word processing operation successful. Upon hiring her, they explained that they want to add three departments to the word processing system and that she has full backing to use any internal or outside assistance she needs to develop an ongoing successful word processing system that will meet management's objectives of increased employee efficiency, faster turnaround time, increased quality of documents, and improved employee morale.

1. Discuss how Helen should go about changing the present unsuccessful system into a successful system that would meet management's objectives.
2. Develop any schedules and support materials you feel would help her in this job.

PART II

FEASIBILITY STUDIES

Applying systems analysis to word processing is referred to as conducting a feasibility study. It serves the same purpose as systems analysis in data processing: to design the most efficient operating system to attain the desired objectives.

This section explains each step involved in conducting feasibility studies and the way in which a firm may achieve its word processing objectives by applying specific techniques.

BENJAMIN / CUMMINGS

WORD PROCESSING SERIES

PEOPLE / PROCEDURES / EQUIPMENT

*"Before setting objectives, one should first deter-
mine the firm's major opportunities and limitations,
identify future potential, define its scope; now one
is ready to determine objectives."*

CHAPTER 3

Planning the Survey

OVERVIEW

Upon ordering a new computer system for Datacom Electronics, President Mark
Jacobs issued a memorandum to employees stating:

> Beginning in the next quarter we will be installing our new computer, and
> we plan to completely computerize our internal operations from the customer's
> placing the order to shipment to the customer. However, it will take at least six
> months to complete the first phase of implementing this new operating system.
> Management will publish periodic announcements as each phase is completed.
> Each employee is encouraged to put forth his or her best efforts so that we may
> achieve our goals on schedule.

President Jacobs knew that ordering the computer and putting it into operation
was not all that was required to accomplish the firm's objectives. The company first
needed to analyze the volume and time schedules to be met and then develop the
necessary procedures.

Word processing operates in the same manner. Purchasing the equipment does
not automatically create a successful word processing system. The firm must learn
what information needs to be acquired, along with its volume and time frame, and
then develop the necessary procedures to put the system into effect. This is done by
conducting a feasibility study to determine whether word processing can benefit the
organization and, if so, how.

The word processing manager may or may not be the person to conduct the
feasibility study. The word processing manager does, however, need to understand the
purpose, ingredients, and expected results from such a study in order to be an effective
word processing manager.

This chapter describes the preparations for conducting a feasibility study and the activities that take place before the study begins.

OBJECTIVES

After completing this chapter, you will be able to:

1. Understand the scope of feasibility studies and the activities that take place before they begin.
2. Describe each step as it occurs and its relative importance.
3. Explain the objectives management may have in implementing word processing.
4. Describe the information gained from the study.
5. Explain the value of the study to the organization.

MIDDLETOWN BANK'S PREPARATIONS

When Middletown Bank's management decided to investigate the feasibility of word processing, they assigned the responsibility to Ron Bies, a systems analyst in their headquarters office. President John Newton told Ron to select two others to serve with him on the study task force.

Middletown Bank's management, including President Newton, Executive Vice President Ronald Stevens, Executive Vice President Jade Lee, and Vice President of Operations John Black, prepared the following list of objectives:

- To establish and maintain a modern, high-quality image.
- To obtain efficient document production.
- To eliminate paperwork backlogs and slowdowns.
- To maximize personnel utilization.
- To control operating costs.
- To provide for controlled growth and expansion.
- To optimize office space utilization.
- To establish and maintain high employee morale.

Management next held a meeting with Ron to discuss the study and its objectives. Topics covered during this meeting were when to begin the survey; what analytic methods to consider; what activities to include; the extent of the study, including which departments to include; and how long they expected the study to take.

Although Middletown Bank had six branch offices, management decided that Ron should study the main branch only, plus document distribution among all the branches.

Following the preliminary management meeting, Ron prepared a list of activities to complete before beginning the study, including:

1. Select two task force members.
2. Walk through the main offices.
3. Prepare a schedule of study events.
4. Select survey techniques.
5. Create written communications, including the announcement of the study to employees.
6. Plan orientation meetings.
7. Obtain all necessary study supplies.
8. Schedule offices and conference rooms for meetings and interviews.

He then prepared a schedule (illustrated in Figure 3-1) to monitor each of these activities while preparing for the study.

Gathering Information

Ron first collected departmental organization charts and floorplans for each of the bank's four floors before beginning his walkthrough. This provided him with a general idea of the overall layout, furniture and equipment locations, working procedures, paperwork volume, and location of and manner in which employees presently performed their specific activities. Ron referred to the charts as he observed employees performing their daily tasks. He began on the top floor, where the executive offices were located, and worked down to the basement, where the bank's data processing was conducted.

Before beginning the walkthrough, Ron took the layout for each floor and marked the location of each person by name and department. Figure 3-2 illustrates Middletown Bank's floorplans, while Table 3-1 lists the employees in each department.

During his walkthrough, Ron stopped to talk briefly with employees at their work stations to make sure the chart was up-to-date. He did not enter private offices but observed whether or not they were occupied. When an employee inquired about the purpose of his survey, he explained that he was conducting a special assignment for the president regarding office space.

Other Preliminary Activities

Management had been approached by marketing representatives from several companies that manufactured office equipment. The vendors had suggested that, by purchasing their word processing equipment, the bank could reduce operating costs, particularly in view of its planned expansion. Some of the representatives marketed dictation equipment, word processing typing equipment, computerized storage systems, and communications links with data processing and remote locations.

President Newton gave Ron the names of the marketing representatives and the vendors' equipment brochures. Ron contacted the representatives to schedule demonstrations of their equipment. After observing various types of word processing equipment in the vendors' offices, Ron requested names of banks and similar organizations that used their equipment. He then visited those offices to observe their word processing systems.

FIGURE 3-1   Middletown Bank Feasibility Study Preliminary Activities

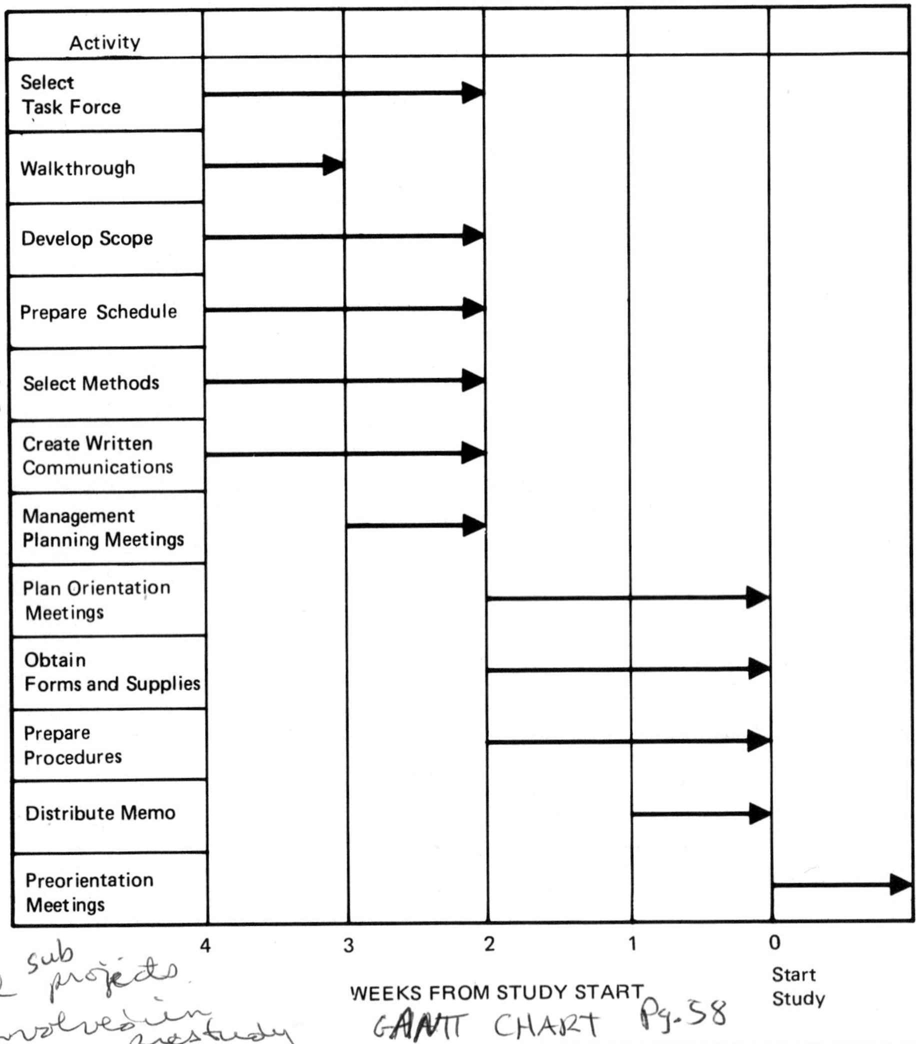

Activity					
Select Task Force					
Walkthrough					
Develop Scope					
Prepare Schedule					
Select Methods					
Create Written Communications					
Management Planning Meetings					
Plan Orientation Meetings					
Obtain Forms and Supplies					
Prepare Procedures					
Distribute Memo					
Preorientation Meetings					
	4	3	2	1	0

WEEKS FROM STUDY START   Start Study

Handwritten annotations: "Plan Study", "all sub projects involved in prestudy", "GANTT CHART Pg.58"

Ron also began to read recommended word processing publications, some of which included *Word Processing Report, Administrative Management, Word Processing World, Modern Office Procedures, The Office, Words, Datamation, Word Processing,* and *Banking Systems and Equipment.* He watched for announcements of seminars and other word processing events in order to meet people already heavily involved in word processing, learn firsthand their viewpoints, and learn more about word processing.

Planning the Preliminary Schedule of Activities

Ron next updated his list of activities for the study and incorporated them into the study schedule. He first listed six key elements:

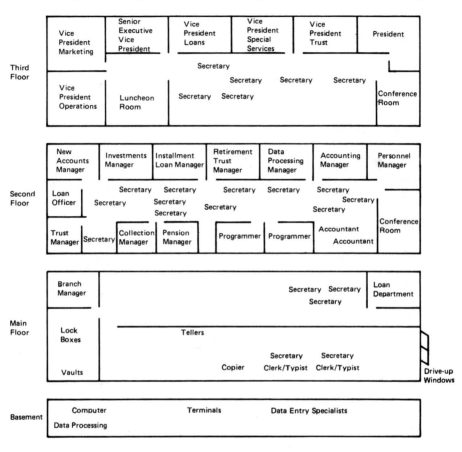

1. Survey preliminaries.
2. Survey orientation.
3. Data collection.
4. Data analysis.
5. New system design and report preparation.
6. Presentation of results of the survey.

In order to plan the amount of time required for each of these six steps, Ron referred to his list of personnel who would be included in the study and scheduled one-half to one hour for each interview. Figure 3–3 shows Ron's schedule.

For his task force, Ron selected Janine Roberts from the Personnel Department and Peter Ross from Accounting. He visited with their managers to explain exactly what he proposed and that he would like their assistance. He said that he anticipated that the study would take from six weeks to over two months of their full time before

TABLE 3-1   Bank of Middletown Organization Chart

Department and Staff	Number of Staff	Secretaries
Executive	7	
President		Mary
Vice President, Executive		Helen
Vice President/Operations		Tomasa
Vice President/Loans		Bridgette
Vice President/Special Ser.		Pamela
Vice President/Marketing		Michelle
Vice President/Trusts		Sumi, Johanna
Personnel	2	
Manager		Peter
Accounting	4	
Manager		Julia
Data Processing	4	
Manager		Sally
Auditing	2	
Manager		Ginger
Trust	2	
Manager		Jenny
		Heather
Legal	3	Helen
Marketing	2	Pedro
Special Services	3	Claudette
Loan	3	Randall
		Rosie
		Alana
Operations	18	Nicole
		Terri
		Dick
		Bonnie
		Hiroko
		25 secretaries

they would be free to return to their regular duties. Their managers agreed to allow them to participate in the study.

SUMMARY OF MIDDLETOWN BANK'S STUDY PREPARATIONS

Once management decided to consider implementing word processing, they proceeded as follows:

Entire **Feasibility Study Schedule of Activities**   **FIGURE 3-3**

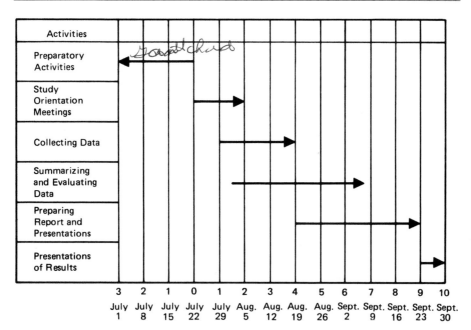

Activities														
Preparatory Activities	*Gantt chart*													
Study Orientation Meetings														
Collecting Data														
Summarizing and Evaluating Data														
Preparing Report and Presentations														
Presentations of Results														

	3	2	1	0	1	2	3	4	5	6	7	8	9	10
	July 1	July 8	July 15	July 22	July 29	Aug. 5	Aug. 12	Aug. 19	Aug. 26	Sept. 2	Sept. 9	Sept. 16	Sept. 23	Sept. 30

WEEKS FROM STUDY START

Pert — calendar of time & events
Ch. 3-10

1. They selected Ron to be the project manager responsible for conducting the study and selecting the task force members to assist in the study.
2. They wrote exactly what their objectives were in implementing word processing.
3. They held a meeting with the project manager to make the following preliminary preparations:
   a. Decide the date the study should begin and when they expected it to end.
   b. Discuss the scope of the study, departments to be included, and functions to be covered.
   c. Discuss the methods to be used.
4. Following the planning meeting, the project manager collected organization charts, floorplans, and personnel listings by locations; and took the information on a walkthrough of the bank's offices to obtain an overview of the current operating system.
5. The project manager attended demonstrations of word processing equipment and visited organizations already using word processing with similar operations to those of the bank. In addition, he read current word processing literature and attended seminars and other word processing events to educate himself in word processing technology.
6. The project manager prepared a schedule of activities for the study.

COMPARING METHODS OF PREPARATION

Let us examine each aspect to see how different organizations might handle each step of preparation before beginning the feasibility study.

Selecting Study Personnel

Middletown Bank's management selected from within the organization an employee who was skilled in systems analysis to conduct the feasibility study. They also delegated to this individual the responsibility to select others to work on a task force.

Alternative Selections   Middletown Bank could have hired outside consultants to conduct the feasibility study. Advantages they might have derived include:

- Objectivity. Since the consultants do not work for the firm, they have no subjective interests. Their reputation is based upon their objective judgment.
- Technical expertise. Word processing consultants have background and training in word processing specialties. Their knowledge and experience therefore should offer the firm expert technical skills and advice.

Other Alternatives   Some of the large word processing vendors, such as IBM, Xerox, Dictaphone, and Lanier, conduct feasibility studies at no cost. The main advantage a firm might derive from using a vendor to conduct its study is the hard dollar savings. Hiring an outside consultant can become fairly costly, while using internal personnel is costly in terms of employee time. Vendors do not charge to conduct studies, since they expect to recover their costs by selling their equipment.

The main disadvantage in using a vendor is subjectivity. Of course that vendor is going to recommend (and sometimes demand prestudy commitment) that the firm purchase, rent, or lease that vendor's word processing equipment.

A second disadvantage is that some vendors might not be qualified in all the areas the firm might want to study. For example, a study conducted by a dictation equipment vendor might not provide representative information for such areas as records retention and communications/distribution.

Using In-House Personnel   Using personnel from within the organization may not always result in objectivity. For instance, if one of the members of the task force normally works in Data Processing, that person might be inclined to make or recommend decisions more beneficial to or representative of the Data Processing Department. In addition, as in Ron's case, in-house personnel (particularly before a firm has implemented word processing) may not have substantial expertise in word processing or the skills required to conduct the study. Should in-house personnel be selected to conduct the study, they must have complete backing of management as well as thorough training in word processing study techniques and technology.

What They Need To Know   Should a firm select in-house representatives, they should be well trained in the following areas:

- Word processing concepts and how word processing benefits the organization.
- How to measure input volume (longhand, dictation, copy) over periods of time.
- How to measure output volume, including revisions, during peaks and valleys.
- How to categorize documents and requirements for each kind of document.
- How to measure personnel factors, including those human qualities, skill levels, and behavioral attitudes required to accomplish productivity objectives while achieving a high level of employee morale.

Who Might Participate on the Task Force   Most firms whose internal personnel conduct the study use more than one person to conduct the analysis. This is more likely to result in objectivity and less resentment or resistance among company personnel, since more departments are represented in the study. If the firm already employs systems analysts, one should participate in the survey. Other departments whose personnel may have the appropriate technical skills include Personnel, Accounting, and Data Processing.

Individuals selected to participate in the study need the technical skills to collect, summarize, and evaluate data. Even more, they need the tact and sensitivity to be objective, enthusiastic, and interested in all those who participate in the study, especially to the secretaries, who frequently feel threatened. Members of the task force need to be highly skilled interviewers, who can listen and perceive without being subjective.

WRITING MANAGEMENT OBJECTIVES

Stating clearcut objectives in written form helps to clarify exactly what benefits the organization, particularly management, wishes and expects to gain. Middletown Bank's management stated that they had five major objectives they wished to achieve through word processing:

1. Maintain high quality communications
2. Provide for controlled growth
3. Maximize space utilization
4. Eliminate paperwork backlogs
5. Control costs

Other objectives frequently expected from word processing are:

- Ability to meet deadlines.
- Increased personnel productivity.
- Reduced turnaround time (from original document creation to completed product).

- Decreased costs of document distribution (mail).
- Faster communication and distribution.
- Quicker accessibility to information.
- Ability to produce phototypeset documents internally.

There is no blanket set of word processing objectives. Each organization has its own needs, problems, characteristics, and applications. Word processing provides such resources as modern equipment, systematized workflow and procedures, and increased personnel productivity techniques. Substantial resources are available through word processing and are waiting to be utilized; it is up to the specific organization to determine exactly what it wants, what it will do, and how it will do it.

The firm must determine exactly what it expects from or wishes to accomplish by implementing word processing. Does it want to improve document quality? produce camera-ready copy? increase production capacity? reduce turnaround time? eliminate overtime and outside personnel costs? transmit documents over telephone lines?

These are some of the results of word processing. It is up to each organization to determine what it wants word processing (or systems integration) to accomplish. Usually, word processing is implemented to achieve more efficient document production from origination to production. Once this objective has been attained, word processing may next set out to perform other functions. Management may set objectives in phases. For instance, one company set its objective in four separate phases:

1. Increase productivity of secretarial personnel while achieving productivity efficiency.
2. Coordinate order entry and shorten the cycle from customer order to product shipment.
3. Coordinate with data processing by using word processing as an input source to data processing.
4. Communicate documents from one location to another.

THE PLANNING MEETING

Before the study begins, management and the task force meet to plan how the study will be conducted. Topics to be covered include the survey time span and schedule, scope (area, departments, applications, and functions to be covered), and methods to be used to conduct the study.

Surveying Time Span, Schedule, and Scope

The length of time depends upon the scope of the study. In order to develop the schedule of study activities, management has to decide the breadth of the study, after which the schedule can be prepared. It could take from two weeks to two months to conduct a study, depending upon what it covers.

Methods Used to Conduct the Study

Management does not select the techniques used to conduct the study. Instead, they delegate this function to the project manager and task force. At Middletown Bank, Ron based his decision upon his experience as an analyst and what he learned about word processing while preparing to conduct the study. Techniques Ron evaluated included secretarial time analysis, action paper analysis, management and administrative time analysis, computer analysis, random sampling, and secretarial interviews.

Ron selected the following methods:

1. Random sampling for two weeks.
2. Computer analysis of daily typing.
3. Secretarial job analysis through secretarial questionnaires and interviews.
4. Administrative support analysis through questionnaires and interviews.

In addition, he planned to obtain such historical data as salary, overhead, equipment, and supplies.

INFORMATION TO BE PROVIDED FROM THE STUDY

When planning the study, one needs to determine what information is desired, including:

* Volume of work.
* The kind of work being done (the applications).
* The form of input (origination).
* The key elements (deadlines, peaks and valleys, and revisions).
* Cost of the present system (sometimes most important), in hard dollars (actual figures available such as salaries, overhead, and equipment costs), soft dollars (intangible costs such as dictator's time), and other invisible costs such as attrition and retraining, employee morale, employee frustration and low productivity, duplicated efforts among departments, personal decision-making, absenteeism, and time away from work stations.

A study can also cover:

* The secretarial stations, including all tasks performed, both administrative and typing.
* Administrative surveys, which include all administrative secretarial tasks performed by secretaries and support needs of management.
* The typing and related tasks only.
* Secretarial work stations and other areas such as reproduction processes, filing and records processing, communications and distribution, phototypesetting, and input to data processing.

SIZE OF THE STUDY

Once the decision to conduct the study has been made and the kind of information desired is determined, the next decisions are:

1. What operations are to be included in the study?
2. Should we start big or small?
3. Should we study one department? one building? the entire organization? one area? one floor? one or more specific applications?

Depending upon the size of the company and its geographical layout, survey size may become obvious once the specific objectives are clearly expressed. A small city government that has several departments, including a Police Department, Public Works, Parks and Recreation Department, Community Relations Department, Buildings Department, City Clerk, and City Manager, might survey all departments that have extensive paperwork, excluding those that process very little paperwork, such as the Fire Department.

In the case of a large company housed in several buildings, the study might encompass three departments located in one building that produce a high volume of paperwork such as engineering, marketing, and executive offices.

A firm might first study the departments that management wishes to change first, usually those that process a large volume of paperwork or have specific paperwork problems. They could be departments needing extensive secretarial overtime or outside help.

Middletown Bank decided to:

- Survey the entire bank and not include the other branches in the original survey except for document distribution between the main bank and its branches.
- Survey document creation, production, filing, and storage.
- Note associated information relating to phototypesetting, reproduction, and communication and distribution.

The relationship between word and data processing would be surveyed at a later time.

FEASIBILITY VERSUS COMPREHENSIVE SURVEY

Sometimes an organization may wish to conduct a preliminary information survey which will provide certain basic information and wait to conduct a detailed analysis. In this case, the organization would conduct a feasibility survey and, should the information provided from the survey favor the company's making the change to word processing, then conduct the comprehensive survey. A feasibility survey is thus for the purpose of measuring work in a specified area to gain enough information for an accurate, intelligent appraisal. The comprehensive survey, on the other hand, is a complete systems analysis of the area, department, or organization for the purpose of restructuring personnel or other resources to improve working methods and attain the particular objectives of the organization.

By comparing the objectives and methods for the feasibility and comprehensive surveys as illustrated in Table 3-2, it becomes apparent that in order to conduct an accurate survey, the same elements are involved; the difference is of degree, number of people interviewed and surveyed, and time involved. In either survey, the following five-step process takes place:

1. *Plan the survey*: write down and schedule objectives; organize the total survey procedures.
2. *Conduct orientation program for employees*: a special presentation should be made to employees and introduced by management, in which the employees are brought into the survey activity and become involved as support for the program.
3. *Collect data*: collect information on ways work is presently done—carbon paper copies (NCR paper), flowcharting, interviewing, random sampling; collect time analysis information.
4. *Interview*: conduct personal interviews with selected personnel (through random sampling or other means) in the areas surveyed.
5. *Analyze*: use flowcharting, graphing, and summarizing.

After these five steps have been accomplished, a better system can be designed.

SUMMARY OF PRELIMINARY ACTIVITIES

President Newton delegated to Ron the following responsibilities:

1. Conduct a walkthrough to gain an overall impression of the current working atmosphere.
2. Suggest the names of other personnel to work with him on the task force.
3. Plan an orientation meeting with bank personnel explaining the survey, its purpose, how it would be conducted, and what would be expected of all personnel.
4. Schedule available offices and conference rooms for interviewing and conducting orientation meetings.
5. Create the study schedule.
6. Provide ample supplies, including work request forms and secretarial and management questionnaires.
7. Evaluate current survey techniques and select those most appropriate for the study.
8. Create written communications to use during the survey, including memos, guidelines, bulletin board notices, survey procedures explanations, printed time schedules, and periodic progress reports.

TABLE 3-2   Comparison of Feasibility and Comprehensive Surveys

---

Feasibility Survey	*Comprehensive Survey*
Objectives	*Objectives*
Measure work in a limited area	Measure work in all departments
Control time of survey	Expand time to include in-depth interviews
Acquire accurate information	Obtain employee input
Measure word processing	Measure all pertinent systems, including:
Typing volume	Typing volume
Typing applications	Origination volume
Priorities	Reproduction volume
Administrative	Data entry volume
Time distribution	Distribution/communications systems
Tasks	Filing and storage
Compare present system to proposed system	Determine potential reduction, enrichment areas, possible combinations of elements
Estimate necessary equipment	Recommend system alternative best suited to meet objectives and needs
Present new system plan	Restructure jobs where necessary
Study Tools (Methods)	*Study Tools (Methods)*
Word processing	Word processing
NCR paper	NCR paper
Document log	Document log
Work sampling	Work sampling
Questionnaire	Questionnaire
Data capsule (1 or 2)	Data capsule (random sampling)
Administration	*Administration*
Questionnaire to selected or random personnel	Questionnaire
Department heads	Interview all managers, selected exempts, secretaries
Section/group leaders	Random sampling
Lead secretaries	
Random sampling	
General Company	*General Company*
Collected by coordinator	Collected by project manager

---

9. Prepare a memo, to be signed by the president, which would include:
   a. An announcement that the survey is going to take place and its objectives and time span.
   b. Names and responsibilities of the personnel who will be conducting the study.
   c. General description of how the study will be conducted.
   d. What is expected to occur and exactly how management expects employees to participate during the study.
   e. Anticipated results and benefits, which might include how the study will

make the work for personnel more efficient for them, saving time and unnecessary duplication and at the same time improving the bank's operating methods; how it will improve the quality of the work and products reflecting the bank; how the bank plans to use the study to establish itself as a leader and active participant in community affairs; and how it will enable the bank to participate more actively in current local issues of importance to the community.

The tone of the management memo should be that all employees who partici- pate in the study are expected to cooperate wholeheartedly to produce a complete and accurate survey which will benefit both the employees of the bank in their daily tasks and bank operations in their endeavor to improve the bank's image in the community. Figure 3–4 is a copy of the memo Ron prepared for President Newton's signature.

Written Communications Used During the Study

While preparing for the study, Ron completed the checklist illustrated in Figure 3–5 and began to collect and evaluate those forms used by other firms for word processing studies. He found many samples in word processing publications and received several from vendors. Some of the forms nearly met his requirements, but not quite; he therefore adapted some for the bank's particular needs. Samples of these forms are illustrated in Chapter 4, "Data Collection Tools and Methods." Forms he planned to use during the study were:

- Principals, and secretarial questionnaires.
- Department head interview forms.
- Work request forms for computer analysis.
- Survey forms for analysis of specific areas such as duplication, records control and retention, and phototypesetting.
- Summary forms for use in computing data from interviews.
- Directives or memos to bank personnel during the study keeping them up-to-date on the status of the study.
- Schedule sheets or appointment calendars for planning activities and scheduling interviews.

Personnel Involved

Ron selected a secretary to handle the appointments for the task force during the study. The secretary was given the responsibility of making and maintaining the appointment calendars for all three members of the task force during interviews and making sure that there was office space free for those interviews. Appropriate tele- phone communications were to be handled by the secretary to keep all parties in- formed: the people being interviewed and the task force members. This would allow flexibility whenever an interview overran the planned time or someone was unable to keep an appointment.

FIGURE 3-4

M E M O R A N D U M

TO: All Middletown Bank   DATE: July 7, 1980
           Personnel

FROM: John D. Newton

SUBJECT: Word Processing Study

Your Middletown Bank management has decided that, in the interests of
our employees, stockholders, and public, we can improve the efficiency
of our office operations. In order to do this, we must first learn
exactly what kinds of problems we presently have in daily operations
and what kinds of improvements can be made in order to increase our
efficiency.

Ron Bies has been put in charge of making an office survey for the purpose of learning exactly what problems you may encounter in your daily
work, what kinds of work duplication might exist that can be handled in
a better manner, the volume of work you process each day, and ways we can
use modern office technologies to improve our internal operations.

For the next two months Ron and his task force, Janine Roberts and Peter
Ross, will be conducting a preliminary survey in which each of us will
participate. Ron will hold several separate orientation meetings during
which he will carefully explain exactly how the survey will be conducted
and how each individual can cooperate.

We will be publishing a schedule of orientation meetings, followed by
frequent news bulletins during the survey.

Should you foresee any problems that might prevent your participation in
this survey, please notify Ron. Your cooperation, suggestions, and
interest in making this survey as accurate and complete as possible will
be greatly appreciated.

Your management is looking forward to this enterprise as an opportunity
to make our organization one of the most modern and up-to-date banking
institutions in the West.

PLANNING THE PRESTUDY ORIENTATION PROGRAM

Ron next planned the prestudy orientation program. In making these preparations, he
set down the following questions.

1. What is the purpose of the orientation program? What should be included in it?
2. How many orientation programs should there be? How many people should
    attend each one? Who should they be? How long should the programs be?

Feasibility Study Checklist   FIGURE 3-5

PERSONNEL

_____ Current job classifications and salary scales
_____ Current overhead factor (including fringe benefits)
_____ Current skills of clerical/administrative personnel
_____ Current absence and turnover rates
_____ Current performance ratings and methods
_____ Current training and development methods
_____ Organization reporting relationships

OFFICE EQUIPMENT

_____ Current inventory per machine type with value
_____ Utilization factor per machine
_____ Maintenance and reliability records for each machine
_____ Operating cost per machine
_____ Facility requirements of equipment (space, energy, etc.)
_____ Compatibility/conversion costs
_____ Other

OFFICE SUPPLIES

_____ Current inventory per item
_____ Current inventory value
_____ Utilization factor per item
_____ Scrap rate
_____ Other

FACILITIES

_____ Workstation space utilization factor
_____ Location of functions according to work flow
_____ Energy and power sources
_____ Lighting output at work levels

---

3. How should the programs be conducted? Who should speak? What should be said? What message must be put across? What visual means can best help convey the message?

4. How should the programs end? Should handouts be distributed during or after the programs? What should the handouts say?

By answering these questions, Ron came up with the following plans for the programs.

1. The purpose of the orientation is to convince each bank employee of the benefits of changing the bank's system or at least of seeing whether it should be changed to improve the way the bank produces documents. The message is that the feasibility study would be made to see if the bank could save money and reduce costs and at the same time make it easier for each employee to conduct his or her work more effectively. After explaining why the study is being conducted it will be necessary to explain how it will be made. Thorough explanations will be made of what will occur and exactly what part each employee can take in the study to make it accurate, thorough, and valuable to the bank and its employees.
2. There will be four orientation programs; one for the departmental managers; one for secretaries; one for staff specialists; and one for other office personnel. The maximum number of people to attend each session will be 12. Each program is planned to take no longer than an hour, the first half dealing with explanations of the purpose and how the study will take place and the second half covering the mechanics and answering questions.
3. Each session will be introduced by the bank president, who will explain the purpose and benefits to be derived. He will then introduce Ron, who will explain the study in depth and answer questions. The main message is the importance of the study to each bank employee to see if word processing can make each person's job better and more effective. Ron decided to show a film from one of the word processing vendors depicting several banks which had implemented work processing and how it had improved their operations and the jobs of their employees. The film is 15 minutes in length and will fit into the time plan perfectly.
4. Ron decided that the question-and-answer session will be concluded by his handing out the schedule of the study and introducing the secretary and the remainder of the task force who will be working with everyone. He will explain how the secretary will schedule the interviews so that everyone can cooperate to make this study a step towards making their bank one of the most modern and efficient banks in the community.

Presentation Facilities

Ron asked the task force secretary to arrange for a conference room for each meeting so that the groups can meet without interruption. He explained that he will be using a film and will need to have the room set up informally so that people can sit comfortably in a casual setting where the film can be shown easily.

Final Plans

After making all of these plans, Ron was ready to meet once again with management to make the final plans for the feasibility study. In preparing for the meeting, he checked the study schedule to make sure that all necessary arrangements had been made. They were:

Conducting the walkthrough to get a general idea of the layout and physical arrangements.

- Recommending people for the task force.
- Laying out preliminary plans for the orientation meetings.
- Preparing a **PERT** (Project Evaluation and Review Technique) schedule to be used to conduct the study.
- Arranging for offices, conference rooms, and telephone contacts and scheduling appointments.
- Preparing supplies, dependent upon the selection of the data collection and survey techniques to be selected.
- Developing suggested written communications to be used during the study.

Prior to this meeting, Ron had carefully evaluated the various data collection and analyzing techniques used to study office systems. Those techniques are described in Chapter 4.

SUMMARY

A feasibility study can cover (a) both administrative and correspondence tasks or areas of a firm (the total secretarial station operation), (b) administrative operations alone, (c) typing/correspondence operations or tasks alone, (d) both administrative and correspondence and other areas as well which might include duplication, records storage and retention, communications/distribution, phototypesetting, and input to data processing.

Information to be gained from the study includes volume, applications, form of origination, key elements, and cost.

The first major decision to be made in planning the feasibility study is its size. Is it to be a comprehensive study of the entire operation or building? Or is it to cover one department, section, area, or application?

The five steps of a study are (a) plan, (b) orient the employees, (c) collect the data, (d) interview personnel, and (e) summarize and analyze the results.

Other preliminary activities to take place during the planning stage are for the project manager conducting the study (along with others participating in the study) to visit vendors to examine kinds of word processing equipment which might be selected and to visit offices in the same business with word processing installations to see how word processing has improved their operations. In addition, the project manager needs to read up on word processing, attend seminars, and learn ways to keep as current as possible on systems available.

Once a company has decided to proceed with a feasibility study, it should:

1. Select the personnel to conduct the study (from consultants, vendors, or internal trained personnel).
2. Write the objectives anticipated through implementing word processing.
3. Have a planning meeting with the project manager in which is determined the survey time span (best time to begin), how long the study will take, and when the results are expected.
4. Discuss various methods which can be used, how each method might affect personnel attitudes, and which method might be most applicable, leaving the selection up to the project manager.

5. Decide what areas are to be studied, what factors will be included, and what functions will be covered.
6. Delegate the preparations to the project manager.
7. Conclude by setting a date for the final planning meeting at which the project manager will present the plan with the **Gantt chart** (a chart used to plan and coordinate an activity involving subactivities) and recommend a study method.

A Gantt chart is very useful in scheduling the prestudy activities, which may include:

- A walkthrough of the area to be studied with floorplans and organization charts for thorough orientation to the tasks/locations.
- Selecting personnel to conduct the study.
- Planning orientation meetings.
- Developing the study PERT chart (schedule of activities to presentation of new system design).
- Arranging all facilities required, including conference rooms and offices for interviewing.
- Arranging for all necessary supplies, including charts, forms, NCR action paper, calendars, and work sampling charts.
- Selecting the survey techniques to be used—work sampling, job analysis.
- Developing written communications to be used in the study, including the management memo to explain the objectives to employees, sell the plan, and gain employees' involvement.

Once all preliminary activities are accomplished, the project manager meets with the firm's management to obtain approval and go-ahead for the study. He or she presents the PERT schedule of study activities, samples of forms to be used in the study, explains how the study will be conducted and by whom, and gets approval to distribute all types of communications. On agreement by all parties, the study is ready to begin.

REVIEW QUESTIONS

1. Name the four concepts of feasibility studies (the study components).
2. What specific information needs to be provided by the study?
3. Outline the feasibility study five-step process.
4. Explain the purpose of developing a schedule before the study.
5. Explain the purpose of a walkthrough and how it is conducted.
6. Name four documents Ron gathered while planning the survey and their value to him in making the study.
7. What other activities did Ron pursue prior to the management planning meeting?
8. Name the six key elements of a feasibility study.
9. Why might a vendor be a poor choice to do the feasibility study? a good one?
10. What does a word processing analyst need to know?
11. Discuss other written communications used in the study besides the Gantt and PERT charts.

DISCUSSION QUESTIONS

1. What is the difference between a feasibility study and a comprehensive study?
2. Why did management decide on their objectives *after* selecting the head of the task force? What is the importance of this?
3. Discuss management's decision to analyze the main branch only and not the other six branches.
4. Discuss the data collection techniques Ron chose and their value in making the study.
5. Discuss the personnel Ron selected and why they would be good candidates to have on the task force.
6. List objectives management of any firm might have for a study.
7. Discuss what would be covered in a word processing feasibility study.
8. Discuss the mood that should be set and what should be stated during the orientation meeting.

CASES

Case 3-1   Instructional Products

Course Development Products, Inc. is a small company which specializes in designing instructional materials for government agencies and private industry. They produce printed and media products for training personnel in government and industry for total enterprises such as aircraft instruction.

Three departments make up the company—Development, Editing, and Production. Table 3-3 shows the personnel alignment of the company.

Personnel Alignment of Course Development Products, Inc.		TABLE 3-3
Development	*Editing*	*Production*
Project Director	Editors (4)	Media Production Manager
Assistant to the Director	Proofreader	Media Coordinator
Project Secretary	Quality Control	Tape/Slide Manager
Manager of Instructional	Secretary	Graphics Supervisor
Development	Typist	Workbook Supervisor
Instructional Psychologists (4)		Illustrator
Scriptwriters (2)		Photographer
Test Writers (2)		Typist
Aircraft Subject Matter		Pasteup Specialists (2)
Experts (20)		Word Processing Supervisor
Secretary		Word Processor
		Production Typist

1. Plan a feasibility study of the entire firm, including both administration and correspondence, including duplication.
2. Develop a schedule for prestudy activities and a schedule for the study.
3. Select the data collection techniques you would use in such a study and discuss who you would have conduct the study. Be prepared to support your decisions and plans for the study.

Case 3-2   Medical Clinic

Holyoaks Medical Clinic is located in a suburb of Philadelphia and has a medical staff of 45 physicians, 3 lab technicians, 4 X-ray technicians, an administrator, assistant administrator, 3 records clerks, and 17 secretaries and typists. The administrator, Julia Reynolds, realizing that there is considerable variance in workload among the secretaries and typists and that the office equipment is outdated, has decided to undertake a feasibility study. How should Julia go about undertaking the study. She is a trained nurse with a minor in business administration and has no background in secretarial work, although she took accounting and management courses in college. She has been working as a nurse and in medical administration for 15 years and has demonstrated considerable administrative and supervisory capabilities.

1. Develop the prestudy and study schedules.
2. Select the study techniques.
3. Determine who should make the study. Be prepared to support your selections and plans.

"A problem well defined is a problem half solved."

CHAPTER 4

Collecting and Summarizing Data

OVERVIEW

A feasibility study is important to a firm in describing its current operating system, isolating problems and weaknesses within the system, and designing a more efficient method of operations. In order to do this, the firm needs to select data collection methods which best provide information while causing as little disruption to the ongoing operations and maintaining as high a level of morale as possible. This chapter discusses the various kinds of techniques used to collect the different forms of information a firm might need and explains how best to administer the data collection process.

OBJECTIVES

After completing this chapter, you should be able to:

1. Describe the information to be provided by feasibility studies.
2. Describe how to prepare and communicate with participants before and during the study.
3. Demonstrate how an accurate and significant study may be conducted.

One of the main decisions to make while planning the study is to select the data collection technique. Which method will obtain the most accurate and viable information and at the same time not cause employee resistance and operational upheaval? When making a study of an office, where employees are mostly knowledge workers, morale can be an important factor.

Techniques used to analyze other situations may not be the most appropriate for analyzing the officeplace. Methods-time-measurement (MTM), because of its scientific nature, is an effective technique to measure manual operations for manufacturing. Will techniques used by systems analysts for records and data processing methods work as well for word processing? A systems analyst defines problems and states the solutions to these problems. How can these same techniques be applied to word processing?

First of all, word processing centers around the work performed by the secretaries and considers the amount of time consumed during secretarial working hours, overtime hours, and additional time taken by supplementary help; the volume of typing produced during working hours; and the problems related to the typing, including the amount of retyping or rekeyboarding.

In the early 1960s, the technique of using carbon sensitized paper (described as action paper) was first used to disclose the volume of typing and the amount of retyping secretaries performed and to isolate factors that caused retypings. By having secretaries keep a copy of each page inserted into the typewriter, one could get an idea of the nature and volume of all typing that secretaries did each day. Today this same method is used in some studies to provide actual copies of all typing activities.

INFORMATION TO BE ACQUIRED

Selecting the techniques to be used depends upon the information one wants to obtain from the study. What are the specific objectives? Questions that may provide the answer include:

- What kind of change is anticipated from the study? Is it a change in the secretarial structure, perhaps to a work group or centralization of typing? Is it simply a change to more productive equipment? If so, what factors are needed to identify the appropriate equipment?
- Is it a possible merging of operations such as keyboarding input to be produced by phototypesetting? or possibly using secretarial input for centralized document revisions to final output? Or is it related to data entry? or communications by means of electronic mail?

Answers to these questions help to isolate the data that is to be studied. One can next determine which technique best provides this information.

Most word processing studies begin with an analysis of the secretarial positions, frequently the total secretarial job and all tasks performed by the secretaries, time distribution, and volume of typing presently being completed.

KINDS OF SURVEYS

A survey may cover (a) the secretarial job itself (where the secretarial time goes), (b) document analysis of typing production and time distribution, and (c) administrative tasks (or everything else secretaries do other than type). In many cases, other areas such as reproduction, filing and storage, and distribution may be covered in the secretarial survey; or they may be done independently.

Questionnaire

To analyze the job of the secretaries, one needs to determine the work they do, the amount of time spent on each task, and problems associated with their jobs in performing those tasks. This survey may be conducted by having each secretary fill out a questionnaire describing that person's position and providing a summary of the secretaries' work. Data from all secretarial questionnaires is summarized and followed up with interviews. Figure 4-1 illustrates a secretarial questionnaire.

Work Sampling

Random or fixed interval work sampling is another technique used to analyze secretarial jobs. In this instance, a surveyor visits the secretary's work area at either random or fixed times. The surveyor marks on a special form (see Figure 4-2) either the task being performed or the fact that the secretary was not at the work station. The tasks performed at these work stations are known ahead of time so that the sampler simply marks a check in the appropriate box at the scheduled sampling time. This information is summarized, and the amount of time devoted to each kind of work or nonwork is derived through statistical analysis.

Document Analysis

To analyze the volume of the complete document production cycle and time required to accomplish all daily typing tasks, analysts often use action paper studies. The action paper is accumulated to determine the exact number of keystrokes per day. In addition, the secretary logs the time involved in typing each page. This technique provides total number of gross typing strokes, lines, or pages; number of retyping strokes; total number of net typing strokes, lines, or pages; and time required to type net strokes, lines, or pages.

Miscellaneous Forms

Other techniques are having secretaries log their time for a defined period on a secretarial typist's form or keeping track of tasks performed on a time ladder.

Administrative Surveys

A survey of administrative work (all work that is not typing) may be done by having the principals (those whose work is performed by the secretaries) fill out questionnaires, indicating work they could delegate to the secretaries. This can be used to enrich administrative secretarial jobs. In addition, the secretaries fill out questionnaires on which they log time devoted to administrative tasks. This time is summarized to

(Text continues on page 67.)

FIGURE 4-1   Example of Secretarial Typing Analysis Questionnaire

SECRETARIAL
TYPING ANALYSIS QUESTIONNAIRE

Name_____Department_____Phone #_____Date_____

Job Title_____Supervisor_____Number of Others You Support:___

Names:_____Typewriter:_____Pica__Elite__

What percent of your time do you spend typing?_____% Name your most frequent typing jobs and their characteristics, starting with the most frequent.

Kind of Document	Form of Input	No. of Times Revised	Amount Revised

How many copies do you normally make when typing?____How are they made? _____Indicate the average number of pages of the kinds of documents you type: Daily correspondence____Form letters___Text___Boilerplate reports___Statistical___Forms____Other (indicate)_____

Indicate the usual turnaround time required by these documents (in hours):

Daily correspondence____Form letters____Text____Boilerplate reports_____

Statistical___Forms___Other_____

What is the error correction policy of your supervisor?_____

Who is responsible for proofreading your typing?_____

How many error corrections per page are allowed before the page must be retyped?____What percentage of your final typing output is changed by the author?____% Have standards of work performance been developed for your typing?____If so, what are they?_____

FIGURE 4-1 (continued)

Describe your most difficult typing assignments_____

_____

_____

Indicate the percent of typing that falls into the categories given below.

Kind of Document	No. of Copies or Carbons	Is Photo-typeset	Requires Special Symbols	Is Revised	No. of Times Revised	Average No. Pages	Rapid Turn-around
Letter							
Memos							
Text							
Forms							
Form Letter							

What is the maximum paper width you use?_____What is your heaviest typing load?_____How do you handle overloads?_____

How often are you backlogged?_____How much typing is periodic?_____

Examine the time you spend doing each of the following activities during an average day. Include personal time and the time you spend waiting for work to account for the total number of hours you work each day.

	Hours per Day
Administrative Duties	
Sorting, Handling Mail	_____
Handling Telephones	_____
Reproduction Work	_____
Clerical Posting, Calculating, etc.	_____
Filing	_____
Research	_____
Assisting Others	_____
Reception Duties	_____
Taking Shorthand Dictation	_____
Special Projects (Describe)_____	_____
Other (Describe)_____	_____
Typing Hours Total	_____
Waiting for Work Total	_____
Personal Time	_____
Personal Service	_____

(Figure 4-1 continues.)

FIGURE 4-1 (continued)

Nonroutine Work: List below the nonroutine work you handle by name of
the principal for whom you perform the task, the kind of task, and its
frequency (monthly, weekly, etc.), and estimate the number of hours the
project requires.

Principal	Type of Project	Frequency	Hours per Project

Narrative: Describe your job briefly, indicating the way you and your
principals work, including their priorities, heavy workload periods, and
ways problems are resolved.

_____

_____

_____

What do you like most about your job?_____

What tasks do you enjoy doing most?_____

What typing jobs do you enjoy most?_____

What form of origination do you find easiest?_____

Why?_____What do you enjoy least about your job?_____

What are your plans for job growth?_____

What kind of job would you like to have?_____

What skills that you do not presently have would this require?_____

_____How do you plan to obtain these skills?_____

What kind of working situations do you like most? Working with others on

a team_____Working directly with one boss only_____Working for several

principals_____Working in small groups close to principals_____

Other_____What suggestions do you have that would

improve your job?_____

Do you like to work overtime?____Do you prefer variety in your work?____

offices to complete the questionnaires, they know how to do so and will want to cooperate by providing accurate and helpful information. This prevents having to follow up on many questionnaires by unnecessary phone calls or interviews because of inadequate information provided by unenthusiastic employees.

During the meeting, the following information is provided:

- Purpose of the questionnaire.
- How to fill it out in detail.
- How it will be interpreted and summarized.
- How it will be used.
- When the participants will learn the results of the survey. What is anticipated from these results.

A blank form is much easier to understand when a sample questionnaire is used to illustrate how to fill it out. However, it is important to be sure that partcipants provide their own answers and do not copy the sample.

Using Random and Fixed-Interval Sampling

Random and fixed-interval work sampling are both based on the theory that a small number of observations or occurrences of a given activity will tend to follow the same pattern as a large number of observations or occurrences of the same activity. For example, if a receptionist who handles phone calls one-fourth of the time is observed during the course of taking an adequate sample, it can be safely assumed that one-fourth of the time is spent at that activity. If one-fourth of the time equals two hours and the phone call volume is known (for example, 75 calls per day), 1.6 minutes is spent per call (two hours divided by 75). This is an oversimplification of how to apply sampling data, but it explains how it can be used to identify time distribution.

Work sampling has usually been conducted on a random basis by scheduling observation times according to a random-numbers table. This assures statistical validity of the sample once the sample size has been calculated.

Fixed-interval sampling uses a fixed time interval between observations. The interval chosen can be anywhere from 25 minutes to 30 minutes or more, depending on the nature of what is being studied and the degree of precision desired.

Fixed interval sampling may be as effective for word processing because office work itself is somewhat random and it is much easier for the analyst to plan and conduct a study in this manner. Because many offices are large and open, the subjects frequently can see the analyst approaching. Therefore, randomizing the observation schedule may not make any difference. Should the subjects try to fool the analyst by pretending to be busy, randomizing will not prevent them from doing so. In practice, those in a group being sampled who fake eventually tire of keeping up the pretenses after a few days and settle back into their routines. In these situations, data from the first few days can be regarded as practice runs and discarded.

To use random or fixed-interval work sampling, the observer needs to:

1. Determine sample size.
2. Select and schedule the random or fixed-interval sample times and accumulation of observations according to accuracy level desired.

3. Meet with participants who will be observed to explain the activity and gain their cooperation.
4. Calculate the cumulative ratio to the total charts.
5. Conduct the observations.
6. Calculate the results.

How Random or Fixed-Interval Sampling Works   The observer uses a sampling observation chart as shown in Figure 4-2 to observe a work station and places a check in the column on the chart corresponding to the activity observed. For example, if the secretary observed is typing, the observer checks that box on the chart. The observer totals information from all such observations to calculate the results of the sampling survey.

Random or fixed sampling terminology describes those elements included during a sampling. In a survey of an insurance company's secretaries located on three floors of an office building, the elements would include:

- *Characteristics.* Attributes which are the objects of the study: work (typing, filing, phoning) and nonwork (waiting for work) and those tasks listed under work are such characteristics.
- *Elementary Units.* Units which possess the characteristics: secretaries who are either working or nonworking.
- *Universe.* Sum of all the elementary units studied in the given time period: sum (or total hours) of those secretaries surveyed in the three-story building.
- *Population.* Sum of the elementary units within part of a universe that will be studied in a given time frame: the study of the first and second floors at one time represents a population of two floors.
- *Sampling Units.* Those units which form the basis of the sampling process: one elementary unit (secretaries) forms one sampling unit as a group. The study is of a

---

Work Sampling Form to Determine Time Distribution of Secretaries   FIGURE 4-2

Name of Secretary	Typing	Filing	Phone	Copy	Mail Process	Calculate	Create (Write/ Dictate)	Other	Idle (Wait)	Away from Desk

work station (a person's work station) which may or may not be occupied; in either case, the work station is being surveyed.

CHARACTERISTICS STUDIED IN WORD PROCESSING

The survey of the Claims Department will observe the characteristics of five secretaries. (See Table 4-1.)

This sampling demonstrates that the five secretaries typed more than they performed any other task (29.7% or 428 minutes of sampling time) and did not work one-fourth (25.7%) of their working hours.

DOCUMENT ANALYSIS

One of the most important aspects of making a study to obtain accurate document production information is also one of the most difficult, particularly when obtaining gross volume of typing versus net amount of typing produced. Therefore, many analysts still use action paper to measure exactly how many keystrokes a secretary types each day in order to produce final net documents.

A typist or secretary who purposely kept a carbon copy of each stroke typed would soon realize exactly how many more strokes were actually typed each day compared to final out-the-door copy. Typing, usually one of the secretary's main functions, is historically extremely inefficient. Let us learn why by studying a typical secretary's working day.

Gina is one of two secretaries working for the Marketing Department of Arbeck Engineering. Gina works for the manager and, along with the other secretary, supports ten salesmen who report to her boss, Ron Okawa. Ron uses a desktop dictation unit; Gina uses a transcribing machine. Since none of the sales representatives have dictation units, they write their input in longhand. Sometimes, when they are out of the office, they phone Gina, who takes information down in shorthand. Gina maintains a heavy workload. As many as five sales representatives can be on trips at a time.

Documents the two secretaries type include daily correspondence (one- to two-page letters and memos), proposals, purchase requests, progress reports, quarterly reports, monthly reports, and standard letters. Each secretary uses a correcting selectric typewriter and has a key phone to handle phone messages. All office personnel have access to four filing cabinets in the office. They send messages on a TWX machine in another building, where they take typewritten messages. The Marketing Department shares an office copier with the Accounting, Order Processing, Data Processing, and Advertising Departments.

Other tasks Gina and the other secretary perform include handling phones, copying, filing, looking up information, coordinating with other departments (particularly during a proposal or report deadline crisis), processing mail, preparing TWX messages, setting up trips and travel arrangements, arranging and attending meetings, and running errands. Gina's morning frequently proceeds as follows:

	Results of Work Sampling of Five Secretaries	**TABLE 4-1**

A. *Characteristics*	*Samples Accumulated*	*Percentage of Total*
Typing	150	29.7
Filing	100	19.9
Telephone	50	10.0
Calculation	34	6.7
Copying	15	3.0
Writing	15	3.0
Other	10	2.0
Nonwork	130	25.7
Totals	504	100.0

B. *Secretary*	*Total Minutes Worked Per Day*
Helen Marke	350
Jane Logan	350
Harriet Myers	350
Robert Morgan	350
Brenda Crossett	240
Total	1440

C. *Activity*	*Percentage of Total*	*Minutes Available*	*Minutes of Activity* [a]
Typing	29.7	1440	428
Filing	19.9	1440	287
Telephone	10.0	1440	144
Calculation	6.7	1440	97
Copying	3.0	1440	43
Writing	3.0	1440	43
Other	2.0	1440	29
Nonwork	25.7	1440	370
Totals	100		1440

[a]Multiply total minutes times percentage of time devoted to each characteristic or subcharacteristic (task)

- 8:00 a.m.—Arrive at office. Check calendars to see what is scheduled for the day and look for messages. Check boss's dictation unit to see if there is any dictation to transcribe from the previous night. Check with TWX operator for messages. Check in box for messages or work left from the previous day.
- 8:45—Begin work, usually backlog typing of reports, proposals, and correspondence. She usually inserts snapout carbon sets for correspondence. The only

problem this creates is that when she makes a correction, the correcting ribbon on the typewriter corrects the top copy only. Sometimes she will correct the carbons. For reports and proposals, Gina types one copy only and makes additional copies on copier down the hall.

- 8:55—Gina inserts original and two carbons and begins to type a letter. The phone rings. One of the sales representatives needs some information. Gina goes to the files and looks up the information. While she is searching the file, her boss arrives and asks her to make a couple of phone calls.

- 9:10—Gina locates the information in the file and finishes the first phone call. Next she checks her Rollodex (a small, spiral desktop file containing cards approximately 4 inches by 2 inches) to locate the desired phone numbers and places the calls. Just as she starts to continue typing the letter, the phone rings. Gina answers the phone; this time it is a sales representative asking that she take down some information, which she does.

- 9:20—Gina hangs up and continues typing. Her boss calls her into his office. He wants her to make some copies for a meeting that he will be attending. She leaves the office and walks to the copier. It is currently being used by an Engineering Department secretary. Gina waits, then makes her copies. When she returns to her office, her boss gives her a rush longhand memo to type.

- 9:30—Gina removes the letter from the typewriter, inserts new paper (memo with carbons), and types the memo. She takes it to her boss, waits for his signature, and hand delivers it as he has requested.

- 9:45—When she returns to the office, Gina reinserts the letter and continues typing. As she is typing, the telephone rings. It is the Travel Department requesting verification of the travel order for one of the marketing representatives. Gina goes to the file cabinet, looks for and locates the travel order, and takes it to her desk to provide the information requested. She returns the travel order to the file. As she returns to her typing, her boss calls her. She goes into his office and he gives her a cassette he has just completed dictating. It is an important rush job. Once again, Gina removes her typing and begins a new project.

9:55—As she starts to type the new project (a report from the previous day's sales meeting), the phone rings. Gina handles the call and returns to her typing, making an error. She removes the paper and inserts another set and continues typing. The head of the Engineering Department comes in and asks her for some information. Gina looks through her papers in the in-box, locates and hands over the information. Gina returns to her typing.

It must be perfect, with no erasures or corrections. It is getting close to the time her boss needs the memo for his meeting, and he needs a copy for each attendee. Gina asks another secretary to handle her phone calls so that she can complete the project on time.

These are not unusual events in many offices, particularly in busy offices where frequent informal meetings and decision-making activities occur. Can this secretary efficiently produce typing? Frequently marketing departments produce a large volume of typing. What is the best way to measure and learn exactly how much?

Action Paper

Action paper is a term applied to all brands of carbonless paper which creates an image from the original sheet of paper without carbon paper. The two most commonly used brands are Action Paper, made by 3M Company, and NCR, manufactured by National Cash Register. Gina could use action paper to make an exact copy of each page inserted into her typewriter, whether or not it became the final product.

Action paper is widely used to measure typing production, because it provides a copy of each page inserted into the typewriter, regardless of whether it becomes the final mailable document. The mailable document could have required several typings (errors, secretarial changes, and author revisions) and therefore consumed a considerable amount of secretarial and author time in order to get it into the mail. Any time the author sends it back for retyping, it must be proofread another time, which is also time-consuming.

Procedures for Using Action Paper Each secretary is provided with a stack of prenumbered sheets of action paper to use during the survey. The secretary is instructed to insert a sheet of action paper behind every sheet inserted into the typewriter to create a copy of everything typed, no matter how brief. This records exactly how much typing occurs at each work station. From these copies, one can learn how much typing is similar in nature and how much has to be retyped because of interruptions, changes, or author revisions. All action copies are normally collected by the analyst at the end of each day to summarize the information. The secretary may also be maintaining a secretarial time log of tasks. If all typing task/time information is being collected from the action paper survey, the secretary is requested to fill out all of the information on the action paper, which usually includes:

- Author of the document.
- Form of input (longhand, machine dictation, shorthand, copy).
- How long it took to type.
- Sequence of the typing (is it the first, second, third typing?).
- If retyped, reason for retyping, e.g., author revision, change in format.

Action paper provides the following information:

- Number of actual typing lines made each day.
- Number of pages typed each day by each typist.
- Number of lines typed in each document classification and on each page by each typist.
- Where mistakes occur (top of page, middle, bottom).
- Kinds of retypings (similar letters, similar paragraphs).

Information from the action paper is summarized into the following statistics:

1. Current (gross) typing volume total.
2. Final (net) output volume (not including retypings).

3. Volume of each category of documents.
4. Volume of each kind of retyping.
5. Volume of each kind of error.

This information is used to determine what improvements and changes need to be made in the office structure and what kind of typing equipment best suits the typing needs.

Instructing Secretaries for Document Analysis

One first needs to decide how long the survey should last and exactly how it will be conducted. Frequently a survey will continue for two weeks, with the secretaries in one department particpating. In this case, the analyst meets with the secretaries and provides each secretary with a pad of prenumbered action paper with the following instructions:

"We have been asked to conduct a special survey to determine your typing volume and related problems such as typing deadlines and interruptions. The purpose of the survey is to see if there need to be some changes in the typing system.

"After considerable research, we feel that probably the most accurate way to determine this is by keeping track of each sheet of paper you have to insert into your typewriter in order to get your typing done. This probably sounds like a great deal of extra work, but we feel that it will be worth it. It will provide you with an opportunity to show how many times you have to retype when work is revised or when errors occur because of interruptions from your typing. We hope it will help draw a picture of your typing tasks in relation to the rest of your job.

"We will be available to provide any assistance, answer any questions you might have, and collect the copy paper at the end of each day. Here is how it will work.

"The special paper is already numbered and has boxes in the lower right-hand corner where you can record information which will be of value to both you and me in making this study.

"Each time you insert paper into your typewriter, place a sheet of this special prenumbered paper behind it. Do this even for envelopes and labels. Whenever you are interrupted and make a mistake and throw away a page, keep the copy and insert the next numbered sheet behind it. This helps demonstrate restarts you have to make because of interruptions.

"Some documents such as tables are more difficult and take longer. We need to know how much longer they take. After you have completed typing a page, write down the date and time in the box in the corner. You will note that you can also write in the number of lines, author's name and department, and any other special information about the document you feel is important. This will take just a few seconds, but it is important to write it down so you will know how much you typed for one person or one department, what form of input you received, or any other special information about each page.

"This prenumbered paper will help keep track of all the typing you do each day, not just your final output. It helps to keep an accurate record of all the retypings you have to do for various reasons. For example, it shows when you are interrupted by a phone call and strike the wrong key or when you have to take out one sheet of paper to do another job. It indicates when you have to reinsert that sheet and it doesn't line up correctly, causing you to have to start over. It lets you know when you have to retype a page because someone changes his or her mind.

"Whatever the reason, it helps to keep track of the volume of typing you do each day, even though you have many other responsibilities. By learning this information, we can find out ways to improve the way you process your work.

"The action paper will be a tool to communicate all of these facts which affect the ability of you and your department to get the typing done. We can find out when you type documents which are similar in nature. We think that you will find the information you learn from this survey helpful. We expect it will help us to decide what changes need to be made to make your typing more efficient."

The meeting should reflect an atmosphere of enthusiasm, cooperation, and team spirit. Most secretaries view this kind of analysis as a threat in which their typing accuracy or secretarial capabilities are being questioned. Instructions should be complete, concise, and clear. The analyst should be available to answer questions and provide support to the secretaries during the survey.

COMPUTER ANALYSIS

Many analysts use a work request form instead of action paper. After typing a job, the secretary can record all the necessary information onto the work request for each typing job. All work requests forms are then read into a computer, which summarizes the information. Figure 4-3 shows a work request form that could be used for a feasibility study or for work measurement to determine what is being produced by the word processing operations.

Use of the work request form requires the same kind of complete cooperation of the study participants as the use of any questionnaire or form that needs to be filled in. A computerized work request form survey may be conducted in one of two manners:

1.   Conducting the survey over a designated period of time.
2.   Continuing the survey until a designated number of forms is used up.

Procedures for computer analysis are begun by deciding what information is to be obtained in the study. For example, each category of documents must be listed. Each organization has its own list of documents. Figure 4-3 illustrates three kinds of origin: handwritten, dictated, and revised. Because some firms might have more, one needs to learn all forms of origination used by the originator making the study. Figure 4-3 also illustrates several kinds of equipment used: electric typewriter, manual typewriter, memory typewriter, or mag card. There is space allowed to indicate other types of equipment used. Only those kinds of equipment used in the organization

FIGURE 4-3   Work Request Form

Center	Work Request Form		
0 0 3	(Put each job on a separate requisition)		

Job Number	Authors Last Name	Dept.	Typist Initials

Origin	Document Typed	Equipment Used

Origin:
- 1 Handwritten
- 2 Dictated
- 3 Revision

Document Typed:
- 1 Correspondence
- 2 Memo
- 3 Procedure Manuals
- 4 Data Proc Manuals
- 5 Lists
- 6 Reports
- 7 Statistical
- 8 Questionnaires
- 9 Labels
- 10 Envelopes
- 11 Pre-Record
- 12 Manuscripts
- 13 TWX Messages
- 14 Form Letters
- 15
- 16
- 17
- 18
- 19
- 20 Other Explain Below

Equipment Used:
- 1 Elec. Typewriter
- 2
- 3 LEXITRON
- 4
- 5
- 6
- 7 TWX-
- 8 Other Explain Below

Date In	Time In	AM 1 / PM 2	Rush	Date Start	Time Start	AM 1 / PM 2
			1			

Date Completed	Time Completed	AM 1 / PM 2	Lunches Worked Through	Weekend Hours & Min. Worked	Total Lines

DO NOT KEY PUNCH BELOW THIS LINE

Typing Interruption: Hrs.   Min.   Indicate type of interruption
- | | Handle Rush Job
- | | Training
- | | Answer Phones
- | | Take Dictation
- | | Clerical
- | | Meeting
- | | Copier Work
- | | Go-fering
- | | Cover During Break / Lunch

© Copyright 1976 · Office Communications Consultants, Inc. | | NOTE SPECIAL INSTRUCTIONS ON BACK

should be listed. Information at the bottom of the form might also differ according to what the organization wishes to study.

After a computer survey is completed, the following results are summarized by computer (summary reports are self-explanatory):

1. *Summary Report.* Production totals for the study period by department: number of typing jobs, authors, lines typed, pages produced, and total operator typing time for the study period.
2. *Office Report.* Results from the work request forms: pages totaled, turnaround time in hours and minutes, operator typing time per job, and typing time per page.
3. *Equipment Origin Output Report.* Comparison of equipment used during the study, by application and origin of input.
4. *Equipment Productivity By Output.* Production, revision speed, and job turnaround time by equipment type and application and specific information relative to the firm (such as surgical and operation reports for a hospital).
5. *Department Client Report.* Author usage and method of origin (volume per author and summary of each origination method).
6. *Operator Typist Report.* Productivity by origin and the equipment used to type the application.

7. *Edit Listing*. Work request forms which were rejected by the computer with the type of error causing that rejection noted.

When using computer analysis, the analyst uses the following procedures in a manner similar to those used with action paper:

1. Provides a supply of forms to the typists.
2. Carefully explains procedures and the importance of providing *all* pertinent information.
3. Remains available to assist and make sure of total understanding and cooperation during each day and collects forms at the end of each day.
4. Summarizes and observes during study.
5. Communicates enthusiasm and cooperative spirit during survey.

All forms of data collecting result in summaries which are then interpreted to determine the productivity of the current system and the improvements that should be made.

Figure 4-4 shows a form used to conduct a study to determine the capability of typing and phototypesetting. This form was used by the participating secretaries to maintain production records for four weeks. The information was keypunched, and the summary in Figure 4-5 reports the current work volume and time distribution needed to arrive at the analysis in Figure 4-6.

Job Control Form   **FIGURE 4-4**

Date	Job No.	Document	Total Lines	Turnaround Time

FIGURE 4-5   **Department Summary Report**

						DATE 08/14/8__
DEPT. NAME	NO. OF JOBS	NO. OF AUTHORS	LINES	WHOLE PAGES	PART PAGES	O TIME HH.MM
EXECUTIVE	27	7	672	15	1/2	7.15
LOANS	9	4	230	5	1/4	4.25
SPECIAL SERVICES	60	4	2055	46	3/4	45.25
MARKETING	78	3	2682	60	3/4	42.12
TRUST	28	3	984	22	1/2	16.57
PERSONNEL	34	3	1386	31	1/2	16.47
ACCOUNTING	95	5	4841	110	1/4	424.19
AUDIT	1	3	44	1		.20
DATA PROCESSING	4	5	17		1/2	.18
LEGAL	60	4	667	15	1/4	9.46
OPERATIONS	2	20	47	1	1/4	1.30
TOTAL	402	61	13771	312	3/4	578.34

Key:
O TIME = TYPING HOURS

INTERVIEWING

During the orientation meeting, the task force explains that some, but not all, of the personnel will be interviewed during the survey. Interviewing everyone would take too much time and is not necessary. If a firm employs five purchasing agents, it is not necessary to interview each one. Personnel to be interviewed may include (a) management, (b) section/department heads (including middle management and supervisors), (c) work originators, (d) staff members, (e) secretaries, and (f) people responsible for certain activities such as mail distribution, telephone and communications systems and equipment, reproduction services, photocomposition or typesetting, data processing, office layout and design, and personnel and salary administration.

Individual interviewing helps to uncover elements that might otherwise have been missed and obtain important management points of view and future strategies.

Management Interviews

Before beginning the survey, management stated its plans for the future, its corporate strategy, and company short-term and long-term objectives. But by interviewing management, the analyst gains an insight into management's operating strategy and policy, the personality or management style, and how this may affect daily work

Summary of Study	**FIGURE 4-6**
Number of departments surveyed	11
Number of typing jobs	253
Handwritten (68.7%)	174
Dictated (9.4%)	24
Revisions (21.7%)	55
Number of authors typed for during study	61
Number of rush jobs (19.7%)	50
Average turnaround time per job	18 hr 35 min
Average typing time per job	1 hr 17 min
Average typing time per page	16 min
Average time job sat waiting to be typed	17 hr 18 min
Total lines typed	13,771
Total pages produced	312
26 lines per page (normal page)	
13 lines per half page	
Average lines per job	54
Average pages per job	1¼
26 lines per page	
13 lines per half page	
Total typing hours	578 hr 34 min
Number of typists	25
Average typing time per typist during study	23 hr 13 min
Total hours available for typing	2030 hr

operations. The interview also provides information as to the projects and paperwork that cross management's desk.

Middle managers provide the interviewer with the workflow information of actual departmental and daily operations. Figure 4–7 illustrates the kind of information that might be asked during a management interview. The interviewer should first determine what executives and departments are responsible, to whom the work or responsibilities are delegated, and what is the related workflow. The interviewer should be sure to learn of any planned changes in the manpower, plant, and equipment acquisitions or other activities reflecting organizational costs and profitability.

Section/Department Heads

The interviewer wants to obtain an overview of the operating department's personnel, kinds of documents, deadlines, priorities, operating status, and any foreseen or planned changes. Specific activities carried on by the department, the flow of those activities, documents produced, and results are studied. The interviewer can draw the workflow during the interviews, chart how the activity begins, its path, its problem areas, spinoffs, and its destination. The interview process allows the analyst to ask

FIGURE 4-7   **Example of Originator's Questionnaire**

ORIGINATOR'S QUESTIONNAIRE

Name _____ Department _____

Title _____ Secretary _____

Date _____ Telephone _____

Is your current secretarial support sufficient? Yes_____ No_____

If not, explain: _____

1. How many originators share your secretary? _____

2. How do you originate your work? Longhand_____ % Shorthand_____ %

    Copy_____ % Machine Dictation_____ %

3. How long do you spend creating documents each day? Average_____

    When _____

4. Do you originate work away from your office? Yes_____ No_____

    How frequently? _____ What type of work? _____

5. What documents do you request in rough-draft form? Correspondence

    _____ Text_____ What percent of your work? _____ % How often? _____

6. How long does it take to get your documents back from typing? _____

7. Do you sometimes send out work that you would like to have revised to

    meet a deadline? Yes_____ No_____

8. Do you sometimes not send out letters because of lack of time to

    originate? Yes_____ No_____ Because your secretary is too busy?

    Yes_____ No_____

9. When are your busiest periods? _____

10. Are there backlogs in your typed documents? _____ How long? _____

11. Are you satisfied with the quality of the documents you author?

    Yes_____ No_____

12. Do you send out similar letters to several addressees? Yes_____

    No_____

13. Do you compose documents that contain paragraphs that are repetitive?

    Yes_____ No_____

FIGURE 4-7 (continued)

---

14. Are you performing tasks that could be delegated to a staff assistant or secretary? Yes_____ No_____ If so, what are they?

_____

_____

15. Are there functions not being performed you could perform if you had more time? Yes_____ No_____ Would they generate typing?_____

---

questions and reexamine to ensure accuracy. Specific volume criteria may be gathered from other interviews with operating staff or secretaries.

Work Originators (Principals)

The people hired to market, engineer, purchase, and perform other work for the organization are the ones whom word processing serves. These people may already have work habits they do not want changed and feel threatened by the study. For example, most engineers have used longhand all their lives to originate their paperwork (memos, letters, specifications, reports, and proposals) and they do not want to change. This works for them—they do it and it gets typed—and they carry on their daily work. Now they may assume that management is thinking of changing these work habits and requiring them to perform their work in a manner for which they have never been trained. Not only is this a threat; they feel it will slow down their work, impede their progress to meet deadlines, and force them to change many of their work habits.

Also, people who use longhand on their jobs and have their own secretaries who can read and interpret their longhand to produce documents resent the fact that someone different may be producing their work—someone with whom they do not have close communication or control over and whose skills may not be as good as their own secretaries'. These originators may not have had time to instruct their secretaries on how to set up a document, who is to receive copies, and how it should be filed or distributed. They have been able to delegate these activities to the secretaries who may have worked for them for some time and proven to be invaluable.

Now things are going to be different. In cases in which the originator was not a particularly good speller or did not know proper punctuation or some other language skill, the secretary always handled those matters. Now the crutch is being removed. Or perhaps the originator always wants letters to be formatted a certain way and sentences and paragraphs to end a particular way. This person may fear that the word processing center or person will make changes in his or her work that the originator does not want. The present secretary always has the correct names and addresses for the originator's usual correspondence; now the originator fears he or she will have to dictate this information to the center, anticipating that it would not have that information. These are fears, not necessarily facts; but they are reasons why people resent having their work habits changed. Therefore, the interviewing of originators must be handled discreetly. The interviewer may need to sell the principal on the value of the survey, explaining that it is not intended to threaten, but that it is meant to help the total organization by saving costs of internal operations and to benefit each person by providing continual high-quality production services.

The questionnaire in Figure 4-7 can be used to interview an originator. Information sought in interviews includes:

- The kinds of activities performed by the person and the resulting paperwork.
- Who does the work for that person.
- Every kind of task performed and skill required.
- Special situations, such as periodic deadlines and priorities.
- How all work is currently performed for that person; e.g., some may be input to data entry through keypunching.
- Planned or foreseen changes.
- The person's special requirements and feelings about his or her work and participation in the organization.

Secretarial Interviews

Guidelines to follow when interviewing secretaries include:

1. Interview a representative portion of the secretaries (or all secretaries, if necessary).
2. Ask to see the form the secretary filled out listing the tasks performed at his or her work station.
3. If the secretary is particpating in an action paper or computer study, refer to the information provided from this study. If not, ask to see sample copies of correspondence, reports, and other documents that he or she prepares. All relevant information for each document should be described on the questionnaire.
4. All interviews should be objective and should avoid confidential personal discussions.
5. The secretary being interviewed should feel that the information is important to the value of the survey and to the total organization. Many secretaries are extremely aware of what is going on in the organization. Their interviews should be meaningful, accurate, and totally descriptive of their work stations. (The interview with the first secretary in a department may be fairly long; after interviewing one or two secretaries, subsequent interviews are apt to provide repetitive information and may require less time.)

Rules for Interviewing

When interviewing secretaries, principals, department heads, or management, it is important to be objective at all times. Interview guidelines are to:

1. Explain your role and what you are attempting to do.
2. Listen. If the interviewee digresses, carefully guide him or her back to the point. Do not cross examine.
3. Do not listen to gossip; cut it off tactfully.
4. Discover what is being done the way that individual does it, not the way others (boss, department head, secretary) think it is being done.
5. Draw the workflow.
6. Obtain all details. Ask questions when you are unsure.
7. Ask the interviewee to phone you if he or she later remembers something essential.
8. Answer all questions as fully and objectively as possible.
9. Note the attitude of the interviewee.
10. Practice interviewing beforehand (important to effective interviewing).

ADMINISTRATIVE SUPPORT STUDIES

An administrative support study provides the volume and time distribution of all nontyping tasks. In addition, an administrator may want to determine other project work that administrative secretaries could be performing. Therefore, both secretaries and principals will participate in this study.

The same techniques as those used in typing analysis, job analysis, or secretarial job analysis may be used in administrative support analysis: questionnaires, work sampling, and interviewing. Questionnaires are specifically designed to learn the amount of administrative support task time being used in the present system and to point out problems or duplications. The manager or principal's questionnaire may be used to upgrade the administrative secretary's job to take over such tasks as dictating routine correspondence or projects the principals find they can delegate. Such tasks might include preparing periodic reports and other documents that may not require the special expertise of the principals or managers.

Many firms are encouraging their marketing representatives, engineers, technical experts and staff personnel to delegate these tasks to their administrative secretaries, thereby freeing these principals' time for management and accomplishments important to the firm.

PREPARING SUPPLIES

Once the data collecting methods are selected, the analyst should make sure all necessary questionnaires and other supplies are on hand for the study. The analyst should set up his or her desk and organize all forms and supplies to make sure preparations are complete before beginning the study.

MANAGEMENT MEMO

Before the preorientation meeting, the management memo should be sent to all participants or affected employees. Communicating with all employees during the study will make them feel involved.

PREPARING TO CONDUCT THE STUDY

During the planning stages, observation of the facilities provides an overview of what to expect from the study. Other preliminary data accumulated beforehand that helps ensure accuracy and provides background includes current salaries, burden factors (fringe benefits, costs of office space), overtime, or outside supplementary help. The documents providing this information include:

- Personnel and salary records, including job classifications and payscales.
- Overtime and temporary help costs for the past year.
- Inventory of office equipment and costs.
- Floorplans and organization charts.
- Attrition rates.
- Burden costs (insurance, vacation pay, sick leave, building space, office equipment attributing to their percentage of overhead).
- Annual report and financial documents.
- Phone directory and personnel listings.

Planning the Orientation Meetings

Prestudy orientation meetings are introduced by top management. Management first explains the study, purpose, and accomplishments expected from the study. Next management introduces the analyst and task force. Separate meetings may be scheduled for each group meeting: management, department and section managers, operating supervisors, principals, and secretaries.

Purpose of Orientation Meetings

The intent of the orientation meeting is to make employees aware that this is a management project, it is important to management and the company employees, and each individual is expected to participate.

Topics To Be Included

The order of topics covered generally conforms to the following pattern:

1. Purpose of the study (by top management). What is expected to be accomplished. Explain the concepts and benefits of word processing and relate them to the organization and to the employees.

2. Who will conduct the study. Introduce project managers and task force.
3. How the study will be conducted (by analyst or project manager of task force). Explain what techniques will be used, how each technique is going to be used, how each person will participate, and what will be expected from each individual. Illustrations of forms used to gather information, the schedule of survey activities, and planned completion time are shown.
4. What is expected on the part of each participant. Clarify the specific objectives anticipated by management from the survey and following implementation of word processing. State who will be responsible for conducting the program and how the participants can communicate with them.
5. What details are pertinent to the survey such as specific survey methods being used, locations where interviews will take place, and ways to communicate any necessary changes in schedule. Conclude with the question and answer session and preparatory schedule and statement.

The idea is to sell each individual on the benefit of the study to the firm (improve productivity and reduce costs) and to each employee (improve the quality of the job). It should be explained that the firm expects to receive benefits in two major ways: from operating more cost effectively in the future to meet specific goals that management sets and from each person's being able to perform his or her work more effectively.

Facilities and Time Span

Presentations usually take about one-half to one hour and take place in a conference room which is free from interruptions, is comfortable and informal, and has adequate seating facilities and visual aids.

Attendees

Each meeting should have no more than 20 attendees. This may mean in some cases splitting one segment into two sessions. For example, there may be 30 department managers. Their meetings will then be divided into two groups of 15 each.

Visuals

Audio-visual techniques used in the presentation might include films, transparencies, slide-tapes, slides, and flip charts, with handouts to be distributed at the meeting's conclusion. Many firms use films from word processing vendors that tell the word processing story—what it is, how it works, and what it has achieved for other organizations. Visuals such as transparencies demonstrate how the survey will be conducted (the forms to be used and how to use them).

Atmosphere

A relaxed atmosphere should be maintained during the presentations, encouraging employee feelings of involvement and participation. Questions should be held until the conclusion of the presentation, which allows attendees the opportunity to ask specific questions without leaving others out. The presenter seeks to maintain control while maintaining an atmosphere of management and employee working together.

SUMMARIZING DATA

During the study, analysts begin arranging information onto summary forms while it is being accumulated. Otherwise, the sheer volume of data being collected may seem insurmountable for efficient analysis. Using a computer to process the summarizing saves considerable time and reduces paperwork. The information summaries then need to be put into appropriate form for interpretation.

What techniques best summarize and interpret the survey data? How can they help management decide what form of word processing is most feasible for the organization? What methods of interpretation are easiest to understand, relate, interpret, and evaluate?

Undoubtedly, visual messages are easiest to relate, interpret, and quickly understand. They must, however, be adequately substantiated. A word processing analyst may use such techniques as floorplans, workflow diagrams, graphs, flowcharts, pie charts, and process charts to illustrate the current system and present the proposed new system.

Charting provides a visual representation of findings and illustrates exceptions to the usual routine. Charting can be used to:

- Collect and present facts about a system in an organized manner.
- Classify and display the facts in an easy-to-read and understandable arrangement.
- Present new proposals in an easy-to-understand form.
- Graphically contrast the old with the new.

Figures 4-8 and 4-9 illustrate different visual methods of presenting summaries of word processing studies for easy interpretation.

Categorizing

Information is first listed by individual secretary and classification, then by the department, and finally by the total group studied. Cross-sorts (the summary of information in two or more ways) are categorized as desired. For example, cross-sorts might include:

- Wait time.
- Document length (average or other).
- Restart ratios (from the action paper).
- Repetitive letters and **boilerplate** (that is, similar information typed repeatedly and easily apparent from an action paper survey).
- Volume of each kind of document (letters, memos, multiple-page text, statistical reports, forms, form letters).

Study of 4000 Secretaries in 13 Companies   FIGURE 4-8

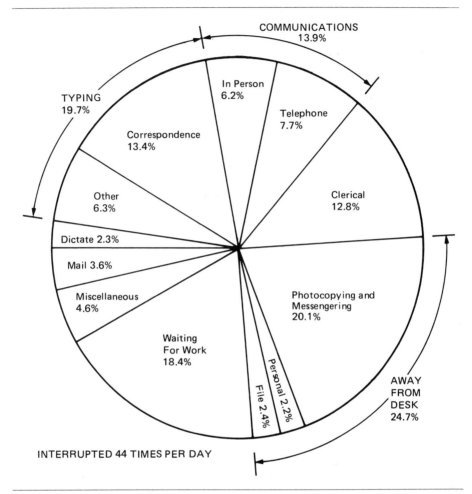

- Task distribution by hour.
- Range of average number of pages per document.
- Kinds, amount, and percentage of errors.
- Volume and percentage of each form of input (copy, longhand, dictation, revision).
- Percentage of revision per page.
- Number of revisions per document or page.

Presenting summarized information in visual form, such as pie charts, flow diagrams, floorplans, or bar charts, makes information easier to explain and to understand. Such charts provide a cross section of how work is distributed. Time distribution is frequently visualized by means of pie charts (see Figure 4-8), while bar graphs may be used to present the distribution of the tasks (typing, work, nonwork,

FIGURE 4-9   Support Requirements Summary

ADMINISTRATIVE HOURS/MANPOWER RECAP

AREA NAM.

ADMIN. HRS.

Support Level	Hrs.	Hrs.	Hrs.	Hrs.	Hrs.	Hrs.		Total Hrs.	Manpower (Total Hrs. ÷ Hrs./Wk.)	Manpower @ %	Work Coordination	Admin. Recap
Current												
Deficiency												
Delegable												
Planned Change												

Special Instructions:

1. To determine Manpower Factor—at the Current Support Level, divide Total Hrs by Manpower =

    Manpower Factor

2. To determine Admin. Equivalent Manpower—for each support level, divide Admin. Hs. by the Manpower Factor.

EQUIV. MANPOWER

Support Level	Admin.	Corr.	Admin.	Corr.	Admin.	Corr.	Admin.	Corr.	Admin.	Corr.	Admin.	Corr.
Current												
Deficiency												
Delegable												
Planned Change												

Correspondence/Administrative Staffing Recap

AREA/GROUP NAME

STAFFING

Support Level	Equiv. Man-power	Secy. Man-power	Equiv. Man-power	Secy. Man-power	Equiv. Man-power	Secy. Man-power	Equiv. Man-power	Secy. Man-power		Secy. Manpower Admin.	Corr.	Work. Coordin.	Total C/AS Staff
Current													
Deficiency													
Delegable													
Planned Change													

administrative tasks) by department. Pie charts or bar graphs may also be used to interpret random sampling characteristics such as time distribution. Manual system charts may be work distribution charts, flow process charts, multicolumn process charts, machine charts, and flow diagrams.

Using Flowcharts

Flowcharts help to point out unecessary steps and duplications in the flow of an activity. One might design a flowchart in either layout, block, or grid form.

Layout   A layout flowchart is made by taking the floorplan and marking arrows to denote the flow of an application or the movement of the people. This method highlights inefficient or inadequate personnel placement and points to where changes in personnel placement or workflow would improve the system. It also points out duplication of effort where steps in the workflow can be eliminated or changed.

Block   A block diagram is made by stringing together a series of blocks, with each block representing an operation in the flow of an application. This highlights all the steps required for an operation or activity and is very useful for recording details during an interview. Most interviewers use flowcharting as an easy means of following the interviewer's description of working routines. The analyst can ask for verification during the interview to make sure that the workflow of the activity is accurate.

Grid   In the case of more complex operations, the grid is most effective. This method ties together the stages of a project as it moves through several departments or stages (from taking an order to shipping a product to the customer). The grid flowchart illustrated in Figure 4–10, follows the path of a sales proposal from the customer's request to the salesperson's handing it to the client.

Checklists

A checklist provides an analyst with a suggestion device and memory aid. A chart or diagram provides the broad spectrum, while a checklist helps the analyst remember important points and relevant facts. Typical checklist questions might be:

- What functions or activities take place most of the time?
- What contribution does each employee make to each activity?
- Where is any misdirected effort?
- Are skills being used properly?
- Are employees doing any unrelated tasks?
- Is work distributed evenly and fairly?

Sometimes a study in one area triggers the need for further investigation into other matters. For instance, when more time is spent on functions other than the department's major function, the reason should be determined, and further study may be necessary.

FIGURE 4-10   Grid Flowchart of Sales Proposal

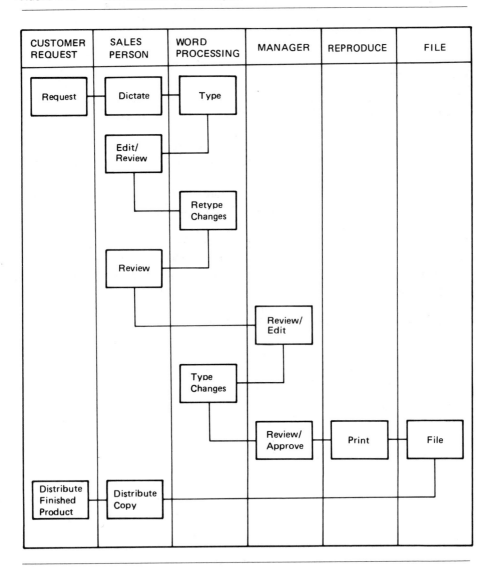

Document Summary Forms

Summaries of information are first listed on the document summary form shown in Figure 4-9. This helps summarize the current system of operations and areas of duplication and presents a quick analysis of high and low volumes. The summaries point out specific points to follow up and question during meetings or interviews.

Summaries of the present system provide the current volume of production by present personnel. A study of correspondence and administrative support provides the total number of work hours currently utilized for each characteristic or subcharacteristic (work or nonwork or kinds of work or nonwork).

OVERVIEW OF THE PRESENT SYSTEM

Once the workflow of the present system is diagrammed and related to the present geographical layout and office structure, an overview may be designed, illustrating the present operating system.

COSTS OF THE PRESENT SYSTEM

By obtaining current labor costs and time volume, the present system operating costs can be determined. This includes overtime or outside help costs. Total present costs include:

- Personnel costs, including salaries, fringe benefits, and burden (office space), as well as costs for overtime and outside help.
- Environment costs, including furniture, space, percentage of overhead attributable, paper, ribbons, media.
- Office equipment and supply costs, including typewriters, dictation units, copiers, terminals, teletypewriters, files.
- Other production costs such as duplicating, printing, distribution.

   After the cost and overview of the present system have been summarized, the analyst determines:

- What changes need to be made.
- How much labor and equipment is needed to achieve present production volume (with a limit in reserve for increased workload).
- What structure best fits the needs, including personnel alignment.
- What equipment best fits the needs and the proposed operating structure.
   Total cost projections for the proposed system.

This information is provided in the following chapters.

SUMMARY

Word processsing analysis of current operations are conducted by (a) collecting management information for the overview, (b) analyzing the time distribution of secretaries, and (c) analyzing the volume of documents produced.

   Secretarial time distribution may be obtained by random or fixed interval work sampling or by having the secretaries log time as they perform their work. Many firms either use consultants or have their own computerized system which tallies this information by having secretaries fill out work request forms for each job typed.

Document analysis may be done by having secretaries fill out logs listing each document, its author and department source, and form of origination with a total number of lines or pages for the document. One technique used to analyze all the varying factors that influence typing productivity is to have secretaries keep action paper copies of each document. This special prenumbered paper contains blocks where the secretaries log such information as author's name, whether it is a retype or new document, typing time, and total number of lines.

Information from these methods is then summarized for interpretation. The total number of hours required to produce documents under the current system provides measurement of current productivity. This is analyzed to determine whether the system can be improved, and if so, in what way. Information provided by collecting typing data includes duplicated typing; kinds and number of errors; and amount of time spent in each typing task, including first time creation, duplicated typing, revision, and error correction.

Administrative surveys analyze secretarial time distribution for all nontyping tasks. These are generally accomplished by having principals fill out questionnaires on which they indicate the kinds of tasks they could delegate, rate the kind of support they are receiving, and designate support areas which could be improved. Secretaries fill out questionnaires listing the kinds of jobs they do, amount of time devoted to them, and how their daily time is spent. Work sampling is also used to conduct an administrative secretarial study.

Many analysts design their own forms to fit the specific organization being studied. At the prestudy orientation meeting, the analyst explains to the study participants and the secretaries the importance of the study to them and to the firm. Their support and desire to participate is important for an accurate and meaningful survey.

In random or fixed-interval work sampling, an observer will visit secretarial work areas and mark on a preprinted chart what task the secretary is doing at that time. All surveyed tasks are tallied to determine the amount of time spent working and nonworking and the amount of time devoted to each task.

Action paper surveys also require complete cooperation and involvement of the secretaries. From these surveys the analyst learns the gross and net volume of typed strokes per day by each secretary, gross and net volume of strokes typed for each document, where mistakes occur, and the kinds of retyping made. These studies help to point out where time can be saved to eliminate duplicated typings and revision typing. It also indicates typing or work problems. For example, if many pages are restarted, the secretary is probably being interrupted while typing. Summaries from action paper studies are used to determine the most appropriate equipment and office structure to improve an office's operations.

Each of these techniques requires well-planned orientation meetings with the participants to allay any fears they may have of losing their jobs or being found inefficient. A study of one's job tends to make one feel that the *person* is being analyzed, and it is important to understand that it is the working situation, *not* the employee, that is being analyzed.

Specially designed work request forms can be used in conjunction with a computer. Computerized studies can be processed in less time and provide a great deal of meaningful information and must be introduced and explained just as carefully to assure complete cooperation and accurate information. Summaries from these reports provide the number of typing jobs, authors, lines typed, pages produced, and total operator typing time during the survey. They may be used for comparison studies, feasibility studies, and work measurement.

Most surveys include interviews with managers, principals, and secretaries. Interviews may be scheduled for one-half to a full hour. Not all employees need to be interviewed, but those interviewed should be representative of the group being studied. Information sought during interviews includes (a) activities performed; (b) resulting paperwork; (c) who performs work and tasks involved; (d) special work requirements; (e) present workflow and methods; (f) changes planned or foreseen; and (g) each employee's perspective of the job, organization, and working methods.

In order to conduct interviews professionally, interviewers need to be good listeners; be tactful, objective, and sensitive; and be able to guide, perceive clearly, flow the activity, and obtain accurate and significant details.

Careful preparations need to be made before the study begins, including (a) working out flowcharts; gathering floorplans, organization charts, and personnel directories with phone listings and location of personnel; and acquiring costs of operations (reproduction, TWX, telephone, filing, salaries, fringe benefits, office space, supplies, purchases of equipment and furnishings); (b) preparing the study schedule by arranging interviews, holding orientation meetings, allowing time to summarize, and presenting the system and activities to take place; (c) preparing the study orientation meeting, including visual aids, format, and schedule; and arranging each meeting with a group of attendees of small enough size for good communications; (d) preparing all forms and other supplies to be used for the study; (e) practicing interviewing if necessary; and (f) having management prepare and distribute the study memo informing employees of purpose and objectives.

During and after data is accumulated, it is summarized onto special summary forms that categorize the information. The summaries provide such information as number of gross and net lines of typing per secretary, per department, and per dictator; percent of each kind of input; and number of lines of each document. This information is interpreted into visual form, such as through charts and graphs which provide visual illustrations of categories of information. Charts help to present facts in an organized manner by classifying and displaying facts and make the information easy to explain and understand.

Checklists may be used to supplement charts in order to support ideas and data summarized on the chart. They also serve as memory checks to facilitate explanations of the visual charts.

Document summary forms graphically illustrate the information accumulated in specific categories, such as total typing time by secretaries, department, and the total group, and help to cross-sort information.

Information from random sampling or action paper surveys might be illustrated on a pie chart where each characteristic or subcharacteristic represents a percentage of the pie.

Flowcharts are extremely effective techniques to present information visually and may be in either layout, block, or grid form. A layout flowchart, or floorplan, places arrows to depict the movement path or flow of an application or people in processing an activity. It points out duplications and roadblocks to smooth operations. A block diagram is made by stringing blocks together, with each block representing an operation in the application workflow. This technique helps interpret during interviews. A grid flowchart illustrates the flow of a project through departments or stages to completion.

A visual representation of the summarized results of the current system and new system design help to interpret the following information.

Current System

- Number of employees producing the current volume.
- Number of required administrative and typing work hours.
- Required volume of output.
- Current volume of other factors included such as reproduction, filing time, TWX/Telex volume.
- Amount of time used to produce a document and a page.
- Workflow related to current working procedures and problems.
- Workflow related to geographical layout and related problems.
- Costs related to the current system.
- How time is used.

New System Design

- Workflow with procedures to solve problems.
- Workflow with layout to save time and increase productivity.
- Costs of new system, including administrative and correspondence work hours, equipment, furnishings, supplies, and startup costs.
- Expected objectives for turnaround time, document productivity, employee productivity.

REVIEW QUESTIONS

1. Name three techniques that are used to study the secretarial job.
2. Discuss two techniques used for document analysis.
3. Name two techniques used in administrative surveys.
4. What information is provided at a meeting at which questionnaires are distributed for secretaries to fill out?
5. How does the theory of random or fixed-interval sampling work?
6. Explain what uses charting serves in summarizing data.
7. How are checklists used?
8. In what way are document summary forms used during the feasibility study?
9. Name the categories of activities used in random sampling.
10. How would you conduct document analysis? Why?

DISCUSSION QUESTIONS

1. Discuss the merits of random and fixed-interval sampling for word processing analysis.
2. Discuss the importance of document analysis in word processing.
3. Discuss some of the interruptions a secretary might experience while typing.

4.   Why would a secretary resist using action paper?
5.   Discuss when pie charts and bar graphs would be more useful than flowcharts.
6.   Discuss when to use the different kinds of flowcharts—layout, block, and grid.

CASES

Case 4-1   Electronics Company

Modern Microsystems, Inc. (MMI), is a medium-size electronics firm which mainly manufactures chips and electronic parts for manufacturers of data processing and word processing equipment and other firms requiring their devices. They have begun to plan a feasibility study of their internal operations, including both administrative and correspondence operations. The study will include 52 secretaries from management through manufacturing and lower level departments and sections.

1.   Select the data collection techniques you would use if you were making the study.
2.   List the necessary preparations for the survey.
3.   Describe how you will conduct the survey from the information provided.

Case 4-2   Law Firm

Miller, Robins, Preston, and Mead is a law firm in San Mateo, California, consisting of 38 attorneys, 4 of whom are senior partners; 32 secretaries; an office manager; a bookkeeper; and a receptionist/telephone operator. In order to be hired, a secretary must have legal experience and be able to take shorthand. Secretarial salaries range from $850 to $1500 per month, depending upon the position of the attorney the secretary works for and the length of time the secretary has been with the firm. All attorneys have their own secretary except for the lowest level and newest attorneys hired.

   The current system consists of:

•   *Origination*: Shorthand, longhand, copy, and desktop magnetic belt dictation units.
•   *Production*: Executive, selectric, or correcting selectric typewriters.
•   *Reproduction*: Xerox 2400 copier.
•   *Filing*: Handled by secretaries in their offices or attorney's offices independently.
•   *Communication/Distribution*: Postage stamping machine or hand delivery to client and court. PBX telephone switchboard with secretaries answering and screening calls.

   The firm is a partnership in which all decisions are made during partnership meetings. However, Mrs. Mead, the fourth senior partner, handles most administrative matters for the firm, including purchasing and hiring of personnel. Mrs. Mead has decided to conduct a feasibility study to determine whether word processing can solve current turnaround problems, improve efficiency, and reduce secretarial turnover.

Current problems include:

- High turnover of secretarial personnel and too many secretaries.
- Morale problems because of conflicts resulting from uneven workflow and varying formats and procedures.
- Overtime by some secretaries to meet deadlines while other secretaries refuse to help out.
- Secretarial time loss waiting for attorneys to return from trial or to be available to transcribe poor longhand.
- Not enough dictation equipment and downtime of the equipment.
- Work delays caused by downtime of the copier and wait time to use it.
- Retypings for minor revisions and frequent retypings of similar documents.

Documents typed include correspondence (memos and 1- to 2-page letters, complaints (2 to 15 pages), summonses (1 to 5 pages), wills and trust (3 to 30 pages), dissolutions (1 to 3 pages), articles of incorporation (8 to 50 pages), by-laws (5 to 15 pages), and answers (5 to 20 pages).

Secretaries perform both typing and administrative tasks for the attorneys, conduct research, run errands, and handle their personal records, particularly for the senior partners.

1. Select the data collection techniques you would use for the study.
2. Write the preparation plans for the study.
3. State your findings from analyzing the information provided.

"The systems approach is revolutionizing business decision making, for it can provide more comprehensive information, faster, at the point and in the form it is needed to make better business decisions."

CHAPTER 5

An Example of a Feasibility Study— The Middletown Bank

OVERVIEW

Management has informed the bank's employees of the upcoming study and its purpose. It is now time for the task force to prepare, conduct, and evaluate the bank's study. This chapter explains how it was accomplished and lists its results.

OBJECTIVES

After completing this chapter you will be able to:

1. List the activities Ron had completed prior to the preorientation management planning meeting.
2. Explain the activities at the preorientation management planning meeting.
3. Prepare a prestudy information memo.
4. Prepare an orientation meeting schedule.
5. List the topics covered at the management and staff orientation meetings.

Quote from Robert J. Mockler, "The Systems Approach to Business Organization and Decision Making," *California Management Review* 11 (Winter 1968): 53–58.

6. Describe ways to conduct the secretarial meetings.
7. List the steps of the bank's feasibility study in order.

PRELIMINARY PREPARATIONS

After he had reviewed each data collection method to determine its applicability, Ron selected the following techniques for Middletown Bank's feasibility study:

*   Job analysis by distributing questionnaires and interviewing managers, principals, and secretaries.
*   Computerized study of document analysis by using work request forms to determine production volume, time distribution, document categories, amount of revision and retyping, and volume of each form of input.

Information Ron expected to obtain from using these techniques included:

*   Current methods of producing documents, document production workflow, and the current operating system.
*   Amount of time each secretary devoted to each secretarial task.
*   Current volume and time distribution of the typing workload.
*   Current problems, duplications, and inefficient procedures.
*   Costs of the present operating system.

Ron visited other banks that had implemented word processing systems to learn what they were accomplishing and what types of systems they used. He learned that most of them had installed word processing equipment and systems because of their large volume of paperwork and the need to process information within short time intervals. Some had installed their word processing centers in the early 1970s, and many had added satellite centers or work groups or had expanded their centers since that time.

Ron discovered that the Trust Department was usually the first department in a bank to implement word processing and often the heaviest user because of the large volume of typing produced. Typical documents produced by Trust Departments included customer correspondence, trust agreements, and documents related to updating clients' trusts.

Ron discovered that one-page repetitive form letters constituted a major typing application in many banks. Such letters were used to alert customers regarding the status of their monthly accounts and quarterly dividends and to solicit further business. (See Figure 5-1.) One bank that he visited employed from 3 to 22 correspondence secretaries in each of its ten word processing centers. (See Figure 5-2.) Some of the centers served one department only, while others served several departments. Centers would share their typing loads with one another when they had a higher volume than they were prepared to handle. The centers treated each department as a

---

Example of Bank Form Letter   **FIGURE 5-1**

MIDDLETOWN BANK
3800 Via Cavallaro
Middletown, Ohio 60750

_____

_____
_____
_____

_____

We wish to extend our sincere thanks for the account you recently opened
in our bank.

You may be certain that we shall do all we can to make your association
with our bank as pleasant and helpful as possible. Our staff is prepared to answer your questions, service your requests, and extend their
experience to meet your needs.

Please do not hesitate to call upon us for any matter in which you
believe we may be of assistance.

Very truly yours,

John B. Newton
President

JBN/pbc

---

customer and kept track of the typing volume and revisions produced for each department. They then charged the cost of producing the documents (by time and volume)
back to the using department. They called this a chargeback method of charging costs
to the using departments, a method commonly used by word processing installations.

Ron learned that many banks used central dictating systems to originate documents so that users could phone in their dictation from any location within the bank.
(See Figure 5-3.) This system was available and convenient for all those who origi-

FIGURE 5-2   **Correspondence secretaries in a word processing center.**
(Photo courtesy of Lanier Business Products, Inc.)

nated typing. It was also the least costly origination method. Ron learned that repetitive letters constituted one major bank typing application; special projects and statistical documents were others. These projects usually were longer and more complex and required several retypings because of the preciseness and accuracy required in the banking industry.

Visits to several banks offered Ron the opportunity to observe a variety of word processing equipment. He learned that many banks had standalone word processing typing units that stored typing on magnetic cards. Supervisors and operators explained that they liked magnetic cards for their form letters because the cards were easy to locate and use. (See Figure 5-4.)

FIGURE 5-3

Dictaphone's Master Mind provides instant information on all word processing jobs.
On-line dictation from Dictaphone's multiple-cassette or endless-loop central
recorder is automatically entered into the computer as soon as an author initiates
dictation from a private-wire, Touch-Tone, or dial telephone. (Photo courtesy of
Dictaphone Corporation.)

Some banks preferred using visual display word processors (see Figure 5-5), because typing was displayed on a televisionlike screen, making it easier to learn and use, since operators could see their work while creating or revising it. They felt that using these machines saved time by making the work easier, particularly for more complex, longer projects.

Ron observed that some banks that used magnetic card typewriters were using **ink-jet** printers for faster speed (see Figure 5-6). Supervisors explained that they could store letterhead, second sheets, and envelopes in the printer, and the system would produce two-page letters with envelopes for the letters to multiple addresses. They found this time-saving capability to be extremely important. They also found the ink-jet printer particularly satisfactory for its speed (92 characters per second versus 15 cps on the selectric typewriter) and its quiet operation.

During this period, Ron also visited vendors' offices to see equipment demonstrations and learn the latest technological advances in dictating and production equipment. He visited four major dictation equipment firms to observe their desktop, portable, and systems equipment and learn how the firms help new dictators learn

FIGURE 5-4   The IBM mag card typewriter makes typing of forms more efficient. Formats may be recorded on magnetic cards and entered into memory, and the machine automatically tabs to the exact location for each fill-in. (Photo courtesy of International Business Machines, Inc.)

dictation skills. When visiting word processing production equipment vendors, he observed standalone units with and without line or word displays, intelligent typewriters, shared-logic systems, and systems that use distributed logic along with large computers.

Ron met with representatives and managers of his bank's personnel, finance, and other departments to obtain suggestions for the task force. He made his selection based upon their suggestions.

The secretary is typing on a visual-display typewriter that displays black characters on   **FIGURE 5-5**
white background. The characters move up the full-page screen the way a piece of
paper moves through a typewriter, allowing for easy concentration and avoiding
fatigue and eyestrain. (Photo courtesy of CPT Corporation.)

Ron also collected the following information:

*   A directory listing personnel and their telephone extensions, job titles, and salary schedules.
*   Current payroll figures, including overhead, burden factor, and fringe benefits.
*   Annual and quarterly reports and supporting financial documents.
*   Floorplans and organization charts.
*   Inventory and costs of office equipment.

Ron's final activity before the management planning meeting was to prepare the schedule of planned activities for the study on a Gantt chart with a supporting checklist.

FIGURE 5-6   **IBM's Office System 6 featuring a high-speed ink-jet printer offers an effective approach to administrative record keeping and processing by storing lists and records on diskettes. Users can easily change, select, sequence, qualify, or reformat records to generate the listings, reports, and documents required for efficient administration. (Photo courtesy of International Business Machines, Inc.)**

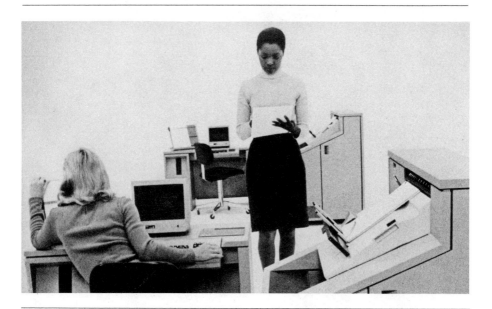

MANAGEMENT PLANNING MEETING

Ron next met with management to describe the status of all preparations. He first presented the names of the two other proposed members of the task force and explained that they were selected because of their skill in dealing with others, their sensitivity and communication capabilities, and their analytic skills. He stated that he felt the three of them could work well together to conduct a successful and meaningful feasibility study. Management at this point approved the selected task force.

Ron then presented the survey schedule, shown in Figure 5-7, explaining that the study would cover a two-week computerized work request survey; the distribution of questionnaires; and interviews with managers, principals, and secretaries. He stated that the activities of the entire study were scheduled to cover a four-week period. Management reviewed and approved Ron's schedule. Ron explained that he believed the computer analysis and questionnaires, along with the interviews, would produce the desired study results. He distributed copies of the forms, stating that any recommended suggestions or changes were welcome. Management made their observations and adapted the forms.

FIGURE 5-7   Study Orientation Schedule

STUDY ORIENTATION SCHEDULE

Executive Conference Room Monday 9 A.M.	Executive Conference Room Monday 10 A.M.	Second-Floor Conference Room Monday 11 A.M.	Second-Floor Conference Room Monday 1 P.M.	Second-Floor Conference Room Monday 2:15 P.M.	Second-Floor Conference Room Monday 3:30 P.M.	Second-Floor Conference Room Monday 4:15 P.M.
MANAGEMENT MEETING	SECRETARIES' MEETING	MANAGERS' MEETING	SECRETARIES' MEETING	STAFF MEETING	SECRETARIES' MEETING	STAFF MEETING
President John Newton	Mary Livingstone	Audrey Johanson	Peter Black	Paula Matthews	Jenny Gallo	Gary Whiteside
Ex. VP Stevens	Helen Dia	Guthrie MacDonald	Julia Myers	David Flaherty	Heather Morrison	Miles Stockwell
Ex. VP Lee	Tomasa Ramirez	Pedro Jiminez	Sally Pedronski	Janet Saluto	Helen Gray	Larry Holmes
VP Black	Bridgette O'Rourke	Gino Cionni	Johanna Gonzales	Melissa Jones	Gino Prado	Irene Torres
VP Garza	Pamela Smithers	Randall Olson	Maria Burruto	Don Vronski	Claudette Lanier	Tom Hall
VP Okimoto	Michelle Bonet	Doris Warner	Florence Gregg	Barry Roberts	Ginger Blake	
VP Rothwell		Ala Morgan	Kris Kroff	Myra Nowells	Randy Orr	
			Maria Sanchez	Harry Cho	Nicole Flaubet	
				Roger Byron	Bonnie Kraft	
				Leon James	Terri Morris	
					Dick Roberts	

Ron next distributed the orientation meeting schedules along with a memo to employees which, in addition to explaining the details of the study and its purpose, stated time and location of the employees' orientation meeting (see Figure 5-8). Ron stated that Lupe Garcia, secretary in the Operations Department, had agreed to act as secretary and liaison for the task force during the study and would maintain the calendar and schedule.

Ron explained that he had assured all department managers that the study would occur at a convenient time for most personnel according to vacation schedules, meetings, trips, and other major events. Management concurred with the study schedule and starting date.

Ron concluded by giving President Newton the draft of the management memo he had written for distribution to bank personnel explaining the study. President Newton reviewed and signed the memo. The meeting adjourned with the understanding that the management and orientation schedule memos would be distributed two days later, and the task force would prepare to begin the study the following week.

THE STUDY

President Newton's announcement and orientation schedule memos were next distributed to bank personnel. The task force began to organize its office for the study, making sure there were plenty of forms to be used in the study and setting up interview times on Lupe's schedule.

ORIENTATION MEETINGS

The task force conducted three types of orientation meetings: a managers' meeting, a meeting with bank operation staff members, and one with secretaries. President Newton opened each orientation meeting by stating the purpose of the upcoming feasibility study (as had originally been stated in the announcement memo) and what the bank expected to derive from the study. His remarks were similar to the following script:

> Your bank has grown very rapidly over the past ten years, with all of the new industry and population growth in the country. Sometimes when a firm is growing rapidly, it does not always have the time to keep on top of the volume of work it expects its employees to handle. We feel that the time has come when we need to take a look at our operating procedures and see if it isn't time to make some changes. Your management has therefore decided to see if it can make some improvements and possibly make some changes in equipment and operating procedures. We have been visiting some banks in the community to see what they have done to improve their operations and have found that some have made remarkable improvements in their paperwork systems. Many of them are

FIGURE 5-8

MEMORANDUM

TO: (Employee Name)   DATE: July 8, 1980

FROM: Ron Bies, Leader
           Word Processing Task Force

SUBJECT: Middletown Bank's
           Feasibility Study

As pointed out by President Newton, all of us who work at Middletown
Bank will be participating in a Word Processing feasibility study for
the next two months. Janine Roberts from Personnel, Peter Ross from
Accounting, and I will work with you to make sure that Middletown Bank's
study is accurate, complete, and meaningful.

The manner in which our study can meet these objectives is to find out
exactly how much work each person processes and possible problems and
duplications currently taking place. We feel very optimistic that, as
a result of the study, we can find better and more efficient and up-to-
date methods to conduct Middletown Bank's business. We expect to discover what improvements need to be made from this study.

We look forward to explaining to you just how the study will be conducted and how each of you can participate in making it successful. We
will meet with small groups to make these explanations at prescheduled
mutually convenient times.

You are scheduled to meet in Conference Room _____ at _____ on _____.
If this time is inconvenient, please contact Lupe Garcia to make other
arrangements.

We will be looking forward to seeing you there.

---

using modern word processing equipment that has helped to make these improvements.

W ord processing may be new to you, as it was to us when we first began
this investigation. You may not have any idea just what word processing means.
Well, I am not going to attempt to explain it to you. We have turned the
complete project over to Ron Bies and his task force. Ron is going to show you a
film and explain just what we expect from word processing and how we will be
going about implementing it. From Ron's study of our operations, we expect to
find ways that will improve the bank's working conditions for everyone in the
organization.

I will now turn the meeting over to Ron Bies, our systems analyst, who
will present a film and explain exactly what will take place at the bank during
the next few weeks.

Ron then showed a film that demonstrated word processing in three different businesses; a law firm, an insurance company, and a bank. The film explained what word processing had accomplished for these firms, how it works, and how it affected the work of the employees.

Following the film, Ron illustrated on an overhead projector the schedule of events to occur during the study. He described the schedule as a "road map of progress" from today to the conclusion, when the task force would present its study findings.

Ron then introduced Janine and Peter and explained that the three of them would be working as a team throughout the study and that they would be available to discuss study activities or answer questions.

Management Meeting

At management's orientation meeting, Ron described the techniques the task force would use in the study, including questionnaires for managers, principals, and secretaries; interviews of representative personnel from each department; and the computerized work request survey. Ron explained the purpose of each technique and how information provided by these three methods would result in summarizing the work being accomplished, time utilization, and related factors.

By illustrating sample workflow diagrams (shown in Figure 5-9), Ron described how information summarized from the study would be interpreted to analyze the present system, isolate areas needing changing, and design an improved system. He then distributed managers' questionnaires, displaying a copy on the overhead projector and explaining details required in filling one out. He then opened up the meeting for questions.

Ron concluded the meeting by introducing Lupe Garcia, the task force secretary, explaining that Lupe would be scheduling interviews and acting as key contact for the task force during the study.

Staff Meetings

Orientation meetings with members of the bank's operating staff were similar to the managers' meeting. Since the attendees ranged from supervisors to staff specialists, Ron made sure they understood that, although they would all be asked to fill out the questionnaires, only some would be interviewed in the interest of time. He stated that they anticipated that representative interviews would reflect the operating conditions for each department without having to take up the time of the entire staff. He suggested that anyone who was not interviewed and who had important data relevant to the study should contact the task force.

After reviewing the questionnaires and introducing Lupe and explaining her role in the study, the meetings were concluded.

Secretarial Meetings

Secretarial orientation meetings were begun by President Newton. After showing the film, explaining the schedule, and introducing the task force, Ron distributed pads of

Distribution Procedures of Word Processing Equipment   **FIGURE 5-9**

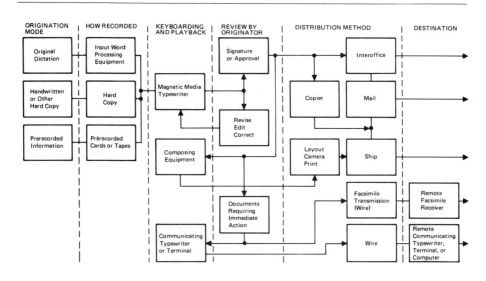

the work request forms and questionnaires. Ron displayed copies of the work request forms on the overhead projector and explained how each block of information should be filled in. He then asked for questions and comments to make sure that the secretaries understood. He covered the questionnaires in the same manner. The secretarial meetings concluded in the same manner as the other orientation meetings.

DURING THE FEASIBILITY STUDY

After the study orientation meetings were completed, Ron, Janine, and Peter prepared the interviews, the first of which were to be with managers to obtain an overview of the activities carried on in each department.

During this period, the secretaries filled in a work request form for each typing job they performed. The task force frequently visited different departments stopping to see if the secretaries had any questions. Because secretaries were also completing the secretarial questionnaires during this period, the task force also answered their questions regarding the questionnaires. The task force picked up the work request forms at the end of each work day, checked them for completeness, and prepared them for data entry. The task force made it a point to be available for assistance and to reflect enthusiasm, interest, and cooperation to everyone participating in the study.

Questionnaires

Bank employees were instructed that either the task force would pick up the questionnaires or they could drop them into the internal mail. As they collected the questionnaires, the task force summarized and tabulated data on the summary forms. Lupe also helped to summarize data from the questionnaires so that it was available for the task force during interviews.

Data from the work request forms was entered periodically into the computer. At the completion of the study, the information would be summarized for evaluation.

Interviews

The task force first interviewed managers so that they could outline departmental activities. Their interviews were scheduled by Lupe, who phoned all scheduled interviewees at least a half day before their scheduled time to make sure they were prepared. Lupe allowed one-half to one hour for each interview, depending upon the department and amount of paperwork and information they expected to cover during the interview.

While conducting the secretarial interviews, the task force explicitly aimed to derive as much how, why, who, how many, which, where, and when information as possible to obtain a clear understanding of the current system. Before they began to interview the secretaries, the task force practiced interviewing each other and made the following list of questions to ask during these interviews:

1. What kind of problems do you sometimes experience when transcribing the various types of input you receive?
2. How do you resolve these problems?
3. How do you believe such problems could be prevented?
4. How do you format each type of document you type? Why is it formatted that way? Who determines these document formats?
5. What kinds of interruptions might you experience when typing? How do you handle these interruptions?
6. When you are working on a rush project and you receive another rush project, how do you handle it?
7. How do you handle a situation in which you are called away from your desk for an important request when you feel your desk should not be left unattended? When might this situation occur?
8. If you are ill or on vacation, how is your work processed? By whom?
9. What kinds of improvements do you believe could be made in the work you are performing? Why?
10. When are your busiest times? lightest? How are these busy times handled if the workload becomes too heavy?
11. Why are some periods particularly heavy?
12. How is your work evaluated? By whom? How do you determine how well you are performing your job? What kinds of changes would you like in this regard?
13. What kinds of changes or suggestions do you have that might improve your working situation? Why?
14. What kinds of changes or suggestions do you have that you feel would benefit the department in which you work? The firm? Why?

By following this list of questions, the task force had a set guideline that made it easy to make sure they were obtaining complete information in a pattern convenient for them to evaluate.

The findings from the survey resulted in the breakdown by types of documents and applications used by departments shown in Tables 5-1 and 5-2.

DEVELOPING THE WORKFLOW

After completing the interviewing, the task force summarized their findings and combined the information with the summaries provided by the questionnaires. They designed completed workflows representing the present system from the preliminary workflows designed while interviewing. Present workflow design helped them to summarize and point out the present operating system, isolate duplications and problems, and observe where changes and improvements needed to be made. Workflow charts are shown in Figures 5–10 and 5–11 on pages 114 and 115. They next planned the new workflow for the purpose of creating an efficient operating system, eliminating duplications, and solving problems.

SUMMARY

After deciding to conduct a word processing feasibility study, Middletown Bank management selected Ron Bies, a systems analyst for the bank, to manage the study. Ron was given responsibility to plan the study and select two other people to work with him during the study.

Ron decided the task force would obtain a departmental activity analysis by using questionnaires and interviews, a secretarial job analysis by using questionnaires and interviews, and a document analysis by using a work request form that each secretary would fill out when typing a document. These would then be entered into the computer for summarizing.

Before beginning the study, Ron visited other banks that already had word processing. From these visits he learned that Trust Departments were the heaviest word processing users; form letters were a major application in every bank; many banks used central dictation systems, some with outside call-in capability; and other major bank typing applications included statistical budgets, forms, forecasts, and special projects that required revisions and retypings. He found that some banks used magnetic card word processors and other used display units, while most used standalone systems, some of which were able to communicate from one branch to another.

Ron gathered documents while preparing for the study that included:

- Personnel listings with phone numbers and locations.
- Job titles with salaries, payroll printouts, fringe benefits, and burden costs.
- Flowcharts, organization charts, annual and quarterly reports, other procedural and financial documents.
- Current operating costs, including equipment, salaries, and supplies.

TABLE 5-1   Types of Bank of Middletown Documents

Originating Department	Types of Documents		
	Daily	Repetitive	Stored

All departments	Correspondence	Open account
		Close account
		Collection letter
		Account statement letter
		Quarterly dividend notice
		Request to provide
		    additional service
		Request for application
		    information	

Marketing		Marketing letters Mass mailings	
Personnel		Personnel letters	
Purchasing		Purchasing letters	
Management	Transactions Reports		
Trust	Funds transfer	Progress reports Letters of credit Letters of transfer Pension funds Stock portfolios	
Executive			Minutes Agenda

Finance			Ledgers
			Profit & loss
			    statements
			Income statements
			Other financial
			    reports

Public Relations		Seasonal mailings Christmas Club	
Operations	Publications Communications to other banks	Tax reports	Manuals Standard practices Bulletins Phone directory Procedures Forms
Records Management	List processing		

Bank of Middletown's Typing Applications	TABLE 5-2
Department	**Applications**
Loan and Loan Servicing	Form letters, correspondence
Trust	Forms, correspondence, reports
Special Services (Deposit, real estate)	Form letters, correspondence, reports
Legal	Reports, stored reports, correspondence
Marketing	Form letters, correspondence
Bank Operations and Administration (Collection)	Internal correspondence, manuals, form letters
Personnel	Form letters, correspondence
Internal Auditing	Internal correspondence
Data Processing	Manuals, specifications, memos, special forms
Accounting	Financial reports, monthly financial updates, memos

At the management planning meeting, Ron presented the following information:

- His selection for the other two members of the task force.
- His survey time schedule, including the prestudy orientation meeting schedule.
- The task force memo to employees.
- Questionnaires and forms to be used during the study.
- The management memo from President Newton introducing the study and explaining its purpose and objectives.

Management approved all of Ron's recommendations and scheduled the study to begin the following week. President Newton began each study orientation meeting by explaining management's commitment. He then introduced Ron, who conducted the remainder of each meeting.

Ron presented a word processing film that showed word processing installations and explained the what, why, and how of word processing. He then introduced the other members of the task force. Using an overhead projector, he explained the various forms and showed how to fill them out. Ron described how the information from these forms would be summarized and used to describe the current operating system with the objective of designing an improved system. He explained that some employees would also be interviewed to make sure the study was complete. After explaining the schedule and questionnaires, Ron asked for questions. Each meeting concluded with an introduction of the task force secretary, an explanation of how to contact the task force during the survey, and the assurance that they would be available to answer questions and assist during the study.

At the secretarial meetings, the work request forms were explained in detail so that the secretaries could fill them out easily and quickly. During the study, the task force visited secretarial work areas to provide assistance and answer questions. With the help of the secretary, they also reviewed the work request forms for completeness before they were sent to computer entry.

FIGURE 5-10   Bank of Middletown's Present Typing System

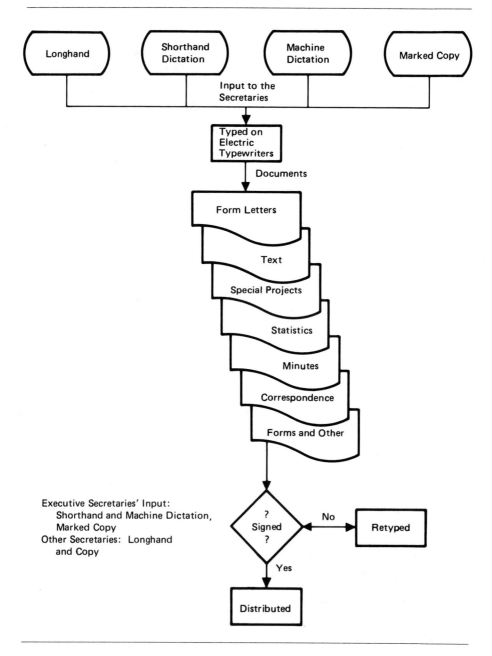

Bank of Middletown's Present Workflow for a Trust Agreement   **FIGURE 5-11**

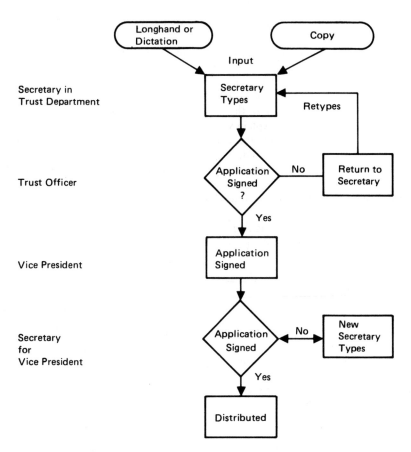

Secretary in
Trust Department

Trust Officer

Vice President

Secretary
for
Vice President

Fact : A trust can be typed more
than 3 times. Average number of
pages is 8 (160 lines) .

Questionnaires were picked up by the task force or returned through internal mail. During this period, the task force began to interview managers and summarize data. Next they interviewed principals and secretaries, asking objective questions to help interpret current working methods, departmental activities, and the workflow. They used these summaries, computer summaries, preliminary workflows, and results from the interviews to interpret and flow the current operating system. By analyzing the present system, the task force designed the new system to solve problems where possible and improve the current system of operations.

REVIEW QUESTIONS

1. What did Ron feel were prime typing applications for bank word processing? Why?
2. Why was it important for Ron to visit banks with word processing before beginning the study?
3. Who launched the orientation meetings? Do you believe this is important to the success of the study? What is your reasoning?
4. Why didn't they interview all the secretaries? Do you believe it would be better to interview all personnel? Explain your reasoning.
5. What activities did the task force accomplish during the study? Discuss why each of these activities was included.
6. Why was it important to summarize data during the study and not wait until it was completed?
7. How should word processing interviews be conducted? Explain the dos and don'ts of interviewing.
8. Explain the purpose of designing workflow during the study.
9. Why did the task force make up a list of bank documents early in the study?

DISCUSSION QUESTIONS

1. Discuss a two-week schedule of interviews and how the length of time might be important to the study.
2. Discuss Ron's memo and whether you believe it had too much or too little information in it. *pg. 102*
3. Discuss the importance of the activities Ron accomplished within the bank before beginning the study.
4. Discuss what might occur during the secretarial meetings and how it should be handled.
5. Discuss how interview time might not always remain as scheduled. How can this be handled?

CASES

Case 5-1   University History Department

The History Department at Leland University has five secretaries: the department secretary, the graduate student secretary, a private secretary to the head of the department, and two others, one of whom holds the junior entry-level job of the more routine clerical tasks. There are 17 professors under the department chairperson and usually 6 teaching assistants. The current operations are as follows.

The department secretary is responsible for running the department, ordering supplies, counseling and advising personnel, and distributing work to the two secretaries who do not have major responsibilities. The secretary who handles graduate students processes requests for admissions, advancement to candidacy, students' graduation requirements, graduations, and student job placement. All related correspondence and document typing is handled by this secretary with occasional help from the other secretaries during periods of peak volume.

The department chairperson secretary handles all of that professor's work, including working with students, hiring professors and teaching assistants, planning the year's schedule of classes, and administering salaries.

The other two secretaries handle department typing and administrative tasks under the supervision of the department secretary. The junior secretary is mainly responsible for the department duplication machine, telephone and office reception, distribution and processing of department mail, and miscellaneous clerical tasks. The other secretary is responsible for administrative tasks and typing for the professors.

As a result of a survey conducted by a university systems analyst, it was learned that the secretaries' time was spent as follows: typing—30 percent, phone—25 percent, waiting for work—10 percent, mail—8 percent, filing—4 percent, errands—3 percent, copying—9 percent, reception and assistance—8 percent, and miscellaneous administration—3 percent.

1. Draw a pie chart showing the work distribution for the department.
2. What is your interpretation of these statistics?

Case 5-2   Pharmaceutical Firm

At Nelson Pharmaceutical Systems, Inc. it was found that the average annual salary of the ten marketing representatives was $35,000. During the study, it was determined that, using longhand, these representatives created an average of 80 letters per day. Using a 50-week work year, what is the cost of their present system of input? What would it be using dictation equipment?

The usual procedure for creating a sales proposal by a marketing representative for the firm is as follows:

1. The representative writes out the proposal in longhand and on marked copy from previous proposals.
2. The secretary (one of five) types up a rough draft of the proposal and submits it to the representative for revision.
3. The representative edits the proposal and returns it for final typing.
4. The secretary types the final proposal.
5. The representative edits again and, in approximately one-half of the cases, has some small changes made which require retyping of those pages containing changes.
6. The changes are typed and the proposal is submitted to the marketing manager, cost accounting, and sometimes top management for approval.
7. Changes are usually made, requiring retyping of 15 to 80 percent of the proposal.
8. Changes are typed and returned to the representative for approval.
9. Usually the proposal is signed by the representative and the manager and sent or delivered to the client.

The five secretaries type the following documents: correspondence (1 page), 41 percent of the time; proposals (3 to 17 pages, revised one to four times) 25 percent; reports (1 to 10 pages, revised 1 to 3 times) 18 percent; repetitive letters (1 page) 10 percent; forms and miscellaneous, 6 percent.

1. Design a flowchart designating the current procedures for creating a sales proposal.
2. Show the document typing distribution on a bar chart.

"A system may be defined as an orderly grouping of separate but interdependent components for the purpose of attaining some predetermined objective."

PART III

DESIGNING THE APPROPRIATE WORD PROCESSING SYSTEM

The study is completed. The data has been summarized, the workflow analyzed, and the present system defined. It is now time to determine the cost of the present system to the organization, its resource availability, and its capability of meeting management's planned objectives. By matching this information to management's objectives and the capabilities of word processing systems, the new system can be planned.

Once the new system and its projected improvements and savings are known, one can select the appropriate structure, job alignment, and workflow that meet the desired expectations.

This section explains how to cost justify a word processing system and design a structure that most appropriately processes the firm's documents, including personnel alignment and work procedures. It also describes how to select origination and production, word processing equipment, followed by reprographic, records processing, and communication/distribution equipment. The section concludes with an explanation of ways to prepare the study report and make a meaningful presentation to management.

"It is the responsibility of management to find the most efficient way of doing any job."

CHAPTER 6

Cost Justifying and Word Processing Costs

OVERVIEW

One of the main objectives management expects to achieve from word processing is to establish a system of document cost control. This chapter explains how to calculate these costs for a proposed word processing system.

OBJECTIVES

After completing this chapter, you will be able to:

1. Indicate elements included in word processing costs.
2. Explain how to determine the number of word processing stations from the summary data.
3. Explain the typing productivity expected from word processing.
4. Explain word processing recurring and investment costs.
5. Explain word processing cost effectiveness.

Evaluations of regular secretarial jobs indicate that although most secretaries are hired mainly to type, they seldom spend half the time at their job typing. For instance, a secretary who works a 7-1/2-hour day frequently types less than four

Quote from James F. Lincoln, *Incentive Management* (Cleveland: Lincoln Electric Company, 1951).

hours. The remainder of the time is devoted to processing mail, handling telephone calls, filing, doing research, calculating, preparing projects, running errands, making meeting and travel arrangements, and being interrupted from one task to perform another. Generally, more than half a secretary's time is devoted to these other-than-typing tasks.

To determine actual typing productivity, accurate analysis requires separating the time devoted to typing from time devoted to performing the other tasks. However, when analyzing the current system, one needs to determine how much typing is produced each day in order to plan the volume requirements for the proposed system. The typing produced each day, therefore, is divided by the total daily working hours, even though many of these hours are devoted to performing other tasks. This indicates the *system* productivity, not that of the secretaries, who may be capable of typing at speeds of from 50 to 90 words a minute. A study of the present system may actually indicate that their average productivity is closer to 5 to 20 words per minute, because the typing is only one of the many tasks being performed over the total daily working hours.

WORD PROCESSING PRODUCTIVITY

If a secretary is equipped with a word processing typewriter, without changing the job, the same interruptions will continue. However, because of the unique capabilities of word processing typewriters, the secretary can still dramatically increase typing output.

Using a word processing typewriter is frequently termed **power typing**. Power typing is premised upon the concept that a secretary who types on a word processor can type at that secretary's **rough draft speed**, the 60 to 80 or more words a minute at which that secretary tested when applying for the job. The reason that one can type on a word processing typewriter at this rough draft speed is that, when typing into memory or onto a magnetic recording medium, any time a typist makes an error, one simply backspaces and types the correct character. This new character automatically erases the wrong character and replaces it with the new one, allowing the typist to type as fast as possible without worrying about making an error. Should the typist make an error and not notice it until later, one can insert a clean sheet of paper and have the word processor type the document again from the recording on the storage medium. Upon approaching the error, the typist will stop the printout, skip the error, and manually type in the correction. Word processing power typing eliminates error-worry slowdown and allows typists to type at their fastest rates. After typing on a word processor for a period of time, typists can increase their typing speeds substantially.

Visual Display Typing

When one's typing is displayed on a line **display** or a visual screen, a person can become even faster. The mechanical action slowdown is eliminated. There is no delay waiting for the typewriter to make such mechanical actions as carrier returns or **tab** in; there is no possible lockup from rapid typing spurts. The characters appear on the display as rapidly as one can type—100 or more words per minute. True rough draft speed becomes even faster.

Corrections of errors that the typist may not have noticed during rough draft typing are later made on a display unit on the screen before printout. The typist will proofread the page on the screen before directing the word processor to print the page. Because it is so much faster to make corrections on the displays, correcting is much faster. Therefore, when planning the equipment configuration for the new system, analysts can anticipate high productivity by the change to word processing display equipment.

Word Processing Production Rates

If a study shows that current typing productivity averages 12 words a minute, what should an analyst expect from a word processing system? Frequently, analysts will use conservative figures to provide for startup and learning curves. Productivity gains that will be achieved depend upon such factors as:

1. Speed of the word processing specialists or secretaries. Some may be able to type as fast as 80 words a minute, while others may produce around 50 words a minute. These speeds will also depend upon the typist's technical expertise in making maximum use of the word processing typewriter's function.
2. Difficulty of the projects. Complex projects that contain several formats and various kinds of data will take considerably longer.
3. Capability of the word processing equipment. Some equipment provides many automatic features that greatly simplify the task for the typist. If these capabilities are easy to learn and use, the equipment is even more productive.
4. Amount of repetitive and stored material. All documents that are created from typing already stored can be printed out automatically at the speed of the printer. Output speeds on word processing typewriters/printers can range from 150 words a minute (or a page in approximately 2 minutes) to a page in a few seconds.
5. The system. No matter how capable the typist may be or how many advanced automatic capabilities the equipment may have, the working procedures will determine how productive each person, and therefore the total system, may be.
6. Management. Finally, the system must be well managed in order to continually achieve its optimum productivity objectives. Procedures need to be enforced daily; standards should be set, measured against, and evaluated.

All of the above factors determine the kind of productivity that will be achieved by implementing the proposed word processing system. In order for the analyst to plan the number of work stations and personnel required in the proposed system, all factors need to be included in calculations. The analyst will automatically plan the proposed system's working procedures so that work can be accomplished at optimum efficiency and anticipate that the system will be well managed. The next step, therefore, is to isolate each kind of document and categorize it into either original or stored typing.

The more typing functions and information that can be stored and recalled, the more productive the system will become.

One insurance company determined that it had the following kinds of documents to be produced by its word processing center:

- original one-time correspondence
- repetitive letters
- stored paragraphs for sales proposals
- stored formatting for checks
- stored formats and information for statistical reports and forms
- test revisions

The company calculated that the work, which had been produced by four secretaries in the past, could be produced by two word processing specialists using visual display word processors because of the amount of information that could be stored.

Costs and Productivity

One way to cost justify word processing system is to compare per-person productivity. The total volume produced by the secretaries under the current system is summarized and divided by the number of secretaries, providing the present per-person volume productivity. The result is compared with the expected productivity under the proposed word processing system. It may or may not imply devoting a full-time word processing secretary using a word processing typewriter. When planning the expected productivity under the new system, the analyst must first decide whether the typing will be performed by full-time specialists.

For example, four secretaries in a traditional office system produced an average of 2000 lines per day. With word processing typewriters and procedures, two secretaries could produce those 2000 lines, reducing the number of personnel by one-half. A comparison of costs of these two systems is illustrated in Table 6-1. This table is a simplified version of costing, since it does not include other factors such as recurring costs of supplies, workspace, and environment.

TABLE 6-1   Comparing System Costs

Present System Without Word Processing		*Proposed Word Processing System*	
4 secretaries at $8400/yr	= $33,600/year	2 secretaries at $8400/yr	= $16,800
(typewriters already paid for)	–0–	2 word processors at $3060 ea.	6,120
Total Cost	$33,600	Total Cost	$22,920
		Savings	$10,680

---

provide the total time distribution of current administrative tasks. Usually the analyst also interviews principals, managers, and secretaries in an administrative study.

JOB ANALYSIS

Many questionnaires have been designed that list every conceivable piece of information concerned with the secretarial job. Some secretaries prepare comprehensive folders or binders containing exact instructions on how to perform each task in case of their absence. However, this type of job description does not provide all the information required in a study, such as how long a task may take and the retypings required to complete the product.

One of the simplest forms to be used is a list on which a secretary lists each task, the time it requires, and weekly volume of work. A task list may serve as an excellent form to use for followup interviews.

Many analysts prepare their own forms before beginning the study, listing each of that firm's specific documents. Analysts maintain a file of questionnaires and forms to use for reference or select those that will provide information desired for the current study.

A questionnaire should provide a clearcut description of the information desired and the opportunity for easy followup. Examples of information requested are:

- Name, department, supervisor, phone number, building location, all of which provide not only the name of the person but all physical information required to locate that person.
- Length of time and jobs held with the firm.
- Major task and next most important task.
- Principals served.

Other sample questions are illustrated on the form in Figure 4-1.

If the study is to include duplication, questions relating to use of copying and duplicating equipment are included on the form. The same is true for communications such as TWX and Telex messages, filing, or other areas such as phototypesetting.

Distributing Questionnaires

The prestudy orientation meeting needs to be well organized so that it will sell participants so that they will cooperate willingly. Questionnaires to be used in the study are distributed during the prestudy orientation meeting. The analyst should carefully explain (a) the purpose and value of the questionnaires (why the information is needed), (b) how they will be interpreted (how the information will be used), and (c) how to fill them out. After providing one for each person, the analyst can cover each point on an overhead projector on which the questionnaire is blown up. Each question and its purpose can be carefully described, and attendees can ask questions to make sure they understood each question. In this way, when they return to their

COSTING THE PRESENT SYSTEM

To determine the total costs of the present system, one first summarizes the cost of total work hours (including overtime and part-time help), equipment, supplies, and overhead. The total of these figures determines the cost of the current volume of work. For example, the four secretaries in the insurance office make an annual salary of $7800 each, excluding benefits, for a total salary of $31,200 per year, or $156,000 over a five-year period.

The feasibility statistics determined that two secretaries provided with word processing typewriters could achieve this work volume at a total cost of $15,600 a year, or $78,000 over a five-year period, not including salary increases or additional staff.

Savings

On a one-year basis, renting the proposed equipment would save $9,480 over the present system. On a five-year basis, the savings totals $47,400; the savings increases to $53,800 if the equipment is purchased. Table 6-2 illustrates how these figures are calculated.

Productivity Factors

The analyst calculated the number of word processing personnel required in the following manner. The four secretaries typed three-quarters of their time during

Calculated Savings Using Word Processing						TABLE 6-2
Present System Costs						
	1 Year		5 Years			
Secretaries (4) at $7,800 each	$31,200		$156,000			
Proposed Word Proceesing System Costs						
	Rental		Purchase		Savings	
	1 Year	5 Years	1 Year	5 Years	1 Year	5 Years
Secretaries (2) at $7,800 each	$15,600	$ 78,000	$15,600	$ 78,000		
Equipment	$ 6,120	$ 30,600				
Total	$21,720	$108,600			$9,480	$47,400
Purchase Cost		$ 10,000 each		$ 20,000		
Maintenance				$ 4,200		
Total				$102,200		$54,800

seven-hour workdays. Rounded off, they typed for five hours a day. Total volume from the study revealed that their daily output was approximately 12 pages per day per secretary. Dividing these 12 pages by 5 hours equals about 2½ pages per hour per secretary, which rounds off to three pages. Dividing 60 minutes by 3 results in 20 minutes to produce each page for an average 250-word letter production rate of 12½ words a minute.

Word Processing Typing Rates

As a result of the ability to power type, a secretary or typist with a word processing typewriter can increase input typing rate dramatically. However, analysts usually use lower input speeds to allow for system implementations and learning stages and avoid unrealistic expectations from the new system.

Using a conservative 45 words per minute as the speed at which the two secretaries can now create their documents, instead of the 12½ words per minute found in the study, the 250-word letter can be typed in 5½ minutes. Rounded off at six minutes, the secretaries can then produce ten pages an hour, or twice as many pages as they did on their electric typewriters. With five hours of typing each day, each of the two secretaries can produce 50 pages a day, a total 100 pages between them a day or 500 pages a week. These statistics are for authored letters which are originated, typed, and signed; they do not apply to previously recorded letters (form letters) or any kind of stored typing, which would be much more productive.

Other Advantages

This system allows for even more productivity because it does not include stored typing when the typist keys in changes only. The 12 pages per day for the four secretaries, or 48 daily pages of production, would have to more than double before an additional secretary would be needed. The new system also provides a future saving of projected salary increases for two secretaries instead of four.

In one Air Force study, administrative personnel estimated the time each person devoted to the various administrative duties and typing during one month. They found that a total of 24,556 hours were devoted to typing and multiplied this sum by hourly salary rates. Productivity and cost figures for conventional administrative systems were compared with those of word processing systems (equipment cost plus cost of necessary personnel).

They next conducted a ten-day line count survey, followed by a time survey of all administrative duties, including typing and shorthand to establish aggregate work hour distribution. From the total work hours required in the traditional system, they subtracted the estimated number of word processing keyboards, personnel, and supervisors required to determine total production time requirements. When they cut back total personnel, those who left transferred to other departments or other positions.

Next, they selected a center location and began personnel and equipment evaluation. The center contained 27 civilian personnel (1 center supervisor, 3 section supervisors, and 23 word processing operators) and 3 military people who served as couriers. Of the original 178 administrative personnel, 51 positions were identified as excess.

Personnel Selection

All interested civilian administrative personnel were offered the opportunity to interview for jobs in the word processing center if they so desired. Twenty-seven were offered positions, while those whose positions were eliminated were transferred laterally to other positions.

This word processing center permits almost unlimited expansion as a result of its structure and organization. They plan to expand its capabilities to support more staff agencies in addition to the eight currently being supported. This system has been so successful that outside subordinate units are being encouraged to form their own centers based on the savings achieved at this installation.

Meeting Volume Requirements

The Marketing Department of Curtiss Electronics employs six secretaries who, from the study statistics, average daily typing production of approximately 500 lines of letters and reports. During peak periods they may have to turn out a volume as high as 20,000 lines within five working days. They accomplish this peak volume by hiring part-time outside help or distributing work to available secretaries in other departments.

The new system was designed to accomplish handling this peak load without hiring outside help. This was accomplished by equipping specialized correspondence secretaries with word processing typewriters. Since they are not interrupted to perform other administrative or clerical tasks, each secretary can produce approximately 900 to 1000 or more lines per day or a total of 5000 lines in five working days. With all six secretaries specialized as word processing typists, they can produce approximately 30,000 lines or more in five days (6 × 5000 lines). The maximum requirement totals 20,000 lines. Therefore, four secretaries produce 20,000 lines (4 × 5000), freeing the other two secretaries to specialize in handling the administrative tasks, including telephone, mail processing, reception, filing, and copying.

This firm maintained the same number of secretaries and eliminated overtime and outside help costs by specializing the correspondence and administrative secretaries.

COST EFFECTIVENESS ANALYSIS

Cost effectiveness analysis is based upon the premise that the cost of the equipment and site preparation of a word processing system can be offset by attaining increased productivity. All other things being equal, secretarial and clerical costs should go down to justify the investment of time and money necessary to convert to the word processing system. If costs under word processing do not decrease, there must be other benefits important enough to warrant these increased expenditures. The cost-effective analysis system that follows is used by the U.S. Army.

Recurring Costs

Expenses for personnel, material consumed in use, operating, overhead, and support services incurred on an annual basis constitute recurring costs. These costs may include:

- Secretarial support, both administrative and correspondence operations, may be categorized as typing, telephone handling, filing, clerical, mail handling, and copying.
- Costs of supervising the quantity and quality of work.
- Costs of author's time devoted to creating, proofreading, and approving typed documents.
- Cost of proofreading the final output copy from typing.

Investment Costs — *should be one-time only*

Investment costs include costs associated with equipment acquisition, property or work space and equipment (furnishings), nonrecurring services, nonrecurring operations, and startup costs. For a proposed system this includes:

- Cost of typing (production) and dictating (origination) equipment.
- Cost of telephone equipment installation and rental.
- One-time moving costs (if required).
- One-time construction costs.
- Accessory costs (supplies, etc.).
- Other costs as incurred (lighting, sound-proofing, air conditioning).

Cost effectiveness is achieved by comparing the current and proposed systems (possibly discounting the word processing equipment over an eight-year economic life). The proposed system will be cost effective if the productivity increase can effect a real cost savings.

Computing Recurring Costs of the Present System

Secretarial Support   List the salaries of secretaries surveyed. If a secretary does not support the work full time, compute that person's percentage (see Table 6–3).

$$\text{Secretarial support cost} = \text{Weekly pay cost per employee} \times \text{Percentage of time engaged in secretarial support}$$

Supervisory Cost   All secretarial work is supervised. Sometimes a senior secretary will supervise one or more typists as a part of the job requirement, or an executive or an

Grade Level	No. of Secretaries	Weekly Pay (Including Burden)	% Support	Total Secretarial Cost
4	2	$150	100	$ 300
5	2	200	100	400
3	3	100	100	300
2	1	50	50	25
6	1	260	50	130
				$1132

Example of Secretarial Support Costs   TABLE 6-3

administrative assistant may perform this task as part-time supervisor. This supervision has a cost that adds to the recurring cost. The percentage of the work week spent supervising can be obtained by interviewing. To compute weekly cost use:

Total weekly supervision cost = weekly pay × percentage of time supervising

Origination Costs   Whatever is typed must first be created (originated). The four major types of origination encountered in most offices are longhand draft, dictation to a stenographer, dictation to a machine, and marked copy. Sometimes copy typing is not included because it has been prepared previously in final form. Self-composition is not included because it is a part of typing and will have been discounted in secretarial time. Standards used for the first three forms are shown in Table 6-4.

The cost of origination also adds to the recurring cost. Information from the study indicates the number of lines per dictator, form of origination, and salary of the author in order to determine cost.

Origination cost for a document =

$$\frac{\text{Total lines per document}}{\text{Factor}} \times \text{Hourly pay cost of author}$$

Example: Assume a document of 67 lines was originated in longhand by Vice President Merriweather and given to his secretary for typing in final form. The cost of

Finished Typing Output   TABLE 6-4

	Factor
Longhand: 1 line per minute	60
Steno Dictation: 2 lines per minute	120
Machine Dictation: 6 lines per minute	360

his time to create that document is: 67/60 × $17.80 = $19.88 where $17.80 represents his hourly pay cost. Cost of origination is computed for each document, and the sum of all origination costs represents total cost of origination to be applied to the typing effort.

Proofreading Costs   Each typed document is proofread before it is signed. The typist's proofreading is included in the typing cost, but when proofing is performed by the author, the time must be calculated separately. The average person can proofread 20 lines per minute[1] while searching for typographical errors (factor = 1200).

$$\text{Proofing cost for a document} = \frac{\text{Total lines per document}}{\text{Factor}} \times$$

$$\text{Hourly pay cost of author}$$

For example, using Mr. Merriweather in the previous example, the proofing cost would be:

$$\frac{67}{1200} \times 17.80 = \$0.99$$

This cost is calculated for each document collected or included in the survey and for each person other than the typist who proofreads it. If both the supervisor and author perform this function, both proofing costs must be applied to the cost of the current system.

To sum up, the total recurring costs for the current system equal typist's costs plus supervisor's costs plus originator's costs plus proofing costs.

Personnel Projection for Word Processing

Before projecting personnel costs, the total salary requirements (including all overhead burden factors) are calculated and totaled for all word processing positions. Based upon these criteria, a projected cost for the typing workload is planned. The cost/benefit analysis remains valid, since it compares the cost of the known workload between the two systems.

Automatic typing (playback of stored information) can be performed at speeds directly proportional to the amount of playback of information stored on the recorded media. Original typing is primarily keyboarding and is accomplished according to typist's speed. Revision of typing already stored is performed at much faster speeds when only corrections need to be keyboarded. Generally repetitive typing (form letter and stored paragraphs, for example) is faster still when only addresses or dates change. General standards used for each level are shown in Table 6–5.

From totals of these three categories, personnel requirements can be established using the standards in Table 6–5 to accomplish the total lines of typing currently being processed.

---

[1] Statistic provided by U.S. Army in AR 340–8, a public document.

Standards for Levels of Typing   TABLE 6-5

	Factor[a]
Original typing: 600 lines per day	3000
Revision typing: 800 lines per day	4000
Repetitive typing: 1000 lines per day	5000

[a]Although equipment and personnel capabilities vary and several methods may be used to determine standards, these factors will be used in the text. Most word processing supervisors use these rates as minimum standards expected from word processing operators.

$$\text{Typing labor} = \frac{\text{Number of lines typed per level}}{\text{Factor}}$$

For example, assume that the survey results indicated that 21,200 lines of typing were produced by all the typists during the survey week, which was considered a typical week. Of this total, 10,350 lines were original typing, 1350 lines were revisions of previous work, and 9500 lines came from repetitive letters being sent to multiple addressees. In this study, a work week for one person is 40 hours.

$$\text{Typing labor—Original} = \frac{10,350}{3000} = 3.45 \text{ Work Weeks}$$

$$\text{Typing labor—Revision} = \frac{1,350}{4000} = .34 \text{ Work Weeks}$$

$$\text{Typing labor—Repetitive} = \frac{9,500}{5000} = 1.90 \text{ Work Weeks}$$

Total typing labor required   =   5.69 Work Weeks

Rounded off to six work weeks or six secretaries

For accurate estimates of staffing needs, this factor should be multiplied by 1.11 to cover normal absences and vacations.

Personnel projection - 5.69 X 1.11
Personnel projection = 6.32 Work Weeks

The 6.3 work weeks is converted to a word processing staff of seven to meet document production requirements found in the study. If the word processing staff includes personnel who are not experienced in word processing techniques and equipment, office procedures, and correspondence terms and formats, initial staffing above the minimum requirement may be necessary. Assume the staffing requirements were established as shown in Table 6-6 for future calculation examples.

TABLE 6-6   Staffing Requirements

	Job Level	Weekly Pay Costs
Supervisor	7	$ 236.80
Editor	6	213.24
Typists (4)	5	765.28
Typists (3)	4	513.00
Total word processing weekly pay costs		$1,728.32

Personnel Projection and Administrative Support   Once the typing tasks have been eliminated, the administrative secretaries may be working either near the principals as previously or in clustered or centralized areas. Major personnel savings and increased administrative support can be realized through specialization, generally allowing one specialist to support five or more authors more adequately than in the past. Assume the requirements in Table 6-7 were established from the survey and the decision was to keep one executive secretary.

Computing Recurring Cost of the Proposed System

Typing Cost   Assume that the word processing typists will produce all the typing. Typing costs therefore will be the sum total of their salary/pay costs.

TABLE 6-7   Administrative Costs   *Non-typing People*

	Job Level	Weekly Pay Costs
Executive secretary	9	$ 289.08
Supervisory administrative support secretary	7	236.80
Senior administrative support specialists[a] (2)	6	426.48
Administrative support specialists[a] (8)	5	1,530.56
Receptionists[b] (2)	3	304.52
Total administrative support weekly pay costs		$2,787.44

[a]Assumes need for support of at least 40 authors; two senior personnel provide capability for more complex demands.

[b]Assumes facilities for centralized receptionist/phone.

Typing cost per week = weekly pay costs × number of typists per grade level

Example

Typing cost for level 5 = $191.32 × 4 = $ 765.28
Typing cost for level 4 =   171.00 × 3 =   513.00

Total typing cost per week   = $1,278.28

Administrative Cost   As shown previously, this is a total of administrative support specialists' salaries.

Administrative support cost =
Weekly pay costs × number of secretaries per grade level

Example

Executive secretary   = level 9 = $289.08 × 1 = $ 289.08
Administrative support cost = level 6 =   213.24 × 2 =   426.48
Administrative support cost = level 5 =   191.32 × 8 = 1,530.56
Administrative support cost = level 3 =   152.26 × 2 =   304.52

Total administrative support weekly cost   = $2,550.64

Supervisory Cost   The cost related to typing or administrative supervision is the weekly pay costs of the supervisor. If the editor has a partial supervisory responsibility, an estimation of this time must be included in the total cost.

Supervisory cost = weekly pay costs of supervisors[2]

Example: Supervisory responsibilities are handled by the word processing supervisor, administrative supervisor, and editor, each of whom receives $236.80 per week. The editor performs lower level supervision for 25% of the time; the others 100% of the time.

Word processing center/supervisory cost = $236.80 × 1   = $236.80
Editor/supervisor cost   = $236.80 × .25 =   59.20
Administrative/supervisory cost   = $236.80 × 1   =   236.80
Total weekly supervisory cost   = $532.80

Origination Cost   A word processing major savings is derived from dictating original correspondence. As illustrated in Table 6–4, machine dictation has a standard production of six lines per minute with a factor of 360. If a central dictation system is proposed, one may assume for the purpose of the cost effectiveness analysis that any document collected during the survey that is two pages or less in length can be dictated effectively. If a central system is not proposed, one must conclude that origination costs will not change from those calculated for the current system.

[2] Include the weekly pay costs of the word processing supervisor and the administrative support supervisor. If other personnel, such as the editors, have part-time supervisory responsibilities, include the pay costs for the percentage of time devoted to these supervisory duties.

Assume Mr. Merriweather's 67-line document was in longhand and less than two pages in length. With central dictation, this is immediately transferable to machine dictation.

Original cost for a document $= \dfrac{67}{360} \times \$17.80$ (hourly salary)

Origination cost for the 67-line document $= \$3.31$

Proofreading Costs   If an editor is used in the word processing system, it is feasible that, based on efficiency, authors will feel it is necessary to give this typed document only a cursory review. However, word processing cannot save all author proofreading. Therefore, to arrive at an estimate of proofreading costs under the proposed system, one should add to the editor's salary one-half of the costs for proofing under the current system.

Proofing costs = weekly pay costs of editors + 0.5 (Current system proofing costs)

Weekly pay cost for editor = 213.24 $\times$ 0.75 (25% of time is supervision in the example) = \$159.92

Proofing costs = \$159.93 + 0.5 (\$0.99) = \$160.43

If no editor is planned for word processing, the proofreading costs will remain the same as stated for the current system.

Table 6–8 is a summary of recurring costs of the proposed system.

Calculating Investment Costs

For each item listed in investment costs, one calculates the amount to be spent during each of the first eight years of the word processing system's life (see Table 6-9).

Calculating Rental Costs

Investment costs for the current system are regarded as sunk cost and usually will not be considered. However, if the current system has leased or rented equipment that will be terminated under word processing, this must be counted. Additionally, if there are

---

TABLE 6-8   Recurring Costs

Summation of Recurring Costs	*Total System Recurring Costs Each Year*	
Typing costs	7 typists' salaries = $1278.28 X 52	= $ 66,471
Administrative costs	13 administrative support = 2550.64 X 52 =	132,631
Supervisory costs	Supervisory (2) + .25 = 532.80 X 52	= 27,705
Origination costs (sum)	50 originators = 2115 X 52	= 109,980
Proofing costs (sum)	Proofing = 645 X 52	= 33,540
Total recurring costs for the proposed system per year		= $370,327

		Example of Dollar Investment Costs (in Years)						TABLE 6-9
	1	2	3	4	5	6	7	8
Rental of automatic typewriters	33,120	33,120	33,120	33,120	33,120	33,120	33,120	33,120
Purchase of dictating machines	3,000	0	0	0	0	0	0	0
Cost of telephone installation	450	0	0	0	0	0	0	0
Moving expenses	0	0	0	0	0	0	0	0
Construction cost	5,000	0	0	0	0	0	0	0
Accessory cost	3,000	0	0	0	0	0	0	0
Maintenance	732	732	732	732	732	732	732	732
Other costs	1,200	250	250	250	250	250	250	250
Total	46,502	34,102	34,102	34,102	34,102	34,102	34,102	34,102

[a]Includes magnetic storage media, typing fonts, ribbons, specialized supplies.

maintenance contracts that will terminate under word processing, this must also be counted. An example of how investment costs are calculated is shown in Table 6-10.

Completion of Cost Effectiveness Analysis

Analysis computations for the current and proposed systems are illustrated in Table 6-11.

- Column b—Investment costs. Place the sum of the investment cost for each year from Table 6-10 on the appropriate line. It is possible that there will be no investment costs for the current system analysis sheet.
- Column c—Recurring costs. Multiply the recurring cost by 52 weeks to get the annual recurring cost under both systems. Place this figure in each year of the analysis sheet.
- Column d—Add investment costs to recurring costs.

	Example of Calculating Investment Costs (Time in Years)							TABLE 6-10
	1	2	3	4	5	6	7	8
Rental Equipment	$5,000	$5,000	$5,000	$5,000	$5,000	$5,000	$5,000	$5,000
Maintenance	420	420	420	420	420	420	420	420
Total	$5,420	$5,420	$5,420	$5,420	$5,420	$5,420	$5,420	$5,420

- Column e—Use the factor given in part A (current system) of Table 6-11 that corresponds with the appropriate year.
- Column f—Multiply the above factor times column d.
- Total project costs equals the sum in column f.

It will be cost effective to install word processing if the total project of the proposed system is *less* than the total project cost of the current system. If costs under word processing do not decrease, the overriding considerations to this very serious objection must be carefully evaluated and documented in the proposal.

Calculating Cost Effectiveness

To determine whether the proposed system is cost effective, one compares costs of the current to the proposed system. The current system costs in the example are:

TABLE 6-11   Comparison of Costs for Current and Proposed Systems

Project Year a	Investment Costs b	Recurring Costs c	Annual Costs (b + c) d	Discount Factor e	Discounted Annual Cost (d X e) f
A. Current System					
1	5,420	840,840	846,260	.954	807,332
2	5,420	840,840	846,260	.867	733,707
3	5,420	840,840	846,260	.788	666,852
4	5,420	840,840	846,260	.717	606,768
5	5,420	840,840	846,260	.652	541,128
6	5,420	840,840	846,260	.592	462,500
7	5,420	840,840	846,260	.538	413,821
8	5,420	840,840	846,260	.489	387,214
Total Project Cost	$43,360	$6,726,720	$6,770,080		$3,625,340
B. Proposed System					
1	46,502	370,327	416,829	.954	397,654
2	34,102	370,327	404,429	.867	350,640
3	34,102	370,327	404,429	.788	318,690
4	34,102	370,327	404,429	.717	289,975
5	34,102	370,327	404,429	.652	263,687
6	34,102	370,327	404,429	.592	236,270
7	34,102	370,327	404,429	.538	208,115
8	34,102	370,327	404,429	.489	197,765
Total Project Cost	$285,216	$2,962,616	$3,247,832		$2,263,796

50 secretaries = 50 × $250 (average weekly salary) × 52 weeks = $650,000
50 originators costs of origination = $3670 × 52 weeks   = 190,840

Total recurring costs   = $840,480

The system is cost effective if the proposed system's total project cost is less than that of the current system. In our example (Table 6–11) the proposed system cost totals $2,263,796, while the current system costs total $3,625,340. From this analysis, we determine the proposed system will save $1,361,544.

Rent/Lease Versus Buy Analysis

When considering investment, explicit recognition must be given to the fact that a dollar today is worth more than a dollar tomorrow because of the opportunity cost related to expenditures occurring over time. Therefore, an annual savings or cash flow projected for tomorrow has a present value less than its undiscounted dollar value. Dollar benefits that accrue in the future cannot be directly compared with investments made in the present because of the time value of money. **Discounted cash flow analysis** (discounting) is a technique applied to convert various cash flows occurring over time as in the case of leasing equipment to equivalent amounts that might be spent for outright purchases at a common point in time considering the time value of money. This results in a valid comparison.

The present value is equal to the cash flow multiplied by the present value factor. For example, a school wishes to decide if it should lease or purchase a word processor that can be leased for $345 a month or purchased for $13,135 with an annual maintenance of $732 and a salvage value of $3000. Table 6–12 compares the costs involved.

One half of the lease price can be applied towards purchase within the first six months, and the word processing equipment has a standard economic life of eight years from the date of initial installation.

Present value of the purchase: (Time = Installation of equipment + 6 months)

The firm must decide whether to lease or purchase the equipment six months after leasing the equipment. At this time, half the lease price paid up to that point may be deducted from the purchase price ($345 × 6 = $2070 ÷ 2 = $1035). Since that price will be paid in the present, the present value of today's dollar = $13,135 – $1,035 = $12,100. The salvage value at the end of the 7½ years must be converted to

	Cost Comparison of Leasing and Buying Word Processor	TABLE 6-12
	Lease Price/Month	*Purchase Price*
Unit price	$345	$13,135
Maintenance	0	732/year
Salvage Value	0	3000

TABLE 6-13   Calculating Present Value (Purchases)

Year	Cash Flow	Present Value Factor	Present Value
0	$13,135-1035	1.000	$12,100.00
7.5	-3000	.513	-1,539.00
0-7.5	732	5.353	3,918.40
			$14,479.40

today's present value and subtracted from the current purchase price of the equipment. The maintenance represents the cash flow in the same amount each year ($732) over the economic life of the equipment, and the present value is added to the investment (see Table 6-13).

To calculate the present value of continued leasing:

0-7.5 (year) $345 × 12 = 4140 (cash flow) × 5.353 = $22,161.42

The present value of the savings of purchase over lease is $22,161.42 minus $14,479.40, or $7,682.02.

Figure 6-1 depicts the present value of this example each year during the economic life of the equipment. The **breakeven point** is the point in this example (4.5 years) where the cost of renting/leasing equals that of purchase.

If the equipment is foreseen to meet the needs of the organization to the breakeven point of 4.5 years, the most economical choice is to purchase. Should the organization be in the process of upgrading to different equipment needs in the foreseeable future and doubts whether this equipment will continue to meet these requirements, it might be more feasible to continue leasing. This allows for changes in the state of the art of word processing equipment. Renting or leasing is the most feasible option when the specified utilization period is less than the economic life unless other requirements are known to extend use of the equipment.

SUMMARY

In determining total costs of a system, all personnel (including fringe benefits) and equipment costs are totaled for a year and a five-year period. The costs of the new system are then determined, including equipment and personnel. This is subtracted to determine the savings of the system (if there is a savings). Generally, because of the increased productivity of word processing, there is a need for considerably less personnel which generally is the main difference in costs.

Productivity desired by the new system determines the number of personnel. First one needs to know the productivity capabilities of the equipment. Present typing volume achieved is determined by either a carbon paper study or a secretarial typing

Example of Breakeven Point Between Leasing and Buying   **FIGURE 6-1**

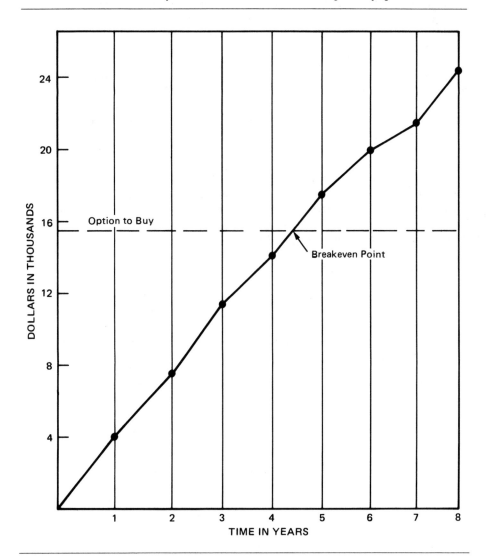

survey (possibly computerized) along with the amount of time required to produce that volume. By dividing the volume by the time required, the present productivity is obtained.

Next, the productivity capability of the word processing typewriters (current ranges are from 150 to 600 words per minute compared to average secretarial ranges from 4 to 15 words per minute) is used to determine how many machines are needed to meet the volume requirements.

Power typing is the term used to describe typing rough draft speed, backspacing, and typing over for errors on a word processing typewriter. Since the new character corrects errors, it frees the typist from the worry of making typographical errors.

Typing on a visual display word processing typewriter is even faster than power typing on a nondisplay unit, because the typist does not have to wait for the typewriter to space, tab, or carrier return.

A secretary who does administrative work as well as typing will end up with a lower productivity rate because of interruptions from typing to perform other tasks. Productivity on word processing typewriters is increased even more when keystrokes can be stored and reused as for revisions of drafts or other documents and original letters to many addressees. Greatest productivity will be achieved in these cases, since the typewriters or printers will move at their fastest speeds, driven by the reading of the stored media. These speeds can be anywhere from 150 words per minute to 600 words or 92 characters per second.

In cost effective analysis the cost of the word processing system and site preparation is offset by the increased productivity attained. Recurring costs are calculated for items incurred on an annual basis and include personnel expenses, operating and overhead expenses, materials, support services, and other items such as supervision, author creation, and proofing.

Investment costs include equipment acquisition as well as space and equipment; startup; and all nonrecurring costs, which may include construction, accessories and costs of lighting, sound-proofing, and air-conditioning.

The proposed system increases productivity, which effects a real cost savings.

In computing secretarial costs, the percent of time the secretary supports the work is included. Supervision costs are included and calculated by determining the percentage of time devoted to supervising the work. Origination costs are the amount of time devoted to origination, which is determined by how long it takes to originate the work. Proofreading costs by the author must also be calculated. This is done by using the standard of average proofreading speed of 20 lines per minute.

All of these recurring costs are totaled to determine the cost of the current system.

To project personnel costs for the typing, the kind of typing required is related to the volume, using the standards for each kind of typing: original (record and playout), revision (playout plus revisions), and repetitive (playout only). To get the hourly rate, the standard of each is multiplied by 60. From the survey, the analysis indicates the amount of original, revision, and repetitive typing, which is divided by its factor to get work weeks. The total number of work weeks is then rounded up to state the productivity required. This number is multiplied by 1.11 to cover normal absences and vacations and is also rounded upwards.

The number of personnel to handle administrative support is also totaled (from the administrative survey), and the numbers established from the system selected (centralized, decentralized). The total typing costs are calculated by adding the salaries of the correspondence secretaries, while administrative costs are the total of administrative support salaries. Again, the supervisory costs are added, as well as costs of origination and proofreading.

Investment costs are calculated for the first eight years of the system's life. This includes rental (or purchase) of word processing typing equipment, dictation equipment purchase, cost of telephone installation, moving expenses, construction costs, accessory costs, maintenance, and other costs which normally covers the cost of storage media, typing ribbon, print wheels, and paper. These are usually considered sunk costs, except for rented equipment and maintenance contracts which terminate.

REVIEW QUESTIONS

1. How is a secretary's productivity obtained?
2. What costs are included in present system costs?
3. Explain power typing.
4. Why can typists type (input) faster on visual display typewriters?
5. Why don't most secretaries produce typing at their top speed capabilities?
6. Explain how word processing typists can produce 900 to 1000 lines or more per day while a regular secretary usually produces less than half that amount.
7. What are the five recurring costs in word processing?
8. List six investment costs in word processing.
9. Explain the three kinds of word processing typing and their factors.
10. Explain how you find the number of people required for the volume need in word processing.
11. Explain administrative costs.
12. Explain how you develop total word processing system costs.

QUESTIONS FOR DISCUSSION

1. Discuss how word processing cost effectiveness differs from the usual secretarial budget.
2. Discuss the comparative costs of the three kinds of word processing typing with and without word processing equipment.
3. Discuss what factors need to be considered in determining administrative costs.
4. Discuss how changing the form of origination from longhand to machine dictation affects costs of internal operations.
5. Explain how to make a rent-versus-buy analysis.
6. Explain why it is important to know how to make a rent-versus-buy analysis.
7. Explain why word processing equipment has no salvage value in a rent-versus-buy analysis.

CASES

Case 6-1   Personnel Agency

The John Riggs Personnel Agency made a feasibility study to see what word processing system would be most effective for them. Their personnel were as follows:

Title	Salary
Manager	$44,000
Recruiters (8)	24,000 (ea)
Secretaries (4)	15,000 (ea)
Typists (2)	9,000 (ea)
Bookkeeper	18,000
Receptionist/Phone	8,000
File Clerk	7,200

They found that the average typing output per day for each secretary was 400 lines for a total of 1600 lines per day, while the typists produced 750 lines each for a total of 1500 lines. The grand total was 3100 lines per day for the six office employees. Origination was all from longhand, and the typing included 400 lines of original typing, 1200 lines of revision typing, and 1500 lines of repetitive form letters.

1. How many word processing secretaries with word processing typewriters are needed to meet the current workload?

Case 6-2   Personnel Agency (continued)

Suppose that the Riggs Personnel Agency decided to get a visual screen system that could be purchased for $14,000 or rented for $360 a month; annual maintenance is $5000.

1. Using the same information as in Case 6-1, if dictation equipment is purchased, how much is needed?
2. What would be the cost of the new system if the staff were reduced according to typing volume needed with one word processing manager and two administrative support secretaries?

"It is the responsibility of management to find the most efficient way of doing any job. It is not the responsibility of the operator."

CHAPTER 7

Designing the Structure, Personnel Alignment, Workflow, and Procedures

OVERVIEW

The purpose of conducting the feasibility study was to find out how work is currently being accomplished and if improvements can be made. Once the statistics are in, the current workflow is diagrammed, problems and current costs are known, and evaluation is completed, it is time to design a better system. One should first determine which type of structure best suits the needs of the firm and what types of jobs and reporting relationships best achieve the desired results. The workflow and procedures should then be designed accordingly.

This chapter studies each element in designing a system, designating how to accomplish the necessary tasks.

OBJECTIVES

Once you have completed this chapter, you will be able to:

1. Design an office structure directed towards best accomplishing an organization's needs.

Quote from James F. Lincoln, *Incentive Management* (Cleveland: Lincoln Electric Company, 1951).

2. Plan personnel alignment accordingly.
3. Diagram and develop those procedures that most efficiently accomplish the firm's objectives.

PRELIMINARY PLANNING

Before designing a new system, one should first determine the firm's major opportunities and limitations, identify future potential and define its scope, and relate these features to available resources. Key considerations to bear in mind when preparing to design a system include:

1. Defining the scope by establishing relative emphasis, priorities, and selectivity among alternatives and concentrating on carefully defined activities.
2. Establishing numerical performance specifications. Such quantification serves two indispensable functions: it provides target objectives for all to achieve; and it gives some precision to decisions regarding resource allocation, including prospective expansion.
3. Devising a strategic plan (a time sequence of conditional moves) in resource deployment. Establishing emphasis and priorities is the heart of such a plan.

A program of implementation and elaboration to be planned might include:

•   Once objectives and goals are determined, analyzing present activities to determine when and how they can be achieved (analyzing results of the study).
•   Calculating personnel resource requirements and physical capacity to meet performance targets (computing requirements).
•   Comparing available resources with those required to accomplish objectives.
•   Developing a critical path problem (scheduling personnel and activities in such a sequence that resource availability matches requirements and performance targets are met).

Three documents to use to schedule the necessary resource procurements and allocations are:

1. A timetable of major strategic moves that indicates the sequence of events, the lead time required before each action can be made effective, and specific times for measuring progress and reviewing plans.
2. A funds flow analysis tied to the timetable, indicating the sources and application of funds necessary to support various planned events.
3. A manning table indicating the key persons necessary to carry out the program and activities assigned to specific individuals.

SELECTING THE APPROPRIATE STRUCTURE

Major features of the present system are clarified through summaries and graphic illustrations. Summaries of current volume of production, distribution of typing and administrative work hours, and current costs provide resource allocation data for the present system. Workflow of major activities delineates problems such as high costs of overtime or high attrition, unnecessary duplications, and low typing productivity.

Graphic representations of current resource allocations are next compared to management's stated objectives. If the current operating system meets management's objectives, there is no need to make any major changes. However, comparing available resources and present workflow activities with stated objectives usually indicates changes or improvements needed to accomplish those objectives. For instance, there may be low productivity in a department where secretaries have a wide variety of tasks to perform. Duplication costs may be excessive, or there may be inadequate office space to meet the growing number of personnel.

Summaries of data obtained from the study provide:

1. Volume of typing production during the study period and an average per day.
2. Kinds of documents produced, ranging from highest to lowest in volume.
3. Division of secretarial time between typing and nontyping tasks, broken down into different nontyping tasks.
4. Amount of wasted time and effort in restarts, duplications, and revisions and errors.

How can this information be interpreted to design the best system to solve current problems while meeting the standards and objectives of the firm? One first must determine which form of office structure will provide the most appropriate working environment and organizational relationship to obtain optimum effectiveness. Keith Davis stated, ". . . different environments require different organizational relationships for optimum effectiveness. No longer is there a 'one best way' whether it is classical or behavioral."[1] This is particularly true for word processing systems.

Word processing structures are usually either (a) a boss/secretary or one-on-one structure (even though the secretary may provide support for more than one person); (b) a single unit or cluster located near the principals, in which the two support services provided by secretarial personnel are separated into personnel who specialize in administrative (nontyping) or correspondence (typing) support; (c) a central support service group in which specialists perform the support function (either correspondence or administrative) placed in a central location; or (d) a combination of centralization and decentralization. Figure 7-1 shows several office arrangements.

Futurists predict that the general secretarial system as we know it today will disappear and be replaced by specialists performing special technical functions. For

[1] Keith Davis, "Trends in Organizational Design," *Proceedings of the Thirty-Third Annual Meeting* (New York: Academy of Management, 1973), p. 4.

FIGURE 7-1   Work Group Office Arrangements

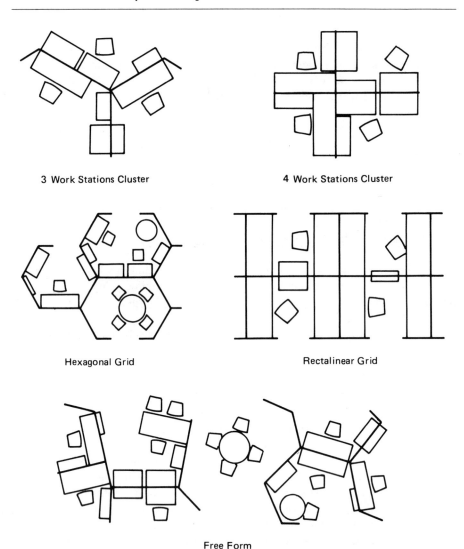

3 Work Stations Cluster   4 Work Stations Cluster

Hexagonal Grid   Rectalinear Grid

Free Form

example, a correspondence specialist produces typing; an administrative specialist performs administrative tasks; a communications specialist handles distribution and communications; a records processing specialist processes documents for storage, retention, and retrieval.

Word processing serves as the key to these specializations, because the capturing or keyboarding of information serves as the nucleus to the total system. A document must be captured before it can be produced, communicated, and stored.

WORD PROCESSING CENTRALIZATION

Originally, the concept of word processing was that of specialists located in a centralized environment working together to produce the firm's typed documents. This structure frees workers from interruptions so that they can devote their time completely to producing the majority of the organization's typing, particularly the long, revised documents, stored boilerplate information, and repetitive letters. Frequently they transcribe information dictated over a central dictating system.

There is no doubt that uninterrupted time in an activity allows an individual to be more productive so long as the individual is motivated and has the appropriate equipment and operating procedures. However, there are several potential problems regarding centralization, the main one being the lack of close communication with other people, particularly those who originate the work.

Centers where specialists produce typing frequently are not located near the work originator. Typing input, such as illegible longhand, poorly marked copy, dictation that is difficult to understand or lacks adequate explanations, or a very complex job, is sometimes difficult to interpret. If a typing specialist must produce the same kind of work day after day without change, boredom is apt to set in.

Everyone has individual preferences. Some people like to work near others so that they can communicate freely and interact frequently with others. Others may prefer to work uninterrupted all day and produce highly technical, difficult projects, which might be typewritten or phototypeset documents, artistic renderings, graphic illustrations, detailed flowcharts, or a combination of typed and graphic presentations. A firm about to implement a word processing system needs to select the structural arrangement best suited to that organization's needs.

> The ideal objective is to create working environments in which employees find job satisfaction while the firm experiences high productivity.[2]

If a firm chooses a centralized typing arrangement, in which correspondence secretaries specialize in producing the firm's typing, the most important second step is to assure that everyone who is selected and who elects to work belongs in this environment. Each individual must have the appropriate behavioral and mechanical aptitudes. Operating procedures need to be designed to use people's abilities so that they will enjoy their work and achieve job satisfaction while the firm's goals of high personnel productivity are achieved.

A firm could structure complete centralization of both the correspondence and administrative operations under one word processing manager. In this case, a different supervisor manages each operation: one over correspondence/typing and one over administration/nontyping. Figure 7-2 illustrates the two types of structures.

---

[2] Fritz J. Roethlisberger, "The Human Equation in Employee Productivity." In *Management: A Book of Readings*, 4th ed., Harold Koontz and Cyril O'Donnell, eds. (New York: McGraw-Hill, 1976), p. 450.

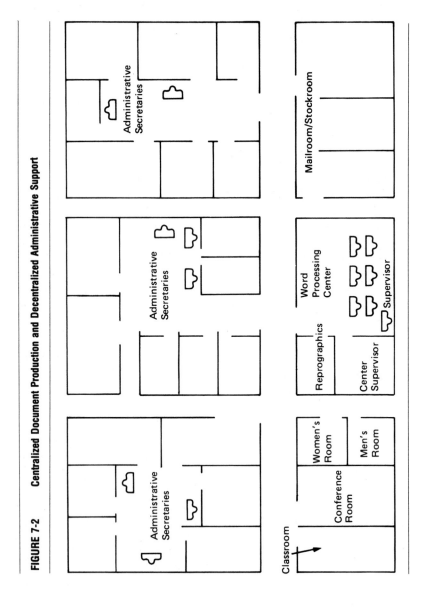

FIGURE 7-2   Centralized Document Production and Decentralized Administrative Support

Administrative Secretaries

Administrative Secretaries

Administrative Secretaries

Mailroom/Stockroom

Reprographics

Word Processing Center

Center Supervisor

Supervisor

Women's Room

Men's Room

Conference Room

Classroom

Centralization Attributes

A team relationship develops among those who can work together and share the work in a social relationship. This is important in working situations so long as a team spirit is encouraged and the workers share the work, which increases productivity. The ability to even out workloads through work distribution prevents instances of some workers' being overworked while others are idle.

Work is more easily controlled when it is centralized. Communication between those who perform the same work but are located elsewhere is less apt to break down, saving costly time and energy. An increased ability to meet emergency situations and deadlines also benefits the organization.

Specialization in one task can lead to self-satisfaction through professional achievement. This is particularly true with those who operate highly technical word processing equipment. The word processing specialist can increase his or her skills through on-the-job-training. Compensation can be linked to reward for accomplishment, which can be a powerful stimulus for top performance.

WORD PROCESSING DECENTRALIZATION

A small firm may find it most efficient to centralize word processing typing and decentralize administration. In this case, administrative support secretaries are located near the principals, which may or may not be most appropriate for larger firms.

Many organizations are changing their centralized typing to units or work groups located near the principals for closer communication (**decentralization**). In some instances, two separate groups service one department: the administrative work group handles all nontyping tasks, and the correspondence group produces the typing.

One law firm provides the legal secretaries with **standalone** word processors (see Figure 7–3) to improve productivity while they maintain their administrative tasks. This way they are knowledgeable and up-to-date in all regards.

Decentralization Attributes

By locating the word processing secretary near the originators, communication gaps are avoided, saving both time and effort, improving working relationships, and boosting morale.

Task identification and ability to perceive the importance of a project are important motivators of top performance. This is usually much more feasible when typing is performed near the principals and the activities taking place.

A correspondence secretary can more easily satisfy needs when located near the originators. Such needs include feeling important, receiving praise, knowing what is expected, and feeling a part of the group. The secretary who is located near the activity and the attorneys knows the value and importance of producing a long, complicated legal document. If located in a separate central area, that secretary may have an idea of a document's importance but will not feel a part of the project and therefore may lack the stimulation of feeling its importance.

FIGURE 7-3   **The AMtext features a full-page display, printer, and dual floppy-disk drives and contains two microprocessors and 48,000 characters of programmable memory. (Photo courtesy of Addressograph Multigraph.)**

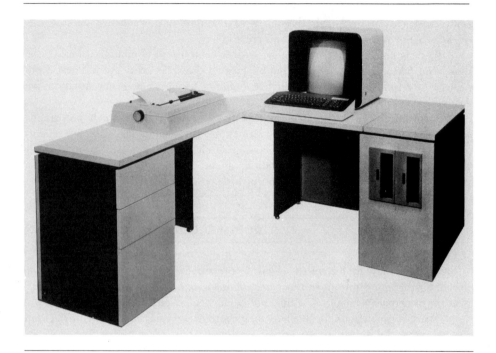

COMBINING CENTRALIZATION WITH DECENTRALIZATION

One large law firm has found it most efficient to provide legal secretaries with their own word processing typewriters to type short, timely documents in addition to performing other legal tasks. The document center, equipped with more sophisticated word processing equipment, produces long, multiple-page, revised documents.

Both legal secretaries and attorneys communicate freely with the correspondence secretaries, either by dictating into their central dictating systems (see Figure 7-4) or by visiting the specialist who produces their documents. Sometimes work that a legal secretary has originated on his or her word processing or intelligent typewriter is transmitted to the center where it is revised or incorporated into longer documents.

BOSS/SECRETARY GENERALIZATION

Many people prefer the combination of administrative and correspondence tasks for the following reasons:

The Norelco automatic dictation system provides around-the-clock dictation availability   **FIGURE 7-4**
from any phone anywhere. All workers in an organization can have complete dictation
capability at their desks and from anywhere in the world. The system features a
full range of dictation controls using conventional telephones and a built-in
intercom for quick communication between dictator and attendant. (Photo
courtesy of Philips Business Systems, Inc.)

1. They like knowing the status of a project. This may be difficult when administrative and correspondence units are separate or are handled by separate individuals. When a generalist handles both functions, that person is continually involved in the total project.
2. Many office workers enjoy their jobs because of the variety of tasks they perform. When they no longer experience this variety, they may become bored or less stimulated by their work.
3. By being involved in both administrative and the typing aspects of the job, there is less communication breakdown. This sometimes is more important to the princi-

pal, who has become used to having one person know all about the work and has built up confidence upon this reliance.

4.   Face-to-face communication and contact is as important in an office as in one's personal life. A secretary located near the principal may find the job more enjoyable and satisfying because of the personal relationship. People who enjoy their work have proven to be the most productive.[3]

SELECTING THE STRUCTURE

To select the most appropriate structure, the following factors also need to be considered:

*   Secretarial organization (secretary/boss; work groups; central typing and work groups; central typing and boss/secretary; or central typing and central administration).   *only self ___ of the ___*
*   Work specialization (separate typing and administration).
*   Job design (activity or manager oriented).
*   Supervision (secretary managed by supervisor or principal).

    The system design components emphasize the following basic considerations:

*   Should secretaries be located next to the principal or in groupings?
*   Should there be a mix or division of tasks (administrative and typing)?
*   Should the job design be oriented towards the principals supported (department, section) or towards the activity (produce form letters, statistical projects)?
*   Who should supervise the secretary, the principal or the supervisor?
*   Should the word processing supervisor report to a function manager or to a word processing manager?

EXAMPLES OF CURRENT SYSTEMS

Centralized Correspondence Support/Decentralized Administrative Support

At the City of Milpitas in California, a central word processing center produces typing for city offices. Administrative services are provided by department secretaries located within the operating departments. A word processing specialist comes to work early each morning to transcribe police reports which are then delivered to the courthouse by 9 a.m. Three other correspondence secretaries, supervised by the word processing supervisor, produce typing for the other city departments, including the City Manager, Attorney, City Clerk, Building and Planning, Public Works, Parks and Recreation, Engineering, Purchasing, and the Fire Department.

[3] Carl Heyel, "Changing Concepts of Human Relations (The Hawthorne Experiments)." In *Management: A Book of Readings*, 4th ed., Harold Koontz and Cyril O'Donnell, eds. (New York: McGraw-Hill, 1976), pp. 437–438.

Principals originate documents by dictating over telephones in their offices in two main buildings or at remote locations. In addition, the police officers carry portable dictation units with them while on duty. Documents are produced on a visual screen shared-logic word processing system using a minicomputer. Documents are delivered to and from the center three times a day by a mail clerk.

Satellite Word Processing Centers

A large law firm in Houston, Texas, finds satellite word processing centers dedicated to producing documents for each floor of the firm extremely efficient. (See Figure 7-5 for an illustration of such a center.) Their objectives included decreasing turnaround time from their former traditional system, maintaining high employee morale, establishing confidence of the attorneys regarding project status, and ability to handle last-minute rush projects and determine priorities.

The ultimate success of the system resulted from the cooperation and support of the attorneys, particularly those in management. Other factors that contributed to its success included standardized procedures and format, in-house training, competent and capable word processing supervision, and word processing management reporting directly to top management.

Although the centers are physically removed from one another, their system offers greater flexibility for control of workflow, ease of solving staffing problems, and continually high-quality output through standardization.

A multifunction office where secretaries are typing on Redactron communicating typewriters and text-editing typewriters. (Photo courtesy of Redactron, a subsidiary of Burroughs.)   **FIGURE 7-5**

They distribute documents from one center to another by means of communicating devices on their word processing typewriters. Another procedure they employ to improve their capabilities is having one person in each center handle minor revisions of six or fewer pages. This allows the centers to push through projects for rapid turnaround while several long projects may be in process. Their safety valve to handle attorneys' last-minute rush projects is a bump system: an attorney with a rush project will discuss this project with another attorney whose work is already in process, requesting permission to bump this rush project ahead of the other job.

Their legal administrative work is processed by the legal secretaries as before, except that they are now relieved of their typing load. This provides legal secretaries with more time to expand their responsibilities and offer services to more attorneys than before, including dictating routine correspondence, as illustrated in Figure 7–6.

WORKFLOW AND PROCEDURES

Diagrams of the current operating system point out duplicated efforts and unnecessary loops in the flow. Frequently a feasibility study will reveal that several unnecessary forms are created during the process of carrying out a project. For example, at General Electric's Motor Plant in San Jose, California, a feasibility study uncovered multiple forms being processed in order to sell a motor and deliver it to the customer. As a result of the study, the plant first cut down from five to one form, dealing with the salesman's delivering a proposal or making a sale, sending the order for processing, designing engineering specifications for the customer, and manufacturing the motor to specifications. After the word processing center was implemented, they tackled the order processing and communications functions between different General Electric facilities.

Some medical clinics and hospitals implement message centers with their dictation systems. These centers can simplify workflow by informing appropriate staff members of current activities. Previously such information was usually lost in the flow and departments were unaware of current activities. A message center can speed up the efficiency of the bed control (or occupancy) system.[4] Often it becomes necessary to notify several departments simultaneously when a patient is discharged or transferred to another area in the hospital. This can be a problem, since in many hospitals only the floor nurse knows when a patient has left and must notify admitting, dietary, pharmacy, and central supply, among other possible areas. By dictating over a telephone or into a desk microphone to a central dictating system, the nurse can have the message recorded simultaneously to all necessary departments or have it transcribed, copied, and delivered. Departments are therefore kept informed up to the minute. (See Figure 7–7.)

In another situation, workflow is simplified when many patients are seen as referrals from other physicians. Large referral centers can implement a system where referring doctors can call in and dictate their impressions and findings of a patient.

---

[4] The bed control objective is to maintain full occupancy.

Lanier's desktop dictating unit features a contoured microphone with a one-hand,   **FIGURE 7-6**
one-thumb control for dictate, pause, reverse, and listen/review functions. The unit
features fully electronic cuing for the executive. The secretary's transcriber
automatically prints out both end-of-letter and special instructions indexing. (Photo
courtesy of Lanier Business Products, Inc.)

This saves the other doctor at the referral center the time involved in doing the initial checkup and saves the patient the cost and time of going through this part of the examination again.

Simplified workflow is being used at the Stanford Medical Center in Palo Alto, California, for medical transcription services. Although the Medical Transcription Center is located in a separate building some distance away from the main medical facilities, the doctors dictate into a telephone or microphone dictation system where the dictation is recorded immediately at the medical transcription center. These recordings are transcribed by skilled medical transcriptionists onto one-sheet report forms, which are then duplicated onto multicolored preprinted forms on the copier.

FIGURE 7-7   **A tone system which turns pushbutton telephones into dictation stations is part of the IBM cartridge system. (Photo courtesy of International Business Machines, Inc.)**

The original is routed to the addressee, the yellow copy is distributed to the Medical Chart Room, the pink copy goes back to the originating department, and the green copy is filed. Charts previously were processed separately by each department, which created its own forms—a very costly process. Now the same form is used for every department in the medical center, saving several thousands of dollars.

Word processing has saved the Air Training Command (ATC) Headquarters at Randolph Air Force Base in San Antonio, Texas, more than $150,000 a year. Their center uses 40 percent fewer people than their previous conventional office system.

After top management had been convinced of the potential for word processing, special forms were designed to use in their feasibility study. These forms were used to summarize the total typing hours recorded at each station studied and the approximate cost of these hours.

PERSONNEL ALIGNMENT

In the mid 1970s, Company A, a growing electronics company in California, installed a word processing center utilizing a supervisor and three word processing operators to produce the typing of multiple-page documents, which consisted mainly of reports, proposals, statistical budgets, and sales forecasts. The company installed a central dictation system in addition to the three word processing typewriters.

Two years later they updated the word processing typing equipment to newer equipment with more capabilities and changed the dictating system to one with automatic stacking of cassettes to handle the dictation. The supervisor was delegated the additional responsibility of supervising the mail distribution system (and later the telephone communications network) in headquarter offices and for branch offices located across the country.

The supervisor now managed the firm's TWX and Telex communicating systems (updating the telephone system) and two additional clerical personnel at this point. The supervisor's title was changed to manager of administrative services. This did not include authority or responsibility over departmental secretaries who typed daily correspondence, short documents, and quick turnaround copy. Those secretaries still reported to the principals whose work they performed.

The manager managed word processing, communications, and electronic mail. Job alignment, shown in Figure 7-8, was designed according to the firm's document production-communication-distribution cycle.

Another large industrial firm, which had first installed word processing equipment in the early 1970s, installed a shared-logic word processing system with six display-screen keyboards. The six correspondence secretaries reported to the manager of word processing, phototypesetting, and mail distribution. The company installed a sophisticated typesetting system designed to read the recordings created by the word processing secretaries on the shared-logic word processing system to produce final phototypeset documents. Before installing the phototypesetting system, phototypeset documents were produced in the Graphics Arts Department or were sent outside. (See Figure 7-9.)

The word processing manager had the following responsibilities: (a) Producing typewritten documents for the Tax Department, Accounting, Legal Department, Public Relations, Advertising, and Marketing; (b) producing phototypeset documents for most of the firm; and (c) communicating and distributing documents within the firm.

At Company C (illustrated in Figure 7-10), a large international firm, the word processing manager is responsible for both administrative and correspondence operations. The word processing manager manages centralized word processing operations along with three additional satellite centers. Administrative secretaries are located near

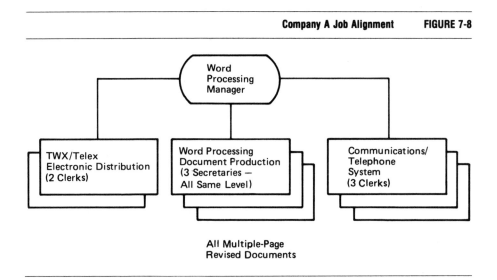

Company A Job Alignment   FIGURE 7-8

FIGURE 7-9   Industrial Firm Job Alignment

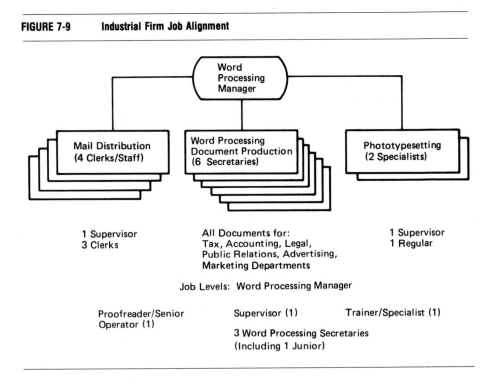

1 Supervisor
3 Clerks

All Documents for:
Tax, Accounting, Legal,
Public Relations, Advertising,
Marketing Departments

1 Supervisor
1 Regular

Job Levels: Word Processing Manager

Proofreader/Senior
Operator (1)

Supervisor (1)   Trainer/Specialist (1)

3 Word Processing Secretaries
(Including 1 Junior)

the principals in the departments they serve including the Engineering Design, Marketing, Order Processing, and Industrial Relations Departments. They perform additional project work and inside sales and purchasing tasks since being relieved of their typing tasks. They do not have typewriters. The administrative secretaries report to the word processing manager but perform work for the managers and principals.

In a followup survey, many of these administrative secretaries expressed opinions that, although they greatly respected their word processing manager, they would prefer to be supervised by the principals whose work they performed. They stated that they also felt these principals were more aware of their performance proficiency on a daily basis. The word processing manager knew that some of the secretaries felt this way.

However, some of these same administrative secretaries preferred reporting to the word processing supervisor because they felt the supervisor was more aware of their needs, job capabilities, and growth potential and was always interested in helping those with the ability and desire to get ahead.

What was the personnel alignment of these word processing operations? How were the jobs managed? How much freedom do these operators and secretaries have in these three separate systems? Which is the best system of job alignment? Should Company C change and have those administrative secretaries evaluated and supervised by the principals whose work they perform each day? Will these principals be as

Company C Job Alignment   **FIGURE 7-10**

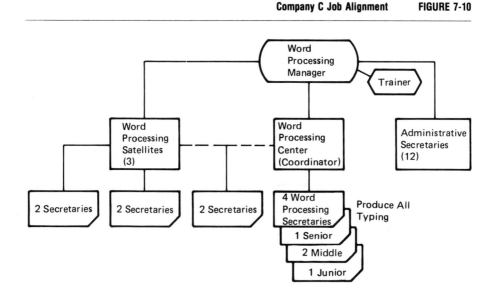

interested in seeing that the secretaries achieve their career objectives and are objectively evaluated?

How do firms achieve their productivity objectives while at the same time helping their employees achieve job satisfaction? What system of job alignment is most appropriate, operates the most efficiently, and at the same time offers employees career opportunities? Many word processing employees wish to better themselves, grow in their jobs, take on more responsibility, and become supervisors and managers.

The old adage "too many chiefs and no Indians" can become a fact if a firm creates too many empires just so that employees can have job titles in order to solve their ego desires and give them a feeling of importance.

Does it make any difference if there are three, four, or five levels of word processing secretaries: senior administrative, administrative, senior, regular, and junior, as opposed to senior, regular, and junior? Are the levels established so that when that six-month review occurs, the individual has the opportunity for a new job title and a six-month pay raise?

When planning a system's job alignment, it is necessary to determine how the system will be managed and design the job structure from there. For instance, at State Compensation Insurance, there are three separate groups that report to the office supervisor, who is responsible for word processing. The structure is shown in Figure 7-11, with a supervisor in charge of each function in close liaison with daily activities, meeting daily turnaround requirements. If this job were eliminated, it might be extremely difficult for the office supervisor to direct all three operating functions and meet deadlines on time.

FIGURE 7-11   State Compensation Insurance Job Alignment

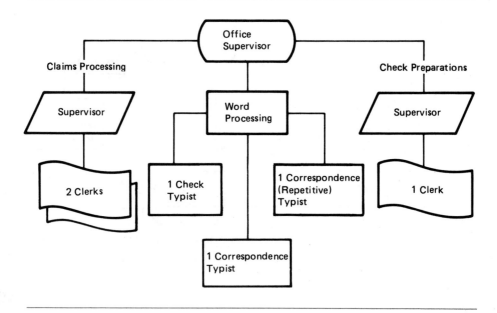

ORGANIZATIONAL FRAMEWORK

One way to keep people motivated is to allow them freedom to plan and carry out their work. However, complete freedom is not possible in situations where people share projects. Work distribution requires team work. Certain organizational restrictions that require a balance between controlled organizational structures and self-motivation become necessary. How well can the principle of predetermination work?[5] A formal organizational structure is based upon functions rather than individuals. It is concerned with authority relationships, controls, plans, and policies. However, controls and policies must be reasonably human so that they do not impede motivation.

A well-planned structure customized according to a firm's character is a basic factor in motivation. Without controlled organization structure, activity can be aimless. Formal objectives and plans provide goals toward which human energies may be directed, policies determine guidelines, and the organizational structure indicates channels of career paths to promotion. The structure recognizes individuals and their places within the organization.

---

[5] Predetermination is the planning and controlling of the job or task by the worker rather than the supervisor.

REQUIREMENTS FOR SUCCESS

To effectively accomplish word processing productivity objectives and effective employee motivation, the structure requires:

1. Organizational objectives compatible with individual objectives.
2. Good leadership.
3. Ability of individuals to identify their interests with those of the organization.
4. Decentralized responsibility and authority.
5. Fair disciplinary action.
6. Good physical conditions.

WORD PROCESSING ORGANIZATION TREND

Although large word processing centers continue to be hierarchical in structure and provide supervisory positions, many firms have changed to satellite centers or less formal work groups. Emphasis on technical proficiency and creative use of the equipment itself may provide longer-range job satisfaction rather than emphasis on career paths. A properly structured organization under efficient management allows employees to find intrinsic satisfaction in their work and in their personal development, not in upward mobility alone.

Organizations that successfully implement word processing expect their word processing secretaries to be highly skilled technicians and imaginative professionals, capable of handling work assignments on their own initiative or in collaboration with word originators. Close supervision should not be necessary. A team leader, rather than a supervisor, might be more appropriate for a professional word processing staff. This leader may be selected informally by team members to handle the function of work coordination when necessary and to act on occasion as intermediary with personnel and management representatives or the users. Predetermination of job objectives may function very effectively in word processing so long as it meets the six requirements for success.

The rapid growth in word processing technology, particularly into the computerized environment, offers a wide diversity and range of applications. As the capabilities of word processing equipment and technology expand, they tend to become more complicated. Typical word processing operations have several levels of correspondence secretaries:

- Those just beginning to produce documents, who process the easy-to-create daily correspondence applications.
- Those who have become adept at using word processing equipment and use most of the equipment capabilities to produce the more difficult documents and needs, such as typing revisions; programming stored documents; and repaginating docu-

ments with headers, footnotes, and other more complicated long document requirements.
- The technicians, whose mechanical and creative abilities make it increasingly challenging to them to find more and more ways in which they can make their equipment take on sophisticated applications.

Word processing secretaries become experts on the job; the on-the-job learning experience in word processing becomes a challenge which intrigues specialists into wanting to become experts in their field and within their companies (see Figure 7-12).

THE EFFECT OF DISTRIBUTED PROCESSING

Rapid growth in the minicomputer industry caused by recent technical breakthroughs in bubble memory and the use of tiny microscopic computers on a chip is greatly

FIGURE 7-12   Career Opportunity Ladder

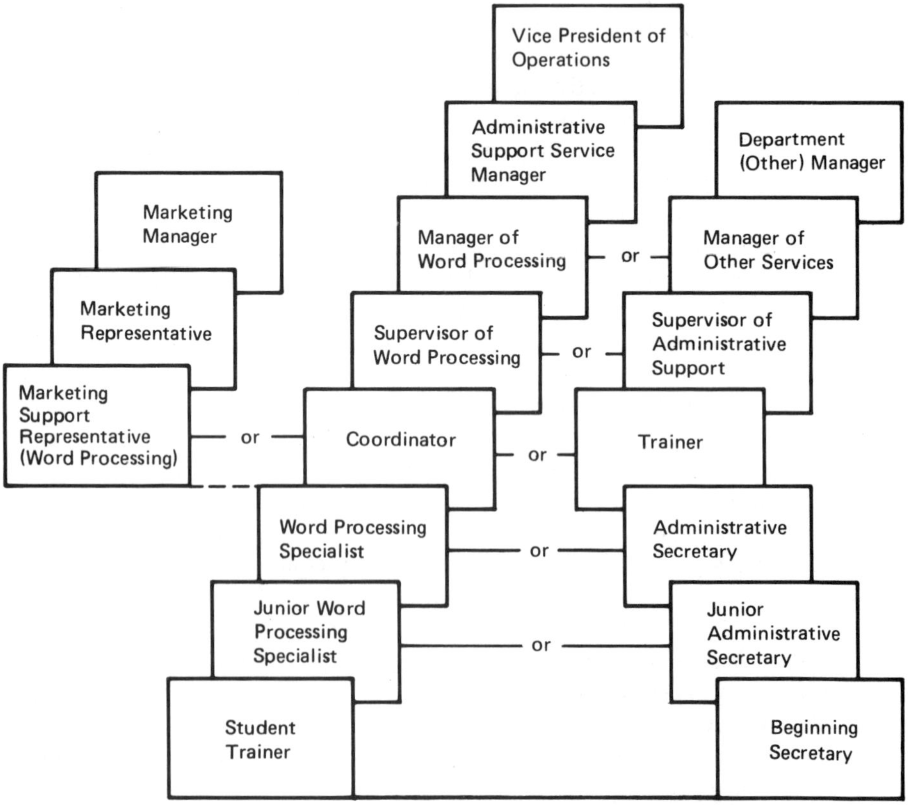

affecting office operations. Many firms are implementing distributed processing networks. By placing computer **terminals** and desktop television screens on the desks of executives and office workers, individuals can handle much of their daily work without changing procedures or sending the work to be done in large central data or word processing centers. Information can be sent directly into the computer system or received from the system from the executive secretary or other individual's desk. As a result, much office information is processed in the traditional operating structure. It is the amount of information workflow that may be changed.

Xerox Corporation sees future offices with small data processors located on executives' desks. These small computers are expected to handle minor problems on their own by means of internal minicomputers and terminals, using an information storage-and-retrieval system. The desk terminals are small, easy to learn and use, and do not require sophisticated techniques or use of special computer languages. IBM's approach is to supply the secretary with a very simple terminal and use the central computer for the processing, relieving the executive of the need to be involved.

Wang's OIS/100 series is a shared resource system (Office Information System). The largest of these systems, the 140, can support 24 work stations and 8 peripherals. The system can produce printed documents ready for duplication on photocomposer and do the printing on Wang's intelligent copier (the Image Printer), daisywheel, or line printers. The system can also use **OCR** input (optical character recognition, a form of data input using an optical scanner) and process electronic mail through **telecommunications**. This system would primarily be used by very large word processing centers and offices implementing true office automation. All Wang systems are compatible, and the System 30 can be upgraded to an OIS/140.

Indicative of future office equipment capabilities, each Wang work station and **printer** has its own microprocessor. Wang's OIS/100 system is supported by 32 K **bytes** of **RAM** (random access memory) per work station and 16 K bytes at each printer. Its distributed intelligence allows most text functions to be completely processed at the work station or printer. The central control unit, which also contains a microprocessor with 64 K bytes of memory and hard disk storage, primarily switches large blocks of text data among the different remote devices.

Because the central unit does not need to interact with each work station for every text-editing command, the Wang system has the ability to sort large volumes of text without slowing response time at the other work stations, reducing the overhead required to communicate in order to accomplish this processing by perhaps as much as 45 percent. This type of system provides such capabilities as:

- Intelligent rather than dumb terminals that add flexibility and power to the system.
- Large **on-line** text storage with additional backup on-line storage.
- Complete compatibility with all Wang equipment and field upgradability.
- **Software** ability to sort lists, make arithmetic calculations, and perform horizontal scrolling (displaying the full page of a document containing several columns by displaying one side of the page and then the other so that an 8½-inch screen width can display up to 15 inches of material).
- Available password security to protect against unauthorized access.

Disadvantages such a system might have are:

- *Size.* How many organizations can support 24 work stations, all within 2000 feet of the central unit? This 2000-foot maximum distance limit is determined by the longest length of interconnecting cable possible without an amplification device. A system this large implies enormous word processing centralization in one building, which may not be organizationally desirable.

- *One controller and disk.* A central control unit failure might disable the entire system, a factor that has always been the major vulnerability of shared resource systems. Larger systems only emphasize this problem.

This type of system will most likely be considered by large firms desiring to lower their overhead for word processing. Large government offices, particularly military, legal, and medical offices with large paperwork volumes are the most likely candidates.

ORGANIZING PERSONNEL ALIGNMENT

In developing the basic method of workflow and staff alignment, the manager needs to organize to eliminate waste in overlapping of jobs, make appropriate job assignments according to available talent, and assign the specific tasks and standards for each job assignment. This includes:

- Establishing functional reporting structures by breaking down responsibilities into statements. Jobs should be neither too large nor too small. The job objectives need to be achievable but challenging.
- Delegating authority and responsibilities, creating accountability for results by writing down what is expected for each job, and establishing control points for each job and insisting on completed work performed to specifications.
- Establishing cooperative relationships, defining critical aspects of each job that requires cooperative interfacing, and explaining how to deal with users (principals) and other services.

FUTURE WORD PROCESSING ORGANIZATIONAL FRAMEWORKS

Because of the opportunity to expand and develop their talents from beginner to advanced word processing experts, word processing specialists may be the forerunners of that ideal organizational structure: one that maintains and allows control along with employee predetermination. Managers in this structure can set the objectives, design the procedures, measure the results, and constantly evaluate the results against planned objectives. They are able to do so because, by stimulating self-motivation, self-learning, and self-evaluation, they are not burdened by the menial daily tasks; they delegate them to the employees. This system works with some employees, but not with all. There are always those who need more direction and monitoring. Therefore, the structure should have the flexibility to handle these situations.

Team leaders must be reliable and accountable to the manager as well as to the work group, or the system may break down.

A VOICE IN DECISIONS

During the 1970s, workers have broadened their interests to include the workplace environment, the investment policies of their employers, and a whole range of social and economic issues.

A positive correlation between participation, productivity, and economic performance was confirmed in the study of employee ownership by the University of Michigan's Institute of Social Research. The 30 employee-owned firms in their survey had higher profits than did conventionally owned firms in the same industry. They found that while minor participation in ownership may not necessarily be associated with higher productivity, in general the more equity owned by workers, the greater the profitability of the company. Worker participation reduces employee-related drags on economic performance: absenteeism, poor workmanship, high turnover, strikes. There appears to be a substantial initial jump in productivity associated with the introduction of substantive worker participation programs. Whether productivity continues to rise faster over time than in conventional firms is as yet unproven. Short-term improvements may prove fleeting if workers do not receive some direct economic gain from participatory work changes. There will be no economic benefits from worker participation if workplace democracy is a sham. If employees are going to participate, then power and the fruits of economic success must be apportioned democratically.

Participatory management requires a new set of values. Management needs to capitalize on the strength of groups, and its leaders must learn to deal sensitively with most people's tendency to remain uninvolved. Successful managers of the future will be enterprising, nonauthoritarian leaders who can mobilize human skills, not just supervise technical know-how, to solve problems.

> Management must be refined, through careful planning, with the full involvement and participation of all segments of society, including unions. There MUST be a new decentralizing process of consultation and decision-making.[6]

> New technology, the rising costs of the factors of production, and expectations that work should be humane as well as profitable are forcing transformations in the marketplace.[7]

> The question is not whether to change work patterns; rather, (it) is which kinds of change are going to be accomplished, how, and by whom.[8]

[6] Umberto Agnelli, Managing Director of Italy's Fiat Company, quoted in American Center for the Quality of Work Life, *Industrial Democracy in Europe.*
[7] Bruce Stokes, "Answered Prayers," *MBA*, December 1978/January 1979, p. 12.
[8] Michael Maccoby, Harvard Project on Technology, Work and Character. Ibid.

Change in the work climate ... cannot be mandated by management or by the union. ... The people affected by the change must have a say in determining the nature of the change as well as planning how the change is to be effected.[9]

Change in the work climate can mean collaboration to improve the physical and psychological work environment, the handling of routine personnel problems, joint consultation on production standards and goals, union representation on company boards, provision of workers' capital for enterprise investments, and worker ownership. Figure 7-13 illustrates the fact that the word processing secretaries selected their team leaders, thereby having the opportunity to participate in making this important decision.

Neither participatory restructuring of repetitive tasks that can lead to boredom nor the introduction of team work will necessarily make it a joy to get up every morning to go to work. There are also rising expectations associated with any experiment in the workplace. Once people are given the opportunity to have a greater say in the organization of their work life, the only way their enthusiasm is maintained is by continuing to expand that control. However, most proponents of job enrichment have no intention of creating workplace democracies. Their aim is to improve working conditions, not to establish new patterns of management and ownership.

FIGURE 7-13   Voice in Decision

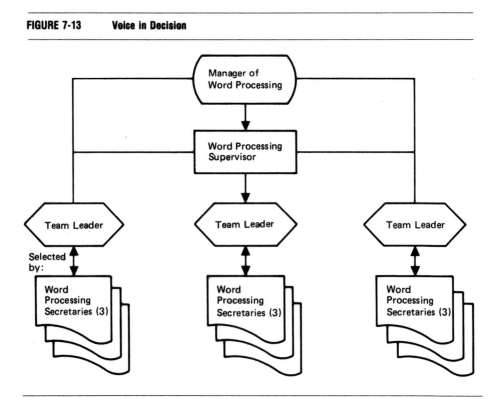

[9] General Motors Vice-President George Morris. Ibid.

Expansion of capabilities and interests of workers will ultimately be stifled unless it is an open-ended process. Experience has shown that it is best if these limits are jointly established by both the workers and their management. There must be room for workers to increase their responsibilities as the program develops.

SUMMARY

After ascertaining features of the present system, including: (a) typing volume, peaks and valleys, and daily average; (b) volume of documents, ranging from highest to lowest; (c) time distribution of secretaries; (d) and wasted time in unnecessary effort, including restarts, duplications, revisions, and errors, the analyst is prepared to design the new system structure.

First, objectives set by management are observed along with the results obtained from the study. The type of structure which best suits the needs of the organization is then selected.

Centralization of typing, which allows for well-controlled monitoring and supervising as well as development of specialized skills, may be selected for a firm requiring high productivity and much work distribution among working groups, particularly for long textual and statistical documents.

Centralization of administrative tasks might also be most effective for the firm, in addition to document production centralization. In this case, both areas might be under the management of one person with a supervisor over each function.

Advantages of centralization are (a) sharing and distribution of work, (b) development of specialized skills linked to performance compensation; (c) increased productivity, (d) increased ability to react to deadlines, (e) easier supervision, (f) easier evening out of workloads.

Decentralization, particularly to small groups located near those for whom they provide service, is becoming more popular. There may be small groups, one for document production and one for administrative support, located near the users, each under its own supervisor.

Combinations of centralization with decentralization sometimes fit the needs most effectively where the centralized document center handles long document production and revision, while the secretary handles daily reactive documents and work.

Advantages of decentralization are (a) closer communication; (b) task identification with the principal resulting in higher task motivation; (c) personal satisfaction derived from working with the originators and face-to-face communications.

Advantages of having a secretary handle both document production and administration are: (a) being kept up-to-date and involved in all aspects, (b) less boredom resulting from a variety of tasks, (c) more communication which maintains a high confidence level, and (d) face-to-face contact and communication for more personal relationship.

The analyst needs to decide the most appropriate arrangement according to the secretarial organization, work specialization, job design, and supervision.

The workflow of the present system should be analyzed to determine where changes can be made to omit duplication and unnecessary loops, always with the aim to simplify the system as much as possible. Ways in which duplication and unnecessary loops can be eliminated may be by designing one form to handle the tasks of several forms, record and store boilerplate information on magnetic media storage on word processing typewriters, and change the flow of the activity. The use of communications on word processing equipment, along with phototypesetting and data entry compatability, can eliminate several steps in a workflow. For instance, if information is keypunched from typewritten sources, it goes through two additional steps. If the typewritten source is recorded directly on a data entry-compatible device, it can be communicated directly to the computer, eliminating keypunching and keypunch verifying, in order to get the information into the computer.

Every time one step is eliminated, it may also eliminate even more time-consuming and costly steps. In the case of a proposal which must be edited by the author, the editor, and then by a manager, three edit checks occur. With the original created on magnetic media, only the *changes* need to be proofed each time, saving critical time of the most costly personnel involved in producing the proposal: the author, the editor, and the manager.

Many people who have been designated word processing management jobs have been given added management responsibilities in activities closely related to word processing, such as mail distribution, phototypesetting, and telecommunications. When the administrative secretaries remain working in the traditional office structure, frequently the word processing supervisor has not been involved. However, in one firm, the word processing manager was responsible for both administration and word processing. In this case, the administrative secretaries reported to the word processing manager while doing the work for the principals in the departments.

In a large international firm, the word processing manager had both administration and correspondence duties. The latter consisted of three satellite centers in addition to a main center, while the administrative secretaries worked near the principals they supported and took on more project tasks, including sales and purchasing. In a survey, these secretaries expressed mixed feelings; some preferred reporting to those whose work they performed, while others liked reporting to the word processing manager, because they felt the word processing manager was more aware of their needs, abilities, and growth potential and was more interested in furthering their careers.

In developing the structure, the manager needs to work towards employee motivation, balancing freedom with controls and policies. The key to this is in making the individual objectives compatible with those of the organization, providing good leadership, motivating employees to organization identification, showing respect for authority, being fair, and maintaining good physical working conditions.

Word processing personnel, by the nature of their work, tend to find job satisfaction and personal development in their work, and not just in the potential upward mobility. The correspondence side of word processing develops highly skilled technicians, who tend to enjoy working in groups where they can select their own leaders. People who do not work effectively in this kind of system generally will not remain in word processing but will seek other work which does not require team work.

At the same time, distributed processing allows people to use terminals at their desks so that those others can accomplish work in the traditional office environment.

In deciding the personnel alignment and structure, the manager needs to plan ways to organize to achieve desired results. The system needs to be structured so that reporting is broken down into responsibility statements, delegation occurs where feasible and where it is well monitored, and cooperation is built in so that the desired service is provided.

REVIEW QUESTIONS

---

1. What are the most important results from the study?
2. Why is the range of volume for each kind of document important to learn from the study? What purpose might it serve in selecting the most appropriate structure?
3. What are the advantages of centralized document production?
4. What are the advantages of decentralized document production?
5. Why did some of the secretaries surveyed prefer to be supervised by those whose work they did?
6. Why did some prefer to be supervised by the word processing manager?
7. How can motivation and control work together?
8. State what is required for effective structure and motivation.

QUESTIONS FOR DISCUSSION

---

1. Explain why the word processing office is frequently structured differently from the traditional one?
2. Discuss why a word processing manager might be able to take on other departments such as mail distribution, telecommunications, and phototypesetting.
3. Explain why word processing secretaries may prefer different reporting alignment from traditional secretaries.
4. What makes the structure of the City of Milpitas most appropriate for the workers?
5. Why were satellite centers best for the Houston law firm?
6. How can forms be used to simplify the workflow of a firm?

CASES

Case 7-1   Law Firm

The staff of Horn, Ashby, Coggs, and Andrews, a law firm with offices in Los Angeles, San Francisco, and San Diego, discerned the following from their feasibility study:

The head office in Los Angeles has 30 attorneys, five of whom are senior partners. They have 25 secretaries, one bookkeeper, one receptionist, and five paralegals. They pride themselves not only on their success but also on the finished quality of their legal documents. Currently they have two word processing typewriters used by two legal secretaries. The other secretaries have either executive or correcting selectric typewriters. Attorneys either dictate to secretaries who take shorthand or use machine dictation. Their other two offices have 20 attorneys, 15 secretaries, and 3 paralegals, as well as a receptionist at each one.

They plan to use computerized legal billing, store boilerplate material on magnetic media, and use word processing typewriters with communications between offices.

1. Plan their most appropriate structure.
2. Support it with the reasons and advantages of the system you select.

Case 7-2 Electronics Firm

A large electronics firm decided it would decentralize all its publications which had formerly been produced by technical typists in a center under the supervision of the production manager. The new system was to have the secretaries in the departments produce the input for the documents on their word processors, which would continue to be edited by the five editors and produced into final phototypeset reports and proposals.

The secretaries would continue to perform the same tasks of handling the phone along with other administrative support and produce the original version of information which would be used in the various sections relating to that department's part of the report. Final phototypesetting and revisions would be done in the Production Department where the editors, illustrators, and printing personnel were located.

- If you were made the manager in charge of the total operation, how would you align the personnel?

"A major growth industry is spawned by a com-
bination of technological development and social
changes."

CHAPTER 8

Selecting Equipment — Origination and Production

OVERVIEW

After designing the new system—its structure, workflow, and personnel alignment—the analyst is prepared to begin equipment selection. First the analyst lists management's expected objectives, current and anticipated volume, document criteria, and working procedures. Next the analyst begins the selection process. This chapter describes word processing origination and production equipment categories and capabilities and concludes with an explanation of how to combine these elements to select appropriate equipment to meet the firm's word processing objectives.

OBJECTIVES

After completing this chapter, you will be able to:

1. State what should be expected of equipment vendors.
2. Categorize word processing equipment.
3. Select dictation and production equipment to meet specific criteria.

Quote from R. L. Katz, *Management of the Total Enterprise* (Englewood Cliffs, N.J.: Prentice-Hall, 1970), p. 211.

SELECTION AND THE ORGANIZATION

In order to select office equipment for the organization, one must analyze the needs of the organization and equipment available. Results from the study provide specific problem areas or areas most in need of improvement. Rapidly changing technology that results in advanced capabilities also may affect equipment selection.

Before selecting either a vendor or equipment, one should determine the selection criteria. For instance, if Arbeck Engineering marketing representatives travel more than half their time and generate most of their paperwork during their trips, they most likely need to carry portable dictation units. (See Figure 8-1.) This would enable them to mail in their dictated material so that the secretaries can type it while they are still away and have it ready for signature upon their return. This system would prevent backlogs, which create peaks and valleys in work volume, and allow the secretaries to produce the documents efficiently. At the same time, the sales personnel can dictate information while it is fresh and avoid heavy workloads when they return to the office. As a result, they can be more effective in their jobs.

Dr. Cowell can dictate directly from a microphone station on his desk immediately after he examines a patient and before he goes to see the next one. This allows him to dictate the information while it is fresh and to record his findings quickly and effortlessly. This recorded information can be transmitted directly to the transcriptionist on a dictation system while he is dictating. If he needs to see a copy of the report before leaving, the secretary can transcribe it while he is dictating and have it ready before he departs. A desktop unit (see Figure 8-2) would not offer him this capability, since the medium would have to be removed and taken to the transcriptionist before it could be transcribed.

A firm such as Koch Insurance Company, which employs several marketing and claims representatives, would probably find a central dictation system (see Figure 8-3) most cost effective and efficient. Such a system would provide each principal with his or her own dictation microphone (or telephone) that records directly into a central dictation medium. This would be efficient and less expensive than a dictation unit for each representative.

Similarly, a firm with a limited budget that wished to provide 20 individuals with dictation capability could satisfy these needs by acquiring a dictation system. This is far less costly than individual desktop or portable units for each dictator. However, cost is only one of the many factors that need to be considered when selecting dictation equipment.

Let us examine production equipment. How can one select the most efficient production equipment to meet the needs of an organization? First, the type of office structure will have a direct bearing on the type of production system selected.

Koch Insurance employs five correspondence secretaries, three in the Claims Department and two in Marketing. What kind of equipment should they select to produce their documents? They must first evaluate their documents by category and by characteristics. Next, they need to survey available equipment and select the kind of equipment that most fits the firm's specific requirements. Before making the selection, they should make a list of the firm's selection guidelines.

Norelco's pocket-size Idea Machine weighs only 10 ounces, is designed for one-hand   FIGURE 8-1
operations, and permits clear, accurate recording. (Photo courtesy of
Philips Business Systems, Inc.)

What guidelines should a firm use to select the appropriate equipment? Each firm's equipment guidelines are derived from the specific needs for that organization, depending upon the size of the office, kind of business it conducts, number of document originators, number of secretaries, and the documents themselves.

A guideline for the top executive's office would include superior quality copy. Accounting Department guidelines would include efficient production of statistical and columnar formats. Some legal application guidelines include documents that are

FIGURE 8-2   An author is shown dictating into a remote microphone of the IBM cartridge system, which includes microphone and telephone systems as well as a desktop recorder, portable recorder, and transcriber, and features a unique cartridge containing 25 magnetic disks which hold six minutes of dictation apiece. (Photo courtesy of International Business Machines, Inc.)

easy to revise and update, rapid information retrieval, and fast production of superior quality documents. (See Figure 8-4.) A publications department that employs five people to type reports, proposals, and manuals might include low cost per work station in its guidelines. If so, a central shared-logic word processing typing system in which each typist's work station shares the central processor would be more apt to meet the guidelines than individual standalone word processing typewriters for each typist.

A low cost per dictator guideline might result in selecting an endless loop dictation system because it would provide each doctor with low-cost dictation capability. The secretaries' equipment guidelines might include a fairly simple, low-cost automatic typewriter or text editor to produce daily work, medical reports, and other medical documents. Figure 8-5 shows a standalone unit with a one-line display.

CRITERIA FOR SELECTING APPROPRIATE WORD PROCESSING EQUIPMENT

Before beginning to plan equipment selection, it is necessary to determine the type of structure the equipment will be expected to fit. Is it a centralized, decentralized, work

The word processing supervisor has an effective management tool in the Dictaphone   **FIGURE 8-3**
Thought Tank system, which monitors the center's daily input, output, total backlog,
and the correspondence secretaries' individual output rates and tells the supervisor
at a glance when peak dictation periods occur and when additional secretaries or
recorders are needed, resulting in improved document transcription turnaround.
(Photo courtesy of Dictaphone Corporation.)

group, or boss/secretary arrangement? After the new system structure is selected, the
category of most suitable equipment may become evident. Other factors may influence the selection as well. In the case of production equipment, the next determining
factor is the characteristic of those documents that make up the largest volume. For
origination, it might be (a) the length of documents, (b) whether originators spend
most of their time in or out of the office, (c) difficulty of format, (d) kind of

---

FIGURE 8-4   Wang's compatible office information system is a hard-disk system with storage of up to 4000 full pages on a master disk. (Photo courtesy of Wang Laboratories, Inc.)

---

information (numerical or alphabetical), and (e) amount of creativity involved in originating.

The simplest way to select equipment is to use a special questionnaire designed for the type of equipment to be selected. One might be selecting equipment for origination, production, reprographics, records processing, communicating, or distributing. Frequently, when first implementing word processing, the only equipment to be selected is for origination and production. Other departments or individuals may be responsible for selecting reprographic, records processing, and communicating and distribution equipment.

Selecting equipment for each phase of information processing depends upon different criteria relating to the process itself. There are certain basic factors to consider when selecting any kind of office equipment, including vendor, cost, human considerations, environment, latest technology, compatibility, and the final consideration that the equipment is selected to meet the specific needs of the organization.

Vendor

The firm may first screen vendors according to whether it desires to rent, lease, or purchase the equipment. Some vendors do not have rental programs or may require outside leasing. Criteria for screening vendors should include:

1. *Reliability.* Does the vendor have an established reliable reputation in the industry? In the specific geographic area, city, or town? How long has the vendor been in business? What is the financial standing of the vendor? Is the vendor well entrenched and able to respond to future technical change? What kinds of equipment guarantee does the vendor offer?
2. *Support Staff.* Does the vendor have a consistently high-quality support staff of

The Artec display system features an easy-to-read display, proportional spacing, and **FIGURE 8-5**
the ability to print justified lines for camera-ready copy. Each floppy disk provides
approximately 80 pages of text storage capacity. (Photo courtesy of
Artec International Corporation.)

representatives who provide marketing, customer engineering, training, and education support.

3. *Response.* Can the vendor respond to customers' needs in each area of marketing, customer engineering, training, and education? How long does it take from the request to the active response? Does the vendor respond quickly to telephone calls? Are the vendor's offices nearby? Can the vendor's support adequately fill requests?

4. *Backup.* In case of problems or complaints, how does the vendor respond? What action does the vendor take? How long does it take the vendor to provide the customer's desired action? If the vendor's marketing, training, or engineering

representative is out of town, what kind of backup is provided? If the customer's equipment is down and cannot be repaired immediately, what kind of backup equipment does the vendor supply?

5. *Knowledge and Experience.* How knowledgeable and experienced are the vendor's representatives? in word processing? on changing technology? of competitors? regarding compatibility with other kinds of equipment? with other vendor's equipment? Are the representatives up-to-date? professional? willing and able to provide current information? How well do they know their own equipment? Can they assist in measurement studies? in writing procedures?

6. *References.* Who is currently using the vendor's equipment? How long have they used it? Do they use it in the same manner and for similar applications? What is their measured productivity (proven productivity records)? Are they accurate? What is their downtime record? Do the other users like the equipment? Why? Do they plan to keep it? plan to get more? Are they planning to change to another vendor's equipment or update to a newer technology?

This type of information is usually obtained through other managers or supervisors of word processing installations, references suggested by vendors, and, most reliably, through word processing consultants with reputed integrity. Positive responses to these questions indicate that the vendor can be on the list of vendors being considered. These questions need to be applied to select equipment for each particular word processing phase. Some vendors could well prove to be more qualified for one type of equipment than for another. A dictation equipment company may have recently announced that it is marketing a word processing typewriter for the first time. This reputable dictation equipment company would have no history upon which to build a base for production equipment in such areas as product reliability, frequency of service calls, and users.

Cost

Companies either purchase, lease, or rent office equipment, depending upon several factors. Because of rapidly changing available technologies, many firms are reluctant to purchase equipment. However, renting is the most expensive way to finance office equipment. Even with changing technology, some firms determine that with writeoffs and government allowances it may prove more financially beneficial to purchase. Sometimes they may plan to move purchased equipment to another area and update the purchased equipment to more recently developed technologies.

The financial criterion necessary to determine whether or not to purchase is price performance. What do you get for the money? How much do you have to spend in order to get what you need? This information can be acquired by asking the following questions:

1. What is the purchase price (with trade-in allowance and resale value of present equipment)?
2. Is there a rental program? If so, how many years in plan (2-year, 3-year, etc.)?

3. Is there a lease plan? If so, how many years in plan (2-year, 3-year, etc.)?
4. Are tax credits obtainable?
5. What is the installation cost (including delivery)?
6. What are the add-on costs: (communications option, another keyboard, another recorder, etc.).
7. What is the cost of updating? (Many systems for word processing typing are software programmed and update the program at no cost.)

Human Factors

Sometimes the ease with which individuals can learn to use the equipment is the most important factor of all. Often people do not take learning time into consideration when selecting their equipment. Frequently it is after their equipment sits idle because none of their secretaries can use it that they discover this problem and have to search for experienced operators. Ease in learning and enjoyment in using word processing typewriters are important.

How do you really know how easy the equipment is to use? In the case of dictation equipment, it might be evident in how readily nondictators change to dictating their daily work. In the case of word processing typing equipment, it shows up in how long it takes a secretary to produce daily documents quickly and effortlessly. Signs of operating difficulty appear when a secretary suddenly cannot take time for breaks, seldom looks up from the work, and might be caught working late, through lunch hours, or on weekends at times when the workload is not any heavier than before.

Questions to ask equipment representatives, current users, and consultants to determine how easy the equipment is to use and learn include:

1. How much time is required to learn? How many days? hours? How is training conducted? How many people will the vendor train without cost?
2. How is the secretary/operator trained? What are the training materials (manual audio cassette)? Are they provided free to the customer?
3. What other training programs are offered? followup seminars? followup in the office, helping each operator to produce applications efficiently? How long does it take to get training help in the customer's office? to get into training class? Does the trainer help with developing procedures? How are firms helped that need more operator followup?
4. What is the break-in period? How soon will the operator be productive? typing what kinds of documents?
5. What skills does the vendor expect from the operator before training? afterwards? Does that person need to be technically or mechanically oriented? What kind of pay is required? Are there available trained operators a firm may hire? What salaries are they asking?
6. What is the attitude of people already using the equipment regarding its simplicity? How long did it take them to learn the equipment? Did firms have to hire special people instead of using secretaries already in the firm?

Environment

What type of office environment does the firm expect the equipment to fit? (See Figure 8-6.) Factors to consider include space, noise level, lighting, electricity availability, location, and temperature changes. One might ask:

1. How loud is the equipment? Will it disturb others working in the same area? Will special noise reduction devices need to be acquired? If so, how much will they cost? How effective are they? Does the room need to be sound-proofed? If so, how—by carpeting the floors, walls, using sound-reduction panels, soundcovers on the typewriters?

FIGURE 8-6   The word processing setup here provides the several benefits of Herman Miller's Action Office open plan. The operator has both visual and acoustical privacy. The special chair provides full back support, adjustability of height and tilt, and comfortable change of posture and has an excellent design for equipment operators who spend long periods of time working at office machines. (Photo courtesy of Action Office System, Herman Miller, Inc.)

2. Is there a possibility of eyestrain on visual displays? Some systems enlarge characters on displays; some displays have less glare.
3. How much space does the equipment require? What are the measurements? Does the equipment include all necessary working space such as a desktop and table space? shelves for supplies? paper holders? drawers or paper stackers?
4. What are the operating requirements? Does the equipment require special electricity (DC rather than regular AC outlets)? Where do outlets need to be located? How are they supplied? (Some word processing desks or work spaces now have electrical outlets.)
5. Are there special requirements? Does the equipment require a special climate (not too hot or too cold)? Is there a possibility that static electricity will affect the equipment? Will power downs cause loss of information? If so, can it be recovered? What kind of lighting is required for efficient working conditions?

Technology

Most people who acquire new equipment or update equipment into a system like to feel that the equipment contains the latest technological capabilities. However, so many technological changes are occurring in so many aspects within the office environment that sometimes an individual decides that not all of the latest advances may be necessary or even appropriate for a firm's particular needs.

If the firm wants to make sure that it is selecting the latest in technology, the following factors should be considered:

1. What is the ability of the equipment to expand? How would it expand? What would be the cost? Will it fit the planned office environment?
2. Is the equipment being considered still being manufactured, or is it reconditioned equipment?
3. Can the equipment be updated? Is it hardwired and therefore unchangeable other than by replacement with different equipment? Is it software oriented? Does software updating cost the customer? How is it accomplished? How often?

Compatibility

Many firms state that their equipment is compatible with all the other equipment they manufacture. What about competitors? In other words, if you already had a mag card II typewriter and obtained an A. B. Dick Magna I (see Figure 8–7), would they be compatible? In this instance, they are, but in most cases they would not be. Many firms state that their equipment is compatible with IBM equipment when they really mean that they will take material already recorded onto IBM media and rerecord the information onto their media. Some equipment is compatible with other equipment. Frequently it means purchasing a converter along with the new compatible equipment. A firm that already has libraries of documents recorded onto their magnetic storage media may want to avoid rerecording this library. Other firms may want to change the manner in which documents are stored and are willing to change. Many firms combine equipment from different vendors, in which case compatibility is definitely an advan-

FIGURE 8-7   Standard features of the A.B. Dick Magna I electronic typewriter include save/recall, line number display, automatic carrier return, and an 8000-character memory. It can simplify draft and revision typing and prints at speeds of 500-plus words per minute. (Photo courtesy of A.B. Dick Company.)

tage. The customer or user should know the various equipment compatibilities when planning the system. Questions to ask are:

1. Is the equipment completely compatible with other equipment made by the same vendor? If not, what changes need to be made? Can one medium be read onto another medium without requiring additional changes or steps? If not, what changes have to be made? (Some systems require additional coding. Some need to be converted through communications devices.)
2. Is the equipment completely compatible with equipment already in-house? What changes need to be made?
3. If a new generation (or family) of equipment is announced, will the equipment under consideration be completely compatible with any upcoming equipment? If

not, what changes will be required? Are additional costs involved? If so, what are they?

MATCHING EQUIPMENT TO NEEDS

You are assigned the responsibility of selecting the most appropriate equipment to meet your firm's needs. One of the purposes of the preimplementation survey is to determine just what the firm's needs are. Summaries of volumes for each aspect help to point out major areas of emphasis. This may apply to each step of the word processing cycle: origination, production, reproduction, filing and storage, and communication/distribution. Thus the office structure that most suitably fits the total organizational system is selected and will influence the kind of equipment selected.

SELECTING EQUIPMENT BY USING QUESTIONNAIRES

Figure 8-8 illustrates the equipment selection process. One can develop a technique to efficiently evaluate equipment by using a questionnaire, which serves to quantitatively measure each system considered, comparing one against the other and eliminating those that do not meet desired requirements. One form can be used as a basic evaluation tool for varying kinds of office equipment, but each category is evaluated by using a special questionnaire designed to analyze that specific kind of office equipment.

Flowchart of Equipment Selection   **FIGURE 8-8**

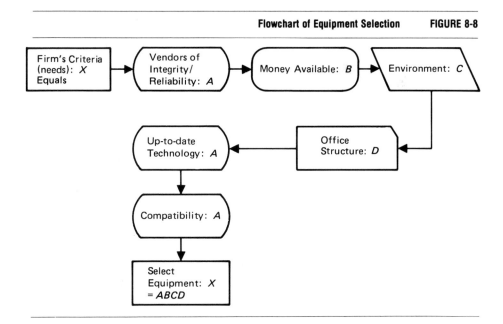

ORIGINATION

Some companies might still rely upon shorthand, longhand, or copy as their major means of input and might therefore not select dictation equipment. In this case, there would be no need to use the questionnaire. However, they might want to use the questionnaire to determine whether they were using the most effective means of origination, the least costly, the quickest to capture the information (originate on the part of the author), and the quickest to produce (fastest and easiest to transcribe by the typist).

The form can be used to determine whether an organization is using the most economical and efficient means of origination. Management can evaluate whether their principals use their time efficiently and whether the transcription is as efficient as it might be. (Rated transcription speeds from machine dictation is higher than longhand or shorthand.)

Modern Dictating Equipment

Computer technology greatly enhances the use of dictating equipment. It can (a) make it much easier for the supervisor to distribute the workload, (b) increase processing capability and speed, (c) simplify selecting rush and special dictation from everyday routine work, (d) provide ability to sort messages from documents to be typed, and, most important, (e) make it easier for the work originator to dictate and communicate. Modern dictation equipment with microprocessors and minicomputers incorporates some of the following devices and features:

- Visual-screen monitors and paper tape printout of current dictation status as illustrated in Figure 8–9.
- A flashing pointer that indicates location on the dictation medium (cassette).
- A light on the panel indicating letter endings and special instructions.
- Ability to phone and dictate from outside the office during any time of day or night.
- Equipment self-diagnosis.
- Minicassettes with visual and electronic indexing.
- Seethrough windows so that dictators and transcriptionists can see the amount of dictation contained on a cassette and location of special instructions.
- A network system that instructs the dictator exactly how to proceed (Figure 8–10).
- VOR (voice operated relay) from any phone. When you talk, it records; when you stop, it stops. On one system, a voice warns when you are nearing the end of your dictation; and when you come to the end, it asks you to stop until it informs you that it is ready for you to continue dictating.
- Automatic fail-safe scanning of cassettes before they are inserted into the carousel, rejecting any broken or incorrectly inserted cassettes.
- Separation of messages from document dictation, automatically ejecting each

Dictaphone's Master Mind has its own word management computer for word processing   FIGURE 8-9
managers. It provides a continuing update of work flowing into and out of the word
processing center, keeps track of up to 2000 jobs, and permanently saves a record
of every completed job. It will print a copy of any desired information, such as a list of
jobs to be done, jobs assigned to each secretary, and unassigned jobs. (Photo courtesy
of Dictaphone Corporation.)

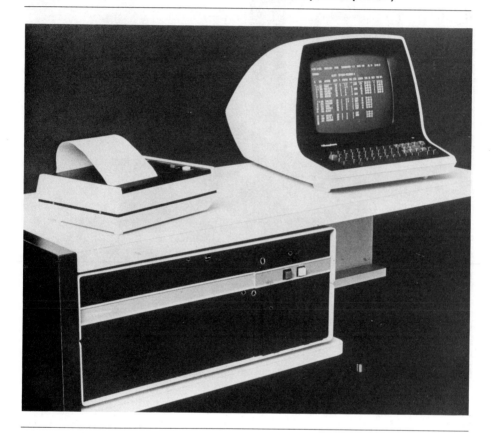

message cassette once the message is ended for delivery, identifying name of person to whom the message goes.

• Automatically ejects rush dictation so it can be processed immediately.
• Automatically produces input data slips that contain such information as ID number of the dictator, time of dictation, time the cassette was ejected from the machine, length of the dictation, and special instructions.

Three Kinds of Dictation Equipment

Work originators may use either desktop, portable, or office systems dictation equipment, depending upon their needs. Many offices will combine equipment in order to

FIGURE 8-10   Supervisor Teresa Glenn is overseeing the operations of the six Sony network dictation units in the word processing center at Mills Hospital in San Mateo, California. (Photo courtesy of Sony Corporation, Business Products Division.)

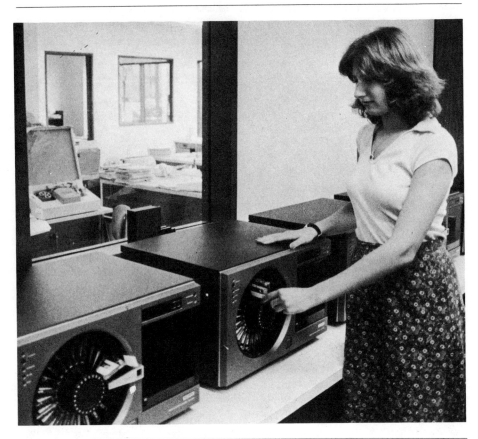

provide the wide range of needs for those who originate work, including top management; department and section managers and supervisors; and those who perform specific professional activities such as marketing, purchasing, engineering, and research. Each type of equipment is most suited to particular needs as described in the following paragraphs.

Desktop Units   Desktop units (see Figure 8-11) should be provided for people with the following dictation needs:

- Long document dictation, particularly creative in nature.
- Confidential documents that cannot be handled outside the immediate work area.
- Complex documents that require considerable revision while dictating.

**The doctor is dictating on his Lanier desktop dictation unit. Its fingertip controls on the   FIGURE 8-11
microphone make it easy to handle reports while dictating. (Photo courtesy of
Lanier Business Products, Inc.)**

- Frequent and high-priority usage. A dictator who dictates frequently and for long time periods generally needs to have his or her own unit.

Portable Units   A small, handheld unit (see Figure 8-12) can be very handy for people who need to originate information, including messages and documents, outside the office. They are most desirable in the following situations:

- Dictating at any time in any location.
- Dictating while on trips.
- Dictating information for reference, taking inventories, conducting library research.

Central Dictation Systems (Telephone and Wired)   A firm or department within a firm may have many people who need to dictate a fairly low volume (up to 600 lines a day) of messages and documents. Such information can be directed to a special group of transcriptionists in a word processing center or work group. Special wired phones or microphones provide any person within the organization the ability to dictate into the

FIGURE 8-12   **This portable recorder records on microcassettes that feature electronic indexing. (Photo courtesy of Dictaphone Corporation.)**

system through regular telephones. (See Figure 8-13.) Advantages of such a system are that:

- It can accommodate many dictators at a low cost per unit.
- It can handle a wide variety of dictation from memos and letters to lengthy reports.
- It requires fewer transcription stations, reducing transcription costs.
- It saves time by eliminating the need to handle dictation media.
- It is more convenient, because it eliminates the need to deliver dictation media.
- One dictation system can cover a considerable distance both within and outside

Dictaphone's Thought Center system features single-step controls that work   FIGURE 8-13
with dial, Touch-Tone, and private-wire phones.
(Photo courtesy of Dictaphone Corporation.)

the organization, saving the cost of purchasing a dictation unit for a number of different work originators.

• It prevents equipment from being lost or stolen.

After determining the type of equipment best suited to meet the needs of the dictators, using the equipment-selection questionnaire can help to make the appropriate dictation equipment selection. (See Figure 8-14.)

PRODUCTION

Selecting word processing production equipment can become quite complex. Not only are there a great many vendors from which to select, but many vendors offer a wide range of word processing typing equipment. For instance, IBM representatives in three different divisions market word processing equipment. A person may select a memory or intelligent typewriter from one sales person, a magnetic card text editor and the Office System VI from another, or a distributed logic text-processing system from a third. Communicating magnetic card or disk typewriters can become input terminals for computerized text editing. Wang offers a wide range of selection from a standalone

FIGURE 8-14   **Origination Equipment Selection Questionnaire**

ORIGINATION EQUIPMENT SELECTION
QUESTIONNAIRE

NAME OF VENDOR_____ADDRESS_____DATE_____

NAME OF CONTACT_____Title_____Other_____

RELIABILITY: Time in Business_____Home Office_____

_____Phone_____

Financial Standing ($ worth)_____Guarantees_____

SUPPORT: Marketing Rep. Support_____Length of time on job_____

Customer Engineering Support_____Length of time on job_____

Training Support_____Programs offered_____Cost_____

RESPONSE: Time to answer service call_____Answer phone calls_____

Distance to office_____Time to office_____Other_____

BACKUP: Answer problems_____Out-of-town support_____

KNOWLEDGE: Word Processing_____Competition_____

In relationship to other equipment_____Other_____

REFERENCES: Current Users--Name of contact_____Company_____

Other Users_____

_____

ASSISTANCE: Procedure Writing_____Volume Measurement_____

Other_____

DOCUMENTS PRODUCED: Major_____Ave.#pp_____Second_____Ave.#pp_____

Other_____Ave.#pp_____Other_____Ave.#pp_____

Creative_____Responsive_____Final_____Draft_____Amount Revised_____

References required to type: Yes_____ No_____

Difficulties for dictating: (Technical)___(Numerical)___(Format)___(Other)____

Where originated: Office_____Out of Office_____

Percentage of typing uses previously typed material_____How soon needed_____

Range in Document Length (pages)_____Number of Revisions_____

PURCHASE PRICES: Desktop price range_____Transcriber Price_____

System Price_____Other Price_____

Lease and Rentals_____

Other Costs_____

EASE OF USE_____TRAINING AVAILABLE_____

RETRAINING_____TIME TO LEARN_____OTHER_____

SPACE REQUIREMENTS_____OTHER REQUIREMENTS_____

TRADE-IN ALLOWANCES_____

MEDIA USED_____

COMPATIBLE WITH_____

RECENT TECHNOLOGY EVALUATIONS_____

SPECIFIC ORIGINATION REQUIREMENTS_____

VENDOR ASSISTANCE_____

unit to shared resource automated office systems. Xerox offers standalone units that may be wired together and a shared-logic system. These are but three examples of the word processing equipment maze.

How does a firm go about determining which is the best or least expensive word processing equipment to select? Frequently it is not easy to determine which is the least expensive. There may be more important factors such as print quality, print speed, unique capabilities, supply costs, trade-in allowance, maintenance costs, service availability, and delivery dates. Is the least expensive system that is used only part of the time less costly than a system that costs $5000 more but is used eight or more hours per day? Some organizations use their equipment during two or three shifts each working day.

In deciding what word processing equipment to select, one should judge by the documents the equipment is designed and expected to produce. Therefore, one must first categorize the documents in their order of volume and importance, list their specific requirements and characteristics, and relate them to the needs of the office structure.

The First Step: Analyzing Document Requirements

There are seven major classifications of documents: one-page letters and memos (correspondence); multiple-page narrative text; columnar formatted documents containing numerical and alphabetical data; documents made up from standardized boilerplate information such as reports and proposals; repetitive form letters with an original for each recipient; preprinted forms onto which information is typed; and miscellaneous cards, labels, envelopes, and small bits of typing.

Each of these seven categories has certain characteristics as follows:

1. *Correspondence.* Usually one page long (may be three, 20 to 25 lines long; reactive (response to request or a request); narrative; requires minimum revision, usually a maximum of one revision cycle; ranges from two to six copies; fast turnaround desired.
2. *Multiple-Page Narrative Text.* More than one page, 25 to 45 lines per page; creative; frequently longhand or copy input; often indented or special format required; frequently heavy revisions and revised more than once; often one original to be copied; usually long turnaround cycle for total document but deadline for each cycle.
3. *Columnar Statistical.* One or more pages with several columns; average of 25 lines per page; frequently longhand or copy input; difficult format with centered headings which is difficult to type; accuracy vital and careful proofreading required; no revision; one original with other copies made by copier.
4. *Standardized Boilerplate Paragraphs.* Multiple-page documents; narrative in nature; frequently from copy or longhand; special format, often indented; creative in nature; one copy; several revision cycles; requires careful proofreading; deadline for each cycle.
5. *Repetitive Letters.* One page long; accuracy important; input dictated or copy; response request-oriented; no deadline problems; carbon copies.

6. *Preprinted Forms.* Accuracy important; one page long, average 25 lines per page; multiple-part form which cannot be corrected; quality important; no revisions.
7. *Miscellaneous.* Small size format to type on (cards, labels, envelopes); accuracy important; no revision; alignment most difficult problem; infrequent typing task; no deadline or copies required.

One should list the firm's specific documents under each category, noting any special characteristics for each. For example, a law firm might have many complaints and cross-complaints which average eight pages in length and which are usually revised at least once. They may be created from marked copies of similar documents. Such documents would be listed under the second or fourth category, depending upon whether there is much boilerplate or possible storage of duplicated typing. These factors help to determine how these documents will be produced on the word processing typewriter and may strongly influence selecting the kind of typing system.

CATEGORIES OF WORD PROCESSING TYPEWRITING EQUIPMENT

Word processing typing equipment can be broken down into four basic categories: intelligent typewriters, standalone text editors, shared-logic systems, and computer text editing. Because of the rapid growth in the number of units that contain a line display or screen as a part of word processing typewriters, any of these four categories could have a one-line display or screen. The screen input ranges in size from five or six lines to a full page.

Intelligent Typewriters   An intelligent typewriter can store a small amount of information and automate many time-consuming typing functions. Examples are the IBM electronic typewriter (see Figure 8-15) and the Qyx (Figure 8–16).

Standalone Text Editors   A text editor is designed to automate the typing of all typical office documents through a wide range of storage capacity and revision capabilities. It has its own microprocessor for text manipulation and does not share its logic with another unit, though it may communicate to another with an added communications device (see Figure 8–17).

Shared-Logic System   A firm that has two or more individuals who prepare the same documents or work together in the same location might consider having two typing stations share the microprocessor or minicomputer. This saves the cost of two individual units and time that normally would be devoted to handling media and paper. This category is expanding, particularly for narrative text and longer documents (categories 2 and 4). (See Figure 8–18.)

Computer Text Editors   Instead of obtaining individual shared-logic systems with their own small computers, a firm might decide to communicate with its own or another computer by sharing computer time. By adding a special text-editing program

FIGURE 8-15

Special models of IBM's electronic typewriter provide such automatic features as centering, word and full-line underscoring and erasing, electronic margins and tabs, column layout and indenting, number alignment, proportional spacing, phrase storage which permits automatic recall of words, phrases, and short letters, and automatic carrier return. (Photo courtesy of International Business Machines, Inc.)

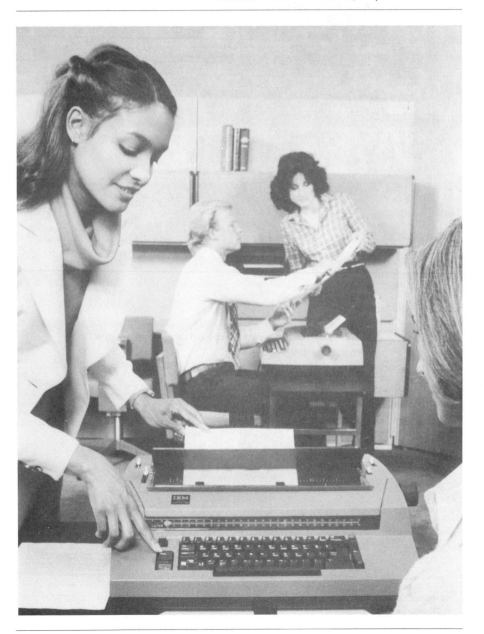

FIGURE 8-16 The Qyx intelligent typewriter Model 1 can be upgraded by adding additional capabilities, including a line display, memory storage, and even two minidisks for more storage capabilities. (Photo courtesy of Exxon Information Systems.)

FIGURE 8-17 Vydec's standalone text editor with optional communicator feature. (Photo courtesy of Vydec, Inc.)

**The A.B. Dick Magna SL shared-logic system allows two or more typing stations   FIGURE 8-18
to share the same minicomputer. (Photo courtesy A.B. Dick Company.)**

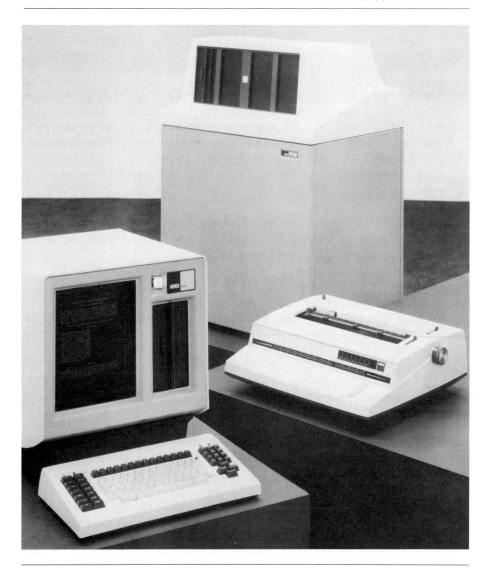

to the computer operating system, the typists simply need an input keyboard device. The keyboard may have a storage medium such as a floppy disk to store the information while initially it is being created and revised. Original information is keyboarded and then communicated into the computer for storage until it is time to revise or create a new document. This technique is used to store mailing lists for later recall to send out special mailings and is especially efficient to sort names or special categories for individual mailings or other file-sorting purposes.

SELECTION CRITERIA

Criteria to keep in mind to determine the most appropriate equipment or equipment category include:

1. Turnaround speed desired.
2. Whether ability to create or edit a document while another is being printed is desired. A display/screen separated from the keyboard has this capability.
3. Print quality desired. Quality ranges from extremely rapid line printers (low quality) to selectric typewriter with carbon ribbon or even to **photocomposition** (high quality).
4. Kind of source (longhand, copy, shorthand, machine dictation).
5. Editing (amount per page, number of times).
6. Proofreading (who does it).
7. Length of documents (for each major application).
8. Need for reuse of information at the next step—through communications, storage, or a shared-logic system.
9. Length of time the document will be stored.
10. Quantity that will be later reused.
11. Peaks and valleys of typing load (range, frequency).
12. Kinds of typing involved (numerical, columnar, technical, medical, equations).

Available Add-ons

Many systems (particularly shared-logic) can add on more keyboards or printers whenever the volume or situation so indicates. Many can add a communications modem to input to a computer or communicate to another such unit at a remote location. Some can add options or update simply through having the service person insert an updated disk into the system. Some vendors offer special programming of more capabilities for their clients or purchase of special programs such as a math package that allows the system to perform such basic calculations as addition, subtraction, multiplication, and division. Some vendors can convert their recordings to another vendor's equipment (to IBM mag cards, for instance), into computers, or into photocomposing systems. Some interface with optical character recognition (OCR) as in Figure 8–19. Figure 8–20 explains how the OCR scanner can output onto microfilm. Figure 8–21 is a questionnaire used in selecting word processing production equipment.

Applications

Table 8–1 shows which category of equipment can be used for which typing applications.

(Text continues on page 200.)

The Hendrix Typereader's optical character recognition scanner reads and duplicates typewritten pages onto the magnetic media of word processing systems. (Photo courtesy of Hendrix Electronics, Inc.)

FIGURE 8-19

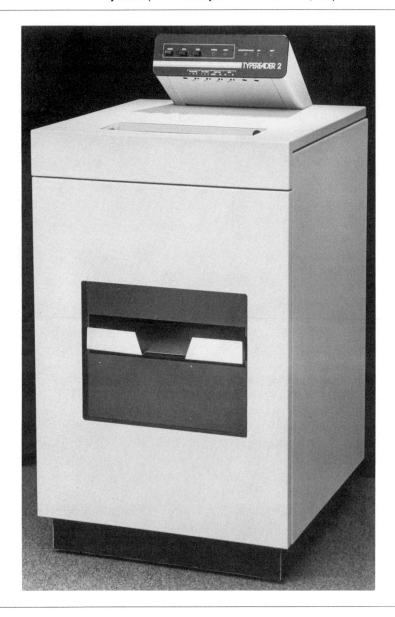

FIGURE 8-20 Kodak's Komstar microfilmer accomplishes data recording by advanced laser technology on a dry laser film. The film processor allows the film to be processed in as little as five seconds after exposure. (Photo courtesy of Eastman Kodak Company.)

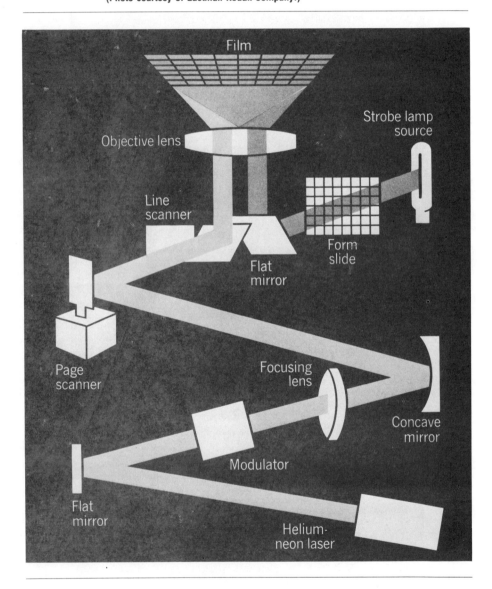

WORD PROCESSING PRODUCTION EQUIPMENT SELECTION
QUESTIONNAIRE

NAME OF VENDOR_____ADDRESS_____DATE_____

NAME OF CONTACT_____Title_____Other_____

RELIABILITY: Time in Business_____Home Office_____

Phone_____Financial Standing ($ worth)_____

Guarantees_____Other Infor._____

SUPPORT: Market Rep._____Customer Eng. Rep._____

Time on Jobs_____Response Time (Msr.)_____(Service)_____

Training Time_____Other Training_____How Trained_____

Programs Offered_____Other Support_____Procedures_____

Distance to Office_____Time to Office_____Other_____

BACKUP: Answer Problems?_____Out-of-town Followup?_____Sales Response_____

KNOWLEDGE: Word Processing_____Know Competition_____

Compatibility Options_____DP_____Photo Comp._____

REFERENCES: Current Users (1)_____Contact_____

(2)_____Contact_____(3)_____

Contact_____(4)_____Contact_____

ASSISTANCE: Procedures Writing_____Volume Measurement_____Other_____

DOCUMENTS PRODUCED: (1)____# pages____# revisions____% revisions____Other___

(2)_____# pages_____# revisions_____% revisions_____Other_____

(3)_____# pages_____# revisions_____% revisions_____Other_____

(4)_____# pages_____# revisions_____% revisions_____Other_____

Other documents_____

Revision cycle time (by document)_____

Number of copies and method (by document)_____

Quality required_____Who Proofs_____Deadlines_____

Other Requirements_____

VENDOR'S EQUIPMENT_____Compatible Equipment_____

Price (Purchase)_____(Lease)_____(Rent)_____Installation Charge_____

Media cost_____Peripheral cost_____Other_____

EASE OF USE_____COST TO TRAIN_____OTHER_____

SPACE REQUIREMENTS_____WIRING_____OTHER_____MEDIA USED_____

OTHER REQUIREMENTS_____COMPATIBLE WITH_____TRADE-IN ALLOWANCE_____

RECENT TECHNOLOGY_____SPECIFIC TYPING REQUIREMENTS_____

VENDOR ASSISTANCE_____OTHER EVALUATION_____

TABLE 8-1   Cross-Reference Matrix of Typing Applications

Category of Equipment	*Applicable Documents*
Intelligent typewriters	Daily correspondence (letters, memos) Up to 20 repetitive letters (requires one-page memory storage) Short time phase storage Small number of stored paragraphs or formats One-time only typing on forms Miscellaneous (cards, labels, envelopes)
Standalone text editors	Daily correspondence (letters, memos) Repetitive letters Short to long time storage Small to large amount of revision Short to long document revision Statistical, columnar formats Stored paragraphs Forms Input to photocomposition and records processing Text
Shared-logic systems, shared-resource systems	Short to long time storage Distribution of long document production Short to long revised documents Statistical columns Stored paragraphs Repetitive letters to multiple addressees (file-list sorting) Text Forms (may be best one for forms, particularly when the format can be stored)
Computer text editors	Long documents, text or statistical Input to data processing Input to photocomposition Repetitive letters to multiple addressees for file-list sorting

DOCUMENT CHARACTERISTICS

Correspondence

The largest proportion of documents typed is that of letters and memoranda, normally one page in length. Numerous measurement surveys made by such organizations as Dartnell Corporation and the U.S. Navy state that correspondence makes up 40 percent of office documents. Their surveys determined that the average page consists of 25 lines of typing with an average number of ten words per line with an average of five characters per word. Allowing for the spaces between words, this results in a

60-space line. Many word processors have a standard margin setting of 60 spaces per line, automatically setting up the word processor's typewriter so that the secretary can begin typing without having to set the margins to type a letter. With 25 lines containing 60 characters, an average page would consist of 1500 characters.

Correspondence usually requires fast turnaround. Criteria for producing daily correspondence are immediate startup and production capability, ease in using and making minor operations, and few complicated operations required.

Input   Most frequently a word processing typist's input is dictated on either an individual unit (desktop or portable machine) or over an internal dictation system. In the first case, the typist must handle the media by inserting it into a transcriber, erasing it upon completion (unless it is to be saved), and removing it from the transcriber. Obviously, productivity is slowed down. A more efficient method would be an internal system that has a tape inside a trunk or a stacked cassette, which would prevent the need to insert and remove tapes or cassettes.

Other   One can also transcribe from shorthand, marked copy, or longhand notes. These are all slower because of the possibility of misreading and misinterpretation. Dictation input requires dictation and transcription skills and well-formulated procedures.

Corrections   Frequently an originator may wish to change the dictation or the dictation may have been misinterpreted. Therefore, the ability to rerun the stored recording of the document is important. A self-contained medium that prevents possible damage by misfiling and is easy to file, locate, and use is desirable for this application.

Text (Narrative Documents)

Text documents may be defined as:

- having more than one page
- being creative in nature
- needing revisions, sometimes quite heavy
- frequently needing more than one revision cycle
- frequently being formatted on pages
- requiring proofreading
- needing accuracy and high quality

As a result of the highly creative nature of text, documents have historically been written in longhand, which allows the creators to see what they are creating and revise during the input cycle. However, as the office environment grows more sophisticated and dictation equipment becomes easier to use, the longhand method is gradually disappearing. More text is being dictated because of the great time savings and rapid turnaround, making it more desirable and convenient to the creator. As a result, the production phase can take less time, since the transcription can often be accomplished much faster listening than reading longhand or edited copy. Additionally, a good text-editing typewriter can save tremendous typing time for text documents.

Format   Text documents are either blocked on the left or indented, depending upon the requirements of the organization or recipient (many government offices have specially required formats). Indentation affects the speed considerably of keyboarding and, even more, of revising. A word processor that contains special indent programming makes creation and revision much easier for the text-editing typist. Video screens are even greater time savers, reducing the possibility of errors and requiring less effort, since the typist can see while revising.

To select the appropriate text editor one should consider:

- Ease of making heavy revisions (minimum operator downtime).
- Ample storage capacity and minimum media handling.
- Minimum nonproductive time. Simplified logging, filing, locating, inserting and removing, and relating copy to media.
- Less mechanical effort.
- Minimum downtime when equipment requires service.
- Reduced amount of learning time and less possibility of making errors.
- Ability to see actual work (codes and special instructions to troubleshoot problems).
- Ability to respond to quick-changing workloads and to distribute workload.

Statistical

Typing numerical data rapidly and accurately is a special skill. The placement of numbers on the upper row of the typewriter makes the typist more apt to make errors. Also, the typing of numbers is done less frequently and therefore does not become habit.

Special formatting requirements add to the difficulty of the rapid and accurate typing of numbers. Columns must be arranged across the page so that they are centered horizontally with equal amounts of space separating each column. Headings need to be centered over each column. As a result, statistical typing is the most difficult and time-consuming typing application. Examples of financial documents include budgets, forecasts, statistical analyses, and accounting data. Ordinarily the typist will count the longest lines within each column, add all columns, and calculate the typewriter setup before typing the document.

If an office produces many statistical documents, the word processor selected should provide capabilities to meet the following needs:

- Automatic alignment within columns around the decimal (decimal tabulation and on the right.
- Easy creating and seeing what is being typed.
- Fast and easy setup.
- Automatic alignment of all columns.

- Automatic centering across page.
- Automatic centering over columns.
- Easy combining of alphabetical and numerical data.
- Easy to revise.
- Easy to read and proofread, resulting in the production of desired document.

Standard Paragraphs

Many reports and proposals and other types of creative documents are or could be created from parts of other documents, which can prevent unnecessary duplicated typing. Storing duplicated typing information (boilerplate) on word processing media can greatly increase productivity. This process requires a word processing system which can rapidly access stored paragraphs and data.

Criteria for boilerplate applications are:

- Easy storing/retrieving.
- Minimum time consumed logging, filing, locating, retrieving.
- Appropriate storage media for specific needs (card, tape, floppy disk, hard disk).
- Minimum time required to learn system.
- Simplicity of system.
- Ability to update system.
- Ease of changing information on media (transferability, automatic duplicator).
- Storage capacity.
- Time required from first draft to creation of final document.

Form Letters

Many businesses use standard letters or find they can standardize some of the letters presently being originated daily by many people within their organizations. Any time an organization can create standard letters for use in its Credit, Personnel, Marketing, Accounting, or Purchasing Departments, it can save considerable time and money for both originators and producers. Creating special form letters can also save originator time and effort, bring in new business, and accomplish work formerly not possible because of lack of time.

A survey of letters produced in specific departments may help provide a list of letters that can be standardized, and stored on media. The users can use a work requirement form or dictate instructions to request each specific letter.

A word processor's ability to process form letters depends upon:

- easy access
- speed and ease of processing
- ability to meet deadlines
- easy filing, logging, locating, and retrieving
- ample storage on media for desired letters
- quality of letter produced
- easy updating and changing

Forms

A form contains preprinted information with blanks to be filled in (usually typed) by user. Forms most frequently have multiple copies either with carbon paper inserted between copies or printed on specially coated paper which automatically imprints on each copy. They are difficult to align in the typewriter and to position appropriately. Because they must be an accurate and readable product, they are tedious to type and require much handling time.

Typing forms historically has been difficult and unpopular among typists. Most forms are not designed by typists, and the designers frequently do not understand the problems encountered when attempting to type onto a preprinted form. Frequently the space between lines is not the same as on a typewriter. As a result, the typing needs to be done *manually* and cannot be done with a word processor. Another example of lack of consideration for the typist is a form that leaves one inch for the address and three inches for the zip code.

Some word processors contain a special forms program. Forms formats are stored, and the typist keys in the special information for each form. The typewriter prints by means of a **pin-feed platen** that holds the forms in alignment and uses continuous fanfold paper. This paper can be quite costly and should not be considered unless the system is designed to fulfill this need.

Perhaps the best way that forms can save an organization time is to have the forms, once they are included in word processing analysis, receive an appropriate analysis by answering such questions as:

- What is the purpose of the form?
- Does it serve its purpose?
- Is this form really needed?
- If it is needed, does it prepare the information so that it is most easily processed? If not, what can be done about it?
- Is it efficient (easy to process, includes typing/inputting information onto the form; easy to read and interpret; easy to accomplish the next step; accomplishes desired task)?
- What is the quality standard? Does it have to be perfect?
- Is the complete form easy to type?
- Is the same information typed on the form frequently? If so, what is the volume?
- If volume is heavy, could it be stored and printed from a medium? If so, how easy is it for a word processor to type on the form?

After applying these questions to each form, firms may decide to implement forms control systems that can result in considerable savings to the organization. If the responses to questions 9 through 12 make it apparent that the forms should be incorporated into the word processing operations, then the appropriate word processor should be selected which is best able to process these forms.

Criteria to keep in mind when choosing equipment for forms are:

- Pin-feed platen for rapid printout compatibility.
- Easy to input (record) information for the form.

- Easy to access the form program (from a second station or storage in a shared-logic or computer system).
- Rapid production capabilities (fast printer).
- Quality requirements met.

Important criteria when determining whether a word processor can adequately produce forms are:

- Ease of operation.
- Ability to produce desired results.
- Time required to produce results.
- Cost factors.
- Turnaround time required.
- Proofreading accuracy and ease.

Miscellaneous

Other kinds of documents typed are typing applications other than the standard ones, infrequent applications, and jobs with unusual ramifications or requirements, such as cards, labels, continuous typing, envelopes, inserts, bulletins, and short forms. Most small items such as a single label or envelope would be typed on a typewriter. However, there are times when labels and envelopes are typed on word processors, particularly when there are repeat mailings to the same address lists. In these cases, the addresses are stored on a medium and run (typed) when needed. Envelope and address list criteria include:

- ample storage on media
- ease of handling media
- ease of updating/changing addresses
- time consumed storing, filing, locating, and retrieving
- ease of recording variable data
- speed of printout
- quality desired
- ability to produce rapid turnaround
- ability to select designated addresses

Information that is typed many times, such as address lists on labels or envelopes, should be stored on a medium (or in memory or storage) to be printed when desired. Library cards can be merged by two stations; labels and envelopes may be continuous or with stop codes to insert the new ones or align on the typewriter/printer. When addresses are recorded for continuous typing, they must be recorded to properly align during printout.

In conclusion, information provided by document analysis provides a list of major documents and their characteristics. One consulting engineering firm produces many multiple-page proposals and reports that include equations and technical typing. In this case, the analyst should select equipment best suited to produce long documents, process heavy to light revisions, including technical capabilities. The system that best processes a firm's technical applications makes the best equipment selection. Selecting equipment implies a logical comparison of needs to available capabilities and selecting the equipment best suited to the particular situation.

SUMMARY

After the survey has been summarized, evaluated, and incorporated with the needs of the organization, one can begin to select equipment best suited to that organization's needs. In the case of dictation equipment, a firm whose employees travel a great deal might select portable units, while a firm with a large number of dictators with low volume would select a central system.

The structure of the secretarial support system has a direct bearing upon the kind of dictation and production equipment selected. For the typing, the kinds of documents and firm's guidelines and policies influence the kind of equipment selected. These include standards to be met such as quality, accuracy, type of information (numerical, alphabetical), and turnaround time. Other criteria such as costs (shared systems cost less per work station than standalone units), ease of use, document cycle, expected turnaround time, and form of origination all have a bearing on selecting word processing equipment.

The best way to select the most appropriate equipment for each category of equipment is by using a questionnaire designed to ask pertinent questions regarding office procedures.

Criteria to be considered in equipment selection include vendor, cost, human factors, environment requirements, latest technology, compatibility, and the ability of the equipment to meet all required needs.

To select the vendor, one should weigh such factors as service calls, response time, average monthly downtime, and quality of vendor support. Support includes the vendor's service record (is it consistent?) and the kind of training and other support offered. Response to needs of the customer includes sales, training, and service followup. Are these available, and if so, how rapid is the response and how complete is the service?

Backup is important. If the sales representative or service representative is unavailable, who follows up, how rapidly, and how well? If the equipment is continually down, can the vendor provide equipment backup?

Also important is how knowledgeable the vendor is in the industry as to compatibility with other equipment and what is available to enhance the equipment. This might include educational training materials and other software. How knowledgeable technically is the vendor? This can be very important with dictation equipment which ties into a phone system. More and more the technology is merging, so that knowledge of other equipment which can merge with equipment that the representative is selling can be extremely important. For example, OCR and phototypesetting both can merge with the word processing input equipment. How knowledgeable is the production equipment sales person of OCR and phototypesetting compatibility?

Frequently, references are contacted to establish confidence in the vendor's product, particularly for new companies. This enables the buyer to identify with the reputation of the vendor as to reliability and integrity, both of which are important in selecting equipment upon which the system will be based.

Cost is frequently given top consideration. In discerning costs of various equipment, purchase, rental, and lease prices should be obtained as well as maintenance costs. Other important costs are costs of storage media, supplies, and additional costs for training. Many vendors charge for the second training cycle on equipment, and some training costs are quite high.

Other costs to consider are tax credits obtainable, installation (and delivery) costs, and add-on and updating costs.

Human factors are also very important and may be concerned with ease of use. In the case of visual screens, some people have found that secretaries who use CRT screens develop headaches and complain of eyestrain. Many factors regarding human use of word processing equipment can be handled and controlled by the manager in the way the system is managed. However, certain aspects are very important, including time required to learn, time required to be fully able to use the equipment and meet production requirements, how the user learns to use it, kinds of training materials or programs available. Assuming there is training followup support, how long is the break-in period? Are there trained operators available? Are ongoing salaries being paid? How well do people who are using the equipment like it?

It is also important to consider the environment in which the equipment will be placed. How noisy is it? Does it require special conditions such as air-conditioning? soundproofing? carpeting? other peripheral equipment such as paperholders? special electricity wiring? possible static electricity problems?

Word processing equipment is considered to have about an eight-year life before it is no longer completely reliable. When getting new equipment, most people like to think that their equipment will not be outdated very soon and that the equipment will continue to do the job for a reasonable length of time. Therefore, whether it uses the most recent technology is also important. If not, why not, and is that important? As technology is considered, such factors as its ability to be updated become important— most current systems are easily and quickly updated at no cost to the customer. How can it be expanded? Is it still being manufactured?

Some kinds of equipment, particularly dictation, have available complete compatibility with all required needs. Many vendors have complete compatibility built in for their equipment: it does not matter whether the input is from one source or another; it can be processed regardless. Some vendors provide compatibility with other vendors, such as A. B. Dick's compatibility with IBM mag cards. If a firm introduces a new generation of equipment, is it compatible with the previous one? If not, how will the customer change over to the new equipment? Some vendors offer services to handle the compatibility problem for their clients.

And, of course, most important is matching the equipment selected to the needs of the firm acquiring that equipment. This is done by selecting the equipment which most fits the structure of the office into which it will be placed.

Equipment for origination is selected according to the way the originators work to meet the requirements they have for originating work.

The most difficult work to process, because of complications which may possibly be involved, is the typing or production of the document. Selection of typing equipment is the most difficult area of equipment selection. Because so many firms offer various types of word processing equipment and systems it can be extremely confusing to the customer even after having used word processing typing equipment for several years. Many firms therefore hire consultants to help them make the selection.

What techniques do the word processing production selectors utilize? First they analyze the document production requirements. Once they know the nature of the documents produced, the task of selecting equipment becomes one of matching equipment which can best handle producing those documents. The kinds and nature of documents are determined, along with the volume of each document. The policies and requirements of the firm regarding those documents are then listed along with each category. This is compared to the various kinds of word processing typing systems: automatic or electronic typewriters (sometimes called intelligent typewriters), standalone word processors with or without screens, shared-logic systems (several terminals sharing a minicomputer), and computer text editors (several terminals sharing a time-share computer or large in-house computer).

The next most important criteria are listed to see which equipment matches the criteria best. For example, if quality is of utmost importance, the typewriter/printer must produce high-quality printing. If speed is most important, the typewriter/printer should be one which meets the speed requirements. Other important aspects are the kind of storage media used (cassettes, cards, floppy disks, tapes, or hard disks). This is important for quick access, ease of filing, locating, and storing long documents, and workload sharing.

Another factor frequently high on the list of desired attributes is the availability of add-ons such as communications, phototypesetting compatibility, conversion to other systems, data entry, and OCR.

Human factors should also be applied during the selection of production equipment, particularly the learning and reliability factors.

REVIEW QUESTIONS

1. How should one begin the equipment selection process?
2. How can the equipment questionnaire help in selecting equipment?
3. What criteria are important regarding vendor selection?
4. What costs should one be familiar with while selecting equipment?
5. What environmental factors are important in selecting equipment?
6. What technological factors are important?
7. What compatibilities are important in selecting equipment?
8. What factors should be considered in matching equipment to needs?
9. What factors are important in selecting dictation equipment?
10. What is the first step in selecting production equipment?
11. Name the four categories of production equipment?
12. Name six criteria which might be important in selecting production equipment.

QUESTIONS FOR DISCUSSION

1. Why might a firm want to hire a consultant for equipment selection?
2. Discuss why production equipment is the most difficult to select.
3. Explain why it is important to learn about the vendor early in the selection process.
4. Discuss how cost affects the equipment selection decision.

5. Explain how environmental factors can affect the ability of the equipment to meet desired objectives.
6. Discuss what effect technology has on equipment selection.
7. Explain what compatibilities might be available in equipment and how they might affect equipment selection.
8. Discuss how failure to see that equipment is matched to needs might affect the organization's selection of word processing equipment.

CASES

Case 8-1   Document Center

Atlas Products, Inc. has a document center which currently produces reports, proposals, specifications, brochures, catalogs, and other long documents. They want to put in equipment which will allow them to produce phototypeset documents ready for printing. They have: ten typists, four editors, three technical writers, two proofreaders, four artists, and a manager.

1. How should they go about selecting their equipment?
2. What kind of equipment do you think they should get? Support your decision.

Case 8-2   Oil Company

Highland Oil Company has a word processing center which wants to update its equipment. They produce daily correspondence, reports, proposals, form letters, forms, catalogs, and directories and want to input to data processing as well as phototypesetting. They want to change the structure from one large center to one medium size center and four satellites on four other floors. They will work independently but will share work during peak periods.

The present center consists of a manager, supervisor, coordinator, two proofreaders, data entry coordinator, two technicians, three data entry specialists, two illustrators, 20 correspondence secretaries, and three clerk/pages.

1. What kind of equipment would you select if you were the manager?
2. Why?

"Word processing is just one segment of a steady movement towards the combination systems which are tying together traditionally discrete offices. . . . Executives are planning for multifunction. . . . Multifunction is growing because package size and price has decreased. Minicomputers are becoming important in the word processing system."

CHAPTER 9

Equipment Selection: Reprographics, Records Processing, and Communications/ Distribution

---

OVERVIEW

Although the word processing system in a firm is generally considered responsible for document origination and production, because of its nature and central role in the information processing of a firm, it may expand into the remaining processes of the paperwork cycle—reprographics or reproduction, phototypesetting, filing or records processing, and document communications or distribution. The word processing manager therefore needs to have a general concept of these other technologies.

This chapter explains the kinds of equipment and processes in other areas and how word processing may merge with them.

Quote from John Dykeman and Charles Ritley, "How Fast Is Word Processing Heading Towards Multi-functions?" *Modern Office Procedures* 21 (June 1977): 46–49.

OBJECTIVES

After completing this chapter, you should be able to:

1. Describe the different ways document copying may be accomplished (reprographics).
2. Describe the modern methods of records processing.
3. Describe different kinds of communications and distribution systems.
4. Relate how best to make equipment selection in each of these categories.
5. Describe how word processing may interface with phototypesetting.

THE INFORMATION PROCESSING CYCLE

Today's technological revolution, particularly the expansion of microcomputers and microprocessors, is closing the gap between the different phases of information processing. The result is a merging of information processing, from the original idea, its means of origination, production, reproduction, storage and retrieval, to final distribution or communication. Total information processing centers upon the continuing development of computer technology.

As data processing technology expands to encompass the various phases of information processing, so do the jobs and skills required of information processing personnel. Many data processing specialists are beginning to learn other technologies. In some firms, word processing is being managed by data processing departments. Figure 9-1 illustrates an IBM information distributor and how it is expected to integrate various phases of information processing. This unit prints with a laser, receives and transmits documents electronically over ordinary telephone lines, and links word processing with data processing. Units such as this will play a large part in the upcoming changes that medium size to large organizations may be making in such areas as originating information, producing, reproducing, storing and retrieving it, and finally communicating and distributing that information. Chapter 8 introduced various means of originating information, including optical character readers, to provide the input or original version. Let us examine other aspects of information processing beyond origination.

TELECOMMUNICATIONS

The science of telecommunications deals with the study of communications at a distance by electronic transmission of impulses such as by telegram, radio, cable, telephone, and television. This field has grown because of rapidly expanding demands and volumes of information, resulting in the need to transmit data from terminals to computers, particularly at remote locations, such as through locating computer terminals in an office to use a computer time-sharing system.

FIGURE 9-1   The multipurpose IBM information distributor represents a new step toward the office of the future. (Drawing courtesy of International Business Machines, Inc.)

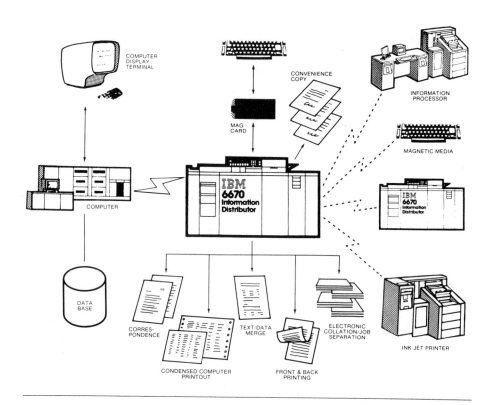

AT&T, the world's largest corporation, dominates the telecommunications industry. Its 23 operating companies handle local and long-distance phone communications and transmit data and information by computers, communicating typewriters, facsimiles, and teleprinters.

AT&T's network is designed to carry the fluctuating *analog* tones of the human voice, not the rapid rat-a-tat signals of a computer's *digital* codes. Therefore, these digital codes must be converted into analog signals for transmission and then decoded at the receiving end. Translation is performed by a device called a **modem**. This process can result in transmission errors and slowdown. As a result, the Federal Communications Commission licensed a number of specialized communications carriers to build data transmission systems, two of which are Datran, founded in 1968, and Microwave Communications, Inc. (MCI).

A telecommunications network can be described as a band of radio frequencies forming a broadband digital network that can act as a communications service within and between cities covered by the band. It can provide:

- Document distribution, data transmission, page/fixed-frame graphics.
- Long-distance phone messages via ground stations and satellites.
- Local distribution via radio links.

It can mean lower entry and operating costs. Potential capabilities a network might provide include:

- Storage and forwarding of messages.
- Conversion between incompatible terminals (analog and digital).
- Priority control.
- Security.
- Address list storage and usage.
- Delivery and acknowledgement such as Western Union's datagram.

Data Communications

The use of computer terminals to communicate data and information over phone lines within an organization, to other organizations, and throughout the world has grown tremendously in recent years. Therefore, the role of AT&T in transmitting data has expanded. Since the computer is equally important, International Business Machines plays a dominant role. Western Union, another common carrier, is also an important participant in this field.

The *key* role is that of the U.S. federal government, whose rulings regarding current, pending, and future legislation affect telecommunications and computer technologies. Many large firms, as well as many small ones, have entered the field or have requested federal permission to do so. One significant firm requesting this permission is Xerox Corporation, who requested federal permission to offer a telecommunications network for common-carrier electronic message services.

Manufacturers of various kinds of office equipment need to be continually up-to-date on technological developments that affect their marketing position. Therefore, firms such as Xerox can be deeply concerned with federal legislation and growing competition.

A Firm's Telecommunications Needs

The following are types of documents or information that a firm might need to communicate or distribute.

- Reports, correspondence, and up-to-date information within its offices.
- Orders, inventory on hand, and equipment to be purchased to its factory.
- New data, deletions of data, changes, new requests, summaries, evaluations, and computer-processed reports and information from its computer center.
- Rapid requests for information, updates, and recent directives from its communications room.

Types of equipment that might be used to communicate or distribute information include telephones, communicating typewriters, dictation equipment (see Figure 9-2), facsimiles, typewriters, photocopying (reprographics) machines, standard terminals, and intelligent terminals containing microprocessors.

AT&T's Bell Data Network/Advanced Communication System (BDN) has been designed to provide these services by means of a packet type of intelligent network. Each user at a communications/distribution point is provided with an intelligent visual screen keyboard containing its own microprocessor. The network would provide intelligence, since it has its own microprocessor and therefore allows dumb terminals to communicate through its intelligent channels.

ELECTRONIC MAIL

It's a concept ready to leave the launching pad for wide-scale integration into office systems.[1]

By using a word processing terminal at each location, a person in one place can send a message or document directly to a person in another (see Figure 9-3). Two important benefits of electronic mail are its speed and direct contact between sender and receiver. It eliminates the typical wait of several days or more between the time a document is sent and received.

When printouts are required, as in most cases, the future office may use ink jet or other nonimpact, rapid printers, possibly merged with facsimile capabilities. In addition, copier/printers with merged facsimile capability will also be popular in medium size to large offices where high volumes of mail and requirements for very high-quality facsimile capability exist (see Figure 9-4).

Quantum Sciences predicts that by 1985 users will be able to choose among a variety of equipment for electronic document transfer, depending upon their needs. Criteria for selection will include volume of message traffic, quality requirements, amount of graphic transmission as opposed to text, and special requirements for speed of output or input.

Ways to Transmit Text and Graphics

Transmission may be direct from word processing typewriting equipment and magnetic media from this equipment, from typewritten or graphic copy transmitted by OCR devices, from remote facsimile scanners, or from the firm's data network.

In addition to high-speed electronic printers, offices may have a wide variety of peripheral equipment designed to expedite transmission of messages. This might include:

[1] Daniel P. Lavery, "Electronic Mail: Circa 1985," *Word Processing*, IBM Corporation, May/June, pp. 3-5.

Dictaphone's Thought Master cassette desktop recorder features electronic   **FIGURE 9-2**
indexing. (Photo courtesy of Dictaphone Corporation.)

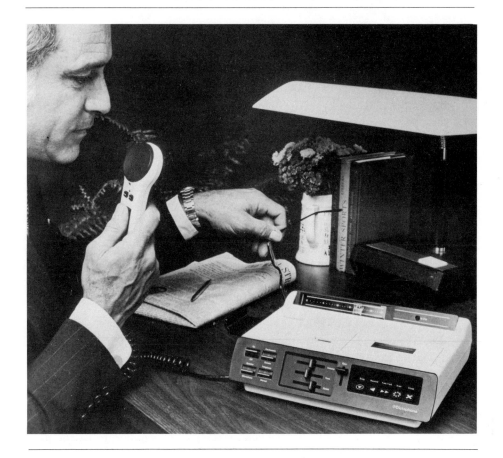

- Copying and duplicating machines (less in home offices than currently). Messages may be sent to branch locations electronically instead of by paper, eliminating the need for home office personnel to distribute paper copies of the message to others in the same branch. At the branch office, copying and duplicating may increase because the message from the home office will then be copied for those personnel who do not have screens or terminals.
- Printing and phototypesetting functions (see Figure 9-5).
- Addressing. A link to a computer will call up special distribution lists, correspondence recipients, and standard name and address storage.
- Postage metering for correspondence to be distributed through the U.S. post office.
- Telex and TWX connections for specialized communications, both input and output.

FIGURE 9-3   **This secretary is about to communicate a document to another word processor or computer on the communicating Redactor I. (Photo courtesy of Redactron, A Subsidiary of Burroughs.)**

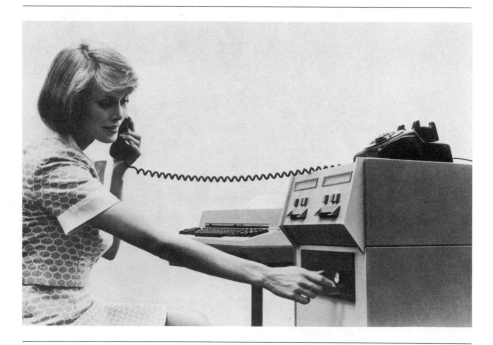

Communications capabilities that companies may select from include:

- Common carriers, including switched message carriers and leased lines.
- Dial-up, **PABX**, and **Centrex** telephone systems will continue to be the most commonly used.
- Specialized carriers, including packet switched networks and links through satellite carriers will become increasingly important, particularly as information is transmitted over data networks.
- Access to the company's data network, including local and remote disk files and the distributed data processing network.
- Communications service companies providing store and forward message switching.

Local work stations or word processing typewriters will probably become terminal nodes on distributed electronic mail systems. The administrative secretarial desk will be equipped with a typewriter that can transmit directly to a computer with terminals on-line to the electronic mail network. Depending upon the size and complexity of the office and network for the company, communications systems might include:

- Computer-controlled PABX.

The Night Caller. Before leaving the office, a secretary stacks documents in the feeder tray of a self-dialing Xerox facsimile system. Automatic dialer (left) will call other unattended telecopier units and send a trayload of documents, in sequence, to designated locations around the country. (Photo courtesy of Xerox Corporation.)

FIGURE 9-4

- PABX.
- Dial-up access to message switched network.
- Access to leased lines or satellite communication.
- On-line communications capability, both within and between word processing centers.

FIGURE 9-5   The Shaffstall photocomposition interface speeds the conversion of Vydec-prepared text into camera-ready galleys. The interface, a floppy-disk read device, transfers stored text onto the photocomposer's visual display terminal. (Photo courtesy of Vydec, Inc.)

A work station with electronic mail capability may serve such functions as input and output capability for text and graphics as well as data. Input may be from magnetic cards, diskettes, and disk packs. Increased memory and storage capacity may be provided by on-line links with data networks and information storage systems. Hard-copy printouts will be produced by the touch of a key on word processing keyboards, electronic mail printers, or on intelligent copiers.

Executives and administrative assistants will have the option of keying in a communications forwarding code to send information to any point in the electronic mail network where it can be printed as hard copy or viewed on a display screen.

Ink-jet and laser printing will be a familiar feature, replacing the mechanical limitations of impact printing, while intelligent copiers will also function as character-generating devices or facsimile printers accessible from work stations for either high-speed or high-quality printout.

Telegram services will be expanded to receive signals from word processing keyboards, magnetic media both on- and off-line, and from data networks.

Output

There will also be a wide range of output devices at the receiving end. The sender may select the desired output device to be used to make the hard copy, depending upon transmission speed, quality of output, and cost of message delivery.

From high-quality ink-jet and laser printers on bond paper to high-speed line printers similar to today's telegram message quality, typewritten and graphic transmission will be available for transmission via facsimile.

First users will be large companies operating on an intracompany basis which will use electronic text and graphics transmission systems; combined data/text/

graphics terminals will open up similar opportunities for small offices. Quantum Sciences predicts that 54 percent of the nation's large and medium size offices will have terminals with electronic mail capabilities by 1985.

RECORDS PROCESSING

Because of the ever expanding growth in paperwork, one of the key areas to be analyzed for increasing efficiency is records processing, the maintenance of records. Many firms have implemented records processing systems, which encompass not only paper records but magnetic media as well, including microfilm and word processing magnetic storage.

Many firms are turning to **micrographics** (a system of storage on microfilm) not only to save space but to save costs through less duplication, more control, fewer supplies, and fewer working hours.

An average four-drawer file can cost over $600, while the annual cost of maintaining it, including floor space, supplies, salaries, and overhead, may range from $250 to $750.[2] Micrographics can cut storage space requirements by 98 percent. Modern records processing equipment includes:

- File cabinets (vertical, lateral with rapid-access characteristics).
- Tub files, making access more convenient.
- Motorized or automated files, including compact, movable—aisle shelves, horizontal mechanized shelves, rollaway filing cabinets, vertical mechanized shelves (power files), and circular rotary files.
- Micrographics (microfilm or microfiche [fiche], called the microform). A microform in the form of roll film can hold up to 3000 pages, containing images stored sequentially along the length of the film. Retrieval depends upon locating a sequence number on the roll. Microfiche mounted on aperture cards provides discrete units of information. Each card contains up to 98 pages, reduced from an 8-1/2 by 11 size page, making indexing very quick and easy. A single fiche tray can hold up to 500 microfiche cards or a total of 49,000 documents—enough to fill four 4-drawer file cabinets.

Capabilities of Micrographics

Because of its adaptability and the need to reduce paper and processing costs, micrographics is expanding dynamically as a tool for integrating management of information. Micrographics offers minispace usage to store documents, rapid retrieval, rapid distribution and reproduction, remote access (ability to make use of documents from a distance), updatability, and ability to purge obsolete material. In addition, micrographics offers the ability to merge word and data processing.

---

[2] "Records Management Goes on Record," *Infosystems* (November 1975), p. 41.

COM (Computer Output Microfilm)

By combining computer and micrographic technology, COM offers important solutions to many modern management system problems (see Figure 9–6). COM is microfilm that contains data produced from computer-generated signals. It may be defined as that recording device that converts computer data into readable language directly onto microfilm.

A document that has been produced on a word processing typewriter can be communicated into the computer, which then converts it to microfilm (computer output microfilm). Through merging word, records, and data processing, COM can solve such problems as the need to retain certain documents and the need of several different people or departments to refer to past records or documents. COM can print at computer tape speed, outputting 10 to 20 times that of electromechanical printers (see Figure 9–7).

COM Recorders   A COM recorder (creator of the microfilm) may be either on-line or off-line. The on-line recorder is directly attached to the computer unit and operates as a substitute for a high-speed printer. An off-line recorder is not wired to the computer and operates independently. It has its own tape drive and accepts magnetic tape from a computer as its input to create microfilm. Off-line units have the advantages of not using computer time and not depending upon each other, allowing more flexibility and computer time-use savings. Computer personnel do not need to be trained in micrographics technology when the COM unit is separate from the computer.

Next Logical Step   Now that the technology for creating microfilm from the large computer is fully developed, what comes next? Logically, that the word processor with its minicomputer will create microfilm. The most efficient way of storing output is by means of ultrafiche.

> Properly planned for and installed, these ultrafiche systems enable users to make significant improvements in EDP operations, distribution, and costs.[3]

Computer output microfilm (COM) is a reprographics process that enables digitized data to be converted from a computer-processable format to roll microfilm or microfiche without first being printed out as hard copy. Since COM systems are capable of processing both alphanumeric and graphic data and operate in either an on-line or off-line mode, they present the data processing equipment user with an attractive alternative to slow, more costly, conventional impact printers.

Three Categories of COM Systems   Alphanumeric printers, used extensively for business applications, produce printout on standard computer line printers on 132-characters-per-side paper, 64-lines-per-page. These printers also print special characters and symbols.

---

[3] Joseph L. Kish, "COM: A Primer on an Important Changing Technology," *Administrative Management* (January 1978), pp. 53–60.

A full size source microfilm reader that offers dual-intensity control, easy fiche   **FIGURE 9-6**
insertion and removal, easy positioning, and extended life lamp. It offers 24,
42, and 48 times magnification and precision focus at natural hand-level height.
(Photo courtesy of Northwest Microfilm, Inc.)

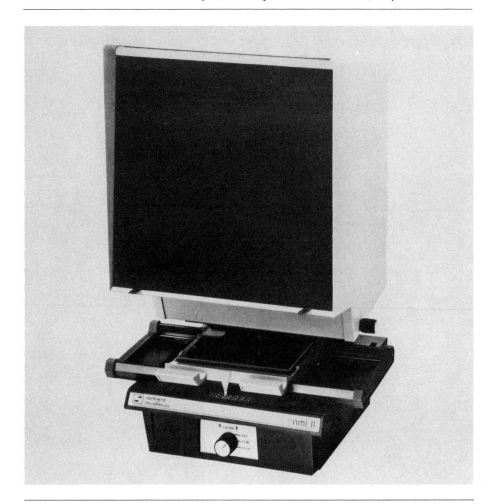

Alphanumeric printers/graphic plotters are used in applications in which alphanumeric and graphic data must appear simultaneously. Typical examples are charts, graphs, and drawings. Business quality, not high graphic quality, is produced. Figure 9-8 shows two printers (one of which is a wide-page printer) that were developed to print from both word and data processing equipment, particularly documents that contain many columns of data.

Precision alphanumeric printers and plotters produce microimages of high resolution and reliability. This category applies to such applications as animated movies,

FIGURE 9-7 **Kodak's Komstar microimage processor combines imaging and processing functions in a single unit. The process completely eliminates the need for a darkroom, processing machine, plumbing, or processing chemicals. Komstar features completely finished frames from print-image tapes in one pass. The operator can remove finished, stacked microfiche from the receiving tray and duplicate them for distribution. (Photo courtesy of Eastman Kodak Company.)**

engineering drawings, and scientific plots and often requires developing and using efficient, frequently complex software.

When properly planned and installed, COM enables users to significantly reduce their EDP operating and distribution costs and improve overall operating efficiencies in the following ways:

- *Time Reduction.* It reduces time required to produce reports and graphs from digitized data, resulting in greatly improved turnaround time.
- *Size Reduction.* COM is far more compact than hard copy, thereby saving a great deal of storage space and costs.

Wang's two bidirectional printers, the Wang Daisy and the Wang Wide-Carriage   **FIGURE 9-8**
Daisy. The Daisy prints at a speed of 40 characters per second. The wide-
carriage printer, with a writing line of up to 18 inches, is ideal for preparing
wide documents such as accounting spread sheets. (Photo courtesy of
Wang Laboratories, Inc.)

Wang's two bidirectional printers, the Wang Daisy and the Wang Wide-Carriage Daisy. The Daisy prints at a speed of 40 characters per second. The wide-carriage printer, with a writing line of up to 18 inches, is ideal for preparing wide documents such as accounting spread sheets. (Photo courtesy of Wang Laboratories, Inc.)

- *Duplication.* COM can be duplicated and distributed faster, easier, and at less cost than hard copy.
- *Reduction of Effort.* Such forms handling as bursting (separating the carbon copies produced by computer printout so that they may be routed), decollating, and binding are not necessary when COM is substituted for hard copy.

A recent study by U.S. Datacorp showed that COM can reduce the cost of computer output anywhere from 35 to 50 percent, depending upon the application.

Disadvantages   The major drawback to the use of microfilm is that there needs to be a reader available whenever a reference is required or made. Nor does using COM eliminate impact printing and hard copy; it merely supplements the hard-copy method. Therefore, it leads to increased capital expenditures for readers and reader/printers, plus the cost of the COM recorder itself. Therefore, there is seldom an offsetting equipment savings.

Although they are not difficult to operate, COM recorders, processors, readers, reader/printers, and duplicators are unfamiliar pieces of equipment to most users and require time and expense to train personnel to use and maintain.

COM Components   Six basic components of a COM system are:

1. *The input system,* which receives the digitized data from the central processing unit (in an on-line mode) or an auxiliary storage device, such as a tape drive (in an off-line mode). The digitized data are converted to an electrical signal, which is transferred to the next component.
2. *The logic section,* where various input data are acted upon by means of the logic section's interpreting various COM control codes and taking the appropriate action, such as formatting the output.

3. *The conversion section* receives the digitized data signals and converts them to analog signals, which in turn are converted to alphanumeric, line, and point symbols.
4. These symbols then pass to the *deflection controls section*, which adjusts their location on the face of the cathode ray tube (CRT) or, in the case of some COM systems, on the face of the microfilm itself.
5. *The display section* receives and then converts the digitized data into readable format through the application of one of the following methods:
   a. *CRT recording*, in which the image is projected on a phosphorescent screen.
   b. *Electron beam recording*, in which the image is written on a dry silver film developed by exposure to heat.
   c. *Light-emitting diode recording*, utilizing banks of light-emitting diodes (LEDs) optical fibers and a translation matrix to generate an image that is subsequently microfilmed.
   d. *Laser beam recording*, by which a laser beam writes directly on a dry silver or vesicular type film.
6. *The film handling section*, which contains the actual equipment (lenses, forms overlays, transport devices) for recording the images on microfilm.

COM output may be either 16mm or 105mm wide roll film, which may be subsequently mounted on reels or inserted into cartridges and cassettes, and microfiche measuring 105mm × 148mm (about 4 × 6 inches). Processed film in either roll or fiche may be duplicated via a roll-to-roll, fiche-to-fiche, or roll-to-fiche duplicator. The COM-generated film is then ready for distribution and use.

Applications   Three basic applications for COM are:

1. Replacing an impact printer for preparing listings and forms. Examples of such applications might be culling and microfilming inactive data from a master file, such as a brokerage itemizing movement of securities in a daily COM-based report.
2. Preparing business graphics, including bar graphs and PERT charts and animated movies.
3. Preparing engineering and scientific plots and drawings and other graphics materials which require accuracy and high image quality.

Analysis   Before implementing a COM system, each current and projected application should be analyzed. When a firm cannot justify its own COM system, it can use a service bureau, which might prove to be the most cost effective.

Modern Technology Developments   One of the most innovative developments is 3M's 715 COM system, which combines a CRT recording method with a dry silver film as well as its wet process microfilm. This advanced CRT development is a spinoff of the U.S. space program. The dry film process provides extremely crisp black images when reproducing copy as well as creating clear microfilm images for records retention.

Improvements in equipment reliability, flexibility, and operational performance are taking place. In addition, improvements are being made in indexing and retrieval techniques and equipment, resulting in COM-generated microfilm becoming a truly viable tool for storage and retrieval of all information, regardless of its frequency of reference or complexity of content.

INFORMATION REQUIRED WHEN SELECTING EQUIPMENT

Reprographics

1. Acceptable quality of appearance. If low quality is acceptable, the most economical method is carbon copying.
2. Range of number of copies—for most economical copy range. When the range is low, a small, inexpensive convenience copier meets the needs.
3. Average number of masters to be reproduced. This affects whether a copier or copier/duplicator best meets the needs and features to be required, such as automatic paper-feeder and duplexing (two-sided copying).
4. Range of paper size to be produced. If small, large, and exceptional sizes are to be copied, equipment selected needs to have those capabilities.
5. Copy cost range. Cost per copy depends upon many factors. Reprographics specialists are trained in making copying surveys and know how to read the monthly duplicating bill to determine the current cost per copy of a system in use. Many factors affect the *true* cost per copy, including average number of copies per run (including wasted copies), supplies cost, and purchase plans or procedures. Purchasing in large amounts costs less per item but can result in copy proliferation and higher costs.
6. Turnaround required or desired. This greatly affects the selection. When rapid turnaround is required, the equipment and system need to be selected that will satisfy this requirement.
7. The system. Will it be a convenience copier used by a large number of personnel, or will it be a centrally located operator-controlled machine? The type of system in which the machine is to be used makes a considerable impact upon the equipment selection.
8. Special requirements, such as duplicating unusual documents, including engineering drawings, computer printout, reducing copies, enlarging small copy, copying from microfilm, making copies from unusual masters, making special masters such as fluid masters.

Once all of this information is provided, a questionnaire should help in making an appropriate selection of reprographic equipment.

Records Processing

1. How frequently are the documents to be referenced? by how many people and in what locations (remote)?
2. What space is available and how much?

3. How long do the records need to be retained for active use? Can they be centrally stored?
4. Is there a duplication of filing?
5. Do the records need to be marked, revised, or notated?
6. Are the documents used with other documents for comparing, creating new documents, or preparing information?
7. Is there a need for access without needing to use a reader?
8. Are records to be frequently updated?
9. How much money is available to purchase equipment?

It is understood that micrographics is the best system because it saves space and can eliminate costly duplications of file equipment and supplies and waste time searching, logging, and filing. However, it does require investment in equipment that is much more costly than other records keeping equipment. Therefore, before deciding to change to a micrographics records processing system, answering these questions helps to place the emphasis in the right place.

When top management becomes involved in seeing that the firm implements a records management system with a retention program, it can begin to implement a program of cost effective records processing.

Telecommunications (Communications/Distribution)

Specialists trained in telecommunications and experienced in managing such systems are delegated responsibilities for selecting and updating the firm's telephone system. Many firms have switched to Centrex systems so that they can eliminate the need for perator intervention for handling incoming and outgoing calls. Firms with offices in remote locations and cities away from their home offices usually put in some sort of special system that eliminates individual long-distance charges for phone calls in outlying areas. Such services might be AT&T's Foreign Exchange of **Wide Area Telephone Service** (WATS) or Western Union's Telestar Broadband Exchange.

Ways in which the communications specialist determines the needs of the firm are by conducting such surveys as a traffic analysis, in which all phone calls are tracked by computer to determine volume and costs.

Questions to ask when selecting equipment for communications distribution, such as facsimile, communicating word processor, teleprinter, or Western Union's mailgrams and datagrams include:

1. What type of information (range) needs to be sent and received rapidly?
2. How fast does it need to be sent or received?
3. What quality is needed at the receiving end?
4. Will additional copies of the received document be needed at the receiving end?
5. Where do the documents to be sent originate? in what form? (on a magnetic medium?)
6. What type of telecommunications system does the firm have that needs to be attached? What compatibility or capability for hookup is required?
7. What daily volume is anticipated?

8. What size documents need to be transmitted?
9. Is 24-hour sending and receiving necessary?

The information obtained from these questions provides a general picture of the factors that influence selection of equipment in these areas. A word processing manager who is required to make equipment selections may ask these questions and use the questionnaires illustrated in Figures 9-9, 9-10, and 9-11 to help make selection decisions.

Table 9-1 illustrates a grid which lists the phases of information processing and the kinds of office structures. This grid provides a basic planning chart to use in selecting each kind of equipment.

SUMMARY

Modern technological developments, especially in computer technology, are merging the various information processing services, particularly through various forms of communications. Telecommunications, the science of communicating at a distance, provides substantial reduction in the time consumed from origination to final distribution. Typing work stations can be used as communications nodes to distribute electronic mail. Output can be received in the form of hard copy from communicating word processors or facsimile receivers or on visual displays and stored on a magnetic medium if so desired.

Records processing is being integrated into the electronic distribution system by means of COM, computer output microfilm, that can store, reproduce, and transmit copies. Some firms are beginning to offer the ability to update microfilm media, which makes the use of micrographics more feasible.

A manager who is given the responsibility for selecting equipment to use in the areas of reprographics, records processing, and communications/distribution needs to develop selection criteria, just as in selecting typing and dictating equipment. A checklist and equipment selection questionnaire can be used to make sure that all pertinent information is obtained for comparison. Many managers use an equipment selection grid in order to crosscheck criteria before making final determinations.

For those managers who are unfamiliar with these technologies, consultants will help in making sure that the firm considers all possible alternatives. Firms that are beginning to develop integrated information processing networks are concerned with selecting equipment using modern, up-to-date technology while meeting necessary component compatibility requirements in order to integrate the system.

REVIEW QUESTIONS

1. What is a specialized communications carrier? Why would this be an expanding business?
2. What kinds of services do telecommunications networks provide?
3. How can communicating word processors function as a part of an information processing network?

(Text continues page 232.)

REPROGRAPHICS EQUIPMENT SELECTION
QUESTIONNAIRE

NAME OF VENDOR_____ADDRESS_____DATE_____

NAME OF CONTACT_____Title_____Other_____

RELIABILITY: Time in Business_____Home Office_____

Financial Standing ($ worth)_____Guarantees_____Other_____

SUPPORT: Marketing Rep._____Time on Job_____

Service Rep._____Time on Job_____

Training Program_____Other Training Assistance_____

Response Time from Service Call_____Distance to Office_____Time_____

Vacation Backup_____Answer Phone Calls_____Solve Problems_____

KNOWLEDGE: Reprographics_____Competition_____In Systems_____

REFERENCES: Current Users (1)_____ Contact_____

(2)_____Contact_____ (3)_____Contact_____

ASSISTANCE: Procedures_____Measurement_____Other_____

LOCATION: Central_____Convenient_____Other_____

Departments Using_____No. Copies Max._____Min._____No. Orig.___

USES: Books, Magazines____1-page masters___Correspondence___Forms___Other____

No. Users____Lockup_____Monthly Volume_____Other Uses_____Departments_____

VENDOR'S EQUIPMENT_____

PRICES (Purchase)_____(Lease)_____(Rent)_____

Trade-in_____Supplies Cost_____Installation_____Other_____

Learn Time_____Retrain Add'l._____Cost_____Followup_____

SPACE REQUIREMENTS_____OTHER REQUIREMENTS_____

KINDS OF PAPER USED: Roll_____Flat_____Size_____Other size_____Other_____

Duplex___Collate____# collate___Feed___Reduce___Enlarge___Other_____

RECENT TECHNOLOGY EVALUATION_____

VENDOR ASSISTANCE_____

RECORDS PROCESSING EQUIPMENT SELECTION
QUESTIONNAIRE

NAME OF VENDOR_____ADDRESS_____DATE_____

NAME OF CONTACT_____Title_____Other_____

RELIABILITY: Time in Business_____Home Office_____Phone_____

Financial Standing ($ worth)_____Guarantees_____Other_____

SUPPORT: Marketing Rep._____Time on Job_____

Knowledge_____Other Support_____

REFERENCE_____CONTACT_____

ASSISTANCE: Procedures_____Volume Measurement_____

RECORDS RETAINED_____

SPACE ALLOWED_____FREQUENCY OF USE_____

WHEN CAN BE DESTROYED_____HOW LONG RETAINED_____

WHO FILES_____HOW OTHERS ACCESS FILE_____

DOCUMENTS FILED: (1)_____Length_____Freq. of Use_____Time to Retain_____

                  (2)_____Length_____Freq. of Use_____Time to Retain_____

                  (3)_____Length_____Freq. of Use_____Time to Retain_____

                  (4)_____Length_____Freq. of Use_____Time to Retain_____

Other_____

LOCATIONS MOST NEEDED_____BY WHOM_____

                  _____   _____

IMPORTANT FACTORS: Immediate Access_____Not Lose_____Take Out of Office_____

Save Space_____Store Over Long Time_____Fire Resistant_____

Use by Many_____Only 1/2_____

Other_____

COMMUNICATION/DISTRIBUTION EQUIPMENT SELECTION
QUESTIONNAIRE

NAME OF VENDOR_____ADDRESS_____DATE_____

NAME OF CONTACT_____Title_____Other_____

RELIABILITY (Time in Business)_____Home Office_____Phone_____

Financial Standing ($ worth)_____Guarantees_____Other_____

SUPPORT: Marketing Rep._____Time on job_____Other_____

Customer Engineering_____Time on job_____Response Time to Call___

Training Support_____Programs offered_____Cost_____

RESPONSE: Phone Calls_____Answer Problems_____Vacation Backup_____

KNOWLEDGE: Word Processing_____Competition_____Other Related Equipment____

REFERENCES: Current User (1)_____Contact_____

(2)_____Contact_____(3)_____Contact_____

ASSISTANCE: Procedures_____Volume Measurement_____Other_____

INFORMATION TO BE PROCESSED_____

PRESENT SYSTEM_____Problems_____

RECOMMENDED SYSTEM_____Solutions_____

Other Peripheral/Related Equipment_____

VENDOR'S EQUIPMENT_____

PRICE: Purchase_____Lease_____

Rental_____Installation Charge_____Other_____

MEDIA USED_____Compatible with_____Ease of Use_____

TRAINING REQUIRED_____Other_____

LOCATION(S)_____

Other Factors_____

Other Costs_____SPECIFIC ORGANIZATION REQUIREMENTS_____

RECENT TECHNOLOGY EVALUATION_____

ENVIRONMENTAL EFFECT_____

VENDOR ASSISTANCE_____

TABLE 9-1   Word Processing Equipment Selection Grid

Word Processing Phase	Office Structure			
	Boss/Secretary	Single Unit	Work Group	Centralized
Origination	Portable, desktop (discrete media), or individual system	Portable, desktop, or individual system (discrete media, or endless loop)	System serving several dictators in one network or individual recorder units, depending upon volume and originators' needs	System mainly, plus portable and individual (depends upon originators' needs)
Production	Intelligent typewriter or standalone text editor	Intelligent typewriter or standalone text editor	Standalone text editor or shared-logic system	Shared-logic system, or computer text editing
Reprographics	Carbon copies or copier	Copier	Copier	Copier/duplicator
Filing/micrographics	File cabinet	File cabinet	Central files or micrographics	Central files or micrographics
Communication/ Distribution	In box (See Chapter 8) Pickup and deliver	In box Pickup and deliver	Mail slots Pickup and deliver	Mail slots Pickup and deliver
Intercompany	Communicating word processor, remote copier, or facsimile	Communicating word processor, remote copier, or facsimile	Communicating word processor, remote copier, or facsimile	Communicating word processor, remote copier, or facsimile

4. What kinds of output might there be on the receiving end of a communicating network?
5. How does COM fit into the information processing network?
6. What are the advantages of micrographics?
7. Why might it be wise to use a consultant when planning the information processing network?
8. List the advantages of using an equipment grid to select equipment?

QUESTIONS FOR DISCUSSION

1. If you were given the responsibility for planning the communications/distribution system for a new company, how would you proceed?
2. If you were asked to take over a communications/distribution system for a company with branch offices in six other cities, how would you proceed?
3. If you were asked to take over the records processing for a new company, how would you proceed?
4. What kinds of output might there be on the receiving end of a records processing network?
5. How would you select reprographics equipment for a firm with 5000 employees, housed in five buildings?

CASES

Case 9-1   Pharmaceutical Company

Littleman Pharmaceutical Company has branch offices in 12 cities. They want to have reprographics equipment that will make copies and transmit between the branch offices. You have the responsibility for making this selection.

1. Write your selection. Write your selection plan, including the checklist.
2. What is your next procedure after the checklist? Write up your implementation.

Case 9-2   University Purchasing Department

River City University's Purchasing Department has decided to establish a centralized records processing department. You have been asked to plan and manage this department.

1. Write your implementation plan.
2. Develop your checklist to select equipment.
3. How would you implement and control the system?

"What we are selling is a more effective way for them to get their job done."

CHAPTER 10

Presenting the New System

OVERVIEW

One of the most important roles the word processing manager plays is that of selling the word processing system to management, middle management, supervisors, principals and company personnel whose positions and daily work will be greatly affected by the change.

This chapter explains how the word processing manager communicates the findings from the feasibility study, the new system design, and benefits to the firm and its employees.

OBJECTIVES

After completing this chapter, you should be able to:

1. Explain how to prepare a presentation of this information.
2. Determine what information to include in the presentations.
3. Prepare a presentation.
4. Substantiate the facts presented.
5. Prepare and use the report and presentation.

Quote from J. Peter Doonan, Systems Manager for Sycor Corp., Ann Arbor, Michigan, in Walter A. Kleinschrod, *Management's Guide to Word Processing*, Dartnell Corp., Chicago, 1975, p. 222.

After evaluating the present system and designing the new system, it is time to arrange the acquired information into a concise and comprehensive format for presentation to top management. If management decides to implement the proposed system, similar presentations will then be made to middle management, supervisors, principals, and the secretaries and other staff members who participated in the survey and are anxious to learn the results.

Sometimes management makes its decision at the conclusion of the presentation. They may first ask questions and then become convinced that word processing will definitely work towards their stated objectives. Other times management may review the information before making a decision after careful consideration. Once the decision is made to implement word processing, top management will want the same information presented to all members of the organization who will be affected by the change. Employees will need to be deeply aware of the results and benefits expected from word processing and to feel involved in any changes that will be made.

Therefore, the following presentations to department managers, supervisors, principals, secretaries, and other participating employees are particularly important. All affected personnel need to be sold on and committed to the program, the success of which depends on their cooperation and backing.

HOW TO PREPARE THE PRESENTATIONS

Begin by assembling the essential information. The analysts first need to decide exactly what information needs to be included in the presentation. The study usually results in accumulating a vast amount of statistics, but the information to be included should describe the strengths and weaknesses of the present system, point out problem areas, and present total productivity costs. In secretarial studies this usually includes:

- Volume of time (work hours) devoted to typing and nontyping secretarial tasks.
- Volume of time (work hours) wasted while waiting for work, away from work station, out of the office, etc.
- Time distribution of tasks for secretarial stations.
- Output volume (typing) for correspondence, reports/text, statistical typing, forms typing, revision typing, and repetitive typing (letters and paragraphs).
- Present workflow, which indicates unnecessary loops and duplications, and the steps required to accomplish each task.

This information is best presented visually by graphic illustrations, such as pie charts, bar charts, floorplans, and workflow diagrams. After evaluating the summaries, one can begin to prepare the presentation, selecting information that is best presented visually.

Preparing the Summary Report

Since most analysts prepare a summary report, they begin by outlining the contents of each page of the report. Once the report is drafted, they select the information they wish to present visually from those pages and draft the visuals. Each report page and its contents are outlined in the following paragraphs.

First page: Objectives of the Study   The purpose of the study was to determine the feasibility of word processing to meet management's objectives, including reduced turnaround time, improved document quality, improved employee productivity, better use of personnel, control of operating costs, and planning for effective productivity during periods of expansion.

Second page: How the Feasibility Study Was Conducted   The task force collected and summarized data by distributing secretarial, principal, and managerial questionnaires; distributing work request forms to collect document analysis; and interviewing secretaries, principals, and managers. The summaries provided information on volume of typing produced and volume of time consumed in its production; task distribution of secretarial positions, with time consumed for each task; task identification by employee positions; and workflow of the present system of operations.

Third page: Scope of the Study—Areas Studied   This page lists departmental personnel included in the study with the number of employees in each department. Other factors included in the study to determine current system operating costs are current salaries, including overhead, overtime, and outside secretarial and related costs; and equipment and supplies costs.

Fourth page: Present System   This page contains a workflow diagram outlining the general workflow of the firm's typing production and performance of secretarial administrative tasks. There may be additional pages diagramming specific workflows, such as a bank's diagram of the current procedure followed when producing a client's trust agreement.

Fifth page: Summary of Findings of Current Volume   This page might use a bar chart to illustrate the relative amounts of time to produce each kind of document. It also might use a pie chart to illustrate the secretarial time distribution by hours and by percentage of time.

Sixth page: Present System Costs   A pie chart might best illustrate the percentage of all cost factors in the current system. This would include recurring and fixed costs for the total system of document production.

Seventh page: Present System Problems   This page lists the most predominant problems discovered during the study. For Middletown Bank, they included wasted time typing revisions and duplications, wasted time waiting for work, waiting to copy, and traveling, costs of overtime and outside help, deadline pressures, personnel attrition and morale, and inadequate communications. In the report, these items are followed by explanations of the resulting effects. The visual leaves this information out and will be explained during the presentation.

Eighth page: Proposed New System   This page might contain an organization chart illustrating the proposed word processing system. Middletown Bank's task force decided to have a main word processing center in the Trust Department, with work groups on the two other floors acting as satellites. All three floors would be supervised by a word processing manager for document production with a coordinator over each of the three groups. Administrative work groups clustered near the departments were planned.

Ninth page: Proposed New Workflow   The workflow diagram in Figure 10-1 illustrates the procedures for document production from origination techniques, production, reproduction, storage and retrieval, and distribution or communication.

FIGURE 10-1   **Bank of Middletown Word Processing System with Word Processing Center on Each Floor**

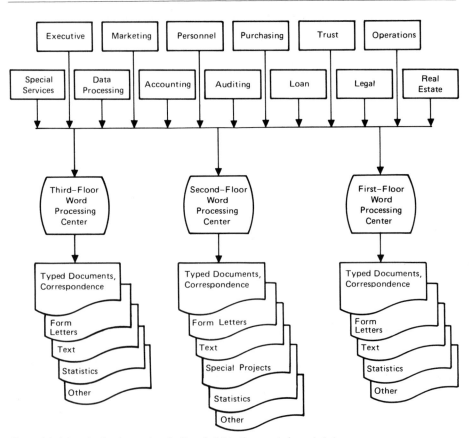

Note: Administrative Services are handled by administrative secretaries and clerks.

Tenth page: Proposed New Equipment   Floorplans of each floor indicating personnel and equipment placement illustrate Middletown Bank's physical plans for the new system.

Eleventh page: Cost Justification   This page of the report, and one of the most important, was used by Middletown Bank for all presentations except the one to the secretaries. Information the bank felt should be included was covered by the following questions:

- How will the new system save money (if it does)? Will it eliminate some jobs? How will personnel be handled? What will the system cost in investment and recurring costs? How long will it take to recover capital investment? Should the equipment be purchased, rented, or leased? Are salary costs changed?

    As illustrated in Table 10-1, this page presents the current system costs at the top, proposed system at the bottom, with the proposed savings on the bottom line. Most cost justifications include personnel, equipment, supplies, and startup costs.

Next page: New System Benefits   Each firm's specific problems and methods of resolving problems may be unique. This page outlines the ways in which the proposed system will resolve those most significant problems, as shown in Table 10-2.

	Middletown Bank's Current System Costs	TABLE 10-1
Item	*One Year*	*Five Years*
Present		
Secretaries at $9600 (25)	$240,000	$1,200,000
Office Equipment (already purchased)	—	—
Total	$240,000	$1,200,000
Proposed		
Secretaries at $9600 (18—9 correspondence and 9 administrative)	$172,800	$ 864,000
Lease of 9 Word Processing Typewriters ($350/mo X 12 X 9)	37,800	189,000
Purchase of Dictation Equipment	3,500	
Investment Costs	5,000	
Startup Costs	2,000	
Total	$221,100	$1,053,000
Savings (based on 5-year equipment lease)	$ 18,900	$ 147,000

TABLE 10-2   Solutions to Old Problems

Present System Problems	New System Solutions
Wasted typing time	Storage of typing which eliminates retyping
Wasted time nonworking	Well-managed work distribution and improved work procedures
Costs of overtime and outside help	More productive system, which prevents overtime and outside help requirements
Deadline pressures	More productive system creating smoother work-flow, evening out work
Personnel attrition, morale	More creative, responsible jobs offering more career opportunity
Inadequate communications	Well-managed procedures and planned communication guidelines

Next page: Implementation Schedule   Figure 10-2 illustrates Middletown Bank's implementation schedule which the task force prepared and all the sequential steps from first-day orientations to the first planned followup review.

Other contents in the report that are not always covered during the presentations might be a list of current office equipment and any costs that can be allocated to the equipment. Even though this might not be included in the report or presentation, the study should have this information included in backup information. Current personnel lists by salary might also have been analyzed and usually are a part of the current system's costs for accurate cost justification analysis. Figure 10-3 is a summary of a report.

Visuals Used in Presentations

Frequently used presentation visuals include flip charts, overhead transparencies, slide-tapes, 35mm slides, films, floorplans, graphic layout drawings, grid charts, pie charts, and flowcharts. Figure 10-4 illustrates how clearly a pie chart communicates information. The quickest and easiest visuals to prepare are overhead transparencies, since they can be typed in large type which will be enlarged further by the projector. So long as the lettering is large and clear and does not contain too much information, transparencies work very well.

The following visual preparation guidelines are recommended for a good presentation:

1. Do not place too much information on each chart.
2. Make sure the letters are large enough for easy readability from the back of the room.
3. Do not read word for word directly from the visuals during the presentation.

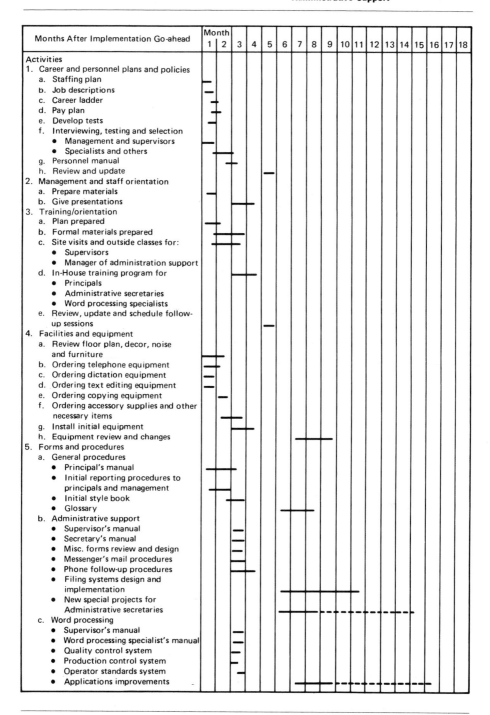

FIGURE 10-3   Study Findings: Report/Presentation

Outlines of a survey report shown below:

I. OVERVIEW OF THE SURVEY containing:

  A. OBJECTIVE of the survey, such as: To learn the present operating system and procedures

  B. SURVEY METHOD (how the survey was conducted)
      Interviews, Work Sampling, Secretarial Task Lists, Copies of Typed Work

  C. AREAS OF STUDY: Originator's Input and Activities, Typing Production, Photocomposition, Copying/Duplicating Volume, Filing System, Communication/Distribution System, Phone System

  D. SCOPE OF STUDY: Analyze present operating system including word processing costs; develop new system and projected costs.

II. SUMMARIZE CURRENT SYSTEM, including:

  A. Work Distribution Summary

  B. Time/Task Distribution

  C. Learn present system:

      Measure current volume and time/work distribution
      Define the present workflow
      Identify problem areas
      Provide solutions
      Plan future system of operating procedures

III. PRESENT COST COMPARISONS

      Present System
      Planned System
      Present Costs of Changeover to New System (Startup costs)
      Present Future Costs and Savings to be Realized

IV. PRESENT IMPLEMENTATION PLAN FOR NEW SYSTEM

---

4. Be prepared to supply details.
5. Use the visual to introduce key points and make sure all points are covered.
6. Do not put *all* information on the visual, only leading or key words.
7. Do not continually look at the visuals; look at and address the audience.
8. Use a pointer so that you can stand to the side and point to each item during the presentation. This helps the audience follow along, because you do not accidentally cover up information on the visual with your body, arm, or hand.
9. Make sure visuals are in proper sequence.
10. Do not divert the audience by leaning on the visual (such as a flip chart on easel) or using distracting mannerisms.
11. Make the visuals interesting and meaningful.

A Pie Chart of Secretarial Time Distribution   FIGURE 10-4

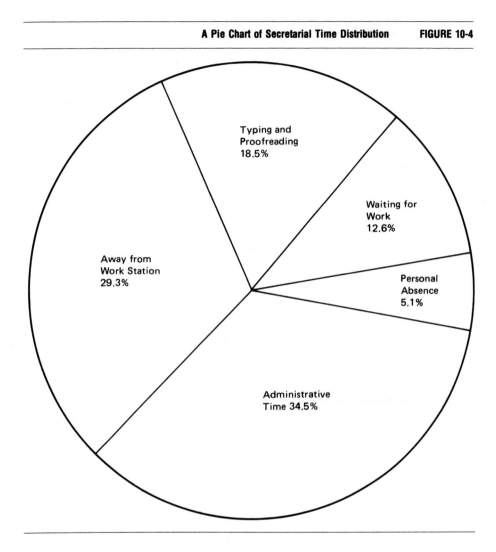

Practice

It is important to practice giving a presentation using visuals so that the presenter is comfortable, relaxed, and confident and avoids being caught off guard or surprised by missing information or inaccurate spellings on the visual which can result in a poor presentation. When people are asked to interrupt important work to observe a presentation, they expect to see a thorough, complete, meaningful, well-organized, and professional performance.

Typewritten Report

Supportive data summaries and other documentation (see Figure 10–5) may be included in the visuals; they are always contained in the typewritten reports. These

FIGURE 10-5   Administrative Support Profile

CURRENT SUPPORT

	Principal Name	Mills	Lyons	Hill	Stone	Lindsey	Gomez	Lee	Wong		Totals	CUMULATIVE TOTALS
1.	Principal Name											
2.	Admin. Hrs./Wk.	20	18	30	22	35	20	16	18		179	
3.	Typ. Hrs./Wk. Unaffected	4	1	1	4	6	4	5	4		28	
4.	Admin. Hrs./Wk. Subtracted (Shorthand, etc.)	2	1	3	3	5	2	4	2		21	
5.	Adjusted Admin. Hrs. (Sum of Lines 2&3 minus Line 4)	22	18	28	23	36	22	17	20		186	186

ADDITIONAL

DESCRIBE LEVEL	Mills	Lyons	Hill	Stone	Lindsey	Gomez	Lee	Wong		Totals	CUMULATIVE TOTALS
Deficiencies		2					3			5	191
Delegables		3		1				2		6	197
Planned Changes			1			2				3	200

	Mills	Lyons	Hill	Stone	Lindsey	Gomez	Lee	Wong		Totals	
Admin. Support-Planned Hours	25	20	29	24	36	24	20	22		200	

STAFFING

Equivalent Administrative Secretarial Manpower	Mills	Lyons	Hill	Stone	Lindsey	Gomez	Lee	Wong			STAFFING NOTES
Secretary Name *Nancy Eben*	10	6			10	3		4			
Secretary Name *Joyce McAuley*	13	5			10	6	5	8			
Secretary Name *Carmen Miller*		9	4	10		6	10				
Secretary Name *Pat Okimoto*			12	12			5	5			
Secretary Name *Peter Dubois*			13	2			5	5			
Secretary Name *Betty Martinez*	2	1			2	8					
Secretary Name											

reports are usually distributed after the presentation is completed to substantiate the information presented and provide a resource document for perusal. Sometimes top management will review the report before it decides whether to go ahead with the program. In instances where management may wish to consider different alternatives, the report serves as the resource upon which to base the final decision.

Summaries included in the visual presentation provide overviews and explain important points. Unnecessary details are not covered in the presentation but may be included in the typewritten report as supportive data. If the report is distributed at the beginning of the management presentation, it should be incorporated as a visual during the presentation. Otherwise it may be distracting to have attendees leafing through the report during the presentation. When handed materials at the beginning of a presentation, many people begin to review them and may continue to do so during the presentation. The speaker then cannot maintain complete interest and control of the audience during the presentation.

Often it is best to avoid using handouts. The typewritten report containing all background and supportive information is distributed at the meeting's conclusion, while the speaker explains what specific study data is contained in the study report.

If handouts are distributed during the presentation, the speaker should provide the attendees time to glance at them. The speaker may then wish to direct attention to a specific point or page and can refer to it at that time and indicate where it is located. Attendees may have questions at this time. If the speaker wishes to hold questions until the end of the presentation, this should be explained before beginning. Otherwise, it is better to distribute supportive documents and address questions at the conclusion of the presentation.

PRESENTATION CONTENT

Top Management

Top management expects to witness a professional, concise, clearcut presentation of how the feasibility study was conducted, and what its findings and recommendations are. This should be kept in mind during preparation. Management is interested only in points that have direct relevance to the new system design or that need to be brought to management's attention.

The presentation should take place in a comfortable conference room. Arrangements need to be made to prevent any interruptions and should be well planned and organized. If a film is to be screened, it should be previewed and the projector tested. The presentation itself should be rehearsed at least two times to ensure its smooth transition, accuracy, completeness, and effectiveness. It should take not more than an hour.

Middle Management

Frequently the presentation to top management and middle management (department heads and supervisors) may be the same unless there are some sections directed to top management only. Sometimes more details need to be covered in the presentation to middle management, particularly regarding specific departmental workflow or new system changes that affect specific departmental personnel. Because they are more involved in the operations, middle management will be more concerned with detailed workflow and operations and may request or desire more complete explanations. All arrangements are the same except that these meetings should be planned to take an hour or more.

Staff

Presentations made to the staff, as those to middle management, may not include cost figures but may provide more detailed workflow procedures. Staff presentations are the most sensitive and should sell the benefits of the proposed change. They should communicate the message that the proposed new system is designed to improve employees' jobs by eliminating unnecessary duplication of effort, inefficient use of their time (over which they have no control), and inadequate methods in the present system: the new system is designed to solve present problems.

The Message

It is important to communicate that all employees, by participating in the new system will help the organization achieve more efficient operations. At the same time, each employee will be able to devote more time to his or her professional tasks. The staff's active involvement and participation are required in order for word processing to succeed. A system designed so that each employee can work more efficiently succeeds only through everyone's cooperation.

The speaker needs to make sure that the secretaries and others who participated in the study feel they are important to the new system's success. Each employee needs to feel the word processing system is designed to improve his or her daily job by allowing the individual to work more creatively. It should be made clear that the proposed procedures and equipment are expected to help accomplish these objectives. The speaker should avoid discussing such negative aspects as the elimination of jobs. If the subject of fewer positions is discussed, explain that any positions eliminated by the new system will not cause employees to lose their jobs. Instead, employees will be offered the opportunity to transfer into positions they prefer and for which they are best suited. Any eliminated jobs will be handled by attrition and job movement.

Communication Attitudes

Too frequently speakers do not thoroughly prepare or rehearse before making presentations. One technique used by accomplished speakers is to prepare a checklist. A checklist itemizes pertinent points, provides a presentation road map when practicing dry runs and helps to make a well-organized and meaningful presentation. Speakers should bear in mind that the attendees are a captive audience who may have other important matters on their minds. They may be annoyed at having to take time away from their work. In addition, some may not believe in the merit of the study or in word processing and are prepared to resist any recommended changes. The speaker therefore should consider the following suggestions:

1. Be completely prepared. The speaker is expected to be thoroughly knowledgeable of all of the facts covered in the study. Each aspect mentioned may be subject to question or controversy. The speaker should be prepared to supply the background and supportive evidence regarding each item covered during the presentation. This may be in the form of notes, summaries, or the study report. The speaker needs to be prepared to answer questions, particularly regarding accuracy of data, workflow, and findings from the study.

2. Be in control. A speaker who arranges for a conference room free from interruptions establishes audience control.

3. Pretest equipment. Make a dry run. The visual equipment should be set up well ahead of time and pretested. Dry-run rehearsals give the speaker confidence. Inadequate organization or incomplete content should come to one's attention by rehearsing in front of a practice audience.

4. Be organized. The speaker should make certain all necessary supportive materials are at hand: pencils and pads for note taking, background data and typewritten reports to distribute at the end of the meeting. An effective presentation does not occur accidentally. The speaker is expected to manage the meeting. One who is well prepared, concise, and accurate, has all necessary information at hand, and is thoroughly knowledgeable and well organized can maintain control and will gain the respect and maintain the interest and understanding of the audience.

5. Use visuals. (See Figure 10-6 for an example.) The visuals help to communicate the message, provided they are presented competently. A speaker who practices using visuals avoids encountering surprises during the presentations. Practicing the use of the visual-aid equipment as well as the visuals avoids most equipment usage problems. A well-rehearsed, and therefore competent speaker, can jokingly handle such situations as equipment breakdowns. If the speaker will use a podium during the presentation, it should be used during the dry run to make sure it is the right height.

6. Explain visuals. After the word processing data was summarized, the analyst prepared a flowchart of the present and proposed systems. A workflow chart, with its supportive data, is illustrated in Figure 10-7. The following script explains the flowchart:

> Secretaries from each originating department type agenda for each city council meeting. The department manager reviews the information, frequently making changes that may need to be typed. Next, the agenda is submitted to the city manager, who reviews it and then submits it to the secretary to be typed. The first revision averages 30 percent.
>
> After looking the agenda over, the manager usually makes a last-minute edit, with approximately 10 percent changes, which the secretary types and submits for final approval. Frequently, secretaries have to work overtime in order to have the agenda ready for each city council meeting.

FIGURE 10-6   A Visual Illustrating Changing Costs

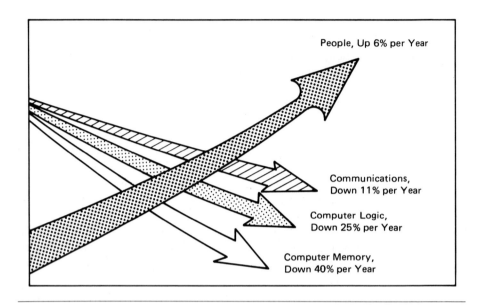

People, Up 6% per Year

Communications,
Down 11% per Year

Computer Logic,
Down 25% per Year

Computer Memory,
Down 40% per Year

Proposed New System. If the city purchased, rented, or leased two word processing typewriters, one for the city manager's secretary and one for a departmental secretary with an accompanying dictation system, it would save time for both the originators and the secretaries as follows:

Department managers (originators) could dictate their information over the telephone to the recorder located near the two secretaries. One or two secretaries could transcribe the first draft of the agenda (which averages 12 pages, approximately 25 lines per page, 10 words per line for a total of 250 words per page).

Once the secretaries type the drafts, the department managers proofread them and make any desired changes. The secretaries make the changes from the recorded drafts stored on disks on the word processing equipment and then present this version to the city manager. The city manager makes the final edit of the changes which are typed from the stored recording by the secretaries and submitted for final proof. Final copy is then duplicated and collated, ready for the city council meeting.

It is apparent that the secretaries will not have to retype any of the old material, only the changes. Just how much time does the proposed new system save compared with the old? What cost savings is involved?

Figure 10-8 illustrates that the proposed new system will save 3.1 hours of secretarial time alone. Table 10-3 breaks down savings of secretarial time and shows subsequent cost savings.

Agenda for Monthly Meetings Workflow   **FIGURE 10-7**

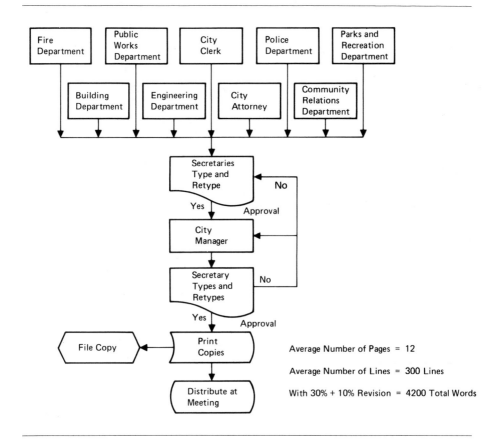

The following script is one example of the type of dialogue this particular illustration would require:

> The difference in the productivity rates of 20 and 50 words per minute is due to the different secretarial procedures proposed for the new system. Currently the secretaries type while performing at least five other major administrative tasks, including handling mail, telephones, copying, filing, and special projects. These duties cause interruptions which reduce their typing productivity to less than half of that in the proposed system: 20 words per minute compared with an average 50 words per minute. Secretaries can produce documents faster with the new system because of specialized tasks in addition to their using word processing typewriters, which make typing easier and faster.

7. Address the audience. Any speaker should look directly at the audience, since people quickly lose interest when a speaker does not look at them. Eye contact helps develop trust. A person is more apt to believe a speaker who communicates

FIGURE 10-8

Productivity Comparison for Typing and Revising a 12-Page Agenda with and without a Word Processor

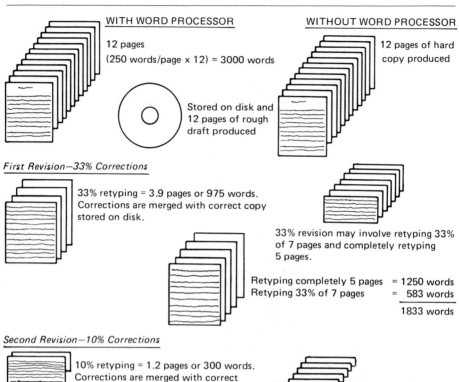

WITH WORD PROCESSOR · WITHOUT WORD PROCESSOR

12 pages
(250 words/page x 12) = 3000 words

Stored on disk and
12 pages of rough
draft produced

12 pages of hard
copy produced

First Revision—33% Corrections

33% retyping = 3.9 pages or 975 words.
Corrections are merged with correct copy
stored on disk.

33% revision may involve retyping 33%
of 7 pages and completely retyping
5 pages.

Retyping completely 5 pages = 1250 words
Retyping 33% of 7 pages = 583 words
                          1833 words

Second Revision—10% Corrections

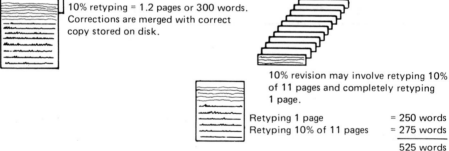

10% retyping = 1.2 pages or 300 words.
Corrections are merged with correct
copy stored on disk.

10% revision may involve retyping 10%
of 11 pages and completely retyping
1 page.

Retyping 1 page = 250 words
Retyping 10% of 11 pages = 275 words
                          525 words

Final Agenda

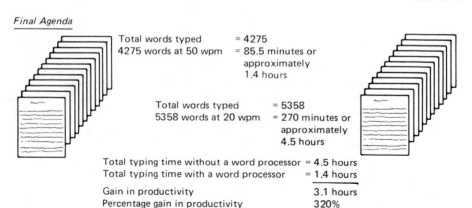

Total words typed   = 4275
4275 words at 50 wpm   = 85.5 minutes or
                          approximately
                          1.4 hours

Total words typed   = 5358
5358 words at 20 wpm   = 270 minutes or
                          approximately
                          4.5 hours

Total typing time without a word processor = 4.5 hours
Total typing time with a word processor   = 1.4 hours

Gain in productivity   3.1 hours
Percentage gain in productivity   320%

		Current System	Proposed Word Processing System
Time and Cost Savings of New Word Processing System			**TABLE 10-3**
Original typing		2.5 hours (20 wpm)	1.0 hour (50 wpm)
First revision — 33%		1.5 hours	.3 hour
Second revision		.5 hour	.1 hour
		4.5 hours	1.4 hours
Time saved	= 3.1 hours		
At average current secretarial cost to company of $10/hour savings (*time only*)	= $31.00		

honesty, knowledge, integrity, humor, enthusiasm, and professionalism. The technique of communicating information is just as important as the information being presented. In order to get all of the facts across with appropriate emphasis, good eye contact is vital. A speaker who is well rehearsed will know the information well enough to look at the audience and not have to read from notes and the visuals. This develops a mutual confidence between the audience and the speaker.

8. Be knowledgeable. By having a thorough knowledge of the subject matter, the speaker can devote more time to addressing the audience rather than reading notes or reading the visuals to the audience. Visuals, an outline, and notes should be used to stimulate ideas and key points and not be read word for word.

9. Answer questions. Sometimes it is difficult to know exactly how much detail will be asked, but the speaker should have appropriate information and data at hand in order to respond to those questions that apply to the study, findings, and recommendations. The speaker should ask attendees to hold unrelated questions until after the meeting so as not to take up the time of the other members of the audience.

10. Provide supportive evidence. A speaker who is prepared with pertinent information in order to respond to questions obtains the respect of the audience. Attendees may think, "That person really does know what is going on around here; maybe something will get done to straighten out _____." Inability to answer or avoiding questions leads to mistrust and lack of belief. The audience will lose confidence in the speaker, in the study, and in the proposed system.

11. Be enthusiastic and positive. Attitudes frequently speak louder than words. An enthusiastic and positive speaker encourages positive responses.

The subject being addressed, word processing, involves change, something which people tend to resist. Therefore, the speaker must be prepared to sell the people in the audience. Why should they change? They need to feel that the change will improve their jobs and careers and make the firm's internal opera-tions more efficient and productive. All negativism such as lack of confidence or competence, controversy, negative or hesitant responses, and personal egotism should be avoided. A person is more apt to buy a product from a salesperson who smiles and communicates the feeling that the product is going to improve the customer's quality of life. The speaker should deliver the same message: word processing will improve each employee's job and working conditions.

THE STUDY REPORT

The typewritten report usually follows a very similar format to the presentation. It should be:

* Concise yet comprehensive enough to provide complete relevant information.
* Well organized, with important information presented first, followed by relevant supportive information.
* Easy to follow and read.
* Accurate and of high quality.

A suggested report outline might be produced in five phases: (a) introduction, (b) study findings, (c) resulting recommendations, (d) summary, and (e) supportive and relevant background data. Contents of the report might answer the following questions.

Introduction

What were the objectives (or charter) of the study? What was the purpose of the study? How was the study conducted? What techniques were used and why? When and for how long was the study conducted? What departments and functions were included? How many people participated? What were their jobs (secretaries, principals, managers)? How many were interviewed? Who made and helped to conduct the study?

Findings

What was the result of the study? What is the current system? its volume of paperwork? How is it performed? What is the workflow? time distribution? What are the current problems or areas for improvement?

Recommendations

What structure would be most appropriate? What job alignment would be most appropriate? How many people are required? What is the system design? What is the workflow design? What kinds of equipment, related jobs, and procedures could be implemented?

Summary *((money))*

What is the comparative cost of the current and proposed system? What are the benefits to be provided by the proposed word processing system? How and when should it be implemented (what is the implementation schedule)?

Supportive Data

What are the background data: personnel listings by job and department category, equipment inventory, current organizational structure and floorplans, other current relevant costs? What are the summary data: all totals and tables prepared as a result of data collection and analysis? What is the cost analysis: how study data were analyzed to prepare the comparative cost effectiveness of the current and proposed systems?

SUMMARY

After the present system has been summarized and evaluated, the workflow is diagrammed. The information obtained provides the basis for the new system design. After all the components of the new system are outlined, one can make the cost justification analyses and outline the new system benefits. This information is then put into final format to prepare the management report and presentation. The survey task force will make a formal presentation to top management, followed by presentations to middle management, staff secretaries, and other personnel who participated in the study.

Analysts usually prepare both a visual presentation and written report. Sometimes the report is distributed during or before the presentation. Usually it is distributed after the visual presentation.

Visuals used in the presentation include transparencies shown on an overhead projector, films, slide-tapes, 35mm slides, or flip charts. They should be well prepared and easy to follow and see and should not contain too much information. Visuals are used to provide leading topics from which the speaker presents applicable supportive facts.

Presentation format usually outlines the path of the study. It begins with management's objectives, explains how the study was conducted, and summarizes data gathered during the study (such as time distribution of tasks, flow of the work, and volume summaries). Next, current workflow and related problems are explained. The proposed new system then is described by showing its structure, workflow, personnel alignment, and distribution of work. Advantages and benefits of the proposed system over the present system are then explained. The management presentation concludes with a description of the cost justification, new system benefits, and implementation schedule for the proposed system.

Speakers need to be well prepared, maintain control, pretest audio-visual equipment, be organized, be able to use and explain visuals, maintain audience eye contact, be knowledgeable, be prepared to answer questions, provide supportive data, and be enthusiastic and positive.

The speaker should keep in mind the importance of word processing to the firm and sell it to the employees (potential users) whose jobs will be affected. The speaker needs to communicate positively with top management, middle managers, supervisors, operating staff, and secretaries. Their understanding, belief and confidence, and—most of all—support and participation are essential for word processing to be successful.

The written report should be concise, comprehensive, well organized, and of top quality. It is generally organized in the same format as the presentation, beginning with the study objectives; describing how the study was conducted; discussing the findings, recommendations, conclusions, and cost effectiveness; and concluding with supportive and background data. It is usually distributed at the conclusion of the presentation to provide management with all necessary information it needs to decide on its implementation plan.

REVIEW QUESTIONS

1. How might management's presentation differ from the one to middle management?
2. How might the presentation to the staff differ?
3. How should the presentation be structured?
4. Name four kinds of visuals are used in presentations?
5. How might the presentation agenda differ from the written report?
6. What kinds of attitudes should the presenter display?
7. How should the presentation conclude?

QUESTIONS FOR DISCUSSION

1. Discuss how presentations may differ among the different groups attending.
2. Discuss how handouts distributed prior to the presentation might affect the presentation.
3. Discuss how the conduct of the presenter can affect the effectiveness of the presentation.
4. If handouts are passed out at the beginning of the presentation, how might the presenter use them to his or her own advantage?
5. If the most important person attending the presentation has to leave, how should the presenter handle the interruption?

CASES

Case 10-1   Unified School District

A task force of three analysts has just completed a study of the Western Hills Unified School District which included 10 high schools, 12 junior high schools, and 15 grade schools. After interviewing all of the secretaries, administrative staffs including counselors, and support services, the task force has decided to recommend implementation of a word processing system with a center in the main high school and satellites at each of the high schools, usually with one corresponding secretary. The center will have five correspondence secretaries under the word processing manager who will also be responsible for the total word processing system. Their monthly cost configuration is shown in Table 10–4. Table 10–5 lists problems of the current system and solutions to be realized from the new system.

Benefits include better service to teachers and administrative staff, more enjoyable jobs and working conditions, and more potential for job growth.

Prepare an outline of the presentation of the study for management.

Case 10–2   Architectural Engineering Company

Upon conclusion of the study of Smith and Pierce Architectural Engineering, Inc., the task force recommended implementing the following word processing system: one main document center with three correspondence secretaries using a shared-logic sys-

		Costs of Current and Proposed Systems	TABLE 10-4

Present System		*Proposed System*	
Secretaries/typists (88)	$80,960	Correspondence secretaries (42)	$39,000
Other present costs	15,500	Word processing typewriters	12,600
		Supervisor	17,000
		Supplies and other costs	1,500
		Administrative secretaries (12)	18,600
Total	$96,460	Total	$88,700
Savings	$ 7,760/month		
Less startup costs (including dictation system)	3,500		
First Month's Savings	$ 4,260		

	Problems and Solutions	TABLE 10-5

Problems	*Solutions and Advantages*
Secretarial overtime averages 22 hr/month	Eliminate overtime costs
Poor quality documents	Improve document quality
Low employee morale	Improve morale with better job conditions
Low productivity	Greatly increase productivity
Duplicated typings because of revisions	Eliminate need to retype for revisions
High secretarial turnover	Reduce turnover by job enrichment and job satisfaction

tem and outputting photocomposed reports and proposals with three small work groups, each with two secretaries using the shared-logic system and dictation equipment. Monthly costs are outlined in Table 10–6. Problems of the present system and planned solutions are listed in Table 10–7.

Prepare an outline of the study report.

TABLE 10-6   **Costs of Current and Proposed Systems**

Present System		*Proposed System*	
Secretaries (28)	$27,000	Correspondence/secretaries (9)	8,100
Other costs	1,500	Manager	1,500
Equipment	2,000	Administrative secretaries (8)	7,200
		Proofreader	900
		Coordinator	1,100
		Equipment	5,000
		Supplies and other costs	900
Total	$30,500 per month	Total	$24,700 per month
Monthly savings	5,800		
Less startup costs	4,100		
First Month's Savings	$ 1,700		

TABLE 10-7   **Problems and Solutions**

Problems	*Solutions and Advantages*
Costs of overtime and outside help	Reduce overtime and outside help and lower those costs
Inability to meet deadlines	Reduce duplicated typing and increase ability to meet deadlines
Low morale	Improve employee morale
Complaints about accuracy and quality	Improve quality and accuracy by ease of proofreading only changes

IMPLEMENTING THE WORD PROCESSING SYSTEM

This section will first consider the events that occur during the period between management's approval of the new system and its implementation. The activities that occur during this period begin with preparing the budget, physical layout, and environment; scheduling equipment and personnel; ordering supplies; and preparing written communications.

Next, job descriptions are written, personnel are screened and selected, and training of the operating staff begins.

During this period, the procedures are planned and written for those who will be the principal users: the operating staff and other departments and services. Training programs are planned, prepared, and conducted.

These preparations are conducted by the word processing management staff but should involve all those who will be working in and with the word processing system.

Part 4 explains how the word processing manager coordinates all these components to prepare to implement the word processing system.

Quote from Carl Heyel, "Changing Concepts of Human Relations," in *Management: A Book of Readings* (McGraw-Hill, 1976), p. 447.

BENJAMIN / CUMMINGS

WORD PROCESSING SERIES

PEOPLE / PROCEDURES / EQUIPMENT

"Forecasting, one of the essential elements in planning, is a prediction of what will happen on the basis of certain assumptions; planning is an attempt to determine what should happen (in very specific terms) and then to take steps that will make it likely to happen."

CHAPTER 11

Planning for Implementation

OVERVIEW

The effective manager is that person who is capable of getting the right things done. A person who is intelligent, creative, and knowledgeable in word processing is not necessarily a successful word processing executive. Effective word processing management requires the ability to know where and how to apply these strengths in the right priorities.

OBJECTIVES

After completing this chapter, you will be able to:

1. State word processing objectives.
2. Explain the importance of setting word processing policies.
3. Explain the value of time lines and schedules.
4. Plan a word processing budget.
5. Explain the kinds of procedures required for word processing.

Quote from Henry C. Egerton and James K. Brown, "Planning and the Chief Executive," *The Conference Board* (1972), pp. 1–11.

6. Explain the sources of and need for support during word processing implementation.
7. Explain the purpose of scheduling periodic reviews.
8. Describe how to plan word processing personnel scheduling.
9. Explain how to select word processing furniture and plan the office layout.
10. State what supplies need to be ordered.
11. Describe what communications should take place during the planning period.

PRELIMINARY PLANNING

Once top management has approved the proposed new system and given its go-ahead, it is time to prepare for implementation. The task force now proceeds to organize a smooth transition from the current system to the new one. Steps to be included while scheduling and preparing for operations include:

1. forecasting
2. setting objectives
3. determining policies
4. establishing timelines
5. delegating accountability
6. determining availability of financial resources
7. designating the distribution of available funds to match needs
8. writing workflow, job descriptions, and operating procedures
9. eliciting support
10. scheduling status review
11. evaluating results
12. reporting results

Figure 11-1 illustrates the implementation schedule checklist developed for Middletown Bank to prepare for its new system. In order to proceed with the planning, Ron and his task force associates followed the necessary steps as explained in the following paragraphs.

Forecasting

Estimate future needs and service requirements. When they began to design the new system, the task force members made sure that any future requirements and plans were included in the system design. They accomplished this by discussing the results of the study with management, department managers, staff, and operating personnel. This allowed them to be assured the new system would meet all necessary specifications. They wanted to make sure they were aware of any changes occurring or anticipated while preparing for implementation. This accomplished two purposes: it helped to avoid surprises that might later result in operating problems (such as under- or over-capacity), and it involved bank employees in planning activities prior to implementation.

1. Start activities.
2. Hold preimplementation planning meetings.
3. Review results of study.
4. Evaluate and test equipment.
5. Select and order equipment.
6. Determine floor space and layout.
7. Determine telephone system.
8. Prepare budget.
9. Plan, select, and order office furnishings (carpeting, desks, chairs).
10. Plan other environmental aspects.
11. Order facilities required: electrical, lighting, air conditioning.
12. Plan supplies facilities, files, storage and retention equipment.
13. Order supplies and equipment.
14. Write job descriptions.
15. Post descriptions to recruit personnel.
16. Interview applicants.
17. Select personnel.
18. Train personnel on word processing and transcription equipment.
19. Write procedures manuals.
20. Design word processing forms.
21. Make final preparation of operating personnel.
22. Conduct orientation and training programs for users.
23. Put system into operation.

Setting Objectives

Review with and obtain agreement from top management exact statements regarding what is expected to be accomplished with the new system. Management's objectives must be consistent with those of the rest of the organization. In order to carry out management's objectives, they must first be concisely formulated so that they may be clearly understood. Objectives should be stated in specific measurable terms. An example of an objective might be: All correspondence (letters and memos) must be (a) free of errors, (b) appropriately formatted according to preset standards, and (c) returned for signature within a maximum of six hours.

Significant objectives should:

- start with the word *to* followed by an action verb
- produce a single key result when accomplished
- specify target date for accomplishment
- specify a maximum cost factor
- be as specific and quantitative as possible

- specify only the *what* and *when*
- relate to the accountable manager's roles and missions directly and to higher level roles, missions, and objectives
- be realistic and attainable, yet challenging

Objectives should not be written until ideas have been solicited from supervisors, subordinates, and peers. They need to be consistent with those of the total organization and the firm's anticipated results. This allows an opportunity for other personnel to participate in planning. People like to know what is expected of them; once they have an exact idea of what they are expected to accomplish, they are more in tune with their work. By helping to set objectives, they know the expected results and have an opportunity to express their opinions. Frequently, employees tend to set higher goals than those set by their supervisors.

Determining Policies

Write down standing decisions which apply to all questions regarding the word processing system. Policies result from decisions made in response to questions and problems. They represent the manner in which matters will be handled in response to such questions as, "How will top priority work be handled?" and "How will daily work be handled along with long projects that require rapid turnaround?"

Word processing requires establishing and carrying out clearcut policies. (See Figure 11-2 for an example.) This applies to the operators and particularly to the users, who previously may have had their own secretaries. In the past, these users felt confident, since they could communicate directly with their secretaries at any time to learn the status of their work.

With a word processing system, especially when a center has been established, this may no longer be the case. Now the users may be instructed to dictate over the telephone into a recorder in a remote location and wait to receive their work. These users may be extremely concerned whether documents will meet their quality standards and desired deadlines. If the users are instrumental in setting policies, they will understand daily working situations which may affect those production factors, particularly how rapidly their work can be processed.

An example of a policy might be, "All dictated correspondence will be given priority over longhand input."

Establishing Timelines and Schedules

Prepare schedules including deadlines and designated turnaround standards to be met and dates when each activity will occur. An important planning task is to schedule work so that word processing can produce documents according to preset standards. This schedule needs to be realistic and meet the following criteria:

1. Allow a reasonable amount of time for the correspondence secretary to produce the document.

Procedures for the Word Processing Center   FIGURE 11-2

Purpose	The Word Processing Center is designed to centralize all typing and process paperwork in a faster, more efficient, and professional manner.
Operation	Normal work schedule is Monday through Friday, 8:30 A.M. to 5:30 P.M. Material received after 3:30 P.M. is considered the next day's work.
	Night and weekend dictation: In case a belt may need changing after hours, the dictator should request instructions from the center manager before after-hours dictation.
Documents to be processed	All original dictation and reports. Specific documents will be listed under the section entitled "Departmental Applications."
Priorities	Work is processed on a first-come, first-serve basis with predetermined exceptions as stated under "Departmental Applications."
Specific deadlines listed below	

---

2. Meet quality standards.
3. Meet the timeline requirements of the originator.

After first setting policies, the task force next scheduled designated timeline standards for each document cateogry.

Some of the decisions to be made when preparing to implement word processing are: Which kind of work will be handled first? Will it be daily correspondence or will it be long, revised projects?

Obvious advantages derived from using word processing typewriters are those which eliminate duplicated typing, including:

- Document revision. Store original versions on magnetic media so the typist needs to type changes only, using the good material saved on the media.
- Repetitive letters, paragraphs, and formats. Store a letter that will go to more than one person so that only the name, address, and any specific variable information needs to be typed for each addressee; the remaining information will be typed from the storage media. Store any formats or paragraphs that are used repetitively to type special documents, such as trust agreements, reports, proposals, budgets, and forecasts. The speed with which these applications can be produced by using word processing typewriters is much greater than a typewriter with no memory or

storage. The advantages derived from the use of word processing equipment in these applications are easily shown in the reduction of document turnaround time.

Daily correspondence is a different matter. Most people can see little or no advantage to using a word processing typewriter to produce a one-time letter (a letter that is typed and signed for mailing without retyping). They do not understand the concept of rough draft speed typing, and it may not apply to extremely rapid accurate typists. Therefore, many firms first begin to record and store boilerplate (repetitive typing) on their word processing media before they begin daily operations. If the form letters and stored paragraphs are already recorded and stored, rapid production of the documents will be achieved.

By comparison, if the word processing system begins by typing daily correspondence (one-time documents), it may be more difficult to prove increased productivity quickly. It is important to sell the users on the advantages the new system has over the old one. Beginning with repetitive documents can therefore be the most logical first application for the new system.

To prepare the word processing schedule, the task force needs to consider which department(s) or application(s) to phase in first. If word processing is going to produce typing for all the bank's departments, will they begin operations by taking work from the entire bank? Or will they begin with one or two departments? Or will they begin with particular applications such as form letters?

The task force needs to schedule phases very carefully, either by application or by department. They definitely would not want to begin the first day without planning. Employees from each department attend an orientation program in which the users (principals) are taught how to use the system, followed by phasing in their work. The second group of users attends the next orientation and training, followed by phasing in their work, and so on.

The bank's task force decided to begin by producing all the typing for the Trust and Loan Department. This included daily correspondence, reports, form letters, statistical work, and forms. All the documents that were formerly typed by the department secretaries were typed by the word processing center located on their floor. Figure 11-2 lists Middletown Bank's policies determined during the planning period.

Delegating Accountability

Determine responsibilities of personnel. Each activity must be accounted for by a responsible person. Each activity is assigned to the person or persons accountable for that project. After designing and writing the job description for each position and allocating the reporting alignment for each position, each activity is defined, including each step in its workflow. Designating accountability and responsibility for each position enables the word processing supervisor to distribute the work and handle various work requests smoothly.

Equally important, this procedure makes it possible to clearly define each function to be performed. Employees who are made aware of their personal job responsibility and accountability are more apt to achieve job satisfaction. An example of delegating accountability could be, "The page is responsible for delivering documents to and from the Word Processing Department."

Determining Availability of Funds

Once the budget is prepared, set priorities for operating requirements according to available funds. Before word processing operations can begin, the funds must first be budgeted. The task force first designed the bank's new system and each component and then planned the budget. The budget included costs for personnel, equipment, floor space, supplies, and overhead. Some word processing systems use a chargeback system, in which the principal users are charged for word processing services performed for them. This is calculated by determining the cost of each part of the total cost to perform the service, including personnel time, equipment time, supplies, and overhead. These costs are allocated to the department being serviced.

A word processing budget must have funds available to cover:

- Word processing equipment (production, origination, and any other equipment assigned to word processing such as OCR, communications, copiers, collators).
- Phone equipment (with any communication modems required).
- Wiring and lighting.
- Furniture (desks, chairs, filing cabinets, counters, tables).
- Sound protection and reduction (including sound partitions).
- Carpeting.
- Space dividers and other peripherals.
- Office supplies (paper, ribbons, print wheels, storage media, reference books, dictionaries).
- Burden (percentage of overhead that covers fringe benefits, vacation pay, and sick leave, as well as cost of office space).

When an organization does not have sufficient funds to acquire all the desired equipment and personnel, it may need to budget in phases according to available resources.

Fitting Available Resources to Requirements

According to available economic resources, develop timelines for scheduling personnel, equipment, and supplies. The task force schedules timelines according to available funds. After determining what funds are available, future additions to the preliminary operation can be planned for later phases and scheduled to be implemented when resources become available.

At the bank, the task force discovered during the feasibility study that it could save considerable time and duplication by implementing word processing communications among branch banks. This would speed up the paperwork processing within the branches and eliminate the need to send work to the main branch for processing and typing. Sufficient financial resources, however, were not available for implementing this equipment during the first phase; therefore, they scheduled this equipment for the second phase, when the funds would be available.

Writing Procedures

Develop standardized methods of performing job functions. To plan a new system, each step from the beginning (originating) to the completion of the cycle (distributing) needs to be outlined. Next, the procedures can be written. These procedures must be carefully and concisely stated so that they are easy to follow.

Resistance to change often results from the fear that one will not be able to function properly in the changed environment and will therefore fail. Each person needs to understand exactly how to accomplish his or her work by using the new system. Once a person understands how it works and how to use it and that it is possible to use it successfully, that person will begin to accept and try it. When a person must change habits that come naturally and easily to new habits, more effort is required. Therefore, each person should be provided clearcut instructions and opportunities to practice and become familiar with the new routine.

We live in a rapidly changing environment in which we are frequently faced with new devices and routines. So long as we know how to use these devices and follow these routines, we find it easier to accept changes. But when this is not the case, we become extremely frustrated and resist making changes. An example was the use of zip codes for mailing. Many people preferred to continue in the old familiar way. It was not until people believed that their mail would get there faster and that it might not get there at all by using the old system that they adapted to the change.

The same is particularly true of the office worker. An engineer may have created in longhand all his or her life. The secretary competently produced long, error-free, top quality engineering specifications, reports, and daily correspondence. The engineer did not have to learn new skills or change any habits. The new (word processing) system may require the engineer to use a telephone or microphone to dictate these documents, not to his or her secretary, but to someone else who may not be located anywhere nearby. The engineer may fear that the new typist will not understand the technical language, know the correct names, type the correct words in the appropriate format, and (most important) produce the document by the required or desired deadline. No wonder this engineer opposed changing to word processing! The engineer needs to know clearcut, concise procedures to follow when originating so that work will be produced exactly as desired and anticipated. Instruction manuals need to specify, in detail, how to produce each principal's documents. All procedures manuals must be prepared before the system is put into operation. This includes procedures for the operating staff. (Procedures writing, as well as other written communications, is detailed in Chapter 14.)

Eliciting Support

While preparing for implementation, the task force should solicit opinions of others to get them involved. The more participation on the part of those who will be using the word processing system, the more apt they are to help it to succeed. Success of the new system depends upon them. If ideas of the users are included in the new system's operating procedures, it becomes *their* system, and they will help make it succeed.

The adage "two heads are better than one" may be applied to designing procedures. Considering several alternatives often leads to more judicious decisions. Ron and his associates responded to suggestions made by participants during the study by later discussing these ideas with them in detail. Many of the new system's procedures were suggested by participants during the study.

The Trust Department manager suggested a way in which paragraphs from various trust documents could be standardized and stored to produce trust agreements, which would save a great deal of retyping time. When planning for implementation, the task force followed this up and, with the help of the Trust Department secretary, designed a procedure to prepare trust documents from paragraphs stored on the word processing medium.

Scheduling Status Review

While planning beginning operations, the task force discussed how soon after implementation the first system review should take place. They felt that to prevent minor problems from becoming major ones, it should be soon enough to make changes and adjustments in areas not functioning adequately, not using the system, or encountering problems. Also, it would prevent failure to use the system and keep minor frustrations from growing into major problems. At the same time, they wanted to give it enough time to settle into a measurable pattern before making an evaluation. They decided to wait until each department had been phased in and operating for four full months before scheduling its first review. They estimated this would take approximately one year.

Evaluating Results

How would they evaluate the system? What standards would they use for status review measurement? Would they expect the system to meet all of management's original objectives by the first review? When would the next review take place? What would be expected at that time?

The task force sat down and wrote their criteria for status evaluation, including the dates reviews would take place, standards to be evaluated, and checkoff points to be covered for interpretation in these evaluations.

Included in the status reviews were:

- Personnel required and available.
- Deadlines required and whether they were met.
- Productivity levels set and whether they were maintained (or what levels were met).
- Users (volume of use by individual or department).
- Applications (volume of each application by department).
- Quality standards set and how well they were met.

After evaluating the results obtained from the status review, the task force determined whether any changes needed to be made. If changes were required, they then decided how to make them. These changes were then incorporated into operating procedures and work standards. Any changes reflected in users' procedures were communicated to the principals involved to aid the word processing system in better serving their needs.

Reporting Results

After completing the status review, the task force prepared to report its findings to management. The evaluation was finalized after the system had been operating for a full year. Prior to full evaluation, the task force reported the results of periodic evaluations of weekly and monthly productivity and work volume.

Statistics used for the one-year evaluation were obtained from their computerized recording/measurement system, which produced daily, weekly, and monthly productivity reports. In addition to these statistics, they periodically interviewed managers, staff, and other personnel (including administrative and correspondence secretaries) to obtain personal attitude feedback. They accumulated the results, had them tabulated by the computer, and included them in their periodic reports to top management. They continually monitored the original objectives against the results obtained to evaluate whether they were meeting original goals.

THE BUDGET

The budget is, simply, the financial plan. In a household budget, the family's sources of income are itemized in an "Income" column, and the ways in which this income will be spent are listed under an "Expense" column. Items include housing, food, transportation, entertainment, medical and dental expenses, education, and sports and recreation. Similarly, the federal budget indicates the government's income sources and allocates funds to national defense, health, education and welfare, agriculture, disaster relief, among other national expenses. In the same way, an organization's budget is a plan detailing how income and available funds will be spent on labor, land, structures, equipment, raw materials, capital goods.

Just as the national budget is used as a device to ensure that the Departments of Defense, Agriculture, and HEW, etc., limit their expenditures to specified or budgeted amounts, a firm's budget can also be used as a device for formulating an organization's spending plans and exercising necessary controls.

Budgeting, then, is a management tool used for both planning and control. Basically, budgeting is a method used to improve operations—a continuous effort that specifies what should be done to get the job completed in the best possible way. It therefore requires a set of performance standards or targets that can be compared to actual results; this process is called controlling to plan. It is a continuous monitoring procedure, reviewing and evaluating performance with reference to the previously established standards.[1]

Established standards require a realistic understanding of activities carried on as opposed to arbitrary standards, which can do more harm than good. Budgets imposed in an arbitrary fashion with impossible targets at one extreme or standards that are too lax at the other can cause frustrations and resentment and result in deteriorating personnel morale. But budgets based on a clear understanding and careful analysis of operations can play an important, positive role.

Planning the Word Processing Budget

Word processing budget costs for workers are determined after the total personnel needs and job alignment are designed. In order to budget the total staff, the job descriptions and number of personnel in each category must first be planned. When the General Electric Motor Plant planned its word processing center, management first designated what positions should be included, wrote the job descriptions, and then budgeted for the personnel. The word processing staff for beginning operations included the word processing supervisor and three correspondence secretaries.

To plan the personnel budget, they set annual salaries as follows: $14,000 for the supervisor and $10,000 for each correspondence secretary; the total personnel budget came to $44,000. This part of the personnel budget was for salaries alone and did not include burden. Burden costs include fringe benefits (vacation time, sick leave, insurance programs) and any other overhead, such as office space.

The next item to budget is the word processing equipment. A major factor to decide at this point is whether to purchase, lease, or rent the equipment. General Electric was installing three word processing typewriters they could purchase for $12,000 each, lease for $370 a month, or rent for $412 a month. After conducting a lease-versus-buy analysis, they decided to lease their word processors. The total budget to lease this equipment was $1100 a month.

They next budgeted their dictation system. They decided from statistics provided by the feasibility study that they needed a system that included four dictation recorders and three transcribers that would be wired into their telephone system so that all office and plant personnel would be able to dictate over the telephone into the word processing center. They decided to purchase this system for $13,000.

They next planned their facilities and office furniture budget. Facilities included office space, electricity, lighting, air conditioning, soundproofing, carpeting, painting, and room decorations. Office furniture consisted of special desks, file cabinets, and a counter for pickup and delivery. Secretarial chairs were already on hand. Their supplies budget included fanfold draft paper, letterhead, envelopes, file folders, ribbons, print wheels, preprinted forms, dictionaries, and reference books.

The correspondence secretaries attended vendor equipment training for one week and were therefore absent from work. If any of these vacated positions had been

[1] J. Fred Weston and Eugene F. Brigham, *Managerial Finance*, 5th ed. Hinsdale, Ill.: Dryden, 1975, pp. 94–95.

filled with outside help, that expense would have been added to the budget. However, since the work was handled by other secretaries, no training cost was added to startup costs.

The supervisor attended a two-week training school that included expenses for air travel, hotel room, and other living expenses. These expenses were attributable to startup and therefore became a part of the startup costs.

PHYSICAL LAYOUT, ENVIRONMENT, AND DESIGN

After designing the word processing structure, appropriate office space must be located. General Electric selected a room 30 feet long by 25 feet wide which had ample space for the four individuals, their office furniture, and the equipment. They decided upon a center; next they needed to locate a room of ample size providing easy access to those using the system. They selected a room at the end of a hall on the first floor of a two-story building near an entrance frequently used by personnel. It was near both the Industrial Relations Department and the plant entrance. Originally the room was not large enough, but they were able to enlarge it by removing a wall separating it from another.

To plan for adequate space, they allowed for desks, chairs, supplies, sound dividers for each secretary, the word processing typing equipment, file cabinets, dictation recorders and transcribers, and distribution system. They installed a long counter with mail slots for departmental pickup and delivery. In addition, they ordered a rolling mail cart with dividers for each department to deliver work to and from principals in the two buildings. Other room preparations included lighting, air conditioning, soundproofing, carpeting, and room decoration. They wanted the room to be a comfortable, pleasant working environment that would provide a cheerful, relaxed atmosphere.

After selecting the location for word processing, a floorplan scaled to size was drawn up and layout designed for equipment personnel. (See Figure 11–3.) They used adhesive stick-ons to represent equipment and personnel. An important consideration was the direction individuals would face: the receptionist would face incoming visitors and the supervisor would face towards the correspondence secretaries. They placed the word processing equipment and personnel in the scaled-down floorplan. This required knowing the dimensions of all office equipment that would be placed in the center.

FURNISHINGS

Many office furniture manufacturers provide consultants who will visit firms implementing word processing to provide customized environmental planning. They specify appropriate equipment to meet a firm's particular needs, including the space available and attractiveness desired. One firm offers extension tables that may be added to clustered work stations to allow more working space for the secretaries. These desks

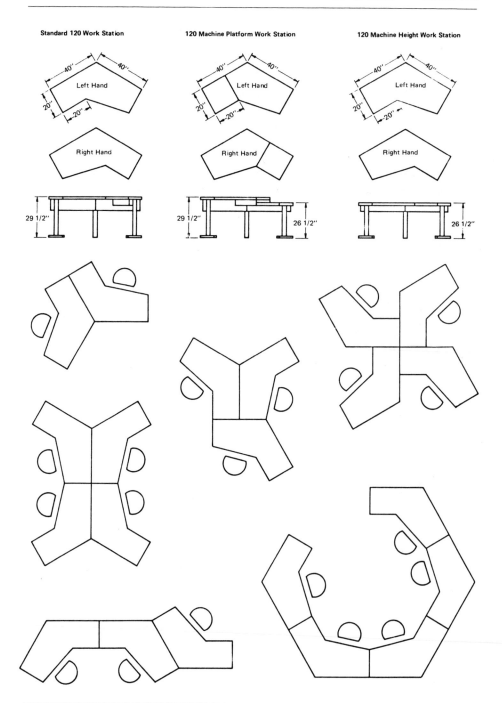

Standard 120 Work Station

120 Machine Platform Work Station

120 Machine Height Work Station

can be arranged in groups of threes by angling 120 degrees for maximum surface access.

Basic modules come in standard, machine, and standard-and-machine heights, with or without recesses for consoles of word processing keyboard equipment and in left- and right-hand configurations.

Another company features specialty desks which can be ordered by components (tops, legs, modesty panels, etc.) which can be knocked down or altered to fit different space requirements. These desks may be ordered in various widths, heights, and depths, allowing the user a choice of several options for cable channels for electricity, varying numbers and arrangements of desk drawers, and colors.

One company features generous storage space, including shelves, dividers, and lateral file drawers, while another features cubicles designed especially for word processing equipment. The cubicles contain work stations with three work surfaces providing ample work space, vertical paper organizers, continuous paper feed shelves, and drawers near the typewriter surface for easy access to filed materials.

Arrangement

As stated by Willoughby Ann Walshe,[2] "Planning the word processing/ administrative support environment entails analyzing and satisfying human needs. Realizing that pleasant and comfortable working conditions increase production by boosting morale and motivation, word processing furniture manufacturers are starting to consult the user on how they can improve their products."

Many furniture supply firms now publish reports and provide consulting services recommending customized arrangements to satisfy each firm's individual environmental and furniture needs.

The Herman Miller Company, a manufacturer of word processing furniture, states that manufacturers of word processing equipment are particularly sensitive to users' needs by designing open office structures based on the premise that the office is a facility based on change. Herman Miller's action office presents an alternative to the traditional combination of private offices and open bullpens. It provides individual work areas for everyone, from president to bookkeeper, by the selective use of easily moved panels of varying heights, plus modular components that attach to these panels, such as work surfaces, drawers, shelves, storage bins, lateral files, mag card trays, and reader stands for correspondence secretaries. Both panels and work surfaces have the ability to accommodate wiring for office machines as well as lights and telephones. (See Figure 11-4.)

Office desks and workspace should allow sufficient space for comfortable working conditions. Secretaries need adequate space for word processing typing equipment, transcribing equipment, and source documents.

In situations where the maximum amount of working space is quite small, the desks may have to be smaller than average so that the space can handle all necessary personnel and their equipment. One Northern California hospital's medical transcription department was confronted with an extremely limited amount of space.

[2] Associate Editor of *Word Processing World*, March 1978 issue.

**The correspondence secretaries in this word processing center have specially   FIGURE 11-4
designed working environments. (Photo courtesy of Lexitron Corporation.)**

Although the transcriptionists, transcribers, and word processing production equipment occupy a small office, the space has been so utilized that they manage to accomplish their work very efficiently. Even more important, they all enjoy their work and maintain extremely high morale.

The secretary's chair affects both productivity and morale. One supervisor stated there was one chair in her department that secretaries particularly liked called the eight-hour chair. Manufactured by Microdyne, it is equipped with a five-legged stand and does not tip easily. An air pressure control level makes it easy to adjust. Although the back cannot be repositioned, it is padded and very comfortable.[3]

Special Features

Partitions and panels are used to offer the secretary privacy and dampen sound. Emma Villalobos, word processing supervisor at State National Bank in El Paso, Texas, states, "After we installed partitions, which separate the operators into clusters of three, we found that there was a lot more privacy and that it also cut down on the noise produced by our six mag card units and System 6 ink-jet printer."

Word processing screens create privacy and dampen sound, and those manufactured by Oxford Pendaflex accept hanging file components. Panels manufactured by Haworth take care of electrical wiring as well. Each panel can handle a total of four outlets, located in power blocks at both ends; a single connection from the paneling to

[3] Twyla Elliott, supervisor of word processing and central files at A. M. Scott and Sons, Marysville, Ohio. From "New Designs Give Work Stations Greater Flexibility," by W. A. Walshe, *Word Processing World*, March 1978.

the permanent wiring can supply five average task stations. This allows the firm to design the office for the people and not according to where power outlets are located and offers the opportunity to create an ideal organizational environment tailored to individual task areas with smooth-flowing traffic and communications patterns and sound control.

Facit Addo features a sound-absorbing word processing desk which has a recessed area for the text editor with a perforated steel sheet underneath that sends the sound from the machine down to the carpet for absorption. By comparison, a traditional desk sends the sound up to the ceiling where it bounces back through the room.

Equipment Designed for the System

Office furniture manufacturers are designing equipment to complement the working environment. Work surfaces are directly linked to the working patterns, and clustered storage and work files are located close-by, allowing the correspondence secretaries to work efficiently.

EVALUATING WORKING NEEDS

In order to plan the working space for word processing production, it is important to consider daily needs as well as whatever is required to make it easy to accomplish the work. The following questions need to be asked:

- How large should the desk space be?
- Should the desks be left- or right-handed?
- Where should supplies be kept?
- What space pattern would best serve the secretaries from the standpoint of efficiency and enjoyment of their work?
- What arrangement works best for the supervisor to maintain open communication with the staff?
- What arrangement serves the communication purposes of the secretaries and the principals?

To answer these questions, it is important to have already made such decisions as: Do you want the principals to feel free to enter the word processing center to discuss with the secretaries the status of their work? Do you want the secretaries to feel free to discuss their work with each other? Do you want the secretaries to get up from their chairs when beginning new jobs for a break from the routine? (This last decision would influence where supplies would be kept—right next to the secretary or at a central location in the office which would require their having to get up and pick up supplies frequently.)

At the IBM San Jose plant, tall square columns with open shelves to store supplies were installed. These units rotated so that a secretary could reach over and spin the column to the appropriate shelf to select whatever supplies (ribbons, print wheels, paper) were required to do the job. Not only was this very convenient, but it saved operator time and increased productivity.

SCHEDULING PERSONNEL

The number of employees in each position and job alignment is decided when planning the proposed new system. Each job description is written, listing the skills required for that position. Many organizations evaluate present personnel capabilities against skill requirements to see whether many present employees fit into the new jobs. Some large firms maintain personnel capability listings in computer storage so that they can obtain printouts of personnel capabilities for career growth and appropriate placement. Many firms advertise job openings within the organization, listing the job title and required skills. This offers employees an opportunity to apply for the jobs they prefer.

Internal employees who apply qualify for jobs by possessing excellent language art, typing and transcription skills, and cooperative attitudes. Those who most fit the designed positions are then selected. Word processing equipment training is provided by either the vendor or internal staff, depending upon each word processing system's training arrangements.

In a manufacturing plant, a word processing work group was incorporated into the Engineering Department where four typists typed original and revised versions to produce all engineering documents and correspondence. The printer and editors in the Publications Department processed the final version for duplication. Formerly they had also performed administrative duties such as handling telephones, filing, making copies, assembling documents, doing research, and arranging for travel and meetings. These duties were now being handled by two administrative secretaries. Before implementation of this new system, the personnel needed to be scheduled for training.

The equipment was to be installed in three months. It consisted of both a central dictation system along with portable dictation units and a shared-logic typing system where each of the four engineering typists created daily correspondence and long documents and stored, revised, and prepared them for final printing in the Publications Department. Considerable learning was involved, not only for the typists, but also for the engineers, the administrative secretaries, and personnel working in the Engineering Department. The questions to be decided were:

- When should the training take place?
- How much should take place at one time?
- Should all personnel be trained together?
- Or should training be conducted on a contingent basis?

Engineers, secretaries, and typists attended training sessions covering dictation and transcription practice; they also worked with the new procedures scheduled over a three-week period. The typists were trained during the week equipment was installed so that they could immediately begin to type their documents on the new shared-logic typing system.

Personnel already employed attended scheduled training sessions. Many times, however, scheduling involves hiring as well as training supervisors, coordinators, technical analysts, editors, authors, and department managers in addition to word processing production secretaries and typists. The word processing manager posts job openings throughout the company and requests the Personnel Department to advertise these openings. Recruitment must be completed and personnel hired before training can be scheduled.

Frequently firms hire supervisors, managers, and experienced operators by advertising in the newspapers or through personnel agencies, schools, and training institutions. If they are able to hire experienced word processing secretaries, less in-house training is required. They still must train new personnel to use their operating procedures, produce specific applications, and use the firm's method of formatting. Therefore, personnel scheduling requires careful forethought and planning.

SCHEDULING EQUIPMENT FOR ORDERING AND DELIVERY

Selected equipment is scheduled so that delivery is coordinated with the time the system's operations will be implemented—either for beginning operations or operational training. If the dictation and word processing typing equipment are to be used for training prior to the actual beginning of operations, the arrival of the equipment should be scheduled to coordinate with the training. All peripheral equipment must also be on hand at that time, including desks, chairs, tables, files, and such supplies as paper, typing ribbons, and media.

Equipment which is scheduled for arrival prior to training or beginning operations includes:

- word processing typing equipment
- dictation equipment
- copying/duplicating and related equipment (see Figures 11–5 and 11–6)
- telephone equipment
- carpeting
- electrical installation, wiring, and cables
- lighting
- sound-proofing and wall dividers
- shelves, storage cabinets
- supplies (paper, media, ribbons)

One way to develop the equipment installation schedule is by working backwards from the planned orientation date. Once that date has been set, the time required for each aspect of physical planning is scheduled to assure that the first steps have been completed so the next step can begin.

The GBC collator can be set next to an offset press, duplicator, or copy machine   FIGURE 11-5
to automatically process rapid collating jobs. The 20-bin collator features
automatic speed control that lets the operator set the pace and assures one-at-
a-time paper feeding, resettable counters, and electronic fail-safe operations.
(Photo courtesy of Ring King Visibles, Inc.)

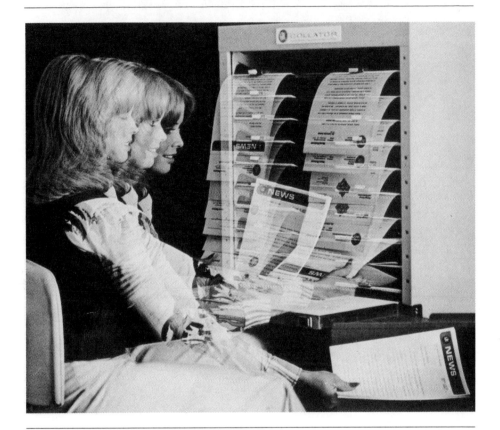

ORDERING SUPPLIES

Secretarial work stations need to be equipped with all necessary word processing
supplies: paper, ribbons, storage media, labels, envelopes, cards, forms, and files.

Suggested Supplies

The following list itemizes categories of essential supplies:

- Typewriter/printer supplies: ribbons, print wheels, correcting tape for word processors which use it (See Figure 11–7).

FIGURE 11-6   The Secretary II-alpha plain paper copier from 3M Company can produce eight copies per minute and is designed for offices turning out 1000 to 5000 copies per month. (Photo courtesy of Minnesota Mining and Manufacturing Company.)

- Printout supplies: fanfold continuous paper, letterhead, preprinted forms, envelopes, and labels.
- Storage media: ample number of storage media to store all of the prerecorded information from which documents will be printed, including form letters and stored paragraphs or original documents used as first versions to produce periodic reports (such as sales forecasts, budgets, financial forecasts, and monthly sales reports). (See Figure 11–8.)
- Secretarial references: dictionaries; word-division guides; operating procedures; technical references, such as legal document formats, government guidelines, and requirements for formatting.
- Principals' references: technical word lists with definitions, spellings, and word

---

Word processing media, including magnetic cards, standard and minicassettes, floppy disks, flexydisks, and hard disks. (Photo courtesy of BASF Systems.)   FIGURE 11-7

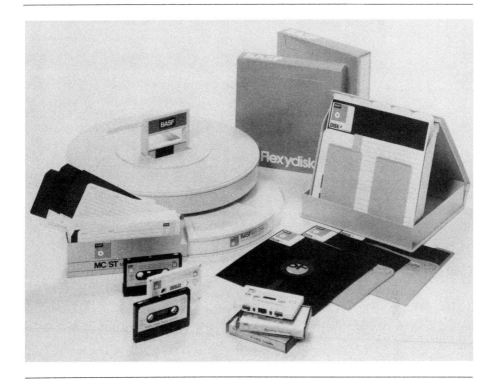

---

division for each department using word processing; address lists for principals; lists of users with their correct titles.

- Files: a filing system which states procedures. (Many firms do not maintain any file copies other than the original version of a document until they know it is completed. They may maintain three-ring binders of stored documents which will be periodically purged.)

COMMUNICATIONS

Before implementing the new system, effective communication should take place in all forms—active, written, and spoken. Any written communication should be carefully scrutinized before publication. All active communications should be positive, inspiring company personnel to be optimistic and enthusiastic about any changes about to take place in *their* organization. Word processing should inspire teamwork, a spirit of *our* company, and pride in the quality of all written products—letters, memos, reports, proposals, manuals, and all internal and external documents.

FIGURE 11-8   A convenient method of storing floppy disks is a container as pictured in this photograph. An operator can store and retrieve diskettes quickly and locate the desired diskette through the clearly visible storage slots. (Photo courtesy of Ring King Visibles, Inc.)

Equally important is the way in which word processing personnel act, particularly the manager and supervisor of word processing. Their way of conducting their daily business is a very effective communications tool.

Written Communications

The word processing manager should distribute memos periodically throughout the organization announcing current status, plans, and the schedule of upcoming events. Top management first distributed the memo announcing their interest in word processing. Management next announced their selection of word processing management—the manager, supervisor, or coordinator. Next the word processing manager circulated written communications, usually with the approval and support of management. Such information might have included the kind of equipment the company has selected, when it will be installed, job openings, schedules for training seminars, or other written announcements which serve the purpose of keeping employees informed of what is happening.

The bank's task force distributed a memo once a week during preimplementation reporting any news they felt would be of interest to employees. They called it "Middletown Bank's Word Processing Bulletin" and used it to publish information regarding job openings, positions filled, names of new hires, equipment that would be coming and when it would be installed, and an open house to be held after implementation.

They began to write their two procedure manuals, one for principals and one for the operating staff. Special forms were designed and printed to use for word processing.

Spoken Communications

Ron and the other members of the task force made it a point to visit with employees occasionally without disturbing their work. Their purpose was to get a feel for the general attitude and acceptance of the impending change and allay any fears they could. They themselves met briefly every morning to discuss new events one might have encountered or simply to plan the activities for the day. They were careful to make sure that they reflected great enthusiasm and a cooperative interest in other employees' questions and fears.

Active Communications

The bank's task force knew that the way they handled themselves with other personnel in the bank was equally important. During this period, they planned exactly how they would proceed each day while preparing for implementation. They were careful not to interrupt other people's work but held their meetings as openly as possible so that those whose curiosity was aroused by the activities would not feel left out. The task force made it their objective to make all bank personnel feel instrumental in implementing the new system.

Avoiding a Word Processing Expectation Gap

An expectation gap may develop between the potential contributions of word processing functions and their actual performance as seen by general management. This expectation gap is characterized by differing interpretations of the following factors:

- top management performance goals and objectives
- functional staff performance capabilities and expectations
- organizational resources provided
- organization performance expectations
- environmental constraints
- controllable elements of the job process
- actual performance attained

Conditions that can lead to misunderstandings and expectation gaps and that should be avoided include:

- Failure of general management to establish performance standards and control procedures.

- Leaving functional operations to internal technical specialists and vendors who operate without planning guidance and focus attention on equipment, introducing sophistication and detail far beyond the need of most users.
- The word processing project director, enamored of hardware, procedures, and efficiency, losing sight of user requirements and dictating to users what they can and cannot have.

Management needs to make sure that the word processing function contributes to improved organizational performance and is properly utilized to maximize benefits. Bridging the expectation gap requires a shared responsibility for the proper utilization of word processing resources. The word processing project director must be a true manager, not just a technician. His or her role must be directed at solving organizational problems, not word processing problems. Available word processing capability needs to be communicated to and understood by the entire organization.

To achieve realistic and common expectations, all affected members of an organization must participate in the development of action plans that support overall organizational goals and objectives.

WORD PROCESSING PLANNING PROCESS

The following planning process outlines key steps and factors to be considered to establish or revitalize a word processing function.

1. Define the word processing functional mission in support of the company mission.
2. Establish clear and specific objectives for the following key areas necessary to achieve the functional mission:
   - marketing strategy
   - innovation process
   - human organization
   - financial resources
   - physical resources
   - productivity
   - social responsibility
   - profit (cost) requirements
3. Establish priorities of (resource) concentration in each key area.
4. Define expected standards of performance in terms of minimum and maximum mission attainment.
5. Obtain top management approval and authorization to continue.
6. Schedule activity deadlines.
7. Make someone accountable for results.
8. Define what satisfies the customer.
9. Obtain information on additional resource requirements, costs, delivery, etc.
10. Obtain top management approval and authorization to continue.

11. Obtain additional resources and install with proper orientation, training, and development activities.
12. Develop methods to sample customer satisfaction and feedback results to key areas in the organization.
13. Implement an organized method to periodically audit and evaluate objectives, performance standards, actual results, and required activity adjustments.
14. Go to work on the plan.
15. Review actual performance versus expected performance.
16. Obtain top management approval and authorization to continue.

When properly used, the word processing planning process will assure that results attained equal the expectations of all people involved. Figure 11–9 outlines the conception and resulting benefits of the word processing mission.

SUMMARY

After management has granted the go-ahead to implement the new word processing system, preparations begin. Steps covered during preparations are to:

- Forecast upcoming events which will affect the system.
- Set objectives in clearcut statements of exactly what the system will do.
- Determine the policies to be followed during all possible events, particularly crises.
- Establish timelines and schedules to be followed.
- Delegate accountability to appropriate personnel who are given responsibilities for projects and communicate the accountable person's responsibility to others.
- Determine availability of funds for the budget.
- Plan the budget according to resources available to fit system requirements.
- Write operating procedures for the users and for the operating staff.
- Elicit support for the system from all sides—management, middle management, supervisors of departments and services, and employees.
- Schedule the first review of system status for feedback and adjustments.
- Determine how evaluation will be made—the standards to be met, expectations, objectives, and schedule.
- Determine how result evaluation will be communicated to management and other members of the organization.

Budgeting is a management tool used both for planning and controlling the operation according to preset standards for continuous monitoring, reviewing, and evaluating. Word processing budgets include all facilities, equipment, supplies, personnel, and peripherals and are usually made for the year.

Planning the facility for word processing originally includes everything from the location of area, carpeting, lighting, electricity, air conditioning, soundproofing, and furnishings. Many office equipment manufacturers feature desks and other office furniture specially designed for word processing containing electricity outlets. Open

---

FIGURE 11-9   Word Processing Principles

I. Conception
    A. Objectives
        1. Maintain high quality in communications
        2. Provide for controlled growth
        3. Maximum utilization of space
        4. Eliminate backlogs
        5. Cost control
    B. Structure of Word Processing System
        1. Equipment (Input [dictation equipment] and output [magnetic keyboard] equipment installed that is designed to function together to handle much more work than was possible before)
        2. Procedures and Controls (procedures: the system or method by which paperwork flows through the bank; controls: a formalized method for determining the volume of work)
        3. Personnel (hiring personnel with the qualifications needed to insure efficiency and a high productivity rate)
II. Benefits
    A. Production Control
        1. Controlled expansion
        2. Workload planning
    B. Written Procedures
        1. Eliminates confusion
        2. Assists in training new operators
    C. Improved Turnaround Time
    D. Consistent Quality of Typewritten Materials
    E. Effective Use of Space
    F. Cost Control
    G. Higher Rate of Production
    H. Equal Distribution of Work
        1. Each operator is knowledgeable in a variety of work.

---

landscaping is used by many firms to improve employee work distribution and to promote teamwork and even workflow.

To plan facilities and furnishings, the planner asks such questions as: How much space is available? How much is required? What best utilizes the space for efficient work performance? What creates the most pleasant working conditions? What will result in the most efficient and productive working situations? What can be updated and changed to meet future requirements?

After preparing the budget, the analyst schedules all the word processing system components so that each event occurs at the appropriate time for smooth implementation. Most organizations phase in by department and work cateogry. The analyst/

manager schedules all necessary equipment so that the system is ready for use when required. This relates to all aspects involved—office equipment, supplies, telephone equipment, physical layout, construction, and preparation, and available storage and supplies.

Providing secretarial services to service users who previously had their own secretaries requires careful planning and coordination. Once the user loses a secretary, that user will rely upon word processing services to provide the necessary services. This means that the correspondence secretaries must be fully trained, equipment working, and the system prepared to accomplish the work, all of which requires hiring, selecting, training, and preparing personnel to perform at the appropriate time.

The users also need to be trained to use the new system procedures, dictation equipment, and any other means of origination when their applications are phased in. The manager schedules orientation training for each person so that he or she can return to the office and begin using word processing immediately.

Word processing should use a checklist that itemizes all supplies which will be needed by word processing. This provides a means of assuring that enough supplies are always available so that all work can be handled smoothly and efficiently. It also prevents expensive overordering.

During the planning and preparation periods, daily communications take place in written, spoken, and active form for the purpose of publicizing the upcoming implementation of word processing. Memos are distributed that keep employees informed of the people selected for certain jobs, new equipment ordered, or new services being offered to users. In addition, the word processing staff also communicates verbally with others in an effort to diminish negative reactions and encourage enthusiasm and interest. Meetings may be held by the word processing manager and supervisors, coordinators, and other staff.

Sometimes an expectation gap develops between the potential contributions of word processing and their performance as seen by management. Avoidance of this gap may be achieved by shared responsibility for word processing utilization by management and the word processing manager. By involving management in the planning process, the word processing manager can be well on the way to achieving the results management expects of word processing. One technique is to have a management statement of the word processing mission within the organization. This might be outlined under two major topics, Conception and Benefits, listing the objectives, structure, and personnel attributes under conception and statements of benefits which are to be gained from the word processing system.

REVIEW QUESTIONS

1. Why should employees be involved in setting objectives? How can this occur?
2. What factors are important when setting timelines?
3. What factors should be considered in scheduling work for word processing?
4. Why is it important to delegate accountability?
5. What funds must be budgeted to cover what word processing costs?
6. What purposes do written procedures serve?
7. How can the support of employees be solicited?

8. Explain the difference between status review and result evaluation. What is covered in each?
9. In budgeting equipment, which are one-time costs and which are continuing costs?
10. What factors should be considered when ordering office furniture for Word Processing?
11. What kinds of supplies need to be ordered for word processing?
12. What personnel scheduling needs to take place?

QUESTIONS FOR DISCUSSION

1. Discuss why forecasting should be included in planning implementation.
2. Discuss reasons users should be involved in setting policies.
3. Discuss the bank's implementation procedures. Do you agree with their phasing-in procedures? Why?
4. Discuss the reasons why you might wish to lease equipment rather than rent; purchase rather than lease.
5. Discuss the different kinds of working arrangements you might have for word processing and which you would prefer as an employee.
6. Discuss three communicating methods the bank's task force used during planning. Do you think they were wise to ask opinions? What kinds of problems might this cause? How would you handle them?
7. Discuss the arrangement in word processing for supplies. Do you think it is best to have all supplies located near the secretaries? Why do you feel that way?

CASES

Case 11-1   Technology Firm

Applied Materials, a medium size, high-technology company, is preparing to implement a word processing system which will consist of five correspondence secretaries using standalone visual screen word processing typewriters, a central dictation system with endless-loop recorders, a Centrex phone system, and a 9400 duplication system. They will need to train all the dictators, who presently use longhand for most of their documents, which are predominantly reports, proposals, specifications, and daily correspondence.

They plan to have three work groups of administrative secretaries who will be supervised by an administrative supervisor, while the correspondence secretaries will be located centrally and supervised by a correspondence supervisor. Both supervisors will report to a word processing manager who is responsible for document duplication and distribution as well as production.

In addition, they plan eventually to cross-train all secretaries in both administrative and correspondence jobs and add a night shift of correspondence secretaries with a head operator in order to meet the heavy volume of document production requirements. They will be using floppy disks, carbon ribbons, and fanfold continuous paper in addition to special bond for the printed documents which will be duplicated on the 9400 which will have a special operator.

Plan their implementation schedule.

Case 11-2   Investment/Real Estate Company

Belmont White is an investment and real estate company which currently has no word processing equipment. They formerly had a mag card II, but returned it when the lease ran out. They are preparing to acquire two word processing terminals which share one printer, along with individual desktop and portable dictation units for the marketing representatives and office staff. In addition, they plan to implement a duplicating system, which will be used by the word processing staff. The office staff will consist of the two correspondence secretaries on the terminals, a supervisor, a clerk/duplication specialist, and two administrative secretaries. Plan their implementation schedule so that they will have the best working conditions in order to meet rapid turnaround requirements of top quality documents.

*"The success and ultimately the survival of every
business . . . depends in the last analysis on its
ability to develop people."*

CHAPTER 12

Planning Word Processing Jobs

OVERVIEW

The key to success of a system is the *human* operation. Therefore, when it is time to
plan who will run the system, in what order and structure, task assignment and
responsibilities, the manager needs to plan well. This chapter encompasses all of the
aspects involved in planning word processing jobs to create a successful system.

OBJECTIVES

After completing this chapter you will be able to:

1. State what responsibilities are delegated by the word processing manager to the
   supervisor.
2. Write a word processing manager's job description.
3. List those attitudes and skills required of word processing personnel (administrative and correspondence).
4. Explain the steps involved in professional personnel selection.
5. List qualifications for a word processing specialist.
6. Explain the importance of each step involved in screening.
7. Explain ways to discover the true capabilities of a job applicant.
8. Describe personal qualities important to word processing personnel.

Quote from Peter F. Drucker *The Effective Executive* (New York: Harper & Row, 1966), p. 99.

9. Describe what should be learned about an applicant in an interview.
10. Explain what determines the contents of a word processing job description.
11. Describe the job of a word processing supervisor.
12. Describe interviewing procedures for a word processing secretary.
13. Plan and conduct an interview.

THE ROLE OF THE MANAGER AND SUPERVISOR

A word processing manager's function is to control the overall word processing operation from initial planning stages through designing and developing, organizing, coordinating, implementing, directing, and evaluating the program to meet growth and changing circumstances. This individual has been the overall responsibility, accountability, and authority for word processing operations.

A word processing supervisor is involved in the daily supervision of word processing operations and in scheduling work and taking necessary action to handle nonroutine situations. The responsibility of the word processing supervisor is to accomplish the word processing objective, which is generally the production of documents, through word processing personnel, equipment, and procedures.

Specific functions of the word processing manager and supervisor may vary according to the nature of the firm, its size and characteristics, and the kinds of documents it produces. An organization will develop those word processing jobs which best fit its organizational needs. It may have such jobs as coordinator, lead secretary, senior secretary, specialist, systems analyst, proofreader, page, and administrative and correspondence secretaries. The variety and types of positions depend upon the size, nature, and structure of the organization. Some supervisors in small firms may be working supervisors, who perform some of the same tasks as those whom they supervise.

Each firm's manager and supervisor will have definite roles within the organization which affect the tasks they perform, their level of authority, responsibility, and accountability. Roles of word processing managers and supervisors can be compared with that of a contractor who is hired to construct a house. The contractor is delegated by you (top management) to manage the project of construction (word processing implementation and operation). In order to build the house, the contractor will hire a supervisor to direct construction activities performed by the builders. The sequence of events taking place is:

1. You (top management) delegated *authority* to the contractor (manager) for the project (management of word processing).
2. The contractor (manager) is *responsible* for building the house.
3. The contractor (manager) is *accountable* for the complete project, including all of the construction operations which take place.
4. When the contractor (manager) hires a supervisor of the daily construction, the authority, responsibility, and accountability are passed on to the supervisor of the project for which that contractor (manager) is accountable to you (top management).

POSITION OF THE MANAGER IN THE ORGANIZATION

The word processing manager may be depicted on the organization chart in relation to four separate entities: top management; other services such as mail distribution, telephone and communications, reproduction, records processing, and phototype-setting; users; and the operating staff who report to the manager (or the supervising staff which is the link between employees and manager). As a result, the effectiveness of the manager is viewed from the four viewpoints of administrative management, parallel management, users, and subordinates, as illustrated in Table 12-1.

How does one measure the successful or effective manager? Simply expressed, it is done through "the ability to get the right things done."[1] That is what the manager was hired to do, just as you hired the contractor to build your house.

The word processing manager has perhaps the most unique position in the organization. The word processing manager accomplishes word processing objectives for the organization through top management, peer groups, users, and word processing staff. Therefore, the word processing manager needs to motivate these four levels within the organization in order to achieve the word processing objectives. The word processing manager could assume three different roles.

The Key Person

Top management views the manager as the key person managing the word processing operations. He or she represents management to the word processing employees and the word processing employees to management. The role can be likened to the hub of a wheel; just as the spokes rotate about the hub of a wheel, so does everything revolve around the manager. Even though this is the acclaimed ideal, research surveys have shown that in most business situations, the manager is seldom the key person.

Person in the Middle

Although far from ideal, this position often occurs in real situations just as the title indicates, as the supervisor in the middle, pressed between the opposing social forces

TABLE 12-1   Manager Effectiveness From Four Points of View

Viewer	Viewpoint
Top management	Person responsible for accomplishing word processing objectives
Parallel management	Person responsible for word processing services as well as coordination
Users	Person responsible for getting their paperwork produced in a timely manner
Subordinates	Person responsible for their job satisfaction

[1] Peter F. Drucker, *The Effective Executive* (New York: Harper & Row, 1966), p. 1.

of management and workers. Management's expectations are largely technical or production-centered: reduce waste, control production, accomplish the job, hire the staff, discipline the employees. The employee's demands are basically matters of feeling: keep oneself out of trouble, present the employee's own desires to management, and be loyal to management or the firm. In this case, the manager is no longer managing the situation but is the victim of it, feeling frustrated, insecure, and unimportant.

Marginal Person

This concept is basically sociological, referring to the fact that the manager is left out of organizational and departmental activities. This individual is not accepted as a member of management, is ignored by staff personnel, and yet is not one of the workers. There is no peer-level support organization, no labor union, board of directors, professional affiliations. He or she tries to act like a manager but does not receive the rewards: decisions are made by management or staff. This role frequently occurs on night shifts, whereas management activities are performed by the daytime staff.

The word processing manager needs the support and continual backing of top management in order to be a key link between word processing and management. Usually this requires confidence and a certain amount of aggressiveness on the part of the word processing manager who should be actively selling the mission of word processing within the organization.

THE SUPERVISION PROCESS

Supervising the word processing operations is predominantly a people-oriented task. The supervisor communicates daily with the word processing staff and the people whom they serve, making sure that all users' needs are being processed according to the procedures currently in use. The supervisor is the personal representative of word processing daily operations upon whom the principals rely to accomplish their work. Where formerly these principals had secretaries sitting outside their offices who typed, copied, filed, and frequently delivered documents, they now rely upon word processing to perform these tasks. The supervisor is responsible for making sure that their specific document requirements are met at the time necessary.

Specifically, the supervisor's responsibilities are:

1. Daily supervision of the word processing operations (by one or two supervisors).
2. Record keeping (setting standards and objectives, tracking their achievement, and recording this information).
3. Work assignment (scheduling of input-work to be produced from machine dictation, longhand, edited copy, or other kinds of input—in order to meet project and daily deadlines).
4. Work distribution (taking the input or work and routing it to appropriate or available personnel and work stations). Some equipment may be used for

specific applications. Work can be routed to departments and individuals by inserting it in mail slots, tub files, or carts on rollers. Principals can also pick up their work personally from the mail slots or tub files that contain Pendaflex files which might be labeled by names of specialists; priority date; department; or typing application, such as statistical documents, forms, form letters, revisions, or daily correspondence.

5. Personnel operations (directing and maintaining a cooperative working atmosphere among the staff, making sure that workloads are shared during peak periods, adjusting to capabilities and daily situations, being aware of personnel climate, attitudes, daily situations, and requirements).

6. Equipment operations (tracking and evaluating equipment utilization, downtime, and whether the present equipment is meeting the work needs; tracking equipment downtime or operator equipment use problems for troubleshooting, and determining appropriate solutions to any problems relative to equipment use, reliability, and ease of meeting productivity requirements).

7. Training of word processing staff and users. Although the overall development, scheduling, and determination of the kinds of training programs, their schedules, and how they are to be administered is the responsibility of the manager, the training itself may be delegated to the supervisor and members of the staff. The more the staff becomes involved in user training and orientation of new personnel, the better the communication between users and working staff—a key to successful word processing operations.

8. Delegating daily requirements (distributing rush jobs, communicating with users regarding input problems, or ensuring that the specific needs of the users are being met). Because of the sophistication of current word processing production equipment, when an organization first acquires its equipment and begins operations, it will settle upon the simplest procedures to get the work done. As the staff members become more experienced with the equipment, they also become more skilled. Analysis of how to accomplish jobs easier, quicker, and better should become an ongoing project. The supervisor usually delegates this responsibility to a member of the staff, giving that person the added responsibility of documenting exactly how to accomplish the longer, more difficult jobs and then instructing other correspondence secretaries. This may be a career growth step among the working staff and at the same time may improve efficiency of the department and the organization, resulting in great time savings, ability to meet deadlines sooner, and use of less personnel time. In brief, it can be an important cost savings.

9. Communicating daily with users, staff, and management (reporting the current status of word processing operations, daily schedule, work status, new capabilities, and techniques which can save time and effort; communicating to the manager the status of current volume production and time distribution for evaluation to determine whether changes or adjustments need to be made).

10. Reporting and advising management of current work status and personnel achievement (tracking individuals' productivity, changes, improvements, and other elements influencing that person's job performance; tracking department's work status, such as volume produced, time required to produce documents,

number of revisions, turnaround time achieved, number of returns for changes of daily correspondence—which may indicate further training required of either principals or operators or both—and other factors relating to satisfying needs of users).

These specific responsibilities of the supervisor summarize the functions that occur in word processing operations. Some word processing managers may delegate some of these tasks to other personnel, such as a coordinator, operating specialist, lead secretary, or senior operator, depending upon the structure of the organization. The previously listed summary provides an overview of the functions that fall into the supervision category. Supervisors need to be well organized in order for the system to continually function properly.

The specific positions in a word processing system depend upon the way the work is to be accomplished. For instance, a large company that produces heavy volumes of lengthy documents requiring revisions in addition to other documents might have job classifications such as proofreader, receptionist, file/mail clerk, page, systems analyst, coordinator, lead secretary, and senior and junior secretaries for both correspondence and administrative operations. The larger the firm, the more apt it is to have more job classifications, particularly if it processes a wide variety of documents.

The need for professional supervision to successfully implement word processing is a lesson well learned by many firms who have had to replace personnel placed in those positions who were not properly prepared or capable of performing the job. Without competent supervision, even the best designed system may falter from inadequate output, high employee turnover, high operating expenses, and poor customer relations.

A word processing supervisor should have the necessary background, interest, and temperament for the task. Few professional secretaries or senior clerks have the capacity or interest necessary to become a supervisor. Good candidates include persons who are informal leaders of their work group or persons who demonstrate leadership traits.

First-line supervisors frequently have to play a number of organizational roles in order to be effective in their jobs. Managers will experience the pressure of being promoted up from the ranks of a peer group. A woman, in particular, is apt to experience even more pressures from her male peers, who generally will be critical of every step she takes.

It is important that supervisors are recognized for their skills as managers; they must plan, organize, lead, coordinate, communicate, and control those activities for which they are responsible. Figure 12–1 lists the major responsibilities of a word processing supervisor.

WORD PROCESSING JOB DESCRIPTIONS

Many organizations may not change the content of secretarial jobs to any large extent even though they implement the change of replacing regular typewriters with word

---

FIGURE 12-1   Responsibilities and Authority of the Managing Supervisor of Word Processing

---

1. Develop procedures for word processing operations.
2. Report to management periodically on word processing status.
3. Receive management direction on up-to-date objectives of the organization.
4. Interact with users with respect to:
    a. current productivity goals
    b. current achievements
    c. successes and failures
    d. changes in workloads
    e. deadline requirements and turnaround times
    f. changing procedures
    g. personnel changes
    h. improvements desired and weaknesses noted
    i. changes in equipment
    j. training schedules and additional training needed
    k. problems (failures to meet deadlines, inability to meet turnaround desired, insufficient instructions, inadequate input)
5. Select, direct, and promote word processing personnel.
6. Conduct internal orientation programs.
7. Communicate with organization and word processing group on status, impending changes, company objectives.

---

processing typewriters or shared-logic systems. In such cases, secretaries handle the same tasks as before and therefore may not need to have new job descriptions.

However, in the majority of offices that implement word processing, the job content *is* changed, which requires designing comprehensive job descriptions and new job categories and pay scales for either centralized or decentralized word processing. Offices which formerly determined the job and salary by whom one worked for now define jobs and salaries according to what tasks are performed.

The job description may be written after the office structure is designed and tasks are defined for each particular job. Job descriptions may be written for separate administrative and correspondence secretaries or for secretaries who perform *both* administrative and correspondence tasks, depending upon the firm's word processing structure. Specific job content is derived from the job analysis conducted during the feasibility study. This information is used to design each job description planned for the new system.

Before detailing job alignment and writing the job descriptions, a word processing manager would refer to the design that explained the recommended job alignment for the new system.

The position description format itself is generally taken from that used by the Personnel Department for the organization. For example, Eastern Airlines has three categories listed for the position description for the manager of Secretarial Services:

basic functions, responsibilities, and relationships. In addition, the position description lists the supervision responsibilities for that job. The manager's job is briefly described in the following paragraphs.

Basic Functions

The major functions to be performed or delegated by the word processing manager are given below. Either the manager or delegated personnel have been hired to accomplish these functions.

1. Provides resources for development, planning, operation, and control of secretarial functions, including word processing as well as administrative secretarial services.
2. Creates, designs, and installs new secretarial services centers.
3. Provides liaison with users and prospective users.
4. Develops and maintains a system-wide program to upgrade and unify secretarial practices and performance including cross-training of personnel.

Responsibilities

Specific activities for which the word processing manager is responsible and held accountable include:

1. Develops long-range plans for new and revised systems to meet the objectives of secretarial services functions.
2. Develops programs and procedures for secretarial services and other administrative areas.
3. Recruits, selects, and trains secretarial services personnel. Determines standards of performance for quality and quantity of output.
4. Develops and maintains cross-training program for all secretarial services positions. Develops cross-training schedules and monitors progress.
5. Ensures performance of assigned function. Develops, ensures proper implementation and maintenance of procedures for proper handling, completion of paperwork, and flow of information. Ensures that proper reports and controls on output are submitted to management.
6. Analyzes complex work situation and breaks it down into workable parts in the framework of a secretarial services organization.
7. Prepares and presents charts as required to System Administration Management.
8. Correlates complex data, determining format of reports, and makes recommendations upon which management consideration and decisions are based; e.g., workload statistics and personnel requirements.
9. Provides financial budgeting for the unit. Reviews and evaluates relationship of expense to projected budget figures and reports findings to next level of management. Performs payroll and salary administration for 50 to 100 personnel.

10.   Develops and trains personnel. Conducts periodic appraisals of system and personnel to ensure conformance with desired objectives.
11.   Determines needs and costs of equipment required to perform objectives.
12.   Provides orientation and makes presentations to new users of administrative secretarial services and word processing concepts. Assists groups serviced in carrying out their objectives.

Relationships (Internal and External)

Interaction of the word processing manager with other personnel both within and outside the organization includes the following functions:

1.   Confers with appropriate company officers and directors regarding the coordination, development, and implementation of new and improved secretarial services systems.
2.   Coordinates with all who use management personnel to carry out the service objectives of the unit.
3.   Through Purchasing, maintains relationships with vendors' representatives on latest office equipment. Participates in industry functions and meetings to keep abreast of latest developments in field.
4.   Maintains contacts with management personnel in other companies involved with secretarial services systems.
5.   Through participation in outside professional activities, maintains technical proficiency in secretarial services concept and equipment and recommends the introduction of these innovations to management.

Supervision

The word processing manager is the head supervisor of word processing personnel. Daily supervision is usually delegated and there may be other personnel, such as a supervisor or coordinator, to whom word processing personnel report directly on a daily basis, but the word processing manager remains the overall department manager.

1.   Delegates responsibilities
2.   Supervises the activities of personnel in the following positions:
  a.   Supervisor of Secretarial Services
  b.   Coordinator of Secretarial Services
  c.   Analyst for Systems and Procedures[2]

Writing Job Descriptions

Each word processing position should have a complete position description detailing exactly what the basic functions or tasks are for that position, the responsibilities to be handled, and internal and external relationships.

[2] These may be handled by the word processing analyst where the firm has established the specific job.

Points to include in a job description are: tasks, career development, reporting alignment, and job requirements (skills and education). Each organization will most likely develop its own job descriptions to fit its reporting structure. Examples of word processing job descriptions that some organizations currently use are illustrated in Figures 12–2 and 12–3. Job description content usually depends upon nature of the work performed, groups supported, applications undertaken, and the character of the

---

Word Processing Manager Position Description   FIGURE 12-2

Division/Department	Administration
Unit	MIS System
Reports to	Director, MIS System
Basic functions	Serves the company by

- Providing resources for development, planning, operation, and control of secretarial functions, including word processing as well as administrative secretarial services.
- Creating, designing, and installing new secretarial services centers throughout the company.
- Providing liaison with users and prospective users of secretarial services.
- Developing and maintaining a system-wide program to upgrade and unify secretarial practices and performance including cross-training of personnel.

Responsibilities   *Planning and policy*—Develops long-range plans for new and revised systems to meet the objectives of secretarial services functions.

Procedural—Develops programs and procedures for secretarial services and other administrative areas.

Other

- Recruits, selects, and trains secretarial services personnel. Determines standards of performance for quality and quantity of output.
- Develops and maintains cross-training program for all secretarial services positions. Develops cross-training schedules, monitors progress.
- Ensures performance of assigned function
- Develops and ensures proper implementation and maintenance of procedures for proper handling, completion of paperwork, and flow of information.

FIGURE 12-3   Position Description for Lead Specialist, Word Processing

---

Division/Department   Administration
Unit   MIS System
Reports to   Coordinator, Word Processing Services
Basic functions
- Leads subfunction of unit with specifically defined objectives in support of designated user group. Plans, establishes, and coordinates priorities within this unit.
- Serves the company by performing administrative or word processing secretarial duties requiring diligent exercise of judgment and initiative.
- In the absence of the Coordinator of Secretarial Services, provides management direction for word processing and administrative services.

Responsibilities
- In addition to performing all the duties of senior and subordinate secretaries, performs more complex work involving a high level of quality and service.
- Implements cross-training schedule.
- Assists Coordinator in delegated duties such as:
  - providing production control and quality control functions
  - instructing secretaries on specific equipment application or administrative procedures
  - servicing selected principals in administrative or word processing activities
  - performing other duties as assigned
- Maintains awareness of Coordinator's responsibilities and scope of operation and keeps her or him informed of production requirements and deficiencies. Also informs Coordinator of procedural changes within the unit. With Coordinator, develops work load schedules for unit.
- Prepares production reports for unit.

---

organization itself. Figure 12–4 is a list of qualifications required of Eastern Airlines coordinators.

SELECTING PERSONNEL AND STAFFING

Historically the process of **staffing** has included the following activities:

1. Procuring employees (recruiting, testing, interviewing, investigating, and evaluating.

Qualification of All Coordinators Selected for Eastern Airlines   FIGURE 12-4
Secretarial Services

- They have a positive attitude toward the concept.
- They believe in the concept. Cannot supervise if they don't believe in it.
- They are able to bring forth ideas and suggestions to improve the overall company and department goals. They are not confined to, "That's the way it has always been, so why change it."
- They are able to get along well with management and nonmanagement and are not reluctant to ask questions which will improve the overall operation and then put them into effect.
- They are able to take constructive criticism and to improve the problem, not dwell on it.
- They can accept disappointments from time to time and don't take them personally. They do not tell others that, "It is unfair. . . ," nor do they involve the rest of the staff.
- They keep confidential matters confidential, as in any management position.
- They are organizers and motivators.
- They are able to plan and implement.
- They are flexible and open-minded. In addition to having the basic skills of secretaries and expertise in an area, coordinators in Secretarial Services are progressive and look for overall improvement of workflow and procedures for the company and the department. Instead of resisting change, they accept the challenge.

---

2. Training and developing employees (skills training, supervisory and executive development).
3. Compensating employees (job description and evaluation, incentive plans).
4. Appraising performance and promoting.
5. Controlling some conditions of work (safety and health hazards).
6. Communicating with employees (newsletters, announcements, suggestion plans, opinion polls).

In short, staffing encompassed activities handled by the Personnel Department. When Labor Relations and employee/management negotiations were also involved, the entire operation was then undertaken by the Industrial Relations Department, which is over the Personnel Department. In such cases, staffing was performed by Personnel Department representatives separate from the departments themselves.

In organizations using systems management procedures, the staffing process can take advantage of computerized personnel records systems and use of quantitative methods of personnel management. For example, by computerizing personnel records, all of an employee's past skills and experiences are stored. Should an opening come up for a position requiring some special skills an employee might possess, regardless of whether that employee was using them for the present job, the information would become available from computer records so that the employee with the special skills could be considered for the specialized job.

A Professional Staffing Program

Recent rising costs, office salaries, and fringe benefits have caused organizations to become more aware of the importance of developing permanent staffs with the appropriate skills for the present job, future jobs, and career development and avoiding attrition whenever possible. The purpose of a professional program is to avoid, through research, the costs of mistakes in hiring. Management is frequently surprised by the large number of employees who leave a job, which becomes very costly to a company. The firm also seeks to discover the factors that lead to stability or instability, or success or failure, in maintaining an efficient work force. Once these factors are known, recruitment efforts are emphasized to screen out (via diagnostic applications forms and tests or professional interviewing) the most unlikely candidates. Early elimination of poor personnel selection makes it possible to spend more time and do a better job on the better prospects in the latter part of the process. The selection process includes:

- recruiting
- screening
- weighted application form and testing
- interviewing
- investigating
- decision to hire or not hire

Recruiting

Recruitment involves:

1. Clearly defining the kinds of persons needed.
2. Selecting sources most likely to yield significant numbers of those types of persons.
3. Advertising and communicating by means of those channels and messages that are most likely to reach that audience.

Constructing a weighted application form requires conducting a correlation analysis to identify the factors (e.g., educational level and amount and type of job experience) that distinguish between successful and unsuccessful employees. The figures are then applied in a rough screening process to eliminate some of the less likely candidates while losing few, if any, of the likely candidates.

There are certain limitations imposed by the government regarding what may be asked a job applicant. Restrictions apply not only to questions regarding race, religion, and sex, but also to physical data, criminal record, and type of military discharge held.

Screening Word Processing Applicants

Most firms preparing to implement word processing need to conduct some personnel recruiting either from internal staff or outside the organization or both.

Those attitudes and skills to look for in screening applicants for jobs in word processing are listed in Table 12-2. They are divided into correspondence and administrative job requirements. However, in a case in which one person performs both kinds of tasks, all those attitudes and skills should be considered when selecting the appropriate candidates for the job.

The word processing manager or task force, along with the Personnel Department, needs to coordinate the job description guidelines to screen applicants. California's Bank of Marin uses the following job qualifications guidelines to select its word processing personnel.

1. Specific skill requirements (typing, transcribing, grammar, spelling, punctuation).
2. Personal characteristics (responsibility, initiative/willingness to learn new skills, diligence, enjoys machines or shows mechanical ability, positive attitude, shows flexibility and thinks progressively, good appearance, able to take criticism, works well with others, reacts quickly to learning situations).

Attrition is a very costly part of business operations, particularly in word processing. Therefore, word processing managers hope to hire employees who wish to stay and grow within the firm. Many firms seek trained applicants by advertising in newspapers; in word processing publications; and with colleges, high schools, and training schools. Once they hire a person, even if already trained and experienced, dead time will still be devoted to training that employee so that the new employee will

---

Word Processing Attitudes and Skills   **TABLE 12-2**

Correspondence		Administration	
Attitudes	*Skills*	*Attitudes*	*Skills*
Follows instructions well	Fast, accurate typist	Handles interruptions well	Good phone skills
Creative	Good powers of con-centration	Takes the initiative	Good people skills
Cooperative	Mechanical	Interest in total organiza-tion/concept	Good at setting priorities
Reflective	Good problem-solving logic	Works well with others	Well-organized
Plans ahead	Produces high-quality typed document	Enthusiastic	Good memory
Prefers to work uninterrupted	Good Business English skills: spelling, grammar, punc-tuation, business letters, vocabu-lary	Not easily frustrated or confused	Good dictator
Likes to type		Looks for ways in which to improve/help	Good proofreader
Methodical		Reliable/responsible	Good English skills
Works well under deadline pressures		Friendly attitude	
Completes project		Good appearance/neat	
Helps others	Good transcriptionist: fast, accurate, listens ahead		

learn all of the firm's particular procedures, formats, and ways of preparing documents. Therefore, careful screening prior to hiring is particularly important for people who work in word processing.

Previous Experience   An applicant who has had previous word processing experience may be more apt to be hired and move more rapidly up the career ladder. (Sometimes, however, previous experience can be a detriment, depending upon the applicant.) Previous office experience generally is valuable to an individual in shortening the break-in time. Some supervisors lean towards hiring people with heavier office experience background, while some find that new trainees just out of school tend to be more flexible. It is important to investigate the background of the applicant to determine just how the applicant has used his or her time prior to applying for the word processing job and how the applicant performed in previous jobs.

Personal Qualities   The personnel manager of Bank of Marin feels that the personal qualities are the final determining factor in selecting the right applicant for the job. Before making the final selection, the manager reviews the application form which the applicant has filled out in longhand and then evaluates the manner in which the applicant presents himself or herself during the interview.

Personal factors are important to anyone's success in all office jobs: those people who work well with others and communicate well make working relationships more comfortable, particularly in word processing, where the ability to share the work is extremely important. High-pressure deadline situations, or crunches are usually a weekly, if not daily, occurrence. Some office jobs may require a person who works best alone handling responsibilities on an independent basis. In word processing, where workers are involved in producing information which may be required on extremely short-range bases at infrequent intervals, working together is crucial. The person who, when not busy, looks around to see who needs help or what needs to be done, is the one who will not only enjoy working in the word processing environment but will succeed in this atmosphere and help the word processing mission achieve its objectives.

As noted in the Bank of Marin's list of personal characteristics, flexibility and enthusiasm, along with the ability to use machines, are important word processing attributes, which today's highly technical office environment requires of most workers. People who enjoy word processing work generally have the attitude of "I want to learn more and do more." Many have advanced from beginning correspondence secretaries to coordinators, supervisors, data entry specialists, systems analysts, trainers, proofreaders, editors, or managers.

Testing

Most tests conducted by a Personnel Department deal with typing production speed and grammatical accuracy (including correct word usage, spelling, and punctuation, as well as word division and format). It has been common practice to have applicants type on standard electric typewriters to test their typing speed and accuracy, frequently during 5- to 10-minute speed tests. More appropriate, of course, would be tests specially designed to test the applicant's net speed on word processing typewriters from creating the draft through final playout. This would be more indicative of the applicant's ability to produce documents on word processing typewriters. Applicants can be judged for accuracy and thoroughput speed.

Some firms have the applicant type a letter in which the applicant is requested to set up the entire letter in a block or modified block format, so that the applicant's ability to produce a mailable letter and the length of time it takes that applicant to produce the letter can be tested. Since this is generally one of the most important aspects of the job, including the ability of the applicant to **proofread** and turn out error-free documents, this type of test would provide better measurement criteria, particularly if the test is conducted on a word processor.

Some supervisors require high typing speeds (as high as 80 or 85 wpm), while others will take lower speeds (as low as 50 wpm) and emphasize the importance of that applicant's accuracy and language arts skills.

Testing Considerations   The applicant's ability to take the input from longhand, copy, machine dictation, and edited copy and turn out the document requested by the originator is a skill of utmost importance in word processing document production. A more accurate test of an applicant's abilities to accomplish this task skillfully and productively would be to have the applicant type from longhand, machine dictation, and perhaps even edited copy. Typing tests in which applicants type from copy are not a very realistic measurement for the job demands. An applicant using a word processing typewriter could be tested for (a) record and playout ability, (b) proofreading ability, and (c) ability to catch his or her own mistakes and correct them, either on playout or by revising during the creation of the typed document. These are fundamental skill requirements for a word processing correspondence secretary.

To measure the individual's command of the English language (grammar, punctuation, spelling, word division, and proofreading), a test could be administered having the applicant write (and then type) a brief memo to the word processing manager/supervisor describing why the applicant would like the job. This would provide an overview of the person's objectives while evaluating the individual's language arts skills and ability to communicate in writing.

Conducting the Tests   The tester needs to be well informed regarding the many kinds of tests (e.g., proficiency, aptitude, interest, intelligence, maturity/personality) as well as each test's job performance credibility. Testers need to be experts at administering tests and using them to determine their validity for a particular position. Many word processing educational training facilities conduct several kinds of tests for their students prior to and following their training for the trainees' information as well as for their future job seeking. Such word processing training is currently conducted in high schools, colleges, state and federally funded training schools, and private schools.

Interviewing

Before interviewing an applicant, the word processing manager should review the completed application form. If the applicant submitted a resume with no application, the applicant should fill out an application form prior to the interview. This allows the word processing manager to have the same format of information for each job applicant. More importantly, a resume allows the applicant to provide only that information the applicant wants known and omit information the applicant does *not* want known. For example, the applicant can leave out years during which he or she did not work for personal reasons.

Information that should be provided on the application include:

- The individual's full name, current address, and phone number (including message numbers if the applicant is hard to contact).
- Position applied for and salary requirements.
- Date available to begin work.
- Names and phone numbers of at least three references (those who know the individual's work characteristics and habits) and authorization for the firm to check those references.

If any of this information is missing, the interviewer should request it during the interview. After this information has been supplied, the interviewer can apply the following to complete the evaluation:

- Amount and type of job experience (including times when not working and what the applicant was doing during those periods).
- Salary history.
- Tenure on previous jobs.
- Special training received.
- Reasons for leaving previous jobs.
- Responsibilities and contributions to previous jobs.
- Education (last time applicant took courses or went to school, degrees, certificates, educational objectives).
- Skills, hobbies, interests, and favorite courses.

The results of any tests taken should be provided to the interviewer.

Prior to the Interview   Upon receiving the application (including tests and resume, if applicable), the interviewer should prepare for the interview by:

1. Listing any questions or circling blank spaces on the application where more information is needed and noting any other questions that should be included in the interview.
2. Setting the scene by arranging for a quiet place without the prospect of telephone interruptions and avoiding physical obstacles such as a large desk between the interviewer and the applicant. (Sitting with a small, round table near both people makes it possible to observe body language and arrange a same-level rather than authoritarian type of atmosphere.)
3. Developing the interview plan and writing it out until the interviewer is comfortable with it.

Interview Questions   The interview is the final key to selection of the appropriate person for an opening. One bank personnel manager makes his final selection based upon the communications skills and attitudes displayed by the applicant during the interview. One should plan exactly what one desires to learn about the application and how to best accomplish these objectives before proceeding with the interview. Using the following list of guidelines can be helpful during an interview:

1. Ask nondirective questions rather than ("yes" or "no" questions) to obtain a meaningful response and avoid giving a cue to the expected answer. Avoid such questions as, "Do you think you would mind retyping a letter for an engineer several times?" The applicant would guess that "no" is the correct answer. Instead ask, "How would you handle a situation when an engineer asks you to retype a three-page letter for the third time when you are in the middle of a rush project?" Use more *how* kinds of questions.

2. Find out what kind of work the applicant *likes to do* and finds most rewarding and least rewarding.

3. Do *not* ask discriminatory questions that are not job related, such as:
    *   How old are you?
    *   What country are you from?
    *   Do you have reliable child care arrangements?
    *   Are you happily married (or recently separated or divorced)?
    *   Do you have physical handicaps?

    You *may* ask questions to obtain information for evaluation such as:
    *   Are you a U.S. citizen or do you have a permanent visa?
    *   Are there restrictions on your activities which will have an effect on your job performance (lifting, carrying, sitting too long)?

Sample Interview

"How do you do. I am _____ . Please be seated.

"There are a few questions you may have missed on the application. Would you mind filling them in for me?" (Applicant writes in missing information where applicable.) "I see you worked at _____, for several years in _____. Please describe your job for me. How does it relate to our opening? What kinds of work did you do?"

(Ask other nondirective questions to get an impression of the applicant's likes, dislikes, goals, and expectations.)

"I am sure that _____ in Personnel explained that we are presently seeking someone in our Word Processing Department. Let me explain to you the kind of job it is and what we do." (Describe the job, number of people involved, tasks involved, requirements.) "What questions do you have about the job (or do you have any questions)?" (Pause.)

"Tell me something about yourself, what kind of work you like to do and feel you do best." (This provides a description from the applicant as to that individual's capabilities and reasons for changing companies.)

"Many of our employees have been with us since we first began in 19__, and today our firm employs 1,200 people in all operations. Since _____ in

Personnel already explained to you our employee activities and benefits, I won't go into them unless you have some particular questions. Do you have any questions in this regard?" (Pause.)

"We offer opportunities for our employees to both learn internally and take time off to take courses at the community college, since we like to see our employees grow and advance in their careers with us. Do you have any questions you would like answered concerning these aspects?" (Pause.)

(Conclusion.) "Thank you very much, _____, for coming in. We will be making our decision within the next few days and will let you know at that time what we decided."

More mistakes are made during interviewing than any other step of the staffing process. In many cases, interviewers have never been trained in sound interviewing methods, which consist of determining what an applicant *can do* (innate talents plus acquired capabilities and experience) and what an applicant *will do* (prediction of actual performance in view of basic habit patterns, personality, and maturity/immaturity).

A systematic approach to these subjects requires an organized method of reviewing the applicant's personal, social, and work history; it involves knowing how to put together the information received in order to bring out the applicant's basic behavior patterns. Further, an adept interviewer knows how to avoid the common errors, such as talking too much or revealing the interviewer's values. The interviewer should realize the importance of obtaining a full and accurate record of the applicant's history so that that information can be used effectively in the investigation process.

Investigation

Investigation is frequently the most penetrating step in the selection process and involves direct contact with the applicant's former supervisors by telephone. A great deal can be learned from conversations with an applicant's former supervisors by telephone, while written inquiries and letters of recommendation are virtually worthless. In order to get the most out of the telephone conversations, the interviewer (or employment specialist) needs to know what exactly he or she is seeking to confirm, how to use the data gathered in order to make the investigation most productive, how to best approach the contact, and how to use the information gained from the contact in order to strengthen the final evaluation of what the applicant can and will do if hired.

After the list of candidates for a position has been narrowed to two or three, references of these final candidates are investigated. Personal telephone contact provides a reliable investigation. It is best to talk with supervisors or instructors who know the candidate well. Before phoning, the investigator should plan the reference check process carefully by making a checklist of questions to ask. The reference investigation for each applicant would include the same questions. The investigation provides a check with those for whom that individual worked or under whom that person studied to validate information on the applications as well as to obtain an impression of the applicant's previous job or school performance.

Evaluating and Selecting Personnel

Sometimes it is very difficult to select one person from several excellent candidates for a position. To solve such a dilemma, the investigator should review all of the written material on the candidate—the application, resume, interview form, tests, reference checklist, and notes taken during reference checks. In addition, the person selecting should consider the applicant's interview responses, personality, and how that applicant would fit into the working environment. Sometimes a second interview solves this selection dilemma. Some investigators obtain the opinions of others, such as the Personnel Department representative who interviewed the candidate, the office receptionist or other personnel who met the candidate, or coworkers or managers. If still undecided, the investigator might make a checklist of desired qualities, list the candidates, and match their qualities against the checklist. This should result in making one final selection.

The Job Offer   Once the candidate has been selected, either the word processing manager or the Personnel Department usually makes the offer. The job offer includes stating these exact terms: job title, salary, starting date, reporting relationships, benefits eligibility, starting requirements (such as a physical examination), starting procedures, when job reviews are due, and any other relevant information. This eliminates the possibilities of any misunderstandings at a later date.

Notifying Unselected Candidates   It is common courtesy to notify applicants for a position if they have not been selected. Some firms send out rejection letters for high-level positions only, such as supervisors and management. Some do not send any at all. Generally, the Personnel Department sends out these rejection letters. However, when the word processing manager must reject someone who might be hired at a later date, the manager then should contact that individual personally, either by telephone or letter. When informing an individual that the job was offered to someone else, one should convey positive feelings by a statement such as, "We selected someone whose qualifications fit the current job's requirements more exactly."

SUMMARY

A word processing manager's functions are to control the overall word processing operation from initial planning stages, through designing and developing, organizing, coordinating, implementing, and monitoring for future growth and technological change. This person is given the overall responsibility, accountability, and authority for these operations.

A word processing supervisor, on the other hand, is involved daily in making the word processing operation work and, when it does not, doing something about it. Responsibilities of the word processing supervisor include accomplishing the word processing objectives—generally production of daily documents—through personnel, equipment, and procedures.

Specific functions of the word processing manager and word processing supervisor may vary according to which ones might be delegated to other word processing personnel, such as a coordinator, lead secretary, senior secretary, specialist, systems analyst, or proofreader. Based upon understanding the *roles* of the manager and the supervisor, one can learn just how to accomplish the specific functions for which that person is responsible.

Supervision of word processing is mainly a people-oriented job and consists of daily supervision. Supervisors need to exercise skills in planning, organizing, leading, coordinating, communicating, and controlling.

Job descriptions should be developed during the implementation phase to define the exact tasks and skill requirements for each position. Attitudes and skills sought when screening word processing applicants include some of the same and some different ones for correspondence and administrative positions.

Hiring personnel should be regarded as a professional program that includes recruiting, testing, interviewing, investigating, evaluating, and selecting. The new hire frequently requires training and development. Other elements of hiring include compensating, appraising, controlling working conditions, communicating, and promoting.

Recruiting involves defining the kinds of persons needed and seeking to fill those positions. Job qualifications are clearly spelled out and include not only skill requirements but personal characteristics as well. It has been proven through industry surveys that an individual's personal characteristics, particularly a businesslike attitude, constitutes the most important criterion for success in the job.

Testing consists of administering tests to determine an applicant's ability to perform the tasks necessary for the position. In the case of the correspondence secretary, typing tests should be administered on a typewriter as similar to the applicable word processor as possible. Some firms test the applicant's ability to produce a mailable letter, which provides evidence of ability to proofread one's work. This quality is extremely important in word processing positions. Word processing tests also need to provide evidence of skills in language arts.

Reference investigations are more reliable when conducted by phoning to check with previous employers or teachers.

Interviews should be well planned, prepared, and coordinated. A checklist of questions prepared prior to interviewing allows comparing applicants and obtaining meaningful information about the applicant, including the way the person responds to the questions. Interviewing is extremely important and requires precise skills that should be practiced.

Selecting the applicant may be done by scrutinizing all the applicants, their applications and how they filled them out, their resumes, interview forms, tests, and reference checks. Sometimes another interview may be required, perhaps by another interviewer to obtain another person's opinion.

Once the employee has been selected, the job offer is made by either the word processing manager or supervisor. At the time of the job offer, one should explain all of the details of the job. Letters or phone calls may be made to the other applicants explaining that the job was filled.

REVIEW QUESTIONS

1. Explain the difference between the jobs of word processing manager and supervisor.
2. State how the word processing manager serves as the key person in an organization.

3. State specific responsibilities of a word processing supervisor.
4. What skills are required of a word processing supervisor?
5. What kinds of jobs might there be in a word processing system?
6. Differentiate the attitudes and skills required of administrative secretaries and correspondence secretaries.
7. What qualifications were required of the Eastern Air Lines supervisors?
8. What is staffing?
9. What is involved in word processing recruitment?
10. What kind of testing is valuable in screening word processing applicants?
11. What steps are involved in interviewing? What kinds of questions should be asked?
12. What steps are involved in investigating?
13. How is the job offer made?

QUESTIONS FOR DISCUSSION

1. Discuss the roles of word processing manager and supervisor and skills most important in these jobs.
2. Explain why word processing requires written job descriptions? How much reliance do you think is placed on them?
3. Discuss the attitudes and skills required of word processing employees and the relative importance of each.
4. Discuss how systems management affects staffing.
5. Explain the requirements of successful interviewing and compare the possible results from well planned interviews with those which occur on the spur of the moment.
6. Discuss the importance of investigating and how it should be carried out.
7. Discuss the followup after selection and why it is important.
8. Why should those who did not get the job be notified? How should they be notified?

CASES

Case 12-1 Electric Company

Mellow Valley Electric Company has had a word processing system for nearly one and a half years. When they implemented the system, they promoted three secretaries to the positions of administrative and correspondence supervisors and word processing manager. These people failed to make the system work and they have encountered critical resistance to and problems with the word processing concept and refusal to use their services. As a result, those three people have been transferred to positions elsewhere in the organization. You have been given the responsibility for staffing those three positions.

1. How will you go about filling the jobs?
2. Present your complete plan.

Case 12-2 Richmond Dairy, Inc.

You have just been hired by Richmond Dairy, Inc. to manage their word processing operations. They had an outside consultant conduct the feasibility study, and this consultant and the administrative vice president hired you to fill the job of managing word processing. You are first faced with the selection of personnel. You will have a word processing center with six correspondence secretaries and two satellites, each with three correspondence secretaries. In addition, you will have four work groups staffed with three administrative secretaries in each, a receptionist, page, and supervisor over both correspondence and administrative operations.

- Develop your staffing plan for the Richmond Dairy, Inc. word processing system.

"Motivational philosophy centers around instilling a sense of belonging and participation in employees. With engineered performance standards these opportunities are enhanced. The supervisor can leave conscientious employees to be their own task masters and concentrate on planning and servicing the department."

CHAPTER 13

Writing Procedures

OVERVIEW

In order for an operating system that requires people to change their working habits to succeed, it must be carefully planned and explained. Each new procedure needs to be described in detail so that each person who is required to use it, understands explicitly how to accomplish his or her part of the activity. This chapter explains what procedures need to be described and how to write them for both the user's manual and the operating manual.

OBJECTIVES

After you have completed this chapter, you will be able to:

1. Explain what sources are used to write procedures.
2. Plan the development of a user's manual.
3. Prepare document request forms.
4. Plan the development of a staff operating manual.
5. Explain the purpose of forms control in an organization.

Writing effective procedures for word processing operations is one of the major activities in preparing for implementation. Principals who now will depend upon word

Quote from James F. Lincoln, *Incentive Management,* Lincoln Electric Company, Cleveland (1951).

processing to produce their typewritten documents, as well as those who type the documents, need to have clear and concise instructions.

Procedures for word processing operations are created from the new system design: the workflow chart, the word processing organization structure which spells out who does which task, the job descriptions of word processing secretaries, and manners in which each document application will be processed.

If the new system is designed so that paragraphs are to be stored on magnetic media for playout to produce trust agreements, the procedures with which to accomplish this task need to be well defined, both for the principal and the correspondence secretary. The procedure for the principal might be using a special request form on which the numbers of the desired paragraphs are written along with information relating to the document. Or the procedure on how to dictate this information into the dictation system might also be defined. The principal may use either technique, whichever is easiest and quickest for that person, to get that information to word processing so that the trust agreement will be typed by the correspondence secretary by the desired time.

Procedures need to be written with the idea that they are subject to continuing changes and updating. As the system develops, new and more efficient techniques are learned or created by the word processing specialists. One of the responsibilities of the senior word processing personnel should be to continually search for better and more efficient ways to produce the firm's documents. In spite of the fact that the procedures are subject to change, they should be written as concisely yet thoroughly as possible so that every principal who begins to send his or her work to word processing finds it easy to do so by following the instructions and receives the desired results.

One of the major goals of word processing is to provide improved secretarial services. The procedures should make this possible. Instruction manuals should be as brief as possible while covering all necessary requirements. Anyone in the organization who wishes to have word processing produce typing should be able to pick up a procedures manual or the appropriate form and transmit that information to word processing for typing without encountering problems.

ORIGINATOR/USER'S MANUAL

Purpose

The originator/user's manual should provide all originators or users with the specific steps required to get their work produced. It should be clear, concise, complete, easy to use, and flexible. It should be designed so that it is easy to update to reflect procedural changes when they occur. These changes may include new ways to get work done or changes in equipment and workflow.

Contents

In addition to forms for requesting specific applications and detailed instructions for each typing application, the manual includes the following:

1. Word processing hours of operation (e.g., 7:00 A.M. to 6:00 P.M.). This would include information regarding shifts, if the organization has more than one daily shift (many firms have incorporated two or three day shifts with a reduction in workforce at night).

2. How priorities are scheduled. Most firms set up a first-in, first-out routine for daily work, scheduling infrequent and long documents according to deadlines that occur at prearranged times, such as monthly budget reports, weekly sales meetings, weekly staff meetings, quarterly reports, annual reports, annual telephone listing, semiannual budget review, and yearly sales forecast. The deadline dates that are known ahead of time are scheduled into operations and listed on a posted schedule so that the Word Processing Department and users are aware of upcoming deadlines ahead of time and they can plan accordingly.

3. Average and planned turnaround time for different kinds of typing applications such as correspondence (one day), medium size reports with some revision, long reports, heavily revised lengthy test, statistical tables, charts, form letters, documents to be created from stored paragraphs, listings to be made from stored material, and special prerecorded forms (purchase orders, etc.).

4. Alignment of responsibilities. What is expected from the originator of work and what will be done by the word processing secretaries. This would include who does the proofreading, who is responsible for making copies, who maintains file copies, when does work have to be received in order to be produced that day, in what form must work be received, what will be provided by the word processing secretary (to return typed copy without typographical errors or misspellings and with correct spellings of names and technical vocabulary), what is expected from the originator (a list of commonly used names and addresses with correct spellings, a list of commonly used technical terms for correct spelling, special paper or forms on which the work is to be typed).

5. Communications tools and techniques, including the following dictation procedures:

    a. Dictator's checklist (small card with clearcut instructions on how to dictate daily correspondence, including how to start dictation, review, redictate, and end).

    b. Detailed instructions on how to dictate each kind of document that each department or section may need.

    c. A walk-through or road map on how to dictate in the same order as preprinted forms such as in-house memoranda.

    d. Instructions on how to dictate a form letter (both the addresses and the letter itself), text, instructions for performing a certain task, a lengthy document with technical vocabulary, a statistical report, engineering and scientific reports (whether to dictate equations and formulas), dictation incorporated with copy for typing (equations might be on copy and not dictated).

    e. Request forms for form letters, stored paragraphs, copy typing, revisions, and other special situations.

6. Sample forms used by word processing with explanations on how to use them.

7. Specific procedures for each kind of document, particularly by department. Example: How to dictate a purchase order (for the Purchasing Department), how

to dictate a will or trust (for the Probate Department), how to dictate a medical consultation, how to dictate an insurance adjuster's report.

8. Copies of all stored material for originator's use and reference.
9. Specific instructions on how to handle special situations, such as whom to contact to solve a particular problem or to change a document already sent to word processing.

Figure 13-1 is a sample format that may be used to design a manual. Figure 13-2 is an example of a user's manual checklist to plan and maintain continual system efficiency. Figure 13-3 is a sample work request form used by Four Phase Systems, Inc.'s word processing center.

WORD PROCESSING STAFF OPERATING MANUAL

An up-to-date operating manual for all word processing personnel is as important as a user's manual. Each member of the word processing staff should have an operating manual within reach to which to refer in order to determine:

*   Correct spellings and addresses for correspondence.
*   Format to be followed for each document typed.
*   Procedures to be followed for each application and specific department.
*   Procedures and techniques used by the firm's word processing personnel.

New personnel who may have worked elsewhere might type some items differently and therefore should refer to the staff operating manual frequently until confident that they are preparing all of the typing as specified in the staff manual. Standardized formats such as line lengths, tab settings, page layout, and other physical characteristics may be a great time saver and even more effective cost saver to the organization, both of which are major reasons for having word processing in the first place.

Purpose and Contents

The staff operating manual should provide word processing secretaries with the procedures to produce accurate, top quality, and professional documents for the organization as efficiently as possible. Included are:

1. Operating schedule (daily working hours, by shift, if applicable); procedures to handle overtime or other off hours.
2. Schedule for infrequent work such as the monthly, weekly, quarterly, semi-annual, annual documents.
3. Format and other procedures to follow for each typing application with samples (for formatting, page layout, etc.).

INTRODUCTION TO MANUAL (How to Use It to Save Time and Get Your Work Done)
I.   WORD PROCESSING OPERATIONS
     A.   Hours: 7:00 A.M. to 6:00 P.M.
     B.   Turnaround Time: Received by 10:00 A.M. (same day)
                           After 10:00 A.M. (next day, depending upon length of document)
II. DOCUMENTS
     A.   Correspondence: Machine Dictation (Use Dictator's Checklist)
          1.   Turnaround time: 4 to 6 hours
          2.   To revise: Use Revision Request Form; 4 to 6 hours turnaround
     B.   Text: Machine Dictation, longhand, marked copy, edited copy (Use Dictator's Checklist/Revision Request/Document Request Forms)
          1.   Turnaround time: Depending upon document length and form of input
          2.   High priorities: Schedule with coordinator
          3.   Rough draft or final: State requirements
     C.   Statistical/Columnar Information: Machine dictation, longhand, marked copy (Use Document Request Form/Dictator's Checklist)
          1.   Provide reference copy for word processing
          2.   Indicate special requirements; whether to be stored for future use
          3.   Turnaround time: one day or by priority
          4.   Rough draft or final
          5.   Revisions: revision request form
     D.   Stored Paragraphs/Data: Document Request Form
          1.   Turnaround time: regular one day, or indicate priority
          2.   Rough draft or final: indicate whether to be revised (use Revision Request Form)
     E.   Form Letters: Request Form or Machine Dictation (Use Dictator's Checklist) Turnaround time: regular one day or indicate priority
     F.   Forms: Machine Dictation (Use Dictator's Checklist or Document Request Form) Turnaround time: Regular or indicate priority
     G.   Miscellaneous: Labels, envelopes, cards, Telex messages, etc. (Use Machine Dictation or Document Request Form)
          1.   Turnaround time: regular one-day or indicate priority
          2.   Indicate whether draft or final and to be revised or stored
     (See enclosures for samples of documents with instructions for machine dictation and filling in forms. Instructions provided by Word Processing supervisor.)
III. FORMS TO USE
     A.   Dictator's Checklist (both in Manual and on Card)
     B.   Document Request Form
     C.   Revision Request Form

FIGURE 13-2   Checklist for the User's Manual

   I. Objectives
     A. Provide Information
     B. Ensure Uniformity
  II. Format
     A. Easy to Use
     B. Allow for Updates
     C. Playscript
     D. Properly Indexed
     E. Concise Language
     F. Professional Appearance
 III. Distribution
     A. After-orientation Training Session
     B. Procedure for All Managers/Exempts/Secretaries
     C. New Employee Distribution
 IV. Content
     See Sample Procedures Manual
  V. Updates
     A. Assign Responsibility
     B. Procedure for Distribution

---

4. Departmental information (names of all principals using the word processing system, their location, job title, and telephone extension; names and addresses of frequently used correspondents for each principal; frequently used technical terminology used by specific departments; and any other information important to know in order to type documents for specific departments).
5. Names, titles, locations, and phone numbers of administrative secretaries and other staff personnel.
6. Sample document request forms and how to interpret them to meet the designated requirements.
7. Organizational standards and guidelines, including regulations to be met.
8. Word processing document standards, specifically in regard to proofreading, language arts, capitalization and punctuation rules and guidelines.
9. Report forms used by word processing in order to document the daily typing volume and time distribution according to department, principal originator, kind of input. Instructions on how to keep and interpret daily statistics. (See Figure 13-4, page 318.)
10. Job descriptions for all word processing personnel positions, listing skills required for each position and next step potential career growth.

WORD PROCESSING CENTER REQUEST

Work submitted by			Date submitted	Time
Telephone	Mail Stop	Department	DATE REQUIRED	TIME

Note: Items marked merely "ASAP" are given LOW priority!

Description of Work:

_____

_____

_____

_____

_____

TYPE OF DOCUMENT

☐ Original Material   ☐ Revision   ☐ Rush

☐ Final Copy Returned with Change   ☐ Standardized Material Codes: _____   ☐ Confidential

---
AUTHOR REQUESTS

☐ Rough Draft   ☐ Multi-Revision Expected   ☐ Extended Retention Until: _____

Other Special Instructions: _____

_____

_____

_____

Date Received	Assigned To	Date Completed

Writing and Recording Procedures

In the operator's (staff operations) manual, such criteria should be included as:

- Type of paper to use (special letterhead, special forms, etc.).
- How long to retain storage of documents.
- Whether and how to file.
- Proofreading procedures (as well as who is responsible for proofreading).
- Language arts rules and procedures for word usage, spelling, hyphenation, punctuation, capitalization.
- Format rules and standards, including setup for letters and memos, indentation rules, special formats used for all documents produced by the word processing operations.
- How stored paragraphs are recorded (what is stored and what is entered for each document). Where stop codes are recorded.

Responsibilities of Personnel

The operator's manual serves as the major reference source of information and guidelines for the operating staff. Each aspect involved in carrying out the daily work needs to be clearly stated, particularly regarding who is to perform each function. This serves as a motivational and supervisory tool that can make the jobs of both supervisor and staff more effective. The following list outlines which functions need to be stated in the manual:

- Who distributes work.
- Who monitors dictation.
- Who decides on how to format a particular document.
- Who is responsible for training new personnel.
- Who handles scheduling and setting priorities.
- Who handles production reporting.
- Who handles workflow procedures.
- Who is responsible for written communications with users.
- Who is responsible for equipment downtime records keeping and communicating with equipment manufacturers for service, ordering, etc.
- Who is responsible for ordering supplies.

OTHER DEPARTMENTS

If other departments need to know what is done in word processing but are not themselves incorporated into the operations, a pamphlet or small manual could be available describing the word processing operations and kinds of work they accomplish. This is more of a *nice-to-know* rather than a *need-to-know* kind of publication; but it is a good sales tool that allows more personnel to become acquainted with the benefits of word processing as implementation gets underway and particularly before incorporating other departments.

OTHER COMMUNICATIONS

In addition to the procedures manuals and a word processing information publication, the company might publish other written documents relating to word processing operations. They could include brief instruction forms to other departments that might use word processing input for such operations as data processing communications between two or more locations, photocomposition, or output (via computer) to micrographics.

When an organization begins to implement a complete information integration system, it is extremely important that the workflow and procedures are carefully planned and implemented. Written procedures are imperative to successful operations, particularly when several services are merged together into a system; tasks and responsibilities need to be clearly defined.

Forms

Organizational personnel who have particular functions tend to create forms for their operations. Without some means of organizational forms control, a firm tends to accumulate more and more forms, which can be a very costly situation. Development of the forms themselves initially may not seem very costly; but the situation can quickly get out of hand, and the firm may suffer from forms proliferation just as many firms discover that uncontrolled copying quickly causes copy proliferation. Allowing each department to develop its own forms is costly because of: (a) the cost of the time spent creating and updating forms; (b) the cost of having the forms printed or the costs of the forms themselves; (c) the cost of using the forms—filling them in, interpreting them, using them for the next step in the process (which frequently results in the creation of a second form in the next department in order for that department to accomplish its task); and (d) the cost of filing, storing, and locating forms.

Paper in itself is a problem in many organizations; modern governmental controls and rules require the use of many forms (more and more, it seems), and this practice takes up space and fills files. The more a firm controls the use of forms, the more it can tighten the processing within the organization. By having a forms control unit as a part of the organizational system bringing together all of the different departmental requirements in order to accomplish the total task, an organization may save a vast amount of costs in personnel time, storage space, and paper.

With a central figure in charge of forms control, any person who wishes to create a new form must submit the suggested form for approval. The forms supervisor makes sure that (a) the form is actually necessary; (b) the form is not a duplicate or duplicating part of another form, which might instead be incorporated into another form; (c) the form is properly designed in order to accomplish the desired task; and (d) the form contains all relevant and required information.

For instance, the word processing manager might decide to design a form for preparing the quarterly financial report for processing to input to the computer (perhaps the input is typed on the word processing typewriter, which then communicates the information into the computer for processing). This form might also be usable by the Data Processing Department for preparation of further statistics. The forms control supervisor therefore would incorporate into this form the information applicable to the Data Processing Department as well.

By coordinating related processing services within an organization, a firm can save considerable personnel and supplies costs. Word processing, because of its central role within these operations, can become the key to improving efficiency and cost effectiveness.

Sample formats, procedures, and forms used by word processing in different kinds of industries are illustrated in Figures 13-4 through 13-9.

SUMMARY

During the preimplementation of word processing, procedures are written for the using personnel and the operating staff who will service those people. These procedures are created from the new system design and its workflow. These procedures need to be planned for flexibility with the thought in mind that, as the system ages, changes will be made to continually improve its service to clients and its effectiveness.

The user's manual explains how work can be accomplished. This manual contains forms to request work, operating conditions, stated responsibilities of the

FIGURE 13-4   An Example of a Line Count Sheet

LINE COUNT SHEET											
Date	Title	Author	Operator	Corres-pondence	Text	Reports	Statis-tical	Forms	No. Rev.	Total Time Elapsed (Min.)	Line Totals
6/1	Acme Letter	Brown	Carole	✓					0	30	60
6/1	Letter #11	Brown	Carole	✓					0	20	75
6/1	Trip Report	Brown	Carole			✓			0	50	100
6/1	Speech	Jones	Stella		✓				3	45	45
6/1	Vacation Memo	Jones	Stella		✓				0	60	225
6/1	Client Billings	Jones	Joan				✓		0	360	500

An Example of a Feedback Form   FIGURE 13-5

To: _____

To improve our service to you, we need your help. Please . . .

☐ DICTATE SLOWER   ☐ SPELL
                                 PROPER NAMES

☐ DICTATE LOUDER   ☐ SPELL
                                 UNUSUAL WORDS

☐ DICTATE DISTINCTLY   ☐ INDICATE THE END
                                 OF THE LETTER

☐ GIVE COMPLETE   ☐ OTHER:
  INFORMATION   (Specified below)

_____

_____

_____

_____   _____
Secretary   *Date*

Now it's your turn. Please tell us how we can improve.

_____

_____

---

originator and operating personnel, planned turnaround time, and written communications techniques.

One of the major components is dictation instructions, a checklist and specific instructions for each kind of document which may be dictated, accompanied by sample documents.

FIGURE 13-6   An Example of a Transmittal Form

TRANSMITTAL INSTRUCTIONS
FOR
PRERECORDED LETTERS

TO: WORD PROCESSING CENTER

FROM: ___SAN RAFAEL MAIN___   ___SGG___   ___10/27/76___
            (Branch)   (By)   (Date)

Letter Category ___1 / 1 / 01___   ___NEW ACCOUNT LETTER___
           (Catalog Number)   (Type of Letter)

SPECIAL INSTRUCTIONS: (if any)

Customer's Last Name	Format Change (salutation, heading, etc.)
Smith	Dear Bill
Allen, Jones and Martin	Gentlemen

Letters Completed_____
                        (Date)

           By_____
1/25/73   (W. P. Operator)

Procedures for the word processing staff are contained in the staff operating manual, which contains specific names and addresses used by work originators and sample document formats and which explains procedures and techniques used by the operating staff. This serves as a reference manual as well as a training manual for new personnel. In addition to containing schedules, formats, addresses, procedures, and sample document formats and request forms, it contains organizational standards, document standards (particularly regarding language arts), report forms to record daily volume and time distribution, and job descriptions of word processing personnel.

In addition to the work originators, there may be departments in the firm which need to have procedures manuals for coordinating work. If this is so, each department should have its own procedures manual.

Other written communications that firms might produce include:

·   Instruction forms used to coordinate with other service departments.
·   Newsletters publishing information about what is taking place in word processing.
·   Internal memos reporting new procedures, new personnel, and other important company information.

FIGURE 13-7   An Example of a Volume Report

BANK OF MARIN
WORD PROCESSING CENTER
VOLUME REPORTS

NAME ___ SAMPLE REPORT

WEEK ENDING ___

DATE	ORIGINAL				STORED			REVISION			
	SOURCE	NATURE	LINES	TIME	SOURCE	LTRS/LINES	TIME	SOURCE	NATURE	LINES	TIME
10/27	SGG	Letter	26	:10	1-1-01	50/950	1:30	JAN	Memo	1	--
TOTALS											

FIGURE 13-8   An Example of a Supplemental Time Sheet

SUPPLEMENTAL SHEET

Date	Time In	Time Out	Total Time	Record	Revise	Correct	P.O.	Addresses			Date	Time In	Time Out	Total Time
								Record	P.O.			PROOFREADING		
Oper's. Initials:		TOTAL									Proofers' Initials:		TOTAL	

Forms control should be considered an important part of the service departments of the organization; since an overuse of forms can be very costly and time consuming. Word processing plays a key role in the services provided principals and therefore needs well-organized written procedures to help users receive the benefits it has to offer.

REVIEW QUESTIONS

1. Explain the purpose of written procedures for the originators of documents.
2. State how these procedures should be written and their important aspects.
3. State what needs to be contained in a user's manual.
4. What is a dictator's checklist and how is it used?
5. What should the staff operating manual include? What is its purpose?
6. What other departments might need the word processing procedures manual? for what purpose?
7. Explain some other written communications word processing might distribute relating to using word processing.
8. Describe the elements of a good form.

QUESTIONS FOR DISCUSSION

1. Discuss what might happen if a firm had no written word processing procedures for the users; for the operating staff.

CONTACT EXT. _____ _____
Alternate   _____ _____

TYPING CENTER REQUEST FORM

Originator_____ Department_____

Date In: _____   Date Due: _____

REQUIREMENTS:

1. Know what the project is to look like.
2. Must be close to finished as possible.
3. Originator must proofread.
4. Photo-ready projects must be final form.

TITLE OF PROJECT: _____
_____

Typing Center Only	Job No._____		
Typist _____		Completion Date _____.	
Type of Project	**Lines**	**Pages**	**Total Hours**
Papers/Reports/Man.			
Straight	____	____	____
Technical	____	____	____
Automatic Letters	____	____	____
Envelopes			
Labels	____	____	____
Cards			
Exhibits	____	____	____
Hard Copy Tape Log	____	____	____
Dictation	____	____	____
Case Study	____	____	____
Booklet			
Brochure	____	____	____
Miscellaneous _____	____	____	____

TW ____   MT/ST ____

COMPOSER ____

TYPE OF PROJECT

TYPED DOCUMENTS

Papers/Reports/Manuscripts	____
Straight	____
Technical	____
Automatic Letters	____
Envelopes	____
Labels	____
Cards	____
Exhibits	____
Hard Copy Tape Log	____
Dictation	____
Erase Tape? Yes	____
No	____

SETUP

Paper size _____
Spacing: Double ____
     Single ____
Grade of Paper: ____
Carbons:
     White ____
     Yellow ____
     Blue ____
DRAFT _____
REVISION _____
FINAL _____

PHOTO-READY DOCUMENTS

Case Study _____
Booklets _____
Manuscript _____
Articles _____
Brochure _____
Exhibit _____
Small job/Misc. _____

SECONDARY CONTACTS
_____
_____

SETUP

Paper size
Margins
Columns
Spacing: Double
     Single

SPECIAL INSTRUCTIONS: _____
_____
_____
_____
_____
_____
_____
_____

TYPING CENTER USE ONLY

MT/SC Information

Type Size _____   Other _____

Type Style _____   Other _____

To be Reproduced: Yes ____ No ____

Save Tape: Yes ____ No ____

Miscellaneous Information:

2. Explain how a word processing supervisor uses the procedures manual when training new hires who are users of word processing.
3. How frequently should procedures manuals be reviewed?
4. How should the updating and changing of procedures be communicated to the users? to the operating staff?
5. Discuss the use of forms in organizations and how they may affect operating cost and operations.

CASES

Case 13-1   Insurance Company

You are a member of a task force which just completed a feasibility study of Wayland Insurance Company and are in the process of preparing to implement a word processing system. You will have a central dictation system which will direct dictation to four different correspondence work groups, each with three standalone word processing typewriters. Dictation will be received on recorders located near the lead secretary who will distribute the dictation and other work received in forms such as longhand, request forms, and copy.

• Outline the procedures manuals for the users and for the correspondence secretaries.

Case 13-2   Community College

Lake Crest Community College has decided to install a word processing center and hopes to expand and have several satellite centers once the first one has proven productive. You have been given the responsibility for managing the word processing operations. You will have a central dictation system which will allow staff and instructors to dictate into the center throughout the campus over telephones and which will have a special outside line which can be accessed through dialing a special number. This number will be given only to department chairpersons and other designated personnel. The center will have six correspondence secretaries, each with a terminal to a shared-logic system sharing two typewriter printers.

• Outline the procedures manuals to be distributed to the users and the operating staff.

BENJAMIN / CUMMINGS

WORD PROCESSING SERIES

PEOPLE / PROCEDURES / EQUIPMENT

*"Top management bought the system, but selling it
to the people who use it is a must if it is to work
effectively."*

CHAPTER 14

Selling the Program— Orientation

OVERVIEW

Selling people on the need to change their work habits is perhaps the most difficult project of the word processing mission. This chapter discusses the reluctance and fears people have and how word processing can overcome these factors and achieve its goal of serving its customers effectively.

OBJECTIVES

After completing this chapter, you will be able to:

1. State how resistance to the new system may be manifested.
2. Understand why people may resist the new system.
3. State actions which should *not* be used to sell the new system.
4. State actions which help sell the new system.
5. Describe the fears the principals have regarding a change to the new system.
6. Describe the building blocks to selling the system.
7. State the importance of word processing service motivation and how to communicate this outlook to the users.

Management made the commitment to implement word processing for the benefit of the organization: to control rising costs, to improve operations, to make better use of their personnel. But if those individuals for whom the system is designed

Quote from Willoughby Ann Walshe, "Insuring that the Paper Work Gets Done," *Word Processing World*, June 1977, pp. 14–15.

refuse to accept and support the system, it will never be truly successful. Many times employees merely go along with the new system because of top or middle management commitment. Some may fight the new system and refuse to change their ways, as evidenced when attempting to change work originators from using paper and pencil to dictation equipment.

In nearly every organization some employees will resist the new way of doing things. This resistance may be manifested in several ways:

* Refusal to use the system.
* Conscious or unconscious avoidance of the system (assuming there are other ways to get the work done).
* Using the system only when absolutely necessary.
* Dumping the more difficult or garbage typing into the system while keeping the easy, everyday typing for administrative secretaries (in situations in which administrative still provide some of the typing).

Most damaging of all is lack of enthusiasm and negative attitudes expressed through the company's grapevine. Informal employee gatherings during breaks, in carpools, or during social functions offer the opportunity to criticize the new system.

Any new system, no matter how well founded or firmly backed, needs to be nurtured during its early development stages. This was true in the early days of electronic data processing and is perhaps even truer in the case of word processing. Word processing hits the employees personally, upsetting their personal empires and introducing a system over which they have no control. In the past, many had control over their secretarial support; now they have none.

Employee negativism during a system's early stages can cause long-term scars and might possibly result in the complete aborting of the system. In addition, negative attitudes may be so subtle that they grow unnoticed until they become dangerously powerful and disruptive.

What kinds of action can one take to become aware of resistance to the new system? Although the system requires management backup and support, it is dangerous to attempt to force employees to use it. This is probably one of the most ineffective techniques. Should management issue an edict to the effect that the new system is here to stay and all employees are expected to give it their full support? In these days of participative management, such an approach can do more harm than good. But if directives cannot assure acceptance of the new system, what can?

TOP MANAGEMENT SUPPORT

First of all, employees need to be aware that management is committed to making the new system succeed. Problems may occur during early implementation, or anywhere along the way, just as they do in any kind of operating activity. Employees must be made aware that management expects ups and downs and is committed to solving problems for continual improvement and development of the new system.

EMPLOYEE INVOLVEMENT

Perhaps the most important factors to a successful system are making the system belong to those who use it and keeping the users involved all along the way—from the beginning of the study to implementing daily operations. If the users participate in making the system into what they see as the best system for the organization, they will find it difficult to dissent and express negative opinions of their own system.

Employees like to feel they are a part of the action and that their opinions and contributions are important in attaining the objectives of the firm. If their advice is sought outright, they find it difficult to resist and instead become involved in planning the system.

By continually pursuing the advice and involvement of these employees who will be using the system, it becomes *their* system, rather than management's new system or the system designed by the task force.

In addition, their advice and comments can be extremely important in ensuring that the new system's planners consider all possible alternatives during planning stages.

THROUGH EXPLANATIONS OF THE NEW SYSTEM

As discussed earlier, employees who have been working in a firm have formed their work habits and established routines. They go to work each day expecting to be able to accomplish their work in a pattern they developed when first working for the firm. Suddenly this is all going to be changed. Some will lose their secretaries. Some will have to do some tasks they formerly delegated to their secretaries, who had learned early how to handle routine tasks, relieving their bosses of mundane routine tasks such as looking up names and addresses for letters or making copies. If the new system does not provide correspondence secretaries with these address lists for each dictator or set up clerical procedures to handle copying, work originators may find a great deficiency in the new system. Such tasks should be planned so that the new system continues to provide services for work originators which can be handled by someone who is delegated these tasks.

The principals, or work originators, do not know how well they will get their work done under this new system. They develop fears that they will lose their jobs or be unable to handle their work effectively. Many firmly believe that they functioned better in the "country-club" atmosphere of the traditional system, and until they learn how to function easily in the new system, they will continue to be reluctant and feel they were much happier in the old system. Those who became adjusted to the relaxed atmosphere must adjust to a new atmosphere in which everyone puts in a full day's work. Once they become adjusted, the principals usually learn that they are much happier when they can see that they have done a full day's work for a full day's pay.

In order to dispel myths and fears about the new system, frequent status reports can be disseminated to inform employees of accomplishments, achievements, and status of operations in the new system.

And, of course, the orientation programs are the first major step in providing all employees with thorough and concise explanations of how the system is designed to make their work easier and produce results for them more efficiently while providing them with the exact steps they need to take in order to use the system effectively.

When individuals fully understand a system and its concepts and realize that it will not cause them to lose their jobs but rather that it will make their jobs more interesting and challenging, their hostility may change to support.

BUILDING BLOCKS

Build Trust

How do you get potential dissenters and uncooperative users to trust in the system? You, the manager or supervisor, need to make them believe in you, and you can do the following to accomplish this.

- Meet with them on their home ground—in *their* offices—and discuss their jobs and needs; then relate how the system can help them accomplish their objectives.
- Learn and discuss their problems and request their suggestions and comments on how they feel the system can solve them.
- Ask them what their fears or objections might be and discuss how best to resolve them.
- Ask their reasons for not using the system and ask how you can help them to make the change.
- Listen to what they have to say before making judgments: they may have some valuable criticism which you need to consider in order to make the system meet their requirements.

Build in System Response

If the new system is designed and the procedures written, and that is considered *the* way the system will operate permanently, you are mistaken. Procedures need to be planned for handling varying situations. Alternatives to the usual situation need to be built in. Keep in mind the law firm in which an attorney who had an emergency job would discuss his needs with attorneys whose work had superseded his, and they would wait for their work until the emergency had been processed. This type of alternative needs to be planned for. In other words, make the system responsive and flexible.

The procedures need to be solid and firm, but they must also be flexible. The system is designed to do the work of those who were hired to market, purchase, engineer, or perform some kind of professional function. It therefore must have definite procedures to be followed for routine and daily work, but it must also be responsive to individual daily needs. Since office needs vary from day to day, the system must be able to fluctuate daily accordingly.

Responsiveness can be accomplished by providing quick turnaround, top quality output, easy-to-use techniques, and flexibility.

Build in Expanding Administrative Support

Secretaries who formerly handled both typing and nontyping or administrative tasks frequently devoted most of their effort to typing. Administrative secretaries who no longer have typing or have little typing to do now have much more time to perform administrative tasks. This can be a great bonus to the principals. But the work must be well organized and directed. The principals must know how to utilize their administrative secretaries' abilities. Too frequently they simply give them more filing, copying, processing, and clerical functions and do not capitalize on delegating those routine tasks the principals had to do themselves before they could get to their more important creative tasks. This might cover responding to requests by letter, requesting information for their jobs, or performing project work which does not demand intensive research.

Offer Dictator Incentive Programs

Some firms have a "Dictator of the Month" award program which has served to promote a closer communication link between word processing and principals. Many have luncheon get-togethers which give everyone the opportunity just to chat and participate in social exchange, but which also break down barriers. Even tongue-in-cheek awards can serve in developing competitive channels which help to promote the system.

Build Morale

Achievement of a team spirit, not just in word processing but throughout the firm, between the principals and those who produce their work can help make the system a success. Word processing organizations and associations have become channels for word processing managers and supervisors to share their daily problems and ideas. This process has helped their morale appreciably, but more importantly, it is contributing towards achieving a feeling of appreciation and devotion to word processing throughout the organization. Perhaps one of the best ways to bring this about is to maintain as much open-door communication as possible while meeting the needs of the users without causing stress on the secretaries.

Provide Service Motivation

customers always right

Word processing, just as data processing, reproduction, communications, and distribution, is a service to be performed for employees within the organization.

Attitude can be one of the most influential factors in developing a cooperative spirit within the organization. When those last-minute report writers bring in their reports with immediate deadlines, it takes considerable self-control to smile and be willing to go that extra mile. However, the supervisor and secretary who maintain the friendly and cooperative spirit while nicely pointing out that they might have been able to add some extras if the work had been received earlier are hard to find at fault.

It seems that departments which service employees are continually faced with last-minute crises and situations. It is in their best interests to provide their services happily and with a friendly smile.

Avoid Criticism

Even though you may be aware of shortcomings in the system and changes that need to be made, do not openly criticize. Always be supportive and dedicated and maintain a positive attitude. There will be enough outside criticism. Besides, your positive feelings can be contagious.

Provide Effective Leadership

The most effective leader makes others in the organization feel that they have done it themselves. If you, the supervisor or manager, can make those who were or might become opponents feel that the system is theirs, just dare anyone to criticize it.

ORIENTATION

During the period of planning for implementation, you learned what the contents of the orientation programs should be and the kind of tone to set while conducting them. Now you will learn exactly how to prepare each program from the beginning to the end, from the first program for top management to the continuing orientation programs for new hires and those who have been participating for several years but need to be kept up-to-date with current operations and functions of the system.

A sample checklist for conducting the program is illustrated in Figure 14-1. By using the checklist, each program can be planned in detail for top management, middle management, supervisors, other employees, and the word processing staff.

Who Conducts the Meeting

Some organizations have the president or a member of top management introduce the first orientation programs to implement the new system. This both provides word processing management with a feeling of management support and backup and makes the employees aware that it is indeed a company-wide program, even though they may be beginning with only one or a few departments. Since it is much easier and practical to phase in a new system rather than make a complete company-wide change at one time, it is important that a phased-in program be kicked off with adequate publicity and employee awareness and support.

Top management previously announced to the personnel that it had decided to implement the new designated system to meet certain objectives. At this time those objectives can be restated so that when the procedures are explained, employees

CHECKLIST
ORIENTATION PROGRAMS

ITEM	TOP MANAGEMENT	MIDDLE MANAGEMENT	SUPERVISORS	OTHER	WORD PROCESSING
WHO					
Introduce Program					
Conduct Program					
Attend Program (No.)					
WHEN					
Date of Program					
Time of Program					
Length of Program					
WHERE					
Place of Program					
WHAT					
Audio-Visuals					
Handouts					

List of Attendees: Top Management _____

Middle Management _____

Supervisors _____

Other _____

Word Processing Personnel _____

Other _____

understand the importance of following those procedures in order to make the system function properly.

Once top management has introduced the orientation program and restated how the organization is now prepared to set out to accomplish its stated objectives, the program should be turned over to the manager of word processing. Management should make sure the word processing manager's role and responsibilities are understood.

Top Management Meeting

Since most of top management has been involved in the decision to implement word processing, this meeting is devoted mainly to the word processing manager's explaining the new procedures, passing out the word processing procedures handbook for management, illustrating how various forms are to be used, and conducting any necessary training.

Most top managers will have been dictating to their secretaries who used shorthand or machine dictation. Therefore, there may be no need to train management in how to dictate. However, the managers may not have used dictation equipment before. If that is the case, machine dictation procedures will need to be included to train those in management in how to use their dictation skills with the equipment in order to get their work accomplished efficiently.

Content of Orientation Meetings

Top management begins with a statement of the organization's objectives for word processing and turns the meeting over to the word processing manager.

The word processing manager explains the responsibilities and duties of the manager in regard to word processing and introduces the supervisors (administrative and correspondence) and explains their duties. Next the manager describes word processing strategy (what is expected to be accomplished over what period of time and how) and policies (what kind of work will be handled first, which departments will be served first, or which categories of documents will be produced first), how phasing-in will proceed, work hours, procedures for exceptions to the usual routine, and feedback procedures.

Getting Attendance at the Training Session

A training session attended by only one-fourth of the work originators would not be very successful. If the other three-fourths do not attend, they will not know the procedures and be able to adapt to and use the new system. Will simply distributing the schedule listing the various orientation meetings result in the attendance of everyone on the list for that session? Without any followup, the answer is *no*. Any time a meeting is scheduled, particularly to train employees in some regard, there are those who will feel that their work is more important and that the meeting may waste valuable time away from the job. They must be completely convinced of the merits of the program. They must feel that if they do *not* attend, it will impede their work performance. They must understand that this meeting will be more than worth the time they take away from their important tasks to attend.

Personal or telephone followup should follow distribution of the orientation meeting schedules. The word processing manager or analyst should make certain that the planned times are satisfactory to each person invited. Otherwise, an alternate time should be arranged for each person who finds it impossible to come at the prescribed time. Once assured that everyone invited is able to attend, the manager or analyst should continue to sell the importance of attending by talking with employees if possible and obtaining verification of attendance just before the meeting is to take place.

In some cases, management distributes memos advising employees that they are expected to attend a training session. Continuing training sessions should then be set up at the time set by the group which will be attending. Some firms have early Friday morning staff meetings. If this is the agreed upon time, the training times for the principals would occur each Friday, with some exceptions such as on holidays, during heavy vacation times, or when they agree they may not need a meeting for a few weeks.

Time of the meetings will differ according to the nature of the business. Some may prefer later hours in the day. One company's marketing representatives return to the office each afternoon after completing customer calls, usually around 4:00 P.M. They scheduled their staff meetings and dictation/communication programs for 4:00 P.M. on Tuesdays. This has worked out very successfully for them, and they use this training session as a tool to bring in outside speakers for other kinds of training beneficial to them in their jobs, as well as to communicate recent information bulletins, air problems for group solving, and improve their communications. They have had guest speakers present talks on motivation, listening skills, organization skills, and new techniques in territory coverage in addition to their usual dictation program.

New Hires: Ongoing Training

Once the word processing orientation programs are concluded and the program is under way, those who attended those sessions know how to use the procedures manuals and can pick up on advanced techniques and skill improvement at periodic staff meetings. However, because the new hires were not around when the first orientation programs took place, they must be brought up to par with the others. The word processing manager or supervisor needs to have a program and method for training each new employee who will be creating documents.

Word processing managers in some firms operate closely with the Personnel Department in training company personnel. Once a person is hired, a memo is sent to Word Processing, giving that individual's name, job title, location, and phone number. Next, the word processing manager or supervisor notifies that person when the next orientation program is being given (large firms which frequently hire new employees hold periodic orientation programs). The employee is then phoned and asked to select the time most convenient to attend the training program. The date is set and a memo, with a copy to the individual's manager, is sent to arrange for the new hire to learn the procedures and the way that work is dictated into the word processing system.

Content of the Orientation Program

The manager first introduces the word processing staff (supervisors, coordinator, specialist, analyst, proofreader, secretaries) and then outlines the working procedures (work hours and planned turnaround time).

Work Hours   Some firms have staggered hours. Flexitime is becoming more and more popular, because it allows firms to have longer working days to recover more of their equipment and labor costs; but it also allows them to offer their employees the ability to plan their own desired working times. At the City of Milpitas, one secretary begins at 6:00 or 7:00 A.M. to prepare the police reports for that day's traffic and other courts which must be ready by 9:00 A.M. This secretary works until 3:00 or 4:00 P.M. The City of Mountain View has several shifts, which allow employees to process all of the city documents (minutes of meetings, agenda, and reports, all of which must meet certain deadlines) as well as to work those hours most convenient to them.

Some married women prefer to work night shifts so that they can be at home with their families during the days. Some firms let the working staff alter their hours to meet personal responsibilities or be able to participate in carpools with others who work flexible hours.

Turnaround Time   When first beginning operations, the manager must decide what kind of **turnaround time** the company will plan for each kind of document: daily correspondence, periodic reports, multiple-page documents, revisions. Many word processing managers plan one-day turnaround for all one-page documents received by a certain time in the day, next-day turnaround for documents received after that time, and other stated number of working hours for lengthy documents according to the number of pages, kind of input, and other factors, which are carefully spelled out in the procedures manual so that all principals know exactly what is to be expected once the new system is underway.

Forms for Certain Documents   Next the manager explains the various forms designed for word processing use and explains how to fill out the work request form to have a document created, stored, reused, or revised. Figure 14-2 is an example of a work (job) request form.

How to Request Certain Tasks   The manager explains that the principals may have word processing maintain certain records which will allow them to process their work efficiently, accurately, and without misunderstandings. These records include:

- Address lists for principals with accurate spellings and titles. These lists allow the principal to dictate the name only and then rely upon the word processing

JOB REQUEST   No. 000001

Requester's Name_____ Dept. No._____ Ext._____

Date Requested_____ Date Needed_____ []a.m. []p.m.

Project Description (Code)_____ (Details) _____

Requester's Signature_____ Approval_____
****

INPUT	OUTPUT	DELIVERY	TYPE STYLE
[] Handwritten	[] Final	[] Client P/U	[] _____
[] Typewritten	[] Final Draft	[] Deliver to	[] _____
[] Dictated	[] Rough Draft	_____	[] _____
[] Other	[] Other _____	_____	[] _____

PAPER	TYPE SIZE	LINE SPACE	COPIES
[] Letterhead	[] 10-pitch	[] Single	[] Carbon
[] Memorandum	[] 12-pitch	[] 1-1/2	[] Photocopy
[] Plain Bond	[] Variable	[] Double	[] Originals
[] Labels		[] Triple	[] Offset Printed
[] Other _____		[] Other_____	No. of Each_____

REFERENCE INFORMATION

[] Presently on Tape/Card #_____ [] Assigned Tape/Card #_____

[] Do Not Retain [] Delete by_____ [] Other
****

JOB ASSIGNMENT

Date/Time Received_____ Date/Time Due Out_____

Priority Code: [] RUSH (Same Day) [] With 24 Hrs [] Within 48 Hrs

Assigned to (Operator) _____ (Proofreader)_____

Supervisor/Coordinator's Initials_____

Date/Time Completed_____ No. Hours _____

Total Units Produced_____Less Errors_____Actual Prod._____

Comments_____

_____

Proofreader's Signoff_____ Supervisor's Signoff_____

White: Operator   Canary: Supervisor   Pink: Requester   (PCS-01-74)

secretary to pick up the correct title and address from word processing files the same way a personal secretary did in the past.

- Lists of technical terms with their definitions and correct spellings. These serve the same purpose, avoiding misspellings, misunderstandings, and misinterpretation in the document content.
- Lists of the principals' stored documents, letters, paragraphs, and any documents which are typed more than once.
- Correct job titles for principals with the appropriate complimentary closing for their correspondence.
- Stationery to be used for certain correspondence. Some principals use executive personal letterhead for some documents. Some departments have different letterheads or forms for specific documents.
- Copies of documents which may be used from time to time to prepare certain departments' or principals' documents for exact format (particularly in the case of government documents, which require an exact amount of space for indents and other specific requirements).

Dictation Training   If the group has not had much dictation experience, a complete dictation training program should be conducted. For orientation and other training sessions when dictation training is to take place, principals should be encouraged to bring with them something they wish to learn how to dictate or get out in the mail. This will allow the trainer to teach that person all of the necessary preparatory and organizational skills before using dictation equipment. Once these skills have been covered so that the trainees are comfortable and understand how to prepare and organize and be ready to dictate, the trainer demonstrates how the dictation equipment is manipulated for dictating. All trainees should devote at least an hour to dictating and preparing a document for typing. New trainees should attend a followup review/problem-solving training session.

Equipment Demonstration/Correspondence Production   The orientation session should allow the attendees to visit the correspondence production operations, watch a demonstration of correspondence being produced, and see the complete operation from how the work is recorded on dictation recorders to how it is distributed back to the principals. Every person who will be using correspondence word processing should have a tour of the operation so that the individual understands the complete document cycle.

Middle Management, Supervisors, Staff

Orientation for the different groups of management and principals who will be dictating and transmitting their typing to correspondence word processing follows a similar pattern. Some sessions to lower staff and management will be more detailed and contain more instructions and training than upper management. It is at the middle management and staff levels where most of the work originates. Their support, cooperation, and understanding of how to make the new system accomplish their work easier and faster is therefore of utmost importance. The manager and word processing staff will want to develop a cohesive teamwork relationship so that these people will always feel free to ask questions, communicate problems they encounter, or suggest changes which would benefit the system. The teamwork of the system depends upon how well the orientation programs are conducted.

Using Visuals

Overhead projection transparencies are used to show and cover in detail each form or procedure in the handbook. Some speakers, when presenting material by means of audio-visual screens, prefer to cover the information without having passed out the material. At the end of the meeting, once explanations have been covered completely and all questions answered, pass out the handbooks. If the handbooks are passed out and the presenter is covering on the screen the same information, the audience can follow along with the forms in the handbook as well as the screen. Generally it is up to the presenter to handle this whichever way is easiest and results in the most comprehensive understanding by the audience. By handing out the copies after having covered them on the screen, the presenter has more control without the audience skipping ahead, and is less apt to have a member of the audience attempt to control the meeting. Figure 14–3 illustrates the procedure form handed out to Bank of Marin users at the end of the orientation program.

Follow-up and Feedback

Before ending the preliminary portion of the program and prior to attending the equipment and production demonstration, the manager should explain to the attendees the way in which followup and feedback will occur. The manager may use questionnaires, memos, news bulletins, and frequent personal visits with the work originators. The more you-oriented the manager is, the more open the communications are. Some managers have rap sessions with special groups at different times; some encourage principals to visit word processing frequently and to feel free to talk over their work with those who process it. This technique is particularly successful in one law firm where all long, revised documents are processed in the document center, while daily work is done by legal secretaries using word processing typewriters and working for the same attorneys they have in the past.

By encouraging the attorneys who bring documents to the document center to first discuss the job with the correspondence secretary, the group has developed an extremely productive and high-morale word processing operation which has been in existence for several years.

Feedback and Follow-up Checklist   The following checklist provides the manager with a means of ensuring that the total operating system is reviewed periodically. This allows for meaningful analysis of actual accomplishments against which to determine how successful the system is and what changes need to be made.

Continue to inform users and word processing staff of management's objectives and how well the word processing system is meeting them.

FIGURE 14-3   Bank of Marin Word Processing Center

Production Categories

The center's production output is divided into five categories:

- *Original (34%)*—Comprised of dictation, i.e., letters, memos, rough drafts, and hand-written projects.
- *Stored (46%)*—Comprised of permanently stored form letters for each of the branches and departments, i.e., new account letters, newcomer welcome letters, personnel department letters, loan department letters, etc.
- *Revision (3%)*—Comprised of actual lines revised (deleted from or added to) projects. After revision is made, the remaining line count is logged in the repetitive category.
- *Statistical (9%)*—Comprised of tabular material, i.e., financial statements, charts, loan reports.
- *Repetitive (8%)*—Comprised of final drafts after revision, miscellaneous form letters (not considered a stored document), etc.

Branch Index Numbers

The stored document binders are separated by branch and department. The center has 254 stored form letters on file in these binders. For example: 1–1–01:

- 1–   The first number indicates branch.
- 1–   The second number indicates department.
- 01   The third number indicates numeric order.

A copy of each stored letter in the binder is sent to the branch/department for their permanent record. This system has proven very effective for locating a particular stored document and processing it in the fastest, most efficient manner.

Volume Reports

To keep track of the center's production, each operator records the work on individual volume report forms. These forms are divided into the five production categories. These categories include the source, nature, line count, and the time it takes to complete the project. These volume reports are turned in weekly.

- Prepare and distribute samples of the work word processing is turning out so that others, upon observing the kinds of work produced and the capabilities of word processing, take advantage of these capabilities to accomplish their work.
- List tasks being performed and those for whom they are performed by person and department (Administrative).
- List the kinds of documents with examples (Correspondence).

- Personally interview principals on a periodic basis to see whether they are receiving the service they desire and if not, why not, and to see how word processing further can service them.
- Analyze the capabilities of each member of the word processing staff to determine if their capabilities are up to par, learn how to improve them, if necessary, and make sure they are performing up to their standards and that their abilities are being used and recognized.
- Match talents to work.
- Maintain availability to meet needs of users.

SUMMARY

Although the first significant criterion for success of a new word processing system is management support and commitment, this is not enough to ensure its success. Many times resistance to the new system by middle management and users will ensure its defeat rather than its success. This resistance may be manifested in such ways as outright refusal to use the system, avoidance of the system, dumping the garbage work into it, and keeping the regular daily work within the department.

Careful nurturing of the program during its early stages is essential. Word processing frequently represents change, which is viewed with a negative eye by most people who are happy with the status quo.

In order to sell the program, management support is required, but not by issuing dictatorial decrees. If people are involved from the early days of planning and they are included in the planning, the system becomes *theirs*, particularly when their ideas may be incorporated into the procedures. The more ownership they feel, the more likely they are to use the system.

People need to have a thorough understanding of exactly how to use the system so that their first attempts are likely to meet with success. The more preparations made before beginning operations which make the work easier for the users, the more apt the system is to meet with early success.

Building blocks to success of the new system consist of such activities as:

- Manager's meeting with the users in their offices and discussing their needs and how word processing can fulfill them.
- Finding out what the users' problems are and solving them.
- Finding out what their fears or objections are and resolving them.
- Inquiring why they refuse to use the system and encouraging them to give it a chance.
- Listening to the users and responding accordingly.

The system should be built with an eye to responsiveness, offering alternatives when the stated procedures are ineffective. The manager should make sure that needs are responded to (e.g., requiring rapid turnaround, providing required quality output, making it easy to use the system, and being flexible). Additional building blocks to success include:

1. Build in more administrative support. If the users, who have lost secretaries who formerly took care of all their needs, are confronted by having to now do these

tasks, they are naturally going to resist the system. Therefore, the administrative secretaries should immediately respond to these needs, particularly since, with their typing responsibilities eliminated, they have much more time to perform administrative support. This may mean showing the principals how they can delegate more work to the administrative support personnel, allowing the principals more time to do their own creative work.

2.   Build in awards such as "Dictator of the Month." Give as much positive feedback to all users as possible. Open up communications channels by having luncheon get-togethers with the correspondence personnel who produce their work.

3.   Build up team spirit and service support, particularly organization identification. Make everyone aware that this is a team, a group of people, who work together to accomplish a specific service they want to do the best possible way for the benefit of the firm and all its employees. Just as data processing turns out reports to managers, supervisors, and staff to help them accomplish their jobs better, so does word processing offer its services to help in its way. In order to motivate the word processing staff towards job improvement, the manager is careful not to criticize people openly, works towards effective leadership of the group so that each staff member is open to suggestions, and is interested in knowing what he or she can do to improve. Supervisors should never criticize their own systems openly.

Preparing to conduct the orientation programs consists of outlining the contents, preparing the facilities, setting the tone, and conducting the programs.

Top management orientation may be the briefest, since it was involved in the decision from the beginning. The main purpose is to explain the procedures to be followed throughout the organization and answer any questions.

Other orientation meetings usually begin with an introduction by top management restating the word processing objectives. Then the word processing manager takes over by explaining his or her own responsibilities and duties and introducing other word processing supervisory personnel. Word processing strategies and policies are explained along with the procedure for phasing in the word processing operating system.

In planning the orientation meetings and the list of attendees at each meeting, people are usually invited through memos scheduling the meetings. The memo is then followed up by telephone calls to make sure everyone possible attends. This may require making some adjustments in order to accommodate everyone. The meetings themselves are scheduled at times most convenient and appropriate to the attendees: sometimes early morning, sometimes noon hour or during the day, and sometimes after hours.

In addition to orientation meetings, followup training sessions are scheduled to update people's knowledge and skills. These also are held to train new hires unless they are scheduled for separate orientation and training programs.

Many firms work directly with the Personnel Department in offering special orientation training to new hires. In a firm which hires only one person at a time, the manager or supervisor might schedule a time when the new hire can work with the trainer on a one-to-one basis or attend a scheduled training session offered periodically for those who have yet to learn the procedures and skills or those who wish to improve their skills.

Visuals are used in the orientation and training programs in order to present information clearly. Procedures manuals are distributed either at the end of the meeting or during it, whichever works most effectively for the trainer and learner.

The outline for the orientation program is:

- Introduction of staff.
- Explanation of policies and strategies.
- Introduction of procedures and schedules.
- Explanation of operating procedures, including turnaround time, use of request forms, address lists, technical terminology, lists of stored documents, lists of job titles, use of special stationery and forms, maintaining sample formats of documents.
- Dictation training.

After the initial orientation of all principals, the manager maintains a followup system and feedback operation in order to evaluate weaknesses and strengths, with an eye to continually improving the service.

REVIEW QUESTIONS

1. In what ways is resistance to the new system expressed:
2. How can management help gain acceptance of the new system?
3. How can the working staff help gain acceptance of the new system?
4. What reasons might the principals have for resisting the new system?
5. How can these be turned around into acceptance?
6. What value does a planning checklist have when preparing the orientation programs?
7. Who might best introduce the first orientation programs and why?
8. Which orientation programs might need to be the most explicit? Why?
9. How can attendance at the orientation programs be ensured?
10. What kinds of visuals might be valuable in conducting an effective orientation?

QUESTIONS FOR DISCUSSION

1. Discuss the nature of resistance to change.
2. How does word processing differ from data processing in introducing change into people's business lives?
3. Explain how the grapevine often builds up resistance and negativism. How can it be used as a sales tool for the new system?
4. How can the attitude of the manager help to counter resistance to the system?
5. How should the supervisor train a group of people, some of whom are used to dictating and some who are not?
6. How can the tour of word processing operations be used to sell reluctant users on the system?
7. How can word processing staff help during orientation and training?

CASES

Case 14-1   City of Hopkins

You have been hired by the City of Hopkins to manage their word processing operations. They had a feasibility study conducted by two different vendors, who wrote the procedures for the dictation system and word processing typing system. They have shown you all the procedures and both offered their films for your use in the orientation programs. You will be giving orientation programs to city managers, working staff, administrative secretaries, and the word processing secretaries.

Outline your program and how you plan to conduct these sessions.

Case 14-2   Research Organization

Lincoln Research Institute is a nonprofit organization which conducts market research investigations for firms all over the world. Some of the outstanding scientists and engineers in many specialties are on their staff. After attempting to centralize their document production, they recently changed to a decentralized operation in which the secretaries and typists in the departments originate and produce all documents which are then printed in their in-house printshop. Their input is output by means of phototypesetting systems. They have many problems with the input from the secretaries where much attrition is experienced on various kinds of word processing keyboarding systems. You have been hired to manage the complete operation up to the printing of the documents. You plan to develop a career growth program for the secretaries, with three levels of jobs ranging from $900 to $1200 per month.

How will you go about turning this into a very successful word processing system?

"Job satisfaction . . . is not the cause of something (for example, increased production) but rather the result of something (the conditions under which the work is done). Hence, job satisfaction is an output, not an input. . . . For long-run operating efficiency it is intelligent to take the position that a balance may well be struck which sacrifices some productivity for job satisfaction."

CHAPTER 15

Developing Training Programs

OVERVIEW

The first step towards development of an efficient operating system is preparing and distributing procedures manuals and other written communications. This becomes the tool necessary to accomplish the daily production routine. However, individuals need to be taught how to use these tools properly. Once they have been shown, they should then practice until they can skillfully use them. This frequently requires feedback and followup until the desired training is accomplished. This process if mandatory in order to develop people so that they can use the system and perform within it successfully. This chapter presents the elements required for successful training programs.

OBJECTIVES

After completing this chapter, you will be able to:

1. Explain the kinds of in-house training programs firms might have.
2. State the kinds of training programs provided by some word processing vendors.

Quote from Carl Heyel, "Changing Concepts of Human Relations," *Management for Business Supervisors*, American Management Association, New York (1972) 44–67.

3. Describe the contents of a word processing supervisor's training program.
4. Explain why principals need to learn to use machine dictation and how it can be accomplished.
5. Explain why work originators might resist changing to dictating their documents to word processing.
6. Explain the two basic word processing training programs.
7. Give the reasons for having continuing training programs for users.
8. Explain how to handle new hires after word processing has been implemented for several years.
9. Explain factors important to planning the training orientation programs.

ORGANIZATIONS AND EMPLOYEE TRAINING

"All [people] want to be part of a group—but they still want to be outstanding in that group. . . . Competition and pride are fundamental urges."[1] The purpose of training is to improve an individual's performance and increase capacity for growth. Organizations traditionally have encouraged and frequently given financial support to their employees to seek training outside their jobs, through night classes, colleges, workshops, and seminars in fields related to their jobs, in order to increase their knowledge and skills. Some firms encourage continual self-development through learning by making it a part of the employee evaluation program.

Many large organizations are implementing career development programs. Some offer in-house training programs which may become ongoing programs once these programs demonstrate their contribution to employee improvement. In order for a firm to maintain internal training in a special skill, it must have adequate attendance, be supported by management, and have job coverage so that the work does not suffer.

The kinds of programs firms are incorporating into their employee development programs are:

1. Language arts or other secretarial skills development: spelling, punctuation, word usage, proofreading, editing, and writing letters and brief documents.
2. Dictation training: learning how to originate documents by outlining and organizing, using dictation equipment, and finally dictating a document so that the typist can type it without questions.
3. Spoken communications skills: getting the message across verbally, working on a team, and acquiring the ability to transact daily business with others.
4. Written communications skills: learning to organize, prepare, and write reports and proposals.
5. Management training: preparing employees for management tasks.
6. Telephone skills: improving present techniques to better serve themselves and the firm or learning to use a new system.

[1] James F. Lincoln, *Incentive Management*, Lincoln Electric, Cleveland (1951).

Many firms send executives to executive development training programs at such institutions as Harvard University and Stanford University Graduate Schools of Business. Some large office equipment manufacturers offer management training programs to their customers. The purpose of these programs is to orient customers to information processing systems by defining and explaining how the concepts are applied to solve traditional problems in the office by offering alternative system designs. These programs are designed to prepare supervisors for word processing management and supervision.

Most large firms with word processing systems have implemented their own in-house training programs. They have come to realize that in-house programs are imperative to continuing success in the use of word processing to its full potential as well as increasing the capabilities of the organization to optimize their personnel time and capabilities of the equipment.

What good is an expensive dictation system consisting of six recorders and six transcribers which can handle dictation of a hundred dictators if they do not use it and instead continue to write out their letters, memos, and reports in longhand? Why did the firm purchase this equipment? Why is it not being used? When it was installed two years ago, a training program was conducted in which those who prepare letters, memos, and reports were instructed in how to use it. A year later another program was conducted, but the majority of work originators did not attend. Most of these originators still use longhand. What can this firm do to solve this problem at this time?

Programs need to become a part of the weekly routine, especially when teaching employees how to be more productive on a daily basis. Work originators need to understand that it is important to use their time efficiently, particularly from management's point of view. Management needs to point out to the principal originators that using dictation instead of longhand can save time for the professional employees in the organization—executives; managers; supervisors; personnel in marketing, purchasing, accounting, engineering, and data processing—who daily are creating those letters, memos, and reports which are produced in word processing. By dictating, they can spend more time doing exactly what their job demands of them and devote less time to laboring with paper and pencil.

The weekly staff meeting is a ritual in many firms, frequently taking place early in the morning before the normal workday begins. Management should establish a weekly staff meeting at which dictation or document creation and communication is practiced and discussed. Through periodic repetition and management-directed procedures, personnel will soon become aware that the skill of dictating documents is expected of those who were hired into the firm to perform managerial, supervisory, and operational functions.

Weekly staff meetings can take place at all levels within the organization—middle management, supervisory, staff, and operating personnel. Everyone who creates documents should be attending the weekly meetings which do not need to take more than 30 to 45 minutes. In this way, the training is more of a communication tool which all will eventually become comfortable with and use out of habit.

Training needs to be offered to *all* personnel in an organization, whatever kind of training that will help each person to improve performance, which in turn improves the performance of that person's group or activity.

Management, supervisory, and staff training programs cover one area of need; the individual who is responsible for producing their documents also needs training for performance improvement. Training programs for word processing correspondence is equally important.

EMPLOYEE TRAINING NEEDS

In addition to losing control over their own secretaries, one of the reasons some principals refuse to dictate is that they feel, or are afraid, that the typist will not type the document correctly. They feel that words written out in longhand will be spelled correctly, while dictated words may not be. Many times these principals are justified because secretaries lack the necessary language arts skills. One of the first aspects of correspondence training, therefore, was the need to improve these skills; supervisors quickly discovered that, unless they set up an expert system of proofreading, they ran into many problems.

Word processing secretaries need to be expert in those skills listed in the job descriptions (listening and interpreting, proofreading, spelling, punctuating, dividing words, setting up documents attractively) in turning out high-quality documents without errors. In traditional systems, their errors did not surface readily, but in word processing they quickly become apparent. Once a person begins transcribing documents from machine dictation, skills in producing high-quality documents with no errors become obvious.

Some firms raise their entry level salaries when hiring word processing specialists, hoping that this will solve language arts problems. Usually, though, they pay higher salaries for secretaries experienced on certain word processing equipment. Unless they give language arts tests, they do not have knowledge of a person's true capabilities in the language arts. They therefore may depend upon the fact that since a new hire has worked successfully in other organizations, the individual will efficiently turn out high-quality work.

Frequently, however, this is not the case. Most supervisors quickly see the need to maintain continual training programs for their staffs. First of all, they want all secretaries to learn to work together, using the same high-quality standards and formatting techniques so that work can be easily distributed and word processing can meet its turnaround deadlines.

In addition, many companies have incorporated several training programs to improve language arts and proofreading skills and to teach the technical language of the various principals whose work they do. Since many supervisors have found that their staffs enjoy variety in the kinds of work they do, they must learn how to produce this variety of work proficiently. If this involves using technical terms, it is important they learn correct usage and spellings. Many times errors in context are made because the secretary did not understand the terminology. In the traditional boss/secretary arrangement, this was easily solved, since the secretary was near the boss/originator and could ask whenever something was not clear. Word processing correspondence secretaries who may not be close to the originators are expected to *know* the correct usage. Usually this means additional learning and training.

One small manufacturing company implemented a word processing system with four correspondence secretaries, who continued to produce the same documents as formerly. For example, the marketing secretary typed documents for that department: proposals, marketing reports, and daily correspondence. The engineering secretary typed engineering documents: specifications, reports, correspondence, and other technical documents.

After six months had elapsed, the supervisor asked the secretaries if they would like to rotate and type other documents. All were eager to make the change. This developed into a rotation system and has expanded to include six correspondence secretaries with an analyst. They now produce the majority of the company's typing. Let us examine the key to the success of this system. The supervisor began weekly training sessions in which each secretary learned the terminology and specific requirements for the department in which he or she would be working. This enabled those secretaries to continue to turn out high-quality, error-free documents for the principals, who then could learn the other operations of their firm. They developed an extremely high morale, and several turned down opportunities to advance to higher paying positions outside word processing because of job satisfaction.

ADMINISTERING TRAINING PROGRAMS

Some organizations have special Employee Development Departments within the Industrial Relations Division which administer their in-house training programs. However, the majority will simply use personnel trainers and representatives to plan and set up training programs most frequently put on by outside consultants in specialty fields, such as personal communications, transactional analysis, and management development. Word processing training programs in most firms are conducted and arranged by the word processing manager or supervisor. If they are handled by the Personnel Department, they will have personnel from Word Processing conduct the training. The majority of firms which have had word processing for several years have their own trainers, whose main job is to train new hires in the department in operating procedures, formatting, methods of communications, and equipment use when necessary.

The Word Processing Department is usually responsible for training both the operating staff and the principals. In some cases, there may be other training required for other service departments or staff. The two major word processing training programs are (a) training the users or principals and (b) training the correspondence and administrative secretaries.

Setting Training Program Times

When deciding when the training programs will be conducted, the manager or analyst is faced with a difficult decision: What time is best for most of the principals? If this affects only a few people, they should be contacted and the time should be planned convenient to the largest number. However, when a large number of persons is involved (as is the case in large firms), the time must be determined by learning from the department managers and supervisors the work schedules and habits of their personnel. Marketing personnel need to be out in the field early in the morning; therefore, staff meetings for them should be scheduled late in the day. Engineering and research personnel frequently become involved in projects later in the day and work overtime. Therefore, perhaps the best time for them would be early in the morning or during the lunch hour.

The important thing for the manager or analyst is to select the time most appropriate for the principals. This can be done by explaining to them that their attending will enable them to do more work out of the office (by phoning in dictation) and get their work back much faster with fewer errors or causes for author editing; therefore, by taking this time away from their jobs, they will receive great benefits in the form of quality and fast turnaround of their typed documents.

PREPARING TRAINING PROGRAMS

In order to develop training programs, the word processing manager or analyst needs to plan, gather information, organize, analyze, and write the final training package. In the previous chapter you learned how to write procedures, the most time-consuming job; the training package has been created and produced, ready for training to begin. Now the most important step must be carefully laid out: how should the training of the users be conducted in order for them to improve their performance and their ability to get their job done by using these procedures? Just how will this training package be administered?

Planning the Program: Setting the Tone

The first training program, orientation to the new system, is the most crucial. It is the tool by which to sell employees on the benefits they will derive by using the new system. The message, "We have prepared these modern time-saving procedures for you to use—now we will explain to you how you can use them," must be presented in a certain way.

Put yourself in the shoes of those who are attending the training and orientation session. They had formerly developed a certain way of getting their work done, which usually was easy to do. They had a secretary nearby who was there to respond to their immediate needs. They had yellow pads and pens and pencils with which they were very capable. Whenever they had an idea they wanted typed by their secretary, they simply jotted down the information, frequently in nearly illegible longhand. But the secretary had become familiar with their squiggles and was able to interpret them and turn out their letters, memos, reports, and other documents in a matter of minutes. What system could be better than that?

Now you are going to tell them they have to change their habits. They no longer have that secretary nearby with the typewriter. They must learn to dictate over a telephone to a secretary they may not know who is not located closeby and expect to get their work done as quickly as before. How can this possibly happen?

How can you convey to these principals that, once they become familiar with it, the new system will eventually make it easier for them to have their documents created and produced and will save them time that they can devote to their professional tasks?

Training sessions with principals need to be casual, comfortable, and open. Communications must maintain a tone cognizant of each principal's resistance to having to change and to losing a secretary. The important aspect of this entire meeting is setting the proper tone. The tone should be one in which sensitivity to each person's situation and needs is most important. Although the system does require learning some new habits and making some changes, the important aspect is that it will allow a person to enjoy the job more once workers have learned to make the system work for them.

Since implementing word processing, many firms have changed from centralized typing locations to work groups located near the principals. One of the chief reasons is to maintain close communication between the secretaries and the principals. Therefore, the change is not so drastic. However, it is a change in the way that the work is done, and in order to sell users on how it will benefit them, setting the proper tone is imperative.

INDIVIDUAL COACHING SKILL: THE ROUTINE

The five steps in coaching include: preparing, explaining, showing, observing, and supervising.

Preparing   Learners must be emotionally ready in order for learning to take place. The most important part of the coaching routine is ensuring readiness by having all equipment within easy reach of the learner and seeing that the learner is comfortable and physically prepared. Teachers also need to know that the learner is capable of learning, or the effort is wasted. For example, if the learner is worried about a personal problem, afraid of failure, insecure in the learning atmosphere, intimidated by the instructor, or otherwise is experiencing emotions which disrupt learning, the student will not learn.

Explaining   First of all, the teacher explains to the student (visually, if possible) what is going to be taught. By demonstrating visually what the student will be taught, the mental stage is set and the student is in tune with what will take place.

Showing   The next step is to show the student the information. The teacher demonstrates the path through the information by means of a workflow chart, demonstrates the equipment, and has the student practice right after being shown. This involves walking the person through each step by showing how one step follows another.

Observing   Next the teacher has the student practice the process as shown by having the student see and correct any mistakes and then reinforcing by verbalizing what he or she did.

Supervising   Next the teacher builds the student's confidence by turning the activity over to the learner and supervising, assisting when the student is in doubt or needs reinforcement or correcting.

This procedure can be applied at each learning step in learning a new skill. The student is the doer and the instructor the coach. In this way, the student becomes self-sufficient and does not depend upon the instructor to perform the activity.

GUIDELINES FOR PLANNING THE TRAINING PROGRAMS

Setting Objectives

When planning the training program, outline the objectives you wish the learners to achieve during that session: for the originators this may be changing their work routine so that they will send their typing to word processing specialists to produce or delegating their administrative tasks to the administrative secretaries.

Planning the Routine

Outline the information that will be included in the presentation and plan its timeline. Try to set a maximum amount of time for each segment. For example, if the training session is scheduled to take one and one-half hours, make sure that each segment has an allotted time and adhere to it during the program. A suggested orientation program follows.

Introduction   Present the way in which work will be accomplished using the new system, including each step that affects those being trained. This may include all five steps—origination, production, reproduction, records processing, and final communication or distribution.

Origination Procedures   Most work will be produced from machine dictation, forms filled in, or marked copy (including revisions). Users need to know how to originate in all three ways, including what needs to go on the forms, how to edit (use proofreader's marks), and how to dictate. Dictation training encompasses learning how to use equipment, to dictate effectively, and to dictate specific applications.

Production Procedures   Both users and operators need to be informed of the turnaround schedule (how much time to expect the work to take from the time it is sent to Word Processing until it is received back), hours when work is being done (e.g., 7:30 A.M. to 5:00 P.M.), and procedures and policies for specific kinds of documents. Most word processing systems use a first-in/first-out system for daily work with scheduled times alloted for periodic reports that must meet certain deadlines.

Other types of information that needs to be communicated during training include:

1. *Information storage policies for daily work and how to request long-term storage.* Supervisors will also need to know when storage media are periodically reviewed for purging and how to notify Word Processing to purge stored information.

2. *Reproduction techniques—carbon copies, copying, duplicating.* Usually the work request form used by Word Processing offers an opportunity for each originator to express how that document should be reproduced, the number of copies desired, etc., in the cases where Word Processing handles reproduction. Many firms may have Word Processing make masters only, and the administrative secretaries make the copies.

3. *Records processing system,* in which copies are kept and storage and retention procedures for media storage.

4. *Communication and distribution of the work after it has been produced.* Some systems have their own delivery carts and personnel who distribute and pick up work. Others phone the originators for pickup.

5. *Revision processing.* Most word processing systems consider a revision of a document as another cycle for production records. In the case in which the transcriptionist has difficulty transcribing the input or other similar types of questions, the originator and transcriptionist need to know how to resolve these problems. The simplest way is to telephone the originator; but sometimes this is not possible, and the procedure therefore needs to be explained.

6. *Acquainting trainees with the system.* During the training program the attendees should work with the forms and practice filling them out for different applications so that they can ask questions and return well prepared to begin sending work to Word Processing. The trainer should observe carefully and request feedback to reinforce learning and make sure the trainees are comfortable with the new system.

7. *Dictation training.* One successful technique used to teach dictation to people inexperienced using machine dictation is to have the originator first create a document in longhand. Then have the originator create the same document by dictating. Before dictating, the learner needs to know how to use the microphone, telephone, or dictation unit. For both types of input, the originator should first outline, write marginal notes, organize, and then originate (write out or dictate). This part of the program should take at least a half hour. Even experienced dictators will want to practice dictating special applications contained in the procedures manual.

The idea that training programs encourage learners because the coach is always around to help solve problems, make the work easier, or make adjustments so that the system performs a service for them is important. Otherwise the training becomes a one-time thing which can be quickly forgotten and never used.

Effective Training Aids

- Audio-Visual: films, slides, overhead projections (transparencies), flip charts, and chalk talks.
- Self-paced: prerecorded audio self-paced learning packages.

- Manuals: procedures manuals, handouts, and workbooks.
- Group participation: case studies, role playing, problem-solving activities, and roundtable discussions.

Advantages and Benefits Gained from Good Training Programs

- Builds confidence in management.
- Builds confidence in the organization.
- Builds self-confidence.
- Contributes to improved staff interest, performance, and growth potential.
- Disseminates information for smooth implementation.
- Builds in ability to use and maintain word processing system.
- Creates a more positive environment.
- Builds employee morale.
- Allows feedback to those managing and operating the system.
- Allows monitoring of skills and growth potential.
- Opens up communications channels between users and those doing their work.

WORD PROCESSING STAFF TRAINING

Most of the discussion thus far has been concerned with training the users who previously worked in the traditional boss/secretary environment. How should continuing training programs be set up for the staff who performs their work? Organizations may have training programs for new hires to teach them formats and production procedures, but generally they do not have followup programs. Centralized document production by specialists who are not located near the dictators creates certain communication problems. Some of these are the need to ensure correct spelling of technical words and names, and interpreting difficult-to-read longhand. If originators are going to dictate those documents that they originally were able to write carefully, they must be assured that they will receive accurately spelled, punctuated, and formatted documents. Therefore, those correspondence specialists must be able to turn out very high quality documents. At IBM's San Jose plant, they seek only executive secretaries to work in their correspondence production centers. They will not hire college students who do not have proven abilities to spell, punctuate, format, and divide words. In other words, secretaries must have extremely fine skills.

Not every firm can afford to pay high salaries to beginning word processing secretaries. Therefore, they set up their own internal correspondence training programs. These programs must test, teach, and measure the abilities of correspondence secretaries to meet the high standards desired for all documents which are to be mailed to the firm's customers and other offices and which represent the firm in the way each person and manager wants that firm to be presented.

What kind of training do employees need to receive? When will it take place? How will it be conducted? How can the secretaries do their work and at the same time upgrade their skills?

Fortunately, there are some fine audio training packages which firms can purchase and use on their transcription equipment to teach these skills. They can be taught during the workday, and workers can be taught skills during slow periods on the job or during special training sessions set up through either Word Processing or Personnel for personnel development. If word processing is to encourage employee development, it must help employees develop through internal training such as by using audio packages.

Discussion Groups

Many word processing managers conduct casual group sessions with both administrative and correspondence secretaries to encourage communications. These sessions are held to discuss areas needing improvement and to offer employees opportunities to discuss how improvements can be achieved. In addition, the manager will evaluate performance and discuss with individual employees the areas which need improving. Rather than formal training programs, more self-paced learning and individualized learning can take place.

Trainers

Most word processing supervisors have a member of the correspondence staff who serves as the trainer. The trainer helps new hires learn the procedures and formats that the organization uses and assists new learners as they begin to produce documents on their word processing equipment. If the equipment is new to the new hire, the individual first learns the system. Sometimes this is done at the vendor's business, but most firms prefer to train their own employees and use the self-paced learning packages obtained from the vendor or purchased from companies who develop these packages, such as Western Tape's memory typewriter and mag card II audio training packages. The new hire can learn the basic equipment and then work with the trainer to produce documents for that organization.

The trainer is usually a secretary who particularly enjoys the challenge of using sophisticated equipment to accomplish difficult jobs. As a result, trainers or specialists are frequently the ones sent to advanced seminars put on by the equipment vendors. Such training helps them to better accomplish their jobs. They learn suggested techniques to help them accomplish difficult jobs which they can pass on to other secretaries. As an example, the Wang shared-logic system has a glossary which can be used to accomplish many kinds of tasks. Usually most firms using Wang equipment have one secretary who specializes in developing various uses of the glossary which that secretary then teaches or assists others with in their daily work.

Outside Consultants

Many firms prefer to use outside consultants to perform training for them. For example, should they wish to conduct followup surveys to find out exactly how much the system is being used by certain departments (if they do not have a computerized measurement system providing this information), they hire consultants to conduct these surveys. Upon learning what areas principals are weak in and the kinds of training which would be valuable to them, they have a consultant conduct the training.

Training programs may last from one to several hours or even more than one session. Seminars and training may be conducted which teach improved dictation skills; organization habits; or listening, proofreading, or telephone skills.

SUMMARY

Most organizations encourage their employees to improve their skills through outside or internal training to enhance their career growth potential. Kinds of internal training firms may offer employees include language arts and other secretarial skills, origination and dictation, spoken and written communications skills, management development, and telephone techniques.

IBM and Xerox Corporation offer many kinds of employee and management development training programs, particularly for their marketing, engineering, and customer training representatives. IBM has several executive development programs as well as customer management seminars presented in their sales training center.

When a firm implements word processing, it needs to plan, set up, and offer orientation training to new users of word processing, in addition to continuing training, particularly in the area of dictation. Since most people still originate their work by writing in longhand, dictation requires a change in work habits as well as learning new skills. Therefore, learning and making the change is frequently resisted by work originators. Convincing them of the benefits of making this change and learning this new skill is important to the success of the new system and to the firm, for word processing can save a great deal of time so that work originators can devote more time to their job activities.

One way to get work originators to use dictating equipment is to have weekly staff meetings at which they can practice and communicate. This way they can share their problems, communicate their reasons for hesitancy, and become a member of the group learning together to use this new skill. This might be one of the best ways to get principals to make the change.

Management needs to make principals aware of the importance it places on efficient use of time. If this message is communicated, principals will become convinced that they need to learn time management in order to perform their jobs efficiently.

Training those who produce those documents is equally important. Frequently the reason most principals do not dictate or resist dictating their work is their lack of confidence in the system. They want their documents to be produced rapidly without any errors and to be of top quality. They may have been able to achieve this very easily and quickly in their former system, where their secretaries were located right next to their offices. They may fear this will not happen with the new system in which they have no control over the secretary to make sure their work is being produced to meet their deadlines. The correspondence secretary may not be near them so that they can check to see the status of their work or give the secretary a brief document they would like right away. They need to see and have proven for them that the new system can accomplish these goals just as well as the former one did—and faster. This, of course, depends upon the efficiency and productivity of the word processing operation and its management to meet their objectives.

Many firms have discovered that when they turn to machine dictation some of the secretaries do not produce high-quality, error-free documents, because they do not have adequate language arts and secretarial skills. Some pay more when hiring from the outside, hoping that this will solve the problem; sometimes it does not. Frequently they hire experienced word processing operators who know the equipment but who still may not have adequate language arts skills.

Firms need to incorporate training programs to improve the skills on the part of the word processing secretaries. Even when they have highly skilled secretaries transferring from traditional jobs into word processing, they need to maintain training programs for cross-training, improving document production efficiency, and promoting operational efficiency.

One firm had secretaries who had worked in departments such as Marketing and Engineering produce those same documents when they transferred to Word Processing. Once the system was operating successfully, they rotated departmental work so that all were cross-trained to work for every department. In this way, they learned how to produce documents for all departments and at the same time they learned more about their firm. This increased their skills and made their jobs more interesting. As a result, some turned down opportunities for higher paying jobs because they found job satisfaction in word processing.

Training programs are frequently administered by the Personnel Department. With word processing, they are generally administered, developed, and conducted by the Word Processing Department. Or sometimes they are administered and arranged by Personnel, while Word Processing conducts the training.

In preparing the programs, it is extremely important to set a tone which results in the enthusiastic participation of all attendees. In addition, it is important that everyone who originates work attend the training sessions. Therefore, it is important to convince personnel of the value and importance of the training sessions. This means that the training sessions must be conducted very professionally, cover all procedures as clearly and concisely as possible, and answer any questions the principals may have.

Prior to the sessions, after distributing the orientation schedule to all principals, followup should be made personally or over the telephone to encourage everyone to attend. Orientation of all those who originate work is important, and they should understand the value of proper orientation to the new system.

Continuing training sessions should be conducted at weekly or other periodic staff meetings to continually communicate ways to improve dictation and get the work done, help with any changes and problems, and suggest ways to improve the efficiency of the system.

A schedule of orientation programs offered on a periodic basis should be maintained to handle all new hires. By working in liaison with Personnel, managers can send a memo to Word Processing with the names, titles, locations, and phone numbers of new hires so that Word Processing can then contact them for arranging their orientation. Managers of work originators should be notified when new hires have attended training sessions (or if they fail to attend).

When attempting to arrange for the best training times for people from many different departments and with different kinds of responsibilities, one frequently discovers that no time is best or perhaps several times are best. Depending upon the size of the organization and number of personnel who will be trained, various times might apply. Such factors as geographical location, nature of the business, and kinds of jobs performed by the trainees may make only one time feasible: the lunch hour. For an organization located at a remote site where employees remain all day and leave only at the end of the day, the lunch hour might be the best solution.

REVIEW QUESTIONS

1. Name five training programs that firms are incorporating into their employee development training.
2. Why does a firm need good dictation training for its personnel?
3. Why is employee training important to an organization?
4. Explain why individuals prefer having a personal secretary to sharing one who is specialized by tasks.
5. Explain ways that language arts skills are important in word processing.
6. How do firms solve the problem of inadequate language arts skills of their correspondence secretaries?
7. Explain how training times should be planned.
8. Describe the tone to be set in the orientation training program meetings and explain why setting this tone is important.

QUESTIONS FOR DISCUSSION

1. Discuss advantages of internal training over outside training for employees.
2. Discuss the reasons for extensive supervisor training programs.
3. Discuss how to make training successful in meeting the firm's development objectives.
4. Discuss who conducts word processing staff training and the advantages of having the training conducted by these persons.
5. Describe the five steps involved in coaching.

CASES

Case 15-1   Law Firm

You have been hired by McAdams, Ross, Gains & Blake, a law firm with offices in Miami, Tampa, and Orlando, Florida, to manage their word processing operations. One of the major responsibilities you have been requested to undertake is to develop training programs for the users, which includes attorneys, operating staff, and administrative legal secretaries who create documents as well as train the correspondence secretaries who produce documents. Their original training programs were developed by the vendors whose equipment they originally purchased which meanwhile has been replaced. The procedures manuals for both areas are seldom referred to, and the office manager who hired you wants you to create a program which will solve their current problems, which are misuse of equipment, lack of dictation input, and frequent misunderstandings as to responsibilities of originators and producers. In addition, they want to upgrade the skills of the correspondence secretaries, who frequently misunderstand legal terminology and the formats for legal documents, causing work to have to be redone. Outline the training programs you would implement.

Case 15-2   Insurance Company

Matterhorn Insurance Company has had a word processing system for approximately five years. You have recently been hired to take over its management. One of your first responsibilities is to plan for phasing in three new departments: legal, sales, and data processing. Previously the word processing center handled work for the claims adjusters only. There is a central dictation system as well as portable units which are signed out by those who wish to take them out of the office. Secretaries in the new departments will remain in their departments and will handle administrative duties. All administrative secretaries, sales personnel, attorneys, and data processing personnel need to be trained to originate their work for production by word processing. You have hired three additional correspondence secretaries who need training in your system. At the same time you wish to include the present correspondence secretaries in order to enhance their knowledge and skills. Outline your training program to handle these needs.

"[The] important aspects of a system must be orderly and hierarchical, ... and ... there must be communication among them. ... Since the system is oriented toward an objective, any interaction among components must be designed to achieve that objective."

PART V

IMPLEMENTATION

This section encompasses the complete implementation program: orientation programs presented to top management, middle management, lower managers and supervisors, staff, other service departments, and secretaries; and training programs including introducing the new system, continual training, and special programs introducing new or changed functions incorporated into the information processing system.

An important aspect of word processing is control and measurement. How do we know whether word processing is meeting its projected production objectives? Is it meeting the planning statistics? What is the average volume being produced? What departments are getting the most use of the system? The least? Is the equipment being fully utilized? Should some equipment be replaced? Are personnel being fully utilized? Are additional or fewer personnel required?

Only by taking some kind of measurement of the system can these questions be answered accurately and comprehensively. Therefore, a control and measurement system is necessary.

What, if any, kind of reporting system should be set up? How should the word processing manager communicate to top management, middle management, lower managers and supervisors, other employees, and the word processing staff?

This section introduces various kinds of reporting methods and how to create and implement these methods.

Quote from Robert J. Mockler, "The Systems Approach to Business Organization and Decision Making," *California Management Review* 11 (Winter 1968); 53–58.

"It is the responsibility of management to find the most efficient way of doing any job. This is not the responsibility of the operator."

CHAPTER 16

Implementing the New System

OVERVIEW

The time has come; the word processing manager's and supervisor's jobs are about to begin. All of the preparations will be put into practice. The true test of word processing as a means of improvement and accomplishment depends upon what occurs next. This chapter explains those activities that should take place.

OBJECTIVES

After completing this chapter, you will be able to:

1. Explain how a firm should plan its word processing measurement objectives.
2. Describe benefits gained from word processing measurement.
3. Describe what information should be provided by work measurement.
4. Explain benefits gained from word processing measurement.
5. Plan a word processing measurement system.

MANAGEMENT SUPPORT

In order for a system to function at top efficiency, it must be backed by top management, just as management sets the criteria for processing and managing finan-

---

Quote from James F. Lincoln, *Incentive Management* (Cleveland, Ohio: Lincoln Electric Company, 1951).

cial data when a firm installs large computer systems. This must be true for any type of word processing system to succeed. Each person should feel confident that management is continually backing up the system and each person's individual efforts, particularly when it is the result of a system that *changes* that person's job and working environment.

A feeling of permanence and the ability to rely upon management as the backbone of the system are of extreme importance. Without management support, a new system will most likely fail.

The process of changing tasks, reporting alignment, and determining responsibilities may be extremely traumatic for those involved. Management's awareness and involvement during the early implementation stages can help achieve a smooth-flowing system in which the employees feel that their participation is important to management and that the goals expected of them are ones in which they participate along with management in meeting the organization's operative objectives.

EXPECTATIONS

One firm should not necessarily expect to achieve the same results as another. Word processing results obtained at an insurance company's headquarters will most likely bear little resemblance to those achieved or expected in a law firm. The insurance company might use word processing to accommodate many dictators who process large volumes of short, routine correspondence and form letters or to maintain large corporate group insurance policies. By applying word processing to achieve these business needs, measurable reductions in terms of lower per-page cost or reduced policy maintenance expenses can be realized.

This will not apply in the field of law. The fact that an insurance company was able to significantly reduce per-page costs may have no relevance to the word processing expectations in the legal climate. A law firm should anticipate different kinds of improvements from word processing—those relevant to producing legal documents (perhaps a faster response time for typing extensive legal briefs, trusts, complaints, summonses, and other legal documents). A main objective in the field of law may be to improve document quality and reduce turnaround time, resulting in providing paralegals and legal secretaries more time to perform legal assistance.

No pat objective should be stated for any organization implementing word processing. Rather, the firm should determine what factors are most important from the new system design and analysis and correlate this information with management's objectives to set measurement goals. Word processing expectations should relate to the specific nature and characteristics of the organization. To establish the correct performance goals in advance of implementation is not simple. One should be cautious before setting firm criteria until the new system has been operating. The word processing supervisor should monitor the system after several weeks of operations before adopting and publishing firm standards for system measurement.

To develop productivity goals, one needs to consider training, learning rates, and anticipated operator skill levels (including the skill sophistication required to operate the equipment). Setting and maintaining appropriate productivity goals, although a complex task, when done well will provide strong incentives for productivity improvements by the employees. Output volume goals must be tailored to meet the situation and not be borrowed from other organizations' word processing systems.

MEASURING PERFORMANCE FOR PERSONNEL EVALUATION

If word processing has an effective measurement system, it can be used to charge back to departments to recover costs of operations as well as to justify the system. A secondary purpose may also be accomplished with appropriate management and applicable statistics by providing the manager a means of evaluating individual performance.

People want to know where they stand and how well they are doing on a continuing basis, not just once or twice a year. When they are not provided with quantitative information, they often assume an improper set of values to measure their own worth. Performance standards of measurement can be used as a specific quantitative motivator. By setting high but achievable standards and continually informing employees whether or not they are achieving these standards, the manager and supervisor maintain continual communication and motivation of their employees. The employee is competing with himself or herself, not the other employees, a factor that creates a more positive cooperative working relationship among the staff.

PURPOSE OF WORD PROCESSING WORK MEASUREMENT

Work measurement is utilized to analyze and control productivity, cost, and effectiveness of the word processing system. Information provided by measuring the system provides criteria to maintain and make necessary adjustments in the system. Work measurement:

- Provides data that can be used to analyze word processing accomplishments and individual achievements. *analyze & feedback*
- Allows monitoring of the system to charge back costs to the users as a profit center, if so desired.
- Provides data to determine areas where improvement, further training, and attention are needed. This may include operating staff, principals, equipment utilization, and services provided.

The new system was designed to meet definite stated objectives and goals. Word processing management needs feedback regarding the achievement of these goals. This requires some type of objective yardstick to measure how well word processing personnel and the word processing department are meeting their goals. A periodic listing of accomplishments and system usage provides a means to determine accomplishments and point out what improvements need to be made.

Work Measurement and Employees

People do not as a rule like to feel that they are being measured while they work. It is therefore important to make employees feel that measurement is a benefit to them. Using work measurement to improve employee relations can be worthwhile and can:

- Improve satisfaction when an employee is given the opportunity to be effective during the total work day.
- Provide satisfaction from performing and attaining specific goals for routine work (e.g., meet turnaround time by typing a high-quality document).
- Provide an opportunity to apply individual incentive programs.
- Attract and keep highly qualified personnel.
- Provide a means of measuring individual performance for those who want to advance their careers. They can see how well they are doing, what exactly is required to get advancements, and receive recognition when they achieve these skills.
- Provide clearcut job definitions so that employees who prefer not to work in the word processing environment will be placed elsewhere, while those who prefer to can be aware of their daily success status.
- Provide much clearer definitions of skills required for the jobs.

The attitude of the supervisor employing work measurement is extremely important. A negative attitude regarding work measurement will be conveyed to the staff and spell failure for the program. A positive attitude will reward the supervisor with an interested, productive staff, enthusiastically working to achieve high-quality standards and improve upon them.

COMPONENTS OF WORK MEASUREMENT

Units To Be Measured

What units will be used for measurement? **Line count** has achieved wide use because of industry acceptance of the average 60-character line, while page content can vary significantly. Other units of measurement may be words, characters, dictation units, or projects. Many systems use units made up of components that relate to the kind of information contained in the document, such as text, columns, statistics, and forms fill-ins.

Standards of Production

Minimum performance levels are to be established for each work category, including transcribing correspondence, printing out form letters, revising a document, producing statistical information, and forms fill-ins.

Quotas

Based upon individual skill levels and experience, each operator should have definite standards adjusted according to the individual's level of development. Quotas may be set for individual projects and categories of documents and should be reviewed periodically to determine whether any adjustments need to be made.

Adjustment Factors

When differing units of productivity are combined to provide productivity rate (for a monthly report), a simplified adjustment rate can be used to compute incentive payments, word processing productivity, and plot productivity graphs.

Productivity Analyses

Many word processing supervisors prefer to provide only a few productivity statistics in order to maintain simplicity. One can evaluate the system and decide what changes and adjustments need to be made by evaluating such reports as:

- Productivity by volume: daily output, weekly output, average output.
- Productivity volume by department: how much is turned out each period (week, month, quarter) for each department.
- Productivity volume by principal (author): how much work was done in that period for each principal user of word processing.
- Productivity by secretary: how much (average, total) work was produced over the measured period (weekly, daily) and for each document category.
- Productivity by document category: how many form letters, revised text documents, statistical reports, forms, etc., word processing produced over the period (weekly, monthly).

Figure 16-1 is an example of a simple monthly control summary report. Figure 16-2 shows a monthly report that provides both hourly and line count figures.

Information from productivity reports can provide total and average output, error levels, new skills required, increased experience or efficiency. These reports are designed to measure the system, not the employee, so that management can judge how well the system is doing. They are also used to point out any changes or additions that should or could be made.

After the system has been implemented and daily work begins, quotas need to be set and monitored. The adequacy of the forms and measurement system also need to be reevaluated.

AN OVERVIEW OF PRODUCTIVITY MEASUREMENT

To efficiently supervise the system's work measurement program, the following needs to take place:

1. Quotas are set.
2. Daily and periodic production is collected and analyzed.
3. System is reviewed.

FIGURE 16-1   **Control Summary Form**

CONTROL SUMMARY											
		Input Category				Type of Output				Proc. Time (min.)	Pages/ Week
Week	Date	Longhand	Dictation	Hard Copy	Edited Text	Original	Draft	Final	Rush		
Totals											

4. Quotas and standards are adjusted.
5. Productivity is analyzed.
6. Incentive programs are implemented.
7. Additional staff and user training occurs (and further programs developed and conducted).
8. System troubleshooting occurs.
9. Additions or reductions may be made to staff, equipment, or shifts.

BENEFITS FROM WORK MEASUREMENTS

What should a supervisor expect to achieve by applying work measurement principles to word processing? Is it worth the time consumed and effort expended? Some benefits to be derived may be to:

- Help determine exact cost per unit by dividing operating costs by production.
- Monitor increase or decrease in usage by customer or project.
- Identify users and nonusers.
- Aid in planning equipment and staff acquisition and double-shift implementation.
- Plot peaks and valleys to plan schedules and overtime.
- Provide a basis for personnel incentive compensation based on accurate performance measurement.
- Provide an accurate chargeback system based on usage rather than $/hour rate.
- Aid in quality and error analysis; pinpoint individual or staff and principal training needs.

WORD PROCESSING MONTHLY REPORT

August, 19

Total Line Output   200,977

    PRERECORDED

        • Revision   97,153
        • Repetitive   48,515

                        145,668

    ORIGINAL

        • Longhand   37,064
        • Copy Type   16,645
        • Machine Dictation   1,600

                        55,309

Average Daily Line Count per Operator   1,928*

Total Number of Jobs   804

AVERAGE TURNAROUND

    Rush   2.21 hrs.
    Daily   7.51 hrs.
    Lengthy   19.04 hrs.
    Weekly**   13.89 hrs.

Available Hours during August   1012.0
Downtime   - 27.8
Backup   -   1.0
TWX   - 106.4
Absences (Vacation, Sick Time, etc.)   - 76.0
Overtime   + 33.0
(Temporary — TWX & WPC)   (18.0 Days)

                                  833.8 Hours

 *Based on 5.5 operators
**Jobs which users have requested be done in two to three weeks. None
  was requested under five working days.

- Monitor quality control of output.
- Provide analysis of projects to develop training procedures and simplify document production techniques.
- Provide equipment downtime analysis to determine equipment reliability, vendor response time, and equipment training weaknesses.

IMPLEMENTING WORK MEASUREMENT

After the new system and procedures have been designed, the supervisor should evaluate what needs to be measured, how to do it, what standards should be set, and what forms should be used. This may require designing several special forms, but it is wise to use as few forms as possible. The more forms used in an organization, the more costly. Forms costs include cost of the forms themselves; cost in time to enter, use, and interpret the information (often to another form); and storage space. Forms can become a cycle of inefficiency and redundancy that can become very costly to the organization. Only six percent of the cost of the system is for the form itself. The majority of its cost comes from those handling costs involved in its use. A breakdown of a form's cost follows:[1]

Category	Percentage
Use	65%
Management	24
Price	6
Procurement	3
Storage	2

Work Measurement Tools

Many supervisors use preprinted pages or plastic overlays with numbered lines on the side for both single- and double-spaced lines. These can be placed next to the copy to count lines in the body of text such as a letter. Any blank space lines are subtracted, and in the case of a letter, three lines are added for headings and closings.

A line length of 60 characters is a recognized industry standard established by measuring average line lengths for text. Many word processing manufacturers program their word processing systems with preset right and left margins and tab settings. The margins are set for a 60-character line. By having the word processor automatically set the margins and tabs when it is turned on, the operator consumes less time preparing to type a document. Word processing supervisors apply the 60-character standard line to all normal documents, including letters, memos, and text, unless they have specific requirements that do not allow them to use a 60-character line. The time saved by eliminating the need to set up formats improves productivity, standardizes procedures, and saves training and setup time.

[1] *Source*: New York State Department of Commerce.

STANDARDS TO SET AND EXPECT

Secretarial capability has considerable impact on standards. Operators who are experienced, particularly on the equipment being used, should be much faster than those who are just beginning. Some secretaries, because of lack of experience or inadequate training may have never learned to use the most advanced sophisticated capabilities of their systems. Obviously, those secretaries will use the techniques they have mastered until they feel secure in learning new techniques.

The supervisor can set standards by having secretaries produce several samples of each kind of document from which the supervisor creates a graph, computing the average time for the slowest and fastest typist. This is then used to calculate average standards to expect for each document.

Consultants Bruce Payne and Associates have developed word processing standard data from predetermined motion time measurements (MTM), the study of a human being at work for the purpose of reducing effort, fatigue, and error so that time and costs can be reduced while production and personal satisfaction are increased. Their program consists of a set of tables that permit the supervisor or controller to put an accurate standard on each job in a matter of seconds per page, according to such factors as the amount and location of editorial changes and category of input.

Standards Related to Equipment

When setting or using preset standards, one should consider the kind of equipment producing the work. Automatic typewriter print speeds vary widely. For instance, average printout speed of the selectric typewriter equals approximately 150 words per minute. Other printers, such as the Diablo or Qume, print at speeds ranging from 350 to 540 words a minute; the ink-jet printer prints at 92 characters per second; line printers are even faster.

Standards therefore need to be related to the speed of the printer. Selection of printers frequently is determined according to the speed and quality (sometimes tradeoffs) desired. Printer technology is experiencing a phase of rapid improvement as far as speed and quality are concerned. Nonimpact printers are being developed that offer not only amazing speed but excellent quality as well. Next to camera-ready composition, the selectric typewriter is rated by many users as top-of-the-line standard print quality.

Standards Related to Classification of Documents

Correspondence (letters and memos) are generally one page long and require original keyboarding and playout. This standard therefore includes time for the secretary to type the information and then print it back out. Some equipment, such as the IBM **mag card** units, uses the correcting selectric typewriter with a **correction** lift-off tape. When the typist makes an error, backspacing not only erases the character in memory (or on the magnetic medium), but also erases from the paper by lifting off that character. In cases where the typist made only backspace errors and there are no revisions, the keyboard copy may be the final copy, eliminating the second step of printing out. This affects the standard for these situations.

Other document classifications as described in Chapter 8, Selecting Equipment, include:

- *Text*   Manuals, guides, reports, proposals. These frequently use an outline format, may contain some statistical tables, generally require at least one revision cycle, and usually undergo heavy editorial changes. Documents that fall into this category include engineering specifications, legal and technical documents, and technical bulletins. The document cycle for these documents includes (a) input (keyboarding) time, (b) playback of first draft, (c) first revision by author, (d) playback of second draft, (e) editor or author final polish revision, and (f) playback of final copy.

  Sometimes there are more revisions, and the amount of revision varies. As a result, many possible variables affect setting standards for the text category. When listing daily production, supervisors list each revision cycle as a new step or document.

  On the category production chart, it is listed as a revision rather than a new document, and the amount of new lines keyboarded may be logged; but playback of all necessary lines must be included in production measurement.

  Setting standards for revised documents depends upon the percentage of revision that takes place. Major revisions may include moving paragraphs, **global replacement** (a single change being made several times with a single instruction) of one term with another, repagination, and other long-document requirements that may be very time consuming. Standards for these specific situations need to be specifically related to the situation and equipment used. Performing major revisions may be much easier and faster on many shared-logic and advanced stand-alone word processors than others. This greatly affects production turnaround and needs to be measured when setting standards.

- *Statistical work*   Generally columns of numbers, frequently mixed with alphabetic characters and column headings, as well as item descriptions. This is the most difficult work to produce for most secretaries, unless they specialize in this type of work. Examples are budgets, forecasts, and financial reports. Some equipment greatly simplifies this work by automatically positioning the typist at the correct position for each column from prerecorded formats which may have been created and stored by the technical specialist. In addition, some systems provide automatic calculation; that is, the equipment will automatically total items and columns—adding, subtracting, multiplying, and dividing—saving time for both those who prepare this work and the typist. Setting standards for this work greatly depends upon the equipment and the operator's abilities to make the best use of the equipment.

- *Forms fill-ins*   Most secretaries find typing forms very tedious and painstaking, mainly because most forms were not designed for typewriters and the secretary has to realign each line in order to type into the spaces provided. Frequently the spaces provided are not large enough to type all necessary information. Many firms with well-established word processing systems have forms specially printed for word processing typewriters. Many word processing typewriters can store each reused format, making it necessary to type the information only. When the word processor prints onto the preprinted form, it will automatically place this information in the appropriate spaces provided. Standards would be set according to the equipment capabilities; a unit that stores the format and allows the operator to key in only information greatly reduces the time required for this application.

• *Stored letters and paragraphs* Form letters are usually the easiest and fastest item to produce. Setting standards on how many can be produced in an hour, for example, is fairly easy because all the secretary has to type is the special or variable information for each addressee. The typewriter/printer will then produce an original letter to each addressee.

Mode of Input

The form of input the secretary receives in order to produce the document greatly influences the time required to transcribe it. Therefore, production standards need to relate to form of input. When St. Luke's Hospital conducted its survey to set standards, transcribing from dictation equipment was found to be the fastest, easiest means of producing documents, so long as the information was well dictated. Dictation techniques and skills also greatly influence the amount of time required to transcribe.

For example, at Stanford University Medical Center, the Medical Transcription Department transcribes documents for the entire facility, which includes not only the permanent medical staff, but medical students and interns as well. Although they conduct dictation programs frequently, many dictators do not willingly attend training sessions, and many could use improvement. For some physicians, English is a second language and they may have strong accents and different means of expressing themselves. Add to that the fact that medical terminology contains many long and difficult technical words.

The Medical Transcription Department is located in a building separate from the main medical center. These medical transcriptionists have been well trained in medical procedures and terminology. Whenever they run into a word which is difficult to understand, they must listen to it until they can come up with what they think that word must be. This greatly slows down their productivity. At one time the supervisor experimented with line counters on the typewriters in order to prove to management their productivity gains resulting from using word processing typewriters. This allowed them to measure the number of typing lines produced each day by each medical transcriptionist. These line counters were later removed because of negative reaction to this means of measurement, and the production volume was not truly representative of the system's capability because of the wide range of dictator's skills.

Setting standards must relate to form of input. The two most frequent forms of input are (a) handwritten or corrected documents and (b) documents dictated from dictation systems or individual units. When using standards, one should screen out materials that cause delays and serious loss of efficiency. These should be regarded as exceptions to the routine.

Methods of machine dictation also can affect standards. Many supervisors feel that **continuous-loop** dictation systems will prove to be more efficient than equipment using **discrete** (cassette, disk, or other individual storage) media, because continuous-loop media are not handled and may be distributed automatically.

Other factors to consider when setting secretarial standards are:

- Keyboard by typing only or by typing and recording (into memory or onto a storage medium).
- Proofreading alone or with another person. *or to a separate*
- Separate playback or at the same time other work is keyboarded. *person*
- Revising according to editorial changes.

Proofreading correspondence usually includes reading the typed copy only, looking for errors. Many other kinds of documents require comparing the typed copy with the original. Important documents frequently require proofreading by two people, one reading to the other. Instances when this may occur include legal implications, important proposals and reports, and documents that will be photo-typeset. When accuracy and quality are very important, many firms have two people proofread together in an effort to prevent errors from slipping through.

Playback, or running edited storage media through the printer to produce clean copy, applies to standalone word processors without screens. Most screen units allow the operator to type and record another page or job while playback is taking place. When this occurs, it is not regarded as using time. But when the operator watches playback, that time is naturally consumed as part of the production process.

The most difficult standards to set are those involving editorial changes. This is because equipment capabilities vary. The same function is frequently performed differently on each vendor's equipment. There may be some word processors which have several ways to perform one task, such as revising multiple-page documents. The mag card II teaches two methods, two-pass or **scanning**, which the operator might use to revise a long document; the training manuals may teach operators more than one way. Even in cases where there may be a special technique that is more efficient, the operator may not understand it and may therefore use a different, more time-consuming technique. The amount or percentage and kind of revision also greatly affects setting standards. If a page is heavily edited, it is usually faster for the operator to rekeyboard that page than to make all the changes necessary.

Standards provide answers to such questions as: How do I know whether my long-term employees are better producers than my newer ones? Is an operator experiencing a problem? Can I be fair and objective in appraising my employees?

Setting Up the System

After documents have been grouped into categories of original typing, revision typing, stored material, and repetitive material, a time study for each category is made using fully trained operators.

Units may be lines per hour or another measurement unit preferred by the supervisor. The measurement may be done by a trained observer or by having each operator keep copies of completed work with the time spent tallied on each document (similar to action paper). Time tracked includes preparation and distribution of each document studied. Each operator should make six samples of each category for an adequate representation of the whole.

This information is recorded onto a probability chart, with minutes as units along the vertical side and number of lines across the bottom. Data is entered as dots across the chart beginning at point 0. Then groups of points that appear to run in a straight line on the chart are identified by means of mathematical formulas or tables, or visually if sufficiently experienced. Dotted lines are drawn to connect these points. The chart will probably produce two sets of straight lines represented by the higher versus the lower producers. Next, from point 0, a third straight line of equal distance between the two dotted lines is drawn. This line determines the best fit, or what a normal operator would normally produce under usual circumstances.

Locate the 60-minute mark on the straight line (125 in Figure 16-3). This represents average lines per hour for satisfactory performance.

SUPERVISING USING STANDARDS

Effective and successful use of standards takes careful planning and maintenance on the part of management, supervisors, and staff analysts. In addition, supervisors should be aware that the employees, as pointed out in the case of using line counters at

A Probability Chart for Original Typing   **FIGURE 16-3**

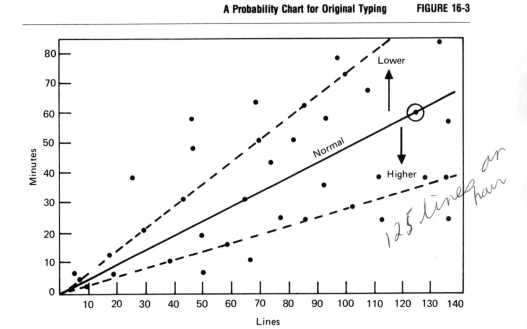

Stanford Hospital, may resist this measurement. Employees may react by fearing their job security, and they may become resistant or negative because of fear of the unknown through lack of information or understanding.

A successful measurement and cost-control program should be carried out from its inception against a background of concern for the individuals and their feelings. Supervisors need to explain carefully that no one will lose a job and this program will allow the employees to measure their own accomplishments and substantiate their efforts and achievements. A well-run measurement standards program will mean cost reductions, higher quality, and better morale.

Some word processing associations, including the IWPA (International Word Processing Association) and APT (Association of Power Typists) have been attempting to develop industry standards for measurements for some time. APT has developed employment standards for typists in the Washington State–British Columbia area for the positions of power keyboard operator I, II, and III. Grade III involves supervision, and APT has a separate standardized test for this position.

Developing standards for the industry is not an easy accomplishment. First of all, there needs to be agreement on nomenclature. The most predominant measurement tool, line count, can be different, depending upon one's definition of a line. Should a line be a carrier return followed by print (which some users currently use)? Should there be a distinction between typed lines for an original draft and lines played back in automatic mode (without operator involvement)? What about more difficult use of foreign languages, technical and mathematical symbols, required changes of typing fonts? And how about more difficult formats for statistical, tabular, and indented material compared to standard text?

EXAMPLES OF WORK MEASUREMENT SYSTEMS

Coppus Engineering

Coppus Engineering Corporation achieved its anticipated results from word processing through good planning and implementation. Their word processing accomplishments included:

- Significant decrease in total typing hours
- Doubled typing capacity
- Substantially improved quality of output
- Improved turnaround

Other unanticipated results were that:

- Users began to mail out improved quality documents they previously mailed out with penned in corrections. This resulted in their appreciation for high-quality documents representing them and increased their confidence in internal operations.

- Revisions and corrections had been a real problem. Correspondence secretaries happily changed to using word processing typing backup correction capability and threw away their correcting fluid.
- Rush jobs, which had nearly always required overtime, were handled easily in the normal workday.

Measurement System   Coppus designers prepared a secretarial **log** to record each job. When work was received, its time of receipt was recorded by a time-and-date stamp. The time was posted onto the log under "day in" and "time in." Time recorded was the time received in Word Processing, not when the secretary began typing. The secretary also logged the originator's name and department.

The secretary then typed the job and recorded its time of completion, total line count, and type of work. The company's work is divided into four categories: longhand, dictation, revision, and statistical. Line counts are determined by templates placed over finished copy. Revisions receive line credit only for lines revised, not for the total job.

Each line on the log sheet is keypunched and becomes a record in the system. These records are sorted and summarized by principal, departmental totals, secretarial production totals, and total word processing output. Information produced by the computer summaries include:

- Turnaround time. They average 235 minutes or about 3-1/2 hours turnaround time for a document.
- Dictation volume total and volume per originator. Obtaining this information indicates who needs individual dictation units (long dictation), who needs additional training, or what letters are similar and can be stored for repetitive typing.
- Volume of production by secretary. This is used to see if each secretary is meeting standard quotas and the average volume per secretary.
- When to expand word processing, either the number of people or equipment or both. They monitor the users and know when other departments are expanding personnel and work and are prepared to supply support when necessary.

Coppus management determined that maintaining a good performance record against turnaround objectives allowed them to control operating costs while maximizing service. Therefore, they decided that they needed to measure consistently and accurately. As a result, management is confident of the efficiency of its word processing system.

St. Luke's Medical Center

At St. Luke's Hospital Medical Center in Phoenix, Arizona, Dr. Harold J. Franceschi, director of the center, decided that in order to provide the best service possible, all dictation regarding patients in the hospital (known as priority dictation) should be transcribed within a maximum of 24 to 28 hours. Transcribed reports were required to have fewer than five errors each.

Dr. Franceschi explained, "In any productivity improvement program, it is important that all concerned know exactly what the objectives of the organization are, as well as what is expected of them individually, from the chief executive down to the line employee performing the individual task."[2]

The center implemented an endless-loop tape dictation system and a monitoring system (see Figure 16-4). Their word processing typewriters print documents at speeds of 540 words per minute. They measured output by reading from the secretarial station meters (transcribers), which record the minutes of dictation taken off the system. Their method of calculating average line transcribed per meter minute produced the following advantages:

- Eliminated some 15 minutes required each day for each transcriptionist to manually count transcribed lines.
- Reduced supervisor time spent verifying line count statistics.
- Became a quicker, consistent, and accurate method for computing lines transcribed each day because one transcriber may transcribe a minute of dictation faster than another.

Dr. Franceschi measures output volume by translating meter minutes on the dictation system into lines transcribed. In order to determine these rates, they conducted a two-month survey in which transcriptionists maintained reports for two months recording their daily line count production and at the same time computed the number of minutes transcribed each day from the meter readings on their work station. Daily meter reading volume was calculated by subtracting the reading at the day's beginning from the reading at the end of the day. The total lines transcribed over the two-month period were divided by the total minutes transcribed over the two months. They found that 5.5 average lines were transcribed for each meter minute. Since the original two-month survey, they have conducted random numerical line counts to verify the theory that calculating the average line count by meters accurately measures the dictation volume transcribed. It has repeatedly proven to be 5.5 lines per transcribed minute.

Using this 5.5 lines per meter minute of dictation, the transcriptionists calculate their line counts each day. Meter readings are recorded on the digital counter and locater part of the endless-loop dictation system (Dictaphone's 193 Thought Tank).

Meter readings on the counter are also used by the transcriptionists to locate material when necessary. The Thought Tank's four-digit, nonresettable counter records only the forward movement of the tape and not the movement when the tape is rewound.

After the transcriptionist has taken the reading at the beginning and end of the day and subtracted to get the difference, this figure is then multiplied by the 5.5 to arrive at the number of lines transcribed each day.

They use the volume guidelines given in Table 16-1 to evaluate the overall performance for each transcriptionist.

[2] Courtesy of Dr. Harold J. Franceschi, Director, St. Luke's Medical Center, Phoenix, Arizona.

Dictaphone dictation monitoring console at St. Luke's Hospital Medical Center,   **FIGURE 16-4**
Phoenix, Arizona. (Photo courtesy of Dr. Harold J. Franceschi, Director of
Medical Records.)

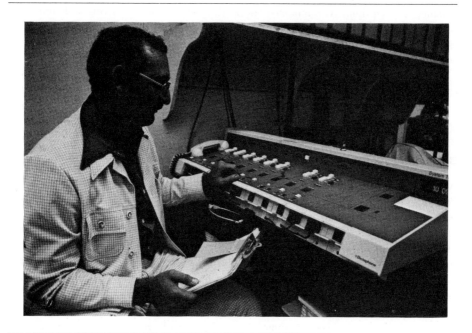

Transcriptionist Evaluation   **TABLE 16-1**

Evaluation	Average Lines Per Hour[a]	Average Lines Per 8 Hours[a]
Outstanding	127	1116
Average	106	848
Unsatisfactory	85	680

[a]Based on 85 characters per line.

St Luke's uses the following records in its work measurement system:

1. Transcriptionist worksheets to record individual daily transcription and locate where medical reports are stored on the dictation media.
2. Transcriptionist monthly production logs that summarize the number of reports and lines transcribed daily and monthly.

From these records, the word processing supervisor prepares individual and departmental reports, monthly summaries, and year-to-date monthly comparisons that are submitted to the director of Medical Records.

The reports have been used for the past five years. As a result, the center has obtained new equipment; remodeled the work space; justified existing and additional personnel; allocated cost of transcription services back to various departments or programs such as Behavioral Health Services, Cardiology, Surgery; and evaluated overall performance of the transcriptionists for merit pay increases. (See Figure 16-5.)

Dr. Franceschi states, "Any program, system or service is only as good as the people who provide it. St. Luke's has one of the best word processing centers in the country because employees are part of the total team which accomplishes the overall goals of the department."

University of California Admissions Office

At the Office of Admissions and Records (OAR) at the University of California in Berkeley, word processing supervisor Frances C. Powell dealt with their special problems in measuring volume and workload by designing a log sheet with accompanying tally sheet which has proven to be highly successful in keeping accurate records of number of lines typed in their word processing center (See Figure 16-6). Under their former system, admissions counselors depended upon secretaries in the departments to type appropriate form letters to applicants from students' folders sent them by the counselors, which consumed considerable time by the secretaries.

The word processing center provides the counselors with a book of standard letters with code numbers. Counselors fill out work request forms by selecting appropriate code numbers for letters to be sent to student applicants. They send these

---

FIGURE 16-5   Word processing center at St. Luke's Hospital Medical Center, Phoenix, Arizona. (Photo courtesy of St. Luke's Hospital Medical Center.)

DAILY LOG SHEET

Name _____   Date _____

Department _____   Hours worked_____

	No.	Description	Variable Lines	Pre-recorded Lines	Time
Pre-Recorded Letters					
Totals					

	No.	Originator	Long Hand	Dictation	Copy Type	Time
Original Letters						
Totals						

	No.	Originator	Revised Lines	Revision Playback	Time
Revision Work					
Totals					

	No.	Description	Long Hand	Dictation	Copy Type	Time
Miscellaneous Work						
Totals						

requests to Word Processing, where the letter is then printed from the prerecorded stored letters. The word processing operators need to type only the student's name and address and other variable information. The letter is returned to counselors for signing and mailing. They have 180 standard letters and 52 variable stored paragraphs for those letters. Variations might include requesting different test scores; whether a student is a nonresident; the college, school, or major applied for; and at what point in the registration cycle the student is requesting admittance. Counselors are free to add or delete as much information as necessary. Approximately two-thirds of the repetitive letters also need accompanying forms that require some typing, depending upon the quarter and point of time within the admission/registration cycle. For the academic year 1975–1976, the center prepared approximately 35,000 pieces of correspondence, of which 70 percent were repetitive letters, with 40 percent containing variables. In addition, they also processed 12,000 other documents: forms, notices, sets of mailing labels, and **hard copy** for offset duplication.

Two of the four word processing secretaries work special shifts to increase equipment usage. Quality of the documents has improved while costs have been reduced approximately $1000 per month since the word processing center first began operations. Because the university is state supported, it will continue to have budget limitations requiring that it take on heavy workloads, with little likelihood of obtaining more equipment or personnel unless it can demonstrate that additional machines will be a cost benefit to the operations. The supervisor must have accurate workload and cost figures with which to make comparison studies while seeking alternative methods to handle work and justify proposals for acquisitions of additional word processing equipment.

OAR is one of several word processing centers on the Berkeley campus. The supervisor serves on a committee that provides assistance to departments seeking to adopt word processing. Therefore, this committee relies upon statistics to provide helpful data.

On the tally sheet devised by Mrs. Powell, form letters are grouped by identifying code numbers and are listed with the basic line count, excluding variables, for each letter. Additional standard paragraphs and special enclosures are also listed, each with the number of lines it adds. While the secretaries **batch** (process similar work in one operation) their work each day, they tally each requested letter, paragraph, or other item in the appropriate space. Special, nonstandard additions are counted as they are typed; then they are entered in the indicated space. The total number of letters is multiplied by the standard established for variable lines (three for the Mag Card II, five for the Linolex because of extra key strokes required for that procedure). At the end of the day, the number of lines typed is easily computed on a calculator. The secretary then enters the totals in the correct spaces on the log sheet.

OAR obtained a transparent overlay that is printed with line counts on a proportional scale in increments of one-inch widths, beginning at 3 inches and ending with 12. This scale has been used as the basis for all line counts, so that statistics are standardized regardless of the varying margins that the different materials require. Using the overlay, secretaries can quickly ascertain the number of lines typed for original documents.

The tally and log sheets have made the task much less frustrating by decreasing the number of hours spent counting lines in individual letters and keeping notes on scratch paper. Management is thus provided with accurate figures on which to base future budgeting and planning decisions.

City of Plainfield

John DiPane, supervisor of communications for the City of Plainfield, New Jersey, devised his own system of measurement. When he first became involved with their word processing system, they were using a page count, which he felt was not telling the complete story of what they were doing, nor did it answer the questions frequently asked by management.

Based on national surveys, the speed of an operator transcribing from machine dictation is 25 words per minute, while transcription of material in longhand is 20 words per minute. These transcription speeds include the time involved in preparing equipment, changing recorded media, and coding material. Because 90 percent of the work is machine dictation, he decided to use the transcription speed of 25 wpm. In addition, the playout speed of the word processing typewriter was considered. Their word processing typewriters print out at a speed of 150 words per minute, which he converted to a line measurement of 12 lines per minute, while the 25 words per minute converted to two lines per minute (12 words per line).

This information was next applied to their operating procedures. Work is transcribed manually at two lines per minute; corrections and revisions are made at one line per minute; work is played out automatically in final form at 12 lines per minute; the total is 15 lines per three minutes or five lines per minute.

Therefore, all factors considered, an operator is capable of producing five lines per minute or 300 lines per hour, which includes drafting and final printout.

An operator's workday (less lunch and coffee and personal breaks) is based on six hours. Therefore, an operator's maximum capacity under ideal situations performing at 100 percent would be 1800 lines per day. This may appear to be extremely high, but it is a figure which can be achieved under ideal conditions performing at 100 percent. With this figure on which to base the center's performance, Mr. DiPane next prepares his monthly report as follows.

Maximum capacity of the center is based on the number of operators per work day for the reporting period. As an example, if three operators each work 20 days a month with no vacations or sick leave, the center's maximum capacity is computed as follows:

1800 lines per day × 3 operators × 20 days = 108,000 lines

Work is recorded by one person to ensure that standards were met in recording and measuring work. In one specific month, 84,000 lines were typed by the center. Since the maximum capacity was 108,000 lines, their productivity/utilization rate was 77.77 percent.

Because Mr. DiPane felt that the more information required of the operators, the less time available for actual transcribing, he preferred to prevent them from consuming time by recording measurement statistics as much as possible.

This form allows him flexibility. In the case of 77 percent productivity, he is able to allow other principals to utilize the center's services without having to worry about backlogs. If productivity were to remain at 95 percent for several months, he could substantiate a request for hiring another operator.

Any word processing system using these procedures would need to revise its figures to meet the particular standards, personnel, and equipment resulting from their own surveys.

CHARGEBACK SYSTEM BASED ON DETERMINING COSTS PER PAGE OR LINE

Word processing can be managed as a business organization. Accurately measured operating costs are charged back to the users. This is accomplished by determining the total costs and distributing these costs among the using departments according to their percentage of total usage. The First National Bank of Chicago charges for each document according to predetermined standards based upon the degree of difficulty and length of the document. By setting standards, a system is established in which the easiest jobs are least expensive and document costs rise with amount of difficulty. A single letter may cost a client $2, while an oversized chart may cost $6. Sometimes other factors are more significant, such as machine usage. Jobs that require heavy editing and use of more expensive equipment, such as a communicating word processor, may cost considerably more. For instance, when the communicating word processor is used, the cost is $13 per hour.

Work is tracked by having each of the bank's 36 operators record his or her work on individual form control sheets that have space for operator name, job number, and type of document. The completed control sheet is turned into the word processing manager at the end of each workday. The manager tallies the totals the first of every month. Monthly overhead costs (salaries, equipment rental fees, light bills, etc.) are calculated and charged back to clients based on their monthly percentage of use. The goal is to come out even. Generally word processing operations are underutilized. When this occurs, they go after more business. During an average month such operations may charge out $30,000 to $40,000.

At Sonoco Products Company in Hartsville, South Carolina, 13 cost centers serve from 2 to 25 principals. In addition to providing word processing correspondence production, they also provide administrative support. The number of secretaries depends upon the number of principals served. They charge back both administrative and correspondence support. Correspondence chargeback is based upon costs per line established from their line standards.

In the case of a letter, everything but the body is considered to be five lines. A line written in longhand which should have been dictated is considered to be 1-1/2 lines; an envelope, two lines. If the typewriter must be changed, each change is counted as an additional two lines. Typing lines for forms and statistical typing up to eight columns is considered twice as difficult, and therefore the line count is doubled; from nine columns up is tripled; revision work is halved.

The center determined these standards based upon experience gained after the systems were in operation. Line counts are collected daily by the word processing manager. Operators use transparencies with sequential numbers running down the side.

These are placed over a transcribed document to count lines, and the operator next calculates each line's worth.

The administrative support cost is based on secretaries' salaries, office expenses, and cost of supplies and is added to the word processing cost at the end of the month. Each department, or client of the cost center, is charged according to the percentage of work performed for it. For example, if a department used the services one month for 32.5 percent, it would pay that percentage of the center's one-month costs.

COMPUTERIZING WORD PROCESSING REPORTS

The same work request form used for computer feasibility studies may be used to measure word processing production. Information marked on the work request form by the operator who types the document is processed to produce reports with the following summaries:

1. Total number of documents produced including time utilization, line count, and time total.
2. Total of each category of document with line count and time total; total of each category of document form (original, stored, revised).
3. Total documents for each department, each principal; total of each kind of document by department and principal with line count and time total.
4. Total documents produced by each operator, each category, line count, and time total.
5. Total documents produced on each kind of equipment, line count, and time total.
6. Total amount of turnaround time and total production time with total wait time.

As a result of obtaining these summaries, the word processing manager can evaluate the productivity of the current system, by document category, by kind of input, and by kinds of production (original document, revised document, repetitive document, and assembled stored information). From these summaries, one can evaluate the system to determine where changes or improvements need to be made, whether the system is over capacity or under capacity, or whether any corrective action should be taken.

Personnel Work Distribution

Some word processing supervisors assume that each word processing secretary can handle a fair share of the workload on an equal basis. If five secretaries are required to keep up with production, each is considered responsible for 20 percent of the workload. In reality, individual differences account for varying levels of competency. Therefore, work should be assigned to fully utilize each individual's skills.

Once work performance standards have been determined, the supervisor can plan work distribution. Cooperation and team spirit should play an important role in the system from the very beginning. Individuals should be motivated, along with the supervisor, to illustrate the ability of word processing to more than meet the objectives set when the system was planned.

Workflow is smoothest when jobs are assigned according to secretarial competencies. A supervisor who ascertains secretaries' preferences and correlates this with productivity goals is on the path to successful word processing implementation. For instance, one secretary prefers and may be most effective when transcribing straight dictation; another may prefer and be particularly adept in producing statistical projects; and another most effective in turning out quick turnaround projects.

Along with establishing smooth workflow, the supervisor needs to standardize methods and provide complete and clearcut instructions. The operating staff procedures manual should be frequently updated according to new, faster, and easier techniques discovered by the secretaries as they become more skillful and knowledgeable on the equipment. Standardized procedures prevent misunderstandings and reduce the number of decisions required.

For an operator who may be a slower typist or one who produces much waste material, on-the-job instructions and training should be implemented. Audio recorded training packages and document production practice can improve the capabilities of these operators. Secretaries should be encouraged to share any shortcuts they learn at the group informal get-togethers or by posting notices on the bulletin board.

Improving Input   The supervisor should plan a periodic evaluation of input. When some authors require more than normal revisions of their daily work, a campaign should be undertaken to cut down on these revisions, which not only take more time in word processing by requiring another turnaround cycle, but take more of the authors' time as well. Instead of revising copy each time that it is read by one of the principals, it should be necessary to provide a clean copy only when the draft is sent out of the office for review, when numerous changes have been made, or when it is in its final stage.

As productivity increases, personnel and equipment can be evaluated. Criteria for hiring and purchasing policies generally become more clearcut. Operators who do not improve through training may have to be replaced by more competent personnel, or new equipment may be needed to produce certain jobs more efficiently.

As the system ages and personnel become more experienced, the benefits gained from measurement in word processing become more and more apparent. Measurement is an excellent and necessary tool to determine employee productivity, operational strengths and weaknesses, usage by clients, amount of usage of each kind of equipment, and the overall volumes of document production accomplished by word processing.

SUMMARY

Word processing systems, in order to succeed and particularly to maintain high employee morale, require complete and continual management support. One firm should not plan its word processing expectations and objectives based upon those of another firm. Because each firm is different, the information learned from a firm's feasibility study should be used in planning those objectives to be expected only from that firm's word processing system.

The word processing supervisor should wait until the word processing system has been operational for at least a few weeks before monitoring and setting productivity standards. Productivity goals need to be determined by considering training, learning rates, and anticipated operator skills which include the sophistication of the equipment. Goals need to be tailored to a firm's particular situation.

Benefits gained from word processing measurement are that (a) data can be used to analyze word processing and individual accomplishments; (b) it provides the ability to charge back costs to the using clients; and (c) it provides data to determine areas which require improvement in training staff or using personnel and equipment.

Although employees do not like to feel that their work is being measured as they work, measurement can be used as a tool to improve employee job satisfaction by giving the employee the opportunity to be effective during the total workday, providing ability to perform and attain specific goals doing routine work, allowing participation in an incentive program, providing a tool for those ambitious to advance in their careers to prove their accomplishments, giving recognition for their work, and providing clearcut job skill needs and definitions of the skills required for the job.

The most widely used measurement unit is line count, although some firms use pages, projects, words, or dictation units. Once the unit is decided, standards and quotas need to be determined for each kind of work: transcription, form letters, statistics, forms, text, revisions, and any other particular kind of document. Each operator should have a specific quota according to the individual's development. This quota should be monitored for adjustment as that employee grows in job capability. In addition, quotas should be set for specific kinds of documents and projects. These also should be reviewed and adjusted periodically. Adjustment factors can be used to provide one simplified measurement rate for the purpose of reporting to the staff, users, and management.

When analyzing productivity, important information to provide includes:

- volume—total, daily, weekly, average
- volume by department
- volume by author
- volume by secretary
- volume by document category

Information from reports provides average total output, error levels, new skills required, and decreases or increases in experience and efficiency. Analyses measure the system, not the employees, in order to make management decisions regarding changes or adjustments to improve the system.

In order for the system to be monitored accurately, a smooth flow of work needs to be maintained by skillful scheduling, which requires setting procedures and methods of handling exceptions to the planned schedule and routine.

Many supervisors set up incentive programs for word processing secretaries and some for users, such as monthly bonus, special awards, guaranteed salary increases for obtaining certain goals, time off, and free luncheons.

Benefits from word processing measurement are that it:

- determines costs per unit of production
- monitors peaks and valleys in usage

- identifies those who use the system
- aids in planning for the future
- provides basis for incentive program and awards
- provides basis for charging back costs to the users
- aids in pinpointing additional training needs
- monitors quality of the system
- provides analysis of present techniques
- identifies areas where techniques need analysis or improvement
- analyzes equipment usage and downtime

Measurement is begun once the system has been operating successfully: quotas and standards are set; productivity is analyzed; incentive programs employed; additional training occurs where necessary; troubleshooting takes place; and any required additions or reductions are made to the staff, equipment, or shifts.

Coppus Engineering reduced its typing hours, doubled the typing output, and improved document quality and turnaround with a word processing system. The measurement technique was to have each secretary record the work produced on a log page which was then keypunched to provide summaries of turnaround time, dictation time and volume for each originator, and secretarial production volume.

St. Luke's Hospital uses the meter readings from an endless-loop dictation system to record transcription volume. The advantages of this system are that it eliminates 15 minutes per day formerly required to do operator line count, saves supervisor's time, and is quick and more consistent and accurate for different operator's capabilities.

Reports are prepared from the calculated 5.5 lines transcribed per recorder per minute to determine monthly colume and evaluate transcribers' performance. As a result of using this system for the past five years, the hospital has obtained new equipment, remodeled their work space, justified additional personnel, allocated costs to using departments, and evaluated performance of transcribers for merit pay increases.

The Office of Admissions, University of California, Berkeley, uses a tally and accompanying log sheet to measure its production. This center, containing four word processing secretaries, has reduced costs approximately $1000 per month and provides production volume on a monthly basis in order for management to accurately determine future budgeting and planning.

The City of Plainfield, New Jersey, uses its transcription from a dictation rate of 25 words per minute (a national standard) along with playout and revision speeds to calculate current lines per minute capability. One person records the work volume and the line count, measured against the total monthly capability of 108,000 lines, to determine the percentage of productivity. If it remains at 95 percent for several months, hiring another operator can be substantiated.

Performance measurement can be an effective motivator. Employees need to know the standards expected of them and how well they are meeting these standards. Standards for each kind of work can be determined by having operators produce several documents in each category while being observed by a trained observer who records the time. The work is then recorded onto a probability chart on which the low performer and high performer are charted. Next the 60-minute mark is recorded and a straight line from 0 is drawn. This represents the satisfactory range from which to plot abilities compared to standards.

In order to charge back costs, all of the costs involved must be determined. Using departments are then charged according to their percentage of usage. First National Bank of Chicago set standards according to a document's difficulty and the time consumed in producing it, as well as the use of more expensive equipment such as communicating word processors (since other costs, including telephone costs, increase the cost of using this equipment). The work is tracked by having the operators record their work on a control sheet which is then summarized at the end of the day by the supervisor. Daily tallies are summarized at the end of the month. Overhead costs are calculated and charged back to clients based on their monthly percentage of use.

Sonoco Products in South Carolina has 13 cost centers each serving 2 to 25 principals. They handle specialized administrative support and correspondence support and charge out one or both services which are charged back to the using clients. Their standards are based upon experience using the system.

Computerizing work measurement is becoming more and more popular since it is one of the most accurate, least time-consuming, and simplified ways of measuring, so long as the system is set up properly and evaluated periodically to keep it current. From the summaries put out by the computer, the word processing manager can evaluate all aspects of the system in order to report how well it is doing, make whatever changes are required, and evaluate individual operators.

Work measurement standards should be set according to each person's current abilities and should be adjusted as secretaries become more experienced with the system.

The word processing supervisor should evaluate the number of revisions by authors in order to see if there is need for improvement and if further training or communications with the users or staff might be required.

Benefits gained from measurement as the system matures are primarily that measurement serves as an excellent tool for the word processing supervisor in determining the health of the system and being able to relate this information graphically.

REVIEW QUESTIONS

1. Why should one firm not pattern its standards and word processing goals after those of another?
2. What needs to be considered when setting productivity goals?
3. What is the purpose of word processing work measurement?
4. Name six benefits that can be gained through word processing measurement?
5. How can work measurement be used to improve employee morale?
6. What are the five components of work measurement and how do they function?
7. What kinds of reports serve the purpose of evaluating the system?
8. What is the purpose of periodic reviews of the system?
9. Explain chargeback systems.
10. What purpose can standards serve to the employee?
11. How can computerizing measurement serve the word processing organization?
12. Explain how work should be distributed among correspondence secretaries.

QUESTIONS FOR DISCUSSION

1. Discuss the positive and negative aspects of word processing measurement.
2. Discuss some of the measurement systems used by various firms mentioned in the text.
3. Discuss why word processing measurement can be a key to employee job advancement.
4. Explain how the word processing manager can use measurement to upgrade a system.
5. Discuss which information can be used by the word processing manager when reviewing the use of the system by clients.
6. Discuss which information provided by measurement is valuable in deciding what kind of word processing production equipment best serves the purposes of the firm.

CASES

Case 16–1 Airlines

Alpine Airlines, after implementing three document centers at its main facilities, in addition to setting up several correspondence and administrative secretary work groups where they formerly had private and department secretaries, has asked you to set up its work measurement system. Recorders for the dictation system are located within the work groups so that the principals can dictate daily work and communicate messages directly to their correspondence secretaries. Special lines are also directed to the document centers so that when the principals wish to dictate long documents directly to these centers, they may do so. Plan the measurement system you would set up to measure productivity so that you know the volume by the two working systems, by type of document, and by each secretary.

Case 16–2 Medical Center

Spring Hills Medical Center has just merged its medical transcription operations with the medical secretarial center so that transcription of most documents originated by the medical staff is produced in the word processing center. You have been given responsibility for designing a work measurement system of the 12 medical transcriptionists who transcribe machine dictation from doctors throughout the center, dictated from the outside as well as inside. Most of their documents are medical reports, charts and memos, correspondence relating to insurance and claims, or doctors' reports and written correspondence. Plan how you would measure the work produced in the word processing center.

"It is our belief that personnel-management training combined with functional word processing knowledge is needed for supervisors to become really effective managers."

CHAPTER 17

Managing Operations

OVERVIEW

This chapter is devoted to activities which take place during daily operation of the word processing system: management and supervision of the personnel and operations by using modern management techniques to solve problems when they occur, plan ahead, adapt to changing situations, and meet the word processing requirements of the organization.

OBJECTIVES

After completing this chapter, you will be able to:

1. Explain what work should be handled when first beginning operations.
2. Describe how managers prepare for beginning operations.
3. State problems managers can encounter in early operations.
4. Describe methods managers use to solve problems.
5. Describe how managers can continue selling word processing services.

It is the word processing system's first day of operations. Management, the staff, secretaries, and the first department to begin using the system have all been oriented. The staff is prepared to begin work. What applications will be the first to phase in? What procedures are set up? What happens next?

Quote from Charles P. Graziani, Manager of Marketing Support for Word Processing, A.B. Dick Corporation, *Word Processing Report* 11 (December 1, 1976), pp. 1–2.

For some organizations, particularly ones such as insurance companies which have in the past used stenographic pools for processing standard letters and daily correspondence, the transition may be minor. Most of the work originators had already been using individual dictation equipment or dictated over the phone and therefore will simply work as they did previously. But for others, it may be quite traumatic. They may have had their own department secretary or even a personal one who made copies, ran errands, and handled many other kinds of administrative tasks, as well as produced all of their typewritten documents. They may no longer have a secretary nearby; perhaps there is an administrative secretary several doors away, but they must now rely upon the dictation system to get their typing to word processing. They may even have been using longhand for origination all of their business careers and now must make the change to dictating over telephones or microphones.

Many firms' word processing systems, during their early stages, still receive considerable longhand input to transcribe. The supervisor may have explained in the orientation program that their procedure was to transcribe all machine dictation before longhand. However, they may not implement this procedure until the system is running smoothly without causing negative reactions.

Before implementing word processing, State Compensation Insurance employed a three-secretary stenographic pool that transcribed all the dictated and longhand input from the claims adjusters. In addition, two other sections each employed two typists to type claims, claims checks, and other insurance forms.

The Sales Department employed two secretaries who spent approximately half their time typing correspondence and sales proposals. After installing the word processing system, they made the following changes:

1. The word processing center, consisting of three correspondence secretaries and a supervisor, produced correspondence for the Claims Department as previously. In addition, they produced correspondence and sales proposals for the Sales Department and payment checks for the Claims Department.
2. The Sales Department maintained one administrative secretary to process administrative tasks.
3. Payment checks for the Claims Department were now produced on a word processing typewriter.

The first change was to centralize the typing for the claims adjusters, sales staff, and check payments. Many claims adjusters still used longhand to create their correspondence. As a result, the correspondence secretaries frequently had difficulty transcribing their handwriting, causing their transcription to take longer than transcribing from machine dictation. After the word processing center had been operating for approximately four months, the supervisor notified claims adjusters that their longhand input would be the last to be processed regardless of priority. Therefore, for top priority work to be processed on time, the claims adjusters had to dictate into their wired desk microphone system. Over a period of time, all claims adjusters discontinued using longhand and changed to machine dictation. The supervisor worked closely with all principals, helping them with dictation or other problems they might have.

THE BEGINNING PHASE

A decision the supervisor must make during the early stages of the word processing system is what work to handle first. If one department is phased in first, all their typing will be processed. However, in the case of one city office in which word processing opened its doors for all city departments, the supervisor and three word processing secretaries (with four pieces of word processing typing equipment) were not able to handle every typing application and meet desired turnaround time. They therefore had to set up a priority system to process top priority documents first. In this case, the city clerk and city attorney had many top priority documents, including agenda and minutes of meetings. Many of their top-priority documents were long (ranging from 7 to 30 pages) and required several revisions. As a result, the word processing secretaries were kept very busy creating these documents and then revising them. Daily correspondence had to wait.

This system soon ran into operating problems, because the workers were not properly equipped to meet the deadlines of long, heavily revised documents; they did not have enough personnel or equipment. If the documents had been phased in later, after the system was operating and producing rapid turnaround documents, it would have been much easier to prove early success.

At KSBW radio-television station in Salinas, California, the word processing center took in typing for the television station manager, all departments (News, Advertising, Public Relations, Programming, Sales, Accounting, and Traffic Scheduling), and for their cable television operations as well. The center employed a supervisor and two operators who worked varying shifts. Before beginning operations, they prepared their monthly schedule and displayed it on the wall. This schedule indicated all periodic deadlines for specific documents they produced. Figure 17-1 shows the Accounting Department flowchart. In addition, they planned to produce sales reports each morning in time for the sales manager's review. Most of the sales representatives would dictate their sales reports either late in the day or early the next morning. Word Processing transcribed these reports first thing each morning, to be ready for the sales manager's review. The Word Processing specialists also produced a daily news bulletin that was distributed by a mail messenger. The supervisor then processed the remainder of their daily work on a first-in/first-out basis.

PRERECORDING STORED DOCUMENTS

Before beginning operations, the word processing supervisor is wise to have the correspondence secretaries, as a part of their final training, record and store repetitive letters and paragraphs. They are then ready to produce those documents created from the stored material whenever the need arises. Principals can request form letters or form paragraphs by either dictating or filling out a request form, and word processing can respond quickly because the information is already keyboarded. See Figure 17-2.

FIGURE 17-1

ACCOUNTING DEPARTMENT DOCUMENT FLOW

@ Closing Date
* Typing - Word Processing Ctr.

† Xerox - Print Shop
+ Mail Out

SUNDAY	MONDAY	TUESDAY	WEDNESDAY	THURSDAY	FRIDAY	SATURDAY
	@Katz Billing	AM *Katz Bk. 1 PM *Katz Bk. 2	AM †Katz Bk. 1 *W Local Bk. 1 PM †Katz Bk. 2 *W Local Bk. 2	AM *Y National †W Local Bk. 2 PM †Y National	PM +Katz & Local Billing	
	AM *Muzak Report PM *W-Y Nat'l Sales Report	AM †W-Y Nat'l Sales Report PM +W-Y Nat'l Sales Report +Muzak Report				
			AM *KNGS Sales Report PM †KNGS Sales Report +KNGS Sales Report			
				AM *Muzak Billing	PM +Muzak Billing	

WORD PROCESSING CENTER
Request for Services

Account #_____   Date_____

Author_____ Phone_____ Location_____

Secretary_____Phone_____

(Please check one) Final Form_____ Draft Form_____ Confidential_____

Already Stored on #_____ Please Store_____ Expiration Date_____

Carbon Copies (Please Indicate No. of Each): Blue___Green___Yellow___

White____Other_____Specify Paper_____Size_____

Envelope_____Label_____Type Style_____

Special Instructions_____

_____

_____

_____

Names, Addresses, and Salutations (Please Write Clearly)

1._____   2._____

_____   _____

_____   _____

Salutation_____   Salutation_____

(Additional Lines On Reverse Side)

FOR WORD PROCESSING CENTER USE ONLY

Description_____Completed by_____

Special Project_____Total Time_____Hours_____Minutes

Your Turnaround In Date_____ In Time_____Number of Lines_____

                 Out Date_____Out Time_____Number of Pages_____

                                                 Repetitive_____

Type of Input: Handwritten_____Typewritten_____Prerecorded_____

               Dictation Disc_____Belt_____Other_____

               Revision Ours_____Theirs_____

393

Many word processing systems can store formats as well, which makes it much easier to produce complex documents that otherwise would require a great deal of setup time. Special formats and related information can be recorded before beginning operations. By planning and preparing ahead, word processing is more apt to prove itself early in the program.

To determine which documents or applications to produce first, the supervisor needs to plan and then set up a priority schedule. The supervisor should consider the needs of the principals, document complexity, and ability to meet rapid turnaround time. Supervisors should be prepared to avoid tying up secretaries and equipment in long, complicated jobs which may prevent meeting planned or expected turnaround of daily documents.

WORK INSTRUCTIONS AND DISTRIBUTION

The supervisor should also make sure the work is properly prepared for transcription and evenly distributed so that some secretaries are not overly burdened while others have little to do. In addition, the secretaries need to be able to identify the work—who originated it, what it is, and what it entails, particularly special instructions and its length. A secretary will sit down and type a short letter knowing that he or she has to leave for lunch in 15 minutes and that it can be produced quickly. However, a secretary who sees several pages of longhand waiting to be typed is more apt to go to lunch and leave the job for later. People prefer to produce smaller pieces of work rather than longer work, for they can see the end of the job. When they are unable to see the end of a job, they are apt to procrastinate. This can be particularly true with dictation when there is no index slip or other visual indication of its length. The secretary does not know whether it is a half page, one page, or several pages. As a result, the secretary is more reluctant to begin that job than one the length of which is visually indicated, just as a person provided with a road map clearly outlining the route to the final destination is more likely to be enthusiastic about departing on a trip.

Scheduling

Routing work in and out of word processing requires daily attention in order for word processing to provide the services intended. With or without a formal measurement system, scheduling is mandatory. Areas that require scheduling include establishing priorities, distributing work, covering absences, and scheduling overtime and periodic events such as monthly reports.

Accounting System

Information obtained from the periodic reports may be converted into management reports. Some word processing systems computerize the data and receive their reports from EDP. This can save a great deal of recording time for the supervisor and secretaries and provide more flexibility. The computer can sort and select information to print whatever report the supervisor desired. Figure 17-3 shows an example of a daily log summary which can be processed for management reports.

Incentive Compensation

Some word processing supervisors have implemented incentive programs. Examples of the kinds of incentives being used include being awarded a monthly bonus by exceeding a quota, winning a special contest, and being awarded a guaranteed salary increase by attaining specific productivity goals.

Other incentives popular with word processing supervisors are time off for achieving certain productivity objectives, free lunch, prizes, honors (name published in the news bulletin), or lunch with the principal whose work the secretary produced. A once-a-month luncheon attended by principals and word processing secretaries during which those who achieved certain goals are honored is particularly effective, since it also affords principals and secretaries opportunities to communicate. Figure 17-4 illustrates a commonly used secretarial history form that records the output of employees.

An Example of a Daily Log Summary   **FIGURE 17-3**

DAILY LOG SUMMARY

Week	Date	Man Days	Rev.	IPE	Hard Copy	Pre. Rec.	Total Pages Per Week
35	6/1-6/4	1.94	23	10	33	1	67
36	6/7-6/11	5.25	122	4	37	17	180
37	6/14-6/18	4.25	58	11	37	47	153
38	6/21-6/25	5.13	70	34	82	8	194
39	6/28-6/30	1.63	50	6	8	0	64
Total		18.20	323	65	197	73	658
Weight		—	.5	1	.75	.15	—
Pages Weighted		—	162	65	148	11	386

Month ——————————

Secretary ——————————

Average Weighted Pages/Day | 21 |

FIGURE 17-4   An Example of a Secretarial History Form

SECRETARIAL HISTORY   MONTH_____ 198_____

SECRETARY NAME	GROSS LINES	CENT. REV.	% REV.	NET LINES	DAYS PRES.	AVG. LINES
TOTAL						

Followup

The supervisor needs to schedule a periodic review of the word processing system to target areas that require improvement or development, plan and budget for the future, make sure the reporting system is worthwhile and that collecting the data is not taking up too much time, and promote communications by keeping the staff up-to-date and asking for their comments and suggestions.

SETTING LEVELS OR PHASES

Firms might set levels ranging from one to five or higher, according to how long their word processing system has been operating and the range of functions accomplished. A firm that has been operating for five years and has added communicating word processors on which operators create data to transmit documents to other communicating word processors or a computer and output to microfilm might be at level five.

At the same time, a firm that opened its doors last month and is beginning operations by producing form letters and daily correspondence might be at level one. Some firms begin word processing with one word processing operator using one unit who transcribes from longhand or marked copy. After this proves successful, the organization realizes the word processor's potential. In order to grow, the company begins to add more equipment and word processing secretaries. A conservative firm may move one step at a time and move up levels gradually over an extended period of time.

Perhaps setting levels or phases is more important to the firm internally than when comparing to other organizations' word processing systems. At General Electric Motor Plant in San Jose, California, management planned to implement in three separate phases:

1. Implement the word processing center to produce daily correspondence, form letters, and multiple-page documents for the plant.
2. Add the capability to communicate with other General Electric locations and use word processing communications for data entry.
3. Automate the complete order entry system.

When they first implemented word processing, they anticipated that attaining level three would be their highest level.

SOLVING PROBLEMS

Morgenthal Electronics Company installed its word processing system in 1966. At first they experienced a period of limited success, then almost total failure, and finally, continuing and growing success. How did they prevent failure? What problems did they encounter? How were they resolved?

The Problems

Supervision was inadequate, normal business practices were not being adhered to, and there was a lack of central control over the work and personnel. Few of the original recommendations, procedures, and methods of operation established when the group was founded were being followed. The supervisor was ineffectual, and the operators appeared to be below par. The system required reorganization, competent supervision, and a qualified staff. Users were not cooperating, and no continual training was being offered them.

How the Problems Were Resolved

A new supervisor was hired who was expected to salvage the operation. The supervisor instigated the following:

- Discontinue loaning personnel from word processing to relieve other departments.
- Update the staff operating manual and make it a vital part of initial orientation and training.
- Enforce strict adherence to company rules, including working hours, attendance, punctuality, and breaks.
- Eliminate split-shift operations when no supervisor was present.
- Establish strict control over personal phone calls and activities.

Results

Within a few weeks the situation began to change. As a result of the improved performance of word processing, principals began to find satisfaction with word processing's products, and new users in growing numbers began to take advantage of its services.

Next, the supervisor developed a program to streamline the system to increase efficiency. Changes were made in personnel, organization, staffing, workflow, controls, services provided, and user communications. These changes were designed to resolve the problems that nearly closed down word processing operations.

The supervisor maintained overall management for the center, including close direct responsibility for high-level corporate projects, while work within the center was broken down into five sections. One section transcribed daily work, another section produced text and revisions, a composing section produced camera-ready documents, another produced art and graphics, while still another section produced statistical documents. Each section had a lead operator who supervised the other operators. An assistant supervisory position was later created to help coordinate activities of the five sections and manage special projects.

Later the supervisor realized the need to control workflow and monitor the quality of work. The supervisor created two jobs to handle these responsibilities, both reporting to the assistant supervisor.

This word processing system nearly failed because the center lacked adequate control and direction. Continual training and communication with users was lacking. After analyzing the problems, the new supervisor acted quickly to turn the situation around. Two major problems needed to be resolved: the users needed to feel confident that the center could produce their work effectively, and personnel needed direction and management control. The supervisor acted to solve these problems by aggressive leadership and meeting the responsibilities of the task at hand.

KINDS OF PROBLEMS

Word processing managers and supervisors encounter varying problems every day; that is the nature of the work. Frequently, they may receive a project that is already late in meeting its scheduled deadline. As a result, they are expected to respond so that the deadline can be met. How does word processing handle this type of problem?

First of all, they provide the expected service and meet the deadline so long as it is possible. For example, a fairly new young attorney in a law firm was given the task of preparing a legal document for a major client. The attorney dictated the document, and it was produced by the correspondence secretary in first draft form. The attorney then reviewed it and returned it for retyping. This was easy, for the secretary had the first version stored on a magnetic storage device and only had to type the changes and make the deletions; the word processing typewriter printed out the new version by incorporating these changes into the stored pages. After reviewing it a second time, the attorney submitted it for approval to a superior, who was out of the office in trial.

The trial did not end for several days, and the document remained on the superior's desk, awaiting review and approval. After returning from trial, the senior attorney reviewed the mail and came upon the document. The attorney reviewed it, made further changes, and had the secretary return it to the younger attorney.

Next, the junior attorney submitted the revised document to the correspondence secretary, who turned out a second revised document from the storage medium, typing in the additions and deleting those words no longer desired. The secretary submitted the new final version to the junior attorney, who reviewed it, and then resubmitted it to the senior attorney, who approved it for distribution to the client.

They met the deadline in spite of the fact that the document was delayed while the senior attorney was out of the office. How? Because it required only a few minutes to print out the final revised document from the word processing typewriter. However, what if the operating procedures had required that this job had to wait until other work was completed (first-in/first-out) before it could be revised? What if the supervisor had enforced this procedure? In this case, it is probable that the document would not have been ready for the client by the promised deadline. Inflexible procedures can result in problems.

Supervisors have to be aware that they will encounter this type of problem very often. Principals will ask to have a document done right away and not want to wait. What jobs can take precedence over others? When can one job be bumped for another? Or can a job be bumped at all?

Posting monthly, weekly, daily or other schedules in the word processing work area provides a visual for all principals and administrative secretaries indicating the current status of word processing work in process. This also allows the supervisor to point out visually to principals who bring their rush jobs that other top priority jobs are already being processed because they were scheduled ahead of time. Perhaps they can follow the procedure adopted by the law firm mentioned previously in which the attorney who needed a job right away conferred with other attorneys whose work was being processed to see whether this new job could take top priority.

A schedule visually presents the current status of work and can become an effective tool to maintain control and at the same time provide flexibility. The supervisor makes the priority decisions or suggests to the principals that they make arrangements among themselves when they have conflicting deadlines. This prevents the secretaries from being caught in the middle. Professional supervision, in which the secretary is supervised indirectly by someone who understands the working situations and problems instead of directly by those whose work he or she processes, offers the secretary more opportunity for job freedom and understanding and less frustration from being torn by making priority rush decisions. In the law firm, when a secretary is supervised by one of the several attorneys whose work he or she produces, the secretary tends to perform work for the supervising or the highest ranking attorney first. This often causes the attorneys who have to wait for their work dissatisfaction with the secretary's work. As a result, the system has several problems, including frequent low morale that affects secretarial productivity.

HANDLING PROBLEMS

Supervisors are required to tactfully inform principals when word processing secretaries continually encounter problems resulting from poor input. Principals need to understand problems and know how to rectify them. The supervisor must be able to communicate and train principals to improve poor input skills.

Complaints about the quality of work produced by word processing may indicate such problems as:

- Poor or inadequate dictation, longhand, or instructions. The supervisor will want to follow up with the principals to help them improve their input.
- Inaccurate spellings of names and technical words. A simple way to handle this problem is to have the originators' administrative secretaries provide word processing with frequently used names and addresses and technical terminology. When the dictator writes to a new person, he or she needs to learn how to spell out the names carefully during dictation so that the secretaries can transcribe them accurately.

A problem caused by the correspondence secretary indicates the need for further training. Although correspondence secretaries are held accountable for catching their errors (proofreading), spot (or occasional) proofing is an effective technique to ensure continuing high document quality. Skills supervisors expect from correspondence secretaries include spelling, punctuation, grammar, word usage, formatting, and listening and comprehending. As an example, a correspondence secretary should be able to tell from the context whether the word dictated is *sight*, *cite*, or *site*.

Correspondence secretaries frequently need training in the special vernacular and requirements of certain departments, particularly when they have not produced their work before. In a San Benito Medical Clinic, they employed three secretaries with from two to ten years of medical experience. However, the radiology secretary had not typed pathology reports before they implemented word processing. When they merged cross-training, the secretary had to learn new terminology in order to be able to transcribe accurate pathology reports.

ORGANIZING

Word processing supervisors and coordinators are responsible for distributing work, meeting deadlines, setting priorities, and meeting all the service requirements of the principals, all of which require good organization.

Good organization requires developing a basic method of workflow and staff communication, which prevents wasteful overlapping of jobs, improper assignments which can waste talent, and customer irritation caused by missed deadlines. A supervisor can establish a well-organized system by adhering to the following three steps:

1. Establish functional reporting structures. Break down center responsibilities into statements of responsibility and group similar statements together. Concise and comprehensive job descriptions establish these grouped responsibilities.
2. Delegate responsibilities and authority. State results expected from each job to establish accountability for the work. This includes well-established control points in each job. Insist that work is complete and performed to specifications.
3. Establish cooperative relationships. Define those critical aspects of each job that require cooperative interfacing with other jobs. Educate the working staff on how to deal with persons outside the word processing system. Make them aware of procedures to follow when dealing with users. Emphasize that they are there to provide *service*.

Word Processing System Activity Planning

Word processing organizing and directing includes six activities: scheduling workflow, assigning projects, determining quality and quantity standards, managing equipment and staff acquisition, handling maintenance and supply requisitions, and budgeting. Figure 17-5 shows a form used to identify problems.

FIGURE 17-5   An Example of a Weekly Error Report Form

WORD PROCESSING
WEEKLY ERROR REPORT

Mini Center Location _____   Week of _____

Secretary's Name	Number of Jobs Completed	Number of Errors	Number of Errors Last Week	Difference Inc./(Dec.)

NUMBER OF ERRORS SHOULD NOT BE THE LINECOUNT OF ERRORS AS SHOWN ON YOUR MONTH-
LY REPORT. THEY SHOULD BE THE ACTUAL NUMBER OF ERRORS TYPED ON ALL DOCUMENTS FOR
THAT WEEK. IF A SECRETARY DID 10,000 LINES FOR THIS WEEK BUT HAD 5 ACTUAL TYPOS FOR
THAT SAME WEEK, THE NUMBER YOU WILL INSERT FOR THIS REPORT WILL BE 5. PLEASE CONTINUE
KEEPING A LINECOUNT OF ALL PAGES WHERE THESE 5 TYPOS APPEARED FOR YOUR MONTHLY
REPORT.

Scheduling Workflow   The word processing supervisor should know at any given time what projects have been received, what projects are in process, who is producing them, their scheduled completion, and available staff. The schedule board can provide this information at a glance and makes it easy to reschedule work when someone is absent.

Assigning Projects   Some word processing systems work on the first-in first-out basis, while others specialize correspondence secretaries by departments or types of projects or subject matter. At Merrimont Medical Clinic, the medical transcriptionists continue to specialize in the types of work they performed before centralizing medical transcription. Some transcribe work from Pediatrics, some for Pathology, and some for other departments. However, the supervisor encourages cross-training, and the transcriptionists have found that they enjoy their work more when they rotate the departments they serve.

Frequently, when first beginning operations, specializing secretaries helps to accomplish high productivity early. Specialization offers the correspondence secretaries opportunities to develop expertise in special terminology and applications for individual departments, particularly those with technical terminology such as engineering, research, and programming. After the system has been operating for some time, cross-training may then become the next step. This provides a staff with more depth and capabilities to meet increasing work demands and handle absenteeism.

Supervisors soon learn which kinds of work are preferred by each correspondence secretary and which secretaries are more skilled in certain applications. Work and job assignments made according to likes and dislikes as well as to capabilities will result in higher productivity and employee morale. Human relations factors also play a part in job satisfaction. At Memorex, each correspondence secretary is assigned to a specific department and develops close relationships with the employees and administrative support in that department. Communication between the correspondence secretary and those whose work he or she is performing plays an important part of job satisfaction, productivity, and overall results.

Determining Quality and Quantity Standards   In addition to setting the productivity standards for word processing measurement, the supervisor aims to achieve those standards expected by the principals. An engineer who writes a technical report may want a rough draft back as soon as possible. At the same time, the Public Relations Manager may want a letter to an executive on letterhead ready for signature. The supervisor needs to make sure that the standards anticipated by those being served are clearly understood and adhered to so that the secretaries can produce documents that meet the requirements of those they are serving.

Expected Performance   Performance criteria expected from a word processing system include: (a) productivity: the amount of work they should be able to accomplish within a given amount of time, (b) responsiveness: how rapidly the work should be performed (turnaround time), (c) convenience: how easy the system is to use and how much principal direction or assistance is required in order to obtain the desired support or response, (d) quality: the proficiency, initiative, and judgment of personnel as well as the quality and accuracy of the finished product, and (e) job satisfaction: how well the jobs are matched to skills and how well personnel practices provide employee job satisfaction over a period of time.

Managing Equipment and Staff Acquisition   After the word processing system has been operating for some time, the supervisor may feel that the volume being processed and the backlog justify more personnel and equipment. A periodic review of the workload and backlog should be documented to justify any such requests. This also pertains to a change in equipment. If the supervisor or manager feels that other equipment would better serve the firm's needs, a request will require justification. This may consist of workload documentation, which usually is derived from the weekly, daily, and monthly production reports.

If the supervisor has to send work outside or bring in outside help, documented evidence will also help substantiate requests for additional personnel and equipment. Some firms have extra shifts to meet increasing volume of work. They also feel that second shifts help them gain more economic return on the high cost of word processing equipment.

Handling Maintenance and Supply Requisitioning   Two logs that provide valuable information are a log that lists maintenance calls and one that tracks supply usage. The latter helps to make sure sufficient supplies are on hand at all times and monitor usage and costs. Logging service calls by machine provides the supervisor with data to evaluate types of equipment or problems occasioned when problems were caused by a lack of operator competency. Sometimes one machine may require many service calls, while another requires very few. In order to determine whether the problem is the equipment or the operator, the supervisor can alternate operators. This should provide the answer and evidence of the problem, particularly if it is an equipment problem. The logs also provide background data to request more vendor support for either training or service and point out the specific problems.

Budgeting   The supervisor is responsible for handling the workload, including increased and decreased workload expectations, new varieties of incoming projects that require special equipment or training, expansion of the customer base, staffing requirements, estimated overtime or temporary help requirements, and other items that require budgeting. Without adequate documentation, budgeting can become a nightmare of estimates. With it, forecasting is a fairly simple process of data analysis. The workload schedules, particularly when planning to process future documents, need to be analyzed to determine volume and plan the forecast.

CONTINUOUS SELL

A truly successful word processing system needs to be supported as well as accepted by the users. One of the major challenges to the manager during the early stages of operating the word processing system is to encourage appropriate use of the system. If the principal work originators participated in the study and implementation preparations and received professional training during orientation, they should be ready and willing to use the system. If word processing fulfills their expectations by producing what they expect—high-quality documents within their desired time frames—they should be well satisfied. Sometimes principals feel that the former system was better, particularly when they have lost very capable secretaries and now depend upon word processing. They may miss the face-to-face contact and find word processing is not conveniently located for them. In this situation, the supervisor needs to sell them and develop their trust in the system.

Supervisors can sell dissenters by (a) visiting with them in their own offices, discussing their needs, and pointing out how word processing can help satisfy them; (b) learning what their problems and their specific requirements may be; (c) allaying their fears about the new system and discussing reasons they may have for not using or planning to use the system; and (d) mostly *listening*. The supervisor should develop a plan to provide dissenters with evidence that word processing can serve them well. The best way to provide this evidence, of course, is by proving to them that word processing can meet extremely rapid turnaround, especially for daily correspondence and stored letters, with top quality output. Making the system very easy for them to use will alone allay many fears, particularly for those reluctant to dictate after many years of using the pen and yellow pad. It is also helpful to demonstrate the flexibility of the system. What does the work originator need done? Word processing can do it (providing, of course, that it is a word processing service). Demonstrating that word processing can meet confidential, rush, and unusual throughput requirements is another method of selling the system. Sometimes Word Processing may have to bend over backwards in the case of resistance, but the foundation must be laid.

AN ABUNDANCE OF WORK

Some supervisors encounter the opposite extreme: once the system begins operations, they are swamped. Frequently supervisors state, "Work came out of the woodwork!" When staff members who seldom created documents before because they did not have a secretary discover that they now have a secretary who can produce documents for them, they begin to create many new documents. In this case, the work did not exist before and therefore was not included in the volume study. As a result, there may not be enough secretaries and equipment to handle the workload.

Supervisors need to be firm, particularly in situations where the planned system may differ from the actual working system. They need to readjust schedules, reset priorities, communicate with work originators, seek more efficient methods, and communicate their problems to management with recommended solutions.

Word processing supervisors need to continually evaluate the workload and seek to resolve problems. Analysis might reveal that many similar one-time letters that could be stored and produced more efficiently, saving time for both the principal and the word processing secretary. The supervisor can demonstrate and explain this capability to the principal.

COMMUNICATING

The marketing representative who is out in his or her territory early each morning calling upon and servicing customers is likely to succeed in making a comfortable living. Why? Because he or she is communicating with those customers on a daily basis. If he or she responds quickly to telephone messages and requests from customers, those customers are likely to want to continue to do business with this representative.

The same is true for word processing. If the word processing supervisor frequently communicates accomplishments, capabilities, current activities, and available services, word processing will most likely succeed. On the other hand, when people do not know exactly what is going on in word processing, how much work is being accomplished, what kinds of work are being produced, the rapid turnaround time being achieved, or how word processing increases document productivity, how likely are they to change their ways and take advantage of this service?

Word Processing needs to get the word out in whatever manner works most successfully for each particular organization. Word Processing might distribute newsletters or bulletins, encourage personal visits and tours, provide periodic equipment demonstrations, or schedule an annual or semiannual open house.

Many supervisors conclude orientation training by taking principals, staff, and other company personnel to visit word processing centers to witness equipment demonstrations. They may suggest that principals visit word processing departments whenever they have special needs or problems. When administrative secretaries frequently communicate with the correspondence secretaries to handle pickup and delivery, department managers and other principals may be less apt to visit Word Processing. Some means of encouraging such visits should be undertaken, particularly in situations in which managers and principals seem to lack an understanding of what is involved in producing documents.

At Chickering and Gregory, a large law firm in San Francisco, attorneys visit the document production center to discuss their special requirements with the correspondence secretaries. This provides face-to-face communication so that the secretaries can make sure they have complete instructions before they proceed to produce the documents. The value of frequent communication to the firm itself, as well as serving the need for rapid document production turnaround, should not be overlooked.

The many benefits that word processing offers a firm may include reduction in operating costs, improved customer service, coordination of operations, reduced turnaround time for important documents, improved document quality, automatic intercompany mail distribution (electronic mail), secretarial time and cost savings, improved time utilization of professional and executive personnel or improved secretarial utilization, and opportunities for women to enter management positions. Whatever the firm's original objectives and goals for word processing, it may accomplish these and much more. The word processing story needs to be told throughout the firm so that fellow employees can participate along with management in knowing that their company is up-to-date and can share in the pride of the firm's word processing accomplishments. Word Processing needs to communicate the firm's success story!

SUMMARY

When word processing managers begin implementing each department, they need to encourage their principals to start using their services right away. For a firm in which the change is not significant, this may be fairly easy. However, for some authors, particularly those used to writing longhand for input, the change may be much more traumatic.

Even for a firm that already has centralized typing facilities, the supervisor should wait until the word processing system has achieved early production objectives before enforcing stringent rules and procedures upon the originators. Supervisors need to decide during early stages what kind of work they are going to handle first. They may want to perform all of the typing for the first departments phased in; some may produce daily correspondence only; others may schedule long, revised documents; some may specialize in repetitive document typing. The supervisor aims to make sure they can meet deadlines without turning down work and to organize a system to accomplish these objectives. Supervisors prepare schedules that display periodic deadlines so that originators know when the deadlines occur.

Prerecorded information for stored letters and paragraphs, formats, or other reused information should be recorded on the storage media before beginning operations so that word processing is ready to produce those documents. To accomplish early productivity objectives, supervisors develop procedures to distribute work evenly and provide the secretaries with the due date and appropriate instructions necessary to produce the work.

Firms may indicate the status of their word processing system by using levels or phases. Phase 1 might indicate a fairly new system that handles origination and production; Phase 2, a system two years or older, might process electronic mail; Phase 3 might include photocompositions; and so forth.

Word processing is expected to meet turnaround deadlines, which requires flexibility while at the same time adhering to established schedules and procedures. It also requires effective work distribution, setting priorities, and providing services expected by those supporting word processing.

Supervisors need to be able to communicate with principals when they need to improve their input so that word processing can accomplish output efficiently. Supervisors should spot proof correspondence secretaries' output to maintain quality and accuracy.

Supervisors need to continually sell word processing services so that principals will support and use the system. By listening to the reasons for resistance or lack of use and support by the principals, the supervisors can learn and plan what to do to remedy such situations. Most of all, the supervisor wants to prove to those reluctant originators that the system will make their work easier for them and improve the document production efficiency.

Supervisors should also be prepared for too much volume. They need to be strong enough to communicate to demanding principals alternatives and solutions to their document production problems. One solution to too much volume is to analyze the volume to see if any letters, paragraphs, or documents are repetitive and can be stored for automatic playout. This eliminates rekeyboarding and saves time for both the originator and producer.

Communicating the success story of word processing is very important. Supervisors might distribute newsletters and bulletins, demonstrate new equipment, or invite principals to visit the word processing center. It is important to communicate the word processing success story.

REVIEW QUESTIONS

1. What decisions does the supervisor need to make when preparing to begin operations?
2. What actions should be taken before beginning operations in word processing?
3. What service do the monthly reports provide?
4. What is the purpose of periodic system reviews?
5. Describe three steps that solved the problems at Morgenthal Electronics.
6. What categories of activities does the correspondence secretary perform?
7. Explain what setting levels or phases means and its value.
8. What kinds of problems might occur with a word processing system?
9. Explain how a new supervisor can solve problems of the word processing system currently in operation?
10. Explain how the manager or supervisor can continuously sell the word processing program.

QUESTIONS FOR DISCUSSION

1. Discuss the value of good management techniques in carrying out a successful word processing program.
2. Explain the kinds of problems that can occur in a new word processing system.
3. How can the supervisor's personality affect the success of the system?
4. Discuss how word processing service relates to problem solving.
5. Discuss how changes in standards and operations might occur as a word processing system moves up to higher levels or phases.
6. Explain how the system's advancement to higher levels affects the jobs of the word processing manager, supervisors, and employees.

CASES

Case 17-1 County Juvenile Probation Office

The County of Chillingsworth has had a word processing center in its Juvenile Probation Department for four years. It is operating successfully and meeting its original objectives; they now have decided to expand and take in the Adult Probation Department as well. They have decided to make it a separate center, since it is located in another building, and pattern it after the Juvenile Probation Department except that they will use a shared-logic production system instead of standalone units as in Juvenile Probation.

How would you prepare for this implementation if you were the word processing manager over these two centers?

Case 17-2 Electronics Manufacturing Company

You manage word processing operations for an electronics manufacturing firm which has the following problems:

1. Eight percent of the input is longhand and the six recorders for dictation are used very little.
2. Principals complain that their documents from word processing often contain wrong context and misspellings, especially of technical terms and names, even though they wrote out the names in longhand.
3. Word processing secretaries complain of hard-to-read longhand and lack of complete information and therefore frequently have to type rough drafts. They also complain of numerous author revisions while trying to meet their deadlines.
4. Some of the administrative support secretaries express their desire to report to the department heads where they work instead of to you, the word processing manager.
5. Indications are that some other firms in your area are promoting word processing secretaries to higher salaries faster than your firm.

How would you go about turning this situation around and solving these problems?

"As the system has progressed, so has the variety of the work we do."

CHAPTER 18

Making Changes

OVERVIEW

After first implementing a word processing system, one begins to find out what kinds of effects word processing has upon the organization. Sometimes new applications are undertaken that were not planned; sometimes new dictators begin to create more documents; sometimes certain problems make it necessary to change procedures, workflow, kinds of equipment, or even the structure of the system itself. This chapter discusses the kinds of changes many organizations have experienced since first implementing word processing and how they resolved them to continue to develop an increasingly productive word processing system.

OBJECTIVES

After completing this chapter you should:

1. Understand what kinds of changes may occur and how they can be resolved.
2. Know how to determine when it is time to change equipment and how to go about it.
3. Know how to handle needs for personnel changes.
4. Understand why the system structure needs to be evaluated to see whether it needs to be changed.

Quote from "Merrill, Lynch Implements Word Processing and Photocomp Simultaneously," *Word Processing World* (September 1977), p. 15.

REASONS FOR CHANGING

Yvonne Hack, word processing manager at Van Swaay Installaties B.V. in the Netherlands,[1] manages one of the early word processing systems in a country where the concept is fairly new. In the Netherlands they call word processing *tekstverwerking*, or text processing. Van Swaay, an air-conditioning engineering and installation firm, created one of Holland's first word processing centers at its headquarters in Zoetermeer, near The Hague.

Since establishing its center in 1972, their production has increased fivefold. They employ 12 administrative secretaries and 9 word processing typists, in place of 31 secretaries who formerly served 12 departments. Yvonne's center first produced form letters and correspondence. They now produce technical quotations and specifications, reports, financial statements, and direct mail campaigns. They have added two Office System 6 systems to their existing six mag card II's. The Office System 6 was installed mainly to process new applications, including filing and preparing weekly expense account records; the company's entire address system; and quotations and specifications from programmed text.

They use the ink-jet printer to print out. Since its speed provides more printout capability than they need for their applications, they plan to expand services to process material for direct mail campaigns.

Their management was receptive to their suggestions for new equipment and procedures. As a result, they were able to change from their former method of typesetting direct mail literature as well as add more new applications to their operations. It is true in any organization that when it comes time to look into changing the system, expanding operations, or adding more equipment or personnel, management support is imperative.

One way in which Van Swaay maintained strong management support was to demonstrate their word processing system to visiting executives. Many of these visitors were so enthusiastic about their word processing system that they began to tell others about it, selling others on its capabilities.

Since first implementing word processing in 1966, Atlantic Richfield Company has made many changes in the work they process, services they provide, and equipment they use. Not only have they made changes and expanded their clientele to some 700 word originators located in three locations in New York City, but they began to experiment with a four-day 35-hour week, offering their operators a choice of hours. They may work either the 7:30 to 4:15 or 8:30 to 5:15 shift four days, leaving Wednesday open.

Some firms that first implemented centralized word processing have changed to decentralization in order to shorten the communication channels or for other reasons. What brought about these changes? How were they felt to be more advantageous? How were these changes implemented? And have they proven more beneficial?

[1] Yvonne A. Hack, "Text Processing—Dutch Style," *Word Processing* (September/October, 1977) pp. 17–19.

CHANGING THE OPERATING SYSTEM

Expanding the word processing system frequently means adding more employees and equipment or adding new departments and phasing them in. When the *system* of operation itself is changed, the reasons usually are either that the former system was inadequate or encountering procedure problems or that they have found a better way.

The rapidly growing technology in word processing itself may offer less expensive and simpler ways to meet word processing goals. For example, optical character recognition (OCR) is rapidly becoming a popular method of input for word processing, as are data processing and phototypesetting. As the technology is perfected, many firms have changed to or added OCR. Information is read from a page typed by a secretary and recorded onto a magnetic medium. This information may be revised to produce final typed output, input to a computer in data processing, or output to phototypesetting. A scanner can read a page in microseconds, certainly much faster than a secretary can type and record a page on a word processing medium.

At American Institute for Research (AIR) in Menlo Park, California, secretaries formerly typed on magnetic tape selectric typewriters to produce their long research reports. These reports underwent several typing revisions before they were considered final. Next they were mailed, and sometimes hand carried, to their Washington, D. C. office. Special operators of the MT/ST's took documents already typed by the secretaries, who work for the various people involved in creating these reports, and retyped them, recording the information onto the magnetic tape. Tapes were updated and information was transferred from one tape to another so that each updated hard copy was recorded onto a new magnetic tape. This method of revision is tedious and requires expert operators.

AIR has implemented a new system using an OCR scanner and the Office System 6 with its rapid ink-jet printer to produce their reports. Copy is typed on the correcting selectric typewriters by the secretaries and then read by the OCR reader that records the information onto a magnetic medium. All revisions are keyboarded by the special operator on the Office System 6 information processor. The operator can see the revisions while typing them on the CRT display and print out drafts and final copy rapidly on the ink-jet printer. Making revisions, the longest step in creating documents that undergo heavy revisions, is much faster and easier this way. This system has proven to save many hours of typing time and, most of all, has shortened the turnaround time so that they can meet critical deadlines. They added communications to the system and now transmit documents from one Office System 6 to another in their Washington, D. C. office.

Benefits from the Change

The benefits they are receiving from making this systems change are:

- Saving keyboarding time (now only one original keyboarding is required instead of two).

- Saving revising time (time is required to keyboard changes only, and there is no waiting for the system to update and transfer information).
- Saving distribution time (where formerly a minimum of one day was required, now it takes a matter of minutes or hours).
- Saving effort (the new system is easier—the secretaries do not have to learn new skills, while the operator has learned to operate a new, simpler word processing system, upgrading word processing capabilities).
- Being able to provide fast, clean draft copy to those who require copy rapidly for editing, approval, and proofreading.
- Saving proofreading time (for typists, for editors, for authors, for those approving the document, since only changes need to be approved and not entire keyboardings).

⑤   The City of Palo Alto implemented a word processing center in the early 1970s. Formerly the secretary for the city attorney and secretary for the city clerk had typed their documents on MT/ST's while they performed their other work. Sometimes they hired a special operator to produce the typing so that the secretary had more time to perform the many administrative duties required in that office.

After conducting an intensive word processing survey of all the city offices, a centralized system was recommended, which would mean moving the two MT/ST's to a word processing center along with an additional MT/ST and an **MT/SC** (magnetic tape selectric composer), which would allow them to print out the many publications being sent out to print shops for phototypesetting. Several city employees had individual desktop dictation units on which they dictated their work to their secretaries. The survey task force recommended that the City install a wired dictation system to enable all city employees who originated documents to dictate into desk microphones into the center.

This system was installed. However, they were unable to handle the work volume and meet deadline requirements for all the dictators, and many refused or failed to use the system and therefore contrived to use secretaries in their offices. In addition, the city manager who ordered the system left to take a job elsewhere, and the new manager failed to understand and support the system. As a result, the system failed and the equipment was moved back to the departments where it formerly had been. A centralized system did not prove successful for the City. An important item in this case is the fact that the City is located in a building in which the various departments are located on different floors. Perhaps work group units on each floor would have been more practical for this type of operation.

The City of Palo Alto changed its word processing operations because:

1. They were underequipped and understaffed.
2. Management failed to support the system.
3. Users were not involved in planning and implementing the system.
4. The geographic layout made it difficult for the system to meet users' needs.

Kaiser Medical Center in Santa Clara, California, is another example of a changed operating system. Kaiser installed word processing typing equipment in two departments: Medical Records and Medical Secretaries. Both used dictation equipment to service doctors throughout the hospital. (See Figure 18-1.) Medical Records transcribed operation, consultation, surgical, and other medical reports that often required immediate turnaround and distribution. The equipment included an endless-loop dictation system and MT/ST's. Medical secretaries employed several medical transcriptionists who typed correspondence and radiology reports. One MT/ST operation produced positive and negative X-ray reports for half the day and transcription the remainder of the day.

The medical transcriptionists transcribed and recorded the reports during the day. A clerk printed out these reports from the recording at night, which allowed

Dictaphone's Thought Master has complete electronic controls on hand microphone. (Photo courtesy of Dictaphone Corporation.)   **FIGURE 18-1**

skilled medical transcriptionists to best use their technical skills, thereby creating the most efficient and productive method of operation.

After some time, management decided to combine the two departments so that one manager would supervise both operations in a centralized working environment. Another change made was to have the medical transcribers run out their own documents.

They made this change because the medical transcriptionists preferred to run out their work and see the reports—their products in which they took a great deal of interest. They have upgraded to new word processing typewriters that are faster and easier to use. As a result, although the secretaries are working in extremely cramped working conditions, they produce large volumes of work, meet the deadlines, and enjoy their work. There is seldom a job opening in this word processing operation.

Kaiser's changes have been to combine two departments into one, upgrade equipment, and have medical transcriptionists produce completed projects, all of which have increased morale and job satisfaction.

AWARENESS OF THE SYSTEM'S EFFICIENCY

Perhaps the most important attitude for the manager regarding his or her word processing system is to believe in its flexibility and its capability to meet new challenges. By keeping up-to-date with new technology, the needs of the word originators, and the capabilities of equipment and personnel, the manager may find many ways to make changes to increase efficiency of the system. Many managers join word processing organizations, subscribe to reports and publications, and keep an eye and ear open in discussions with other managers and vendors, always alert to finding new and better ways to accomplish word processing services.

By maintaining open communications links within the organization, the manager also learns more about functions within the firm which word processing might be able to accomplish as in the case of filing and preparing the weekly expense account records at Van Swaay.

Because of its central document production, word processing can spin off into other services. One example would be to schedule meetings by automatically collecting and comparing business calendars. A calendar reservation service could resolve conflicts as well as make conference room reservations.

Wise managers suggest that their supervisors, coordinators, secretaries, and other staff members become active in associations where they know what is going on as well as communicate within the firm, keeping up-to-date with activities in other departments and seeking ways in which they can improve their services to their firm.

CHANGING EQUIPMENT

One of the most prevalent changes in word processing systems is to upgrade and change equipment. The rapidly advancing technology has encouraged many firms to rent or lease and not purchase their equipment. However, some feel, that in comparing costs of renting and leasing to purchasing, they may be wise to purchase, in spite of increased capabilities of newer equipment. More and more word processing production equipment is software designed, which allows the vendors to upgrade their customers' equipment. Wise purchasers explore such promises cautiously, as sometimes it still means replacing one unit with another and ends up costing more than anticipated. Firms expect the word processing manager to determine when is the best time to change, which change to make, and how to make the change. The decision is extremely complicated because of the increasing number of manufacturers and increasing numbers and wide ranges of products they offer.

IBM has many different products to offer its customers at varying price levels, including their simple correcting selectric typewriter, electronic typewriter (see Figure 18-2), memory typewriter, mag card typewriters, Office System 6, System 32, and 3790 distributive processing systems. Xerox offers card, cassette, one-line and full-page display, and a shared-logic system. Wang's product range is probably the widest of all, from their small System 5, 10, 20, 25, and 30, to its new 100 series. Most firms also offer varying systems for their equipment. For example, several, such as Vydec, offer OCR readers in their product line. All offer some forms of communications. (See Figure 18-3.)

When a word processing manager decides it is time to look into changing equipment, it is no simple matter. One might seek the advice of a consultant or have the consultant conduct special selection research. One firm's manager made a list of what the firm wanted in its new system and asked the consultant to provide them with a list of up-to-date equipment, comparing systems and vendors from which to select and including the consultant's recommendations.

Selection of equipment should depend mainly upon what the firm or manager expects from the new equipment. Once this decision is concisely stated, it is much easier to decide which equipment best fulfills the need.

One large law firm first established a word processing system supplying each legal secretary with mag card I's and word processing secretaries with mag card II's located in their document center. This allowed the legal secretaries, who typed and recorded documents on the mag card I's, to turn those cards requiring revisions over to the word processing secretaries. Attorneys took their long documents directly to the document center and informed the word processing secretaries of their needs, deadlines, and any relevant information. This allowed direct communication, making sure their instructions were clearly understood before word processing secretaries began to produce the long documents.

The firm has changed to new standalone visual screen word processing typewriters for the word processing secretaries. They did not provide these units for the legal secretaries; instead, they kept the mag card II's and eliminated the mag card I's. They no longer have compatibility between the legal secretaries' work and that of the word processing secretaries, but the new equipment is much faster, easier to learn and operate, performs many functions previously not available, and allows secretaries to increase their turnaround time and handle more work. The firm is planning to make further changes and include legal billing and communications from the word processing typewriters in the future.

FIGURE 18-2 The IBM electronic typewriter has a 94-character keyboard (upper left), which contains sculptured keybuttons 25 percent larger than regular size. The machine features format storage (upper right), automatic operational capabilities (lower left), and special storage for instruction cards (lower right). (Photo courtesy of International Business Machines, Inc.)

The A.B. Dick magna I features the communication option that communicates   **FIGURE 18-3**
with other magna I's, other word processors, or computers. (Photo courtesy
of A.B. Dick Company.)

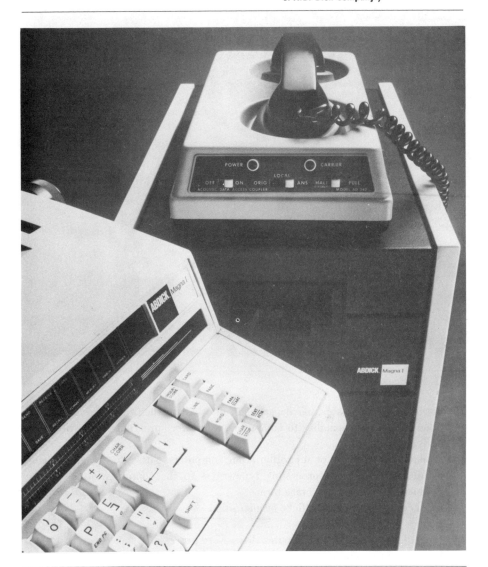

Kinds of Equipment Changes Being Made

Firms are changing word processing typing equipment because of new technologies. Other reasons firms make these changes are:

•   New dictation equipment capabilities (see Figure 18-4), including automatic visual screen monitoring and paper printout for volume productivity analysis per

FIGURE 18-4   Dictaphone Time Master produces summary reports of word processing activities. (Photo courtesy of Dictaphone Corporation.)

machine, per originator, per department, or whatever the firm wishes to monitor.
- Communications capability to computers, other word processing typewriters, and outlying areas.
- Producing microfiche or microfilm from computers. These documents are communicated from word processing typewriters to the computer, which in turn produces the records in storage form.
- Produce copies from microfiche or microfilm.
- Copiers with CRT screens.
- Inputting information to computers from word processing typewriters.
- Inputting information to computers and word processing (and storing) by optical character recognition (scanners).
- Inputting documents to phototypesetting equipment from word processing typewriters.
- Typing from voice recognition (it is developed and being used to a small extent but is still in early development stages).
- Merging telecopying (sending documents from one location to another over telecopiers) with word processors.

• Improved and faster printers using new technologies such as laser, fiber optics (see Figure 18–5), and ink-jet.

Equipment changes and advancing technology is covered in Chapter 19. One firm is currently implementing communicating word processors throughout its headquarters and other locations to process their internal mail. At the same time, this firm has analyzed its records retention and storage needs and is merging this with their computer operations and word processing. It plans to integrate their information system consisting of dictation equipment, word processing typewriters, computer processing, and microfiche storage.

PERSONNEL CHANGES

When Nationwide Insurance Company discovered it was under capacity, it added personnel and equipment. However, some of the present personnel were unable to cope with the demands of the complicated kinds of work and transferred to other departments or left the firm. Many times word processing managers discover that some

---

The VQC compact copier from 3M Company utilizes Lensar® fiber optics in a simplified, trouble-free copying system that eliminates the lenses, mirrors, baffles, high-energy lamps, reflectors, and cooling devices found in conventional copiers. Copies are automatically cut to size, matching the original. Standard 8½ by 11 inch documents are produced at the rate of 15 per minute. (Photo courtesy of Minnesota Mining and Manufacturing Company.)   **FIGURE 18-5**

of their staff are not suited to word processing jobs—the deadline pressures, the last-minute demands when authors bring work in at the end of the day, or other pressures inherent in word processing production services.

The sooner a person who does not find the word processing working atmosphere enjoyable realizes it, or the manager realizes it, the better. This allows the manager to help that employee change to a more suitable working situation and is less apt to cause friction or other problems within the department.

Adding personnel to an expanding operation is one of the more pleasant tasks, so long as the manager is able to locate applicants with the necessary skills and attitudes. Adding new personnel to an existing staff is very important, and the manager wants the new employee to fit into the team. The manager already has a well-organized program to train new hires and bring them to the level of the other secretaries.

Having to reduce staff, perhaps because of economic conditions, is much less pleasant and can be more difficult. If all secretaries are extremely competent, the manager has to decide who should be the one to leave, so long as all are particularly happy there. If someone has expressed an interest in working elsewhere, there is no problem. But in the case in which it is a happy working situation for all, the manager will have to select the one to move on.

When one employee is leaving and another has been hired to replace that person, the new employee should learn the job from those responsible for training. Most word processing managers have a word processing secretary who is responsible for training new hires, rather than expecting the new hire to learn from the person leaving. This prevents the possibility of wasted time and poor habits being passed along.

Word processing managers frequently promote secretaries within the department or to other positions within the firm. When filling vacant positions and adding more staff, managers need to be very careful that the team spirit tone is well understood by newcomers and that their personalities adapt well into the working atmosphere.

Should another department be merged into the word processing center, as in the case at Kaiser Medical Center, the manager expects and wants to make sure that all secretaries are compatible and work well together. Sometimes this may take considerable counseling and requires the employees to learn to work with others, particularly those with whom they have interpersonal conflicts.

UPDATING THE SYSTEM BY LEVELS AND PHASES

Successful early operations tend to be those that start simple and gradually implement more complex applications. The word processing system that begins by processing daily correspondence and form letters gives itself plenty of breathing room before tackling more complicated, long documents. Handling daily correspondence does require one very important item: developing and meeting daily turnaround times and continually responding to peaks and valleys from the users.

When the City of Palo Alto began operations by producing long, complicated documents that had to meet certain deadlines and consisted of input from several sources, their first phase failed because of the complicated elements involved. If this application had been left to a second or third phase in its development, they would have had more opportunity for success.

Updating the system includes (a) analyzing the application, (b) creating the step-by-step procedure, (c) obtaining the appropriate equipment for the application, (d) training personnel to accomplish the work, and (e) phasing this application into the daily schedule of operations.

Analyzing a New Application to Be Phased In

Before phasing in the next application, the manager should make sure that it has been carefully analyzed so that the coordinator can prepare each step of the procedure to produce that application. Just as in any word processing analysis, the application needs to be analyzed to determine (a) its nature of input (longhand, marked copy, dictated matter), (b) its average length, (c) its quality requirements, (d) its revision cycle (number of revisions and amount of revising most likely to occur in each cycle), and (e) its deadline cycle. This information helps the supervisor to determine who should handle the job on what kind of equipment and what kind of output can be used in each stage (in the case of three revisions before final copy, perhaps a rough draft can be played out on continuous paper on a rapid document printer while the final copy will be printed on a slower printer that produces higher quality results). Some documents have special requirements such as footnotes, formulas, and equations, changing formats, and other specifications that greatly affect the system selected to produce the document. These factors also greatly influence the turnaround time standards to be set and ability to schedule this application along with other work.

When management decides to phase in capabilities that merge word processing into other phases of the information integration system, the word processing manager needs to be able to include the effect this will have upon the daily word processing operations as well. For example, if word processing will be preparing data entry for data operations, an operator needs to be trained to handle this application. If one of the units is going to have communications capabilities, an operator needs to be trained and perpared to communicate documents. This needs to be scheduled into the daily workload. If one operator will be creating input for phototypesetting, that is another application that requires training, scheduling, and interfacing with the person responsible for taking that input and processing it.

FOLLOWING A STEP-BY-STEP SCHEDULE

Western Publishing, largest creator, producer, and publisher of juvenile books in the United States, is also a major commercial printer of paperback books, road maps, catalogues, and educational material. As a result, their word processing requirements include manuscript typing with emphasis on superior quality. In addition, they have the usual corporate headquarters applications of financial, legal, and personnel reports and correspondence, as well as correspondence for marketing and consumers.

They installed MT/ST's and MT/SC's after a feasibility study in 1973 and placed the equipment at scattered centralized locations throughout several departments. In addition, they installed a telephone dictation system in a center where ten secretaries were located.

They began to phase in departments on a predetermined schedule with the full backing of senior management. They changed supervisors when their phase-in program was still in progress.

The new supervisor who took over a two-year-old system was totally new to the concept of word processing. When evaluating the existing system, the supervisor found that many of the old procedures did not meet current needs: existing record keeping procedures were inadequate, and new applications were needed. Management expressed some concern over the effectiveness of the center. Productivity and quality, while satisfactory, were below the levels they expected, and the new supervisor was given the responsibility of improving the center's overall performance. A moratorium was therefore instituted until the situation had been assessed.

SELECTING APPROPRIATE EQUIPMENT

An analysis was conducted, just as though they were conducting an original feasibility study. Results verified that the equipment was appropriate for the applications and quality requirements, but their use of continuous form paper sacrificed some quality standards. They therefore changed to the mag card II to obtain its high quality. When the ink-jet printer became available in 1976, they replaced old equipment with it so that they could meet their speed and quality requirements.

First the new supervisor set up a logging system to record the work received, to whom it was assigned, the time and date, time completed, and equipment used (see Figure 18-6). This way, the supervisor could track daily activity, identify problems, reorganize workflow, recognize peak volumes, and measure productivity and turnaround time. Next the supervisor eliminated records that were not necessary and maintained only those records that would provide information vital to proper system management and future development and serve as a history of the center's growth.

TRAINING PERSONNEL

These records indicated that few principals were using the telephone dictation system and most of the incoming work was in longhand. All users were retrained in dictation techniques, and top priority was assigned to all dictated work. They established a goal of same day turnaround for anything dictated before noon.

Next they discovered that the word processing secretaries used different techniques to operate the equipment. They therefore developed standard operating procedures manuals for the secretaries, which resulted in consistent quality. Users now knew the quality they could expect. The standards had to be completely adhered to in order to take advantage of the 92-characters-per-second speed of the ink-jet printer.

DAILY LOG SHEET										
Control Number	Author	Type of Input	Type of Output	Category	Rush ($\checkmark$)	Rev. No.	Operator (min.)	Turn-around (min.)	Processing	No. Pages

When the supervisor realized that some of the secretaries lacked adequate language arts skills and were unable to participate as members of a working team, coping with deadline pressures and required flexibility, the supervisor redefined criteria for hiring new personnel to make sure that when new personnel were hired, they were qualified to meet the demands of the job.

Their present training program for new hires dictates the first six weeks to learning the operations of the center and the company, equipment, and procedures. This is followed by a week's training at the vendor's location learning to operate the equipment in which they take samples of the company's work to practice while training. During the remainder of the six-week break-in period, the new secretaries' work is closely checked.

PHASING INTO DAILY OPERATIONS

In addition to the original word processing center in the main plant, they added a second center five miles away. Their current system consists of 18 secretaries, one supervisor, and one group leader to support 300 principals.

The results are that they consistently produce phone dictation within a four-hour turnaround time and are endeavoring to reduce this to two hours. Accuracy rate averages approximately 98 percent; standardized procedures allow work sharing, even between the two centers; and productivity averages approximately 250,000 lines monthly.

Although they are still phasing in some of the departments, they were able to improve a system encountering serious difficulties by stopping and measuring the current system to see that their system was meeting its objectives.

EXPANSION

Nationwide Insurance implemented word processing in 1972 following an in-depth study.[2] Several months following implementation, the center was fully operational and was producing more lines than were originally expected from the equipment configuration. However, a problem developed at this point in spite of the fact that some of the areas included in the survey had yet to be incorporated into the operations. It became apparent that the workload survey had been conducted during a very slow period which was not representative of the typical workload. Once the system was implemented, the company entered a peak workload period. As the center progressed, the workload grew to 68 percent higher than during the survey period.

As a result, expansion was mandatory. More machines and operators had to be added to handle the total typing requirements for departments to be serviced, including the Systems Department, in which 200 authors generated work involving complex outline formats and many statistical charts as well as highly technical data processing terminology. The expanded staff devoted its efforts to continually seeking more efficient methods to perform the work. As a result, some of the staff left the center and were replaced by employees more receptive to the change and demands of the work. In addition, the supervisors learned to check work entering the center, establish new formats when needed, and define unusual applications for the equipment.

The company also added a full-time copy editor/proofreader. Initially, this word processing center was established to serve only the Systems and Data Processing Departments. Since 1972, it has tripled in size and has been reorganized into two units which currently serve 20 percent of the staff office departments and some subsidiary and affiliated companies. Nationwide's present system hardly resembles the original installation; equipment, people, procedures, and locations have changed, and the company anticipates further expansion and evolution of the system.

SUMMARY

When a manager wishes to make changes in the existing system, top management support is necessary. One firm maintained management support by inviting executives in that firm to show their word processing center to visiting executives. Another firm has changed to operating a four-day work week.

Operational changes occur because either the former system was not working or was inadequate or there is a better way of operating. Sometimes an equipment change can cause a system change, as in the case of using OCR scanners as a means of input for word processing, data processing, or phototypesetting.

Some systems change because they are not properly equipped and the centralized concept is inappropriate for them. One system had to expand to meet the expanding workload. It became apparent that the study did not represent the typical

[2] N. Elizabeth Fried and Mary K. Kohlbacher, "Nationwide's Word Processing Policy Pays Off," *Words* (Summer 1978), pp. 42–43, 45.

workload, and they therefore needed to add to their capability in order to meet their increasing workload.

One medical facility combined two departments so that one manager could direct the work. Some systems designed for top operating efficiency may be changed because the people are not happy under such automated procedures as having a clerk run off the work transcribed by a secretary instead of the secretary play back her own work. In order to maintain job satisfaction, the manager changed to a somewhat less productive system in order to increase the secretaries' enjoyment of their jobs.

Managers need to be alert for ways in which they may want to change their system in order to increase efficiency or job satisfaction. They can learn from other managers, vendors, and publications as well as from observing possible applications within the firm. Managers should encourage their staff to keep abreast of what is going on both inside and outside and always seek ways to improve their word processing services.

Because of rapidly changing technology, many firms do not purchase their equipment; instead they rent or lease. Some word processing manufacturers offer many different models of equipment. As a result, it is not easy for managers to decide which is best for them. Many firms use consultants to help them select equipment. They may present the consultant with a list of their requirements and request advice to select equipment best suited to meet these needs. Some firms simply upgrade to equipment with more capabilities to increase productivity and the number of functions it can perform. This allows a firm to handle more applications as well as produce larger volumes.

Firms may change equipment for dictation, word processing typing, copying and duplication, forms retention and storage, data entry, input into phototypesetting, and telecommunications and distribution.

Many firms add personnel when they are understaffed or replace those who do not fit into the word processing environment. Such firms train new hires to use that firm's procedures by including trainers on their staff. Those who may not fit into a word processing environment should be moved early. Administrative secretaries should be trained by other administrative secretarial trainers, not the departing secretary. In correspondence training, some managers send new hires to the vendors and some managers use self-paced training manuals to teach equipment operations once secretaries have learned the firm's word processing procedures from the staff trainer.

When merging two departments into one, managers need to be sensitive to possible personality conflicts and help employees learn to work together happily.

Managing the expanding operation requires delegating appropriate tasks to those on the staff who are ready and capable to help merge the new operations, equipment, and personnel into the present operating system.

REVIEW QUESTIONS

1. State the key facts required when attempting to change a system.
2. What kind of changes might a firm make to their word processing system?
3. Explain four reasons a firm might have for changing their word processing system.
4. What is required of a word processing manager regarding his or her word processing system?

5. What change is a firm *most* apt to make in its word processing system? Why?
6. Name seven kinds of equipment changes some firms make.
7. Describe how several changes in a word processing system can affect its personnel.
8. What can the manager do to keep operating personnel up-to-date with changing technologies?
9. Describe the steps involved in updating a system.

QUESTIONS FOR DISCUSSION

1. Discuss what a manager can or should do to ensure that the changes in the firm's word processing system are supported by management.
2. Discuss what techniques a manager can use to ensure support throughout the organization in making changes to the word processing system.
3. Discuss how changes in managerial personnel can affect the word processing system.
4. Discuss how the manager can ensure that company personnel are aware of what the word processing system is doing for them and the firm.
5. Discuss how changing technology affects the operating procedures of the firm.
6. Discuss how changing technology affects personnel, their jobs, and morale.
7. Discuss what can happen if a firm fails to continually review the system as to its currency and adequacy in providing the firm's services.

CASES

Case 18-1 Insurance Company

Golden Gateway Insurance has had a word processing center for four years. The former manager has been promoted to manager of office services, a position over word processing, communications/distribution, and reproduction operations. You have been hired to be word processing manager with the major tasks to handle as well as the management of word processing operations. You are to select a new, more effective word processing production system to replace magnetic cassette typewriters and develop an interface to electronic mail distribution.

Explain how you plan to handle these two responsibilities.

Case 18-2 Research Institute

Sawyer Research Institute has decided to implement a word processing system consisting of production equipment for the secretaries which allows them to create work for the production of reports and proposals as well as their own daily work. Secretaries work for one to three managers, engineers, scientists, and executives and other departmental personnel. They use shorthand, longhand, marked copy, and individual desktop dictation units as a means of input.

You have been hired to manage the word processing operation and its interfacing with the editors and production staff who are responsible for final production of all reports and proposals. Explain how you will go about making the system work and what changes you will make to meet the firm's objectives which are to improve the quality of all documents, reduce overtime costs, and shorten the turnaround time from origination to final production and distribution of these documents.

BENJAMIN / CUMMINGS

WORD PROCESSING SERIES

PEOPLE / PROCEDURES / EQUIPMENT

*"At work, everything will be computerized except
the coffee breaks. Letters will be typed, orders will
be placed, bills will be paid, and files will be searched,
all by computer."*

CHAPTER 19

Growth and the Future

OVERVIEW

This chapter discusses the continuing technological changes that affect office personnel and operations, particularly as a result of growing paperwork demands and
decreasing equipment costs. The impact of miniaturization is being felt in all aspects of
information processing—telecommunications and electronic mail, records processing,
reprographics, and document origination and production. This chapter discusses the
fact that word processing managers and supervisors will be in positions greatly
influenced by the continually changing technologies.

OBJECTIVES

After completing this chapter, you will be able to:

1.   Understand the roles that AT&T and IBM play in telecommunications.
2.   Conceive of the various means and uses for electronic mail.
3.   Comprehend the various means of production input and output.
4.   Understand how the many and varied methods available to process information
     make the role of the word processing manager increasingly important to an
     organization.

Quote from John Fletcher, "The Next Computer Revolution," *Mainliner Magazine* (June 1978).

CHANGES IN THE OFFICEPLACE

Some of the changes predicted, as well as those actually taking place in some firms today, are discussed in the following paragraphs.

Flexitime   People select their own daily working hours, go to work four days a week, vary their shifts by days or weeks, in short, work flexible schedules according to times most convenient to them.

Location   Many large firms move their headquarters or other offices out of the cities into outlying areas, away from downtown congestion. This is more convenient to their employees and helps them to conserve energy.

Environment   Offices are **open landscaped**, in which the few actual offices provided for senior executives are movable modules. Other employees work in areas with movable partitions allowing freedom of movement and communications.

Administrative Support Centers   Teams of workers offer such administrative support to executives and staff employees as typing daily correspondence (word processing specialists), storing and retrieving information (information specialists), and communicating information to and from other locations as well as into and from computers (communications specialists) under the supervision of team supervisors. In addition, administrative support specialists assist executives in routine projects, relieving them for more management-oriented tasks. These specialists make up teams that provide support to individual groups of executives and staff employees.

Word Processing Centers   Highly trained specialists produce lengthy, heavily revised documents in the word processing center that is equipped with a high-speed duplicator so that documents can be printed and published directly from this facility.

Administrative Support Equipment   Word processing specialists in the administrative support work group units keyboard correspondence on their visual display intelligent typewriters that can communicate to other centers and groups as well as into and from the computer. In addition, the unit has a convenience copier and microfilm reader.

The Executive's Office   The executive, in this case a middle manager, has a telephone with a message signal device that indicates when calls or messages are waiting and a button which allows diversion of calls to message centers or another extension. The phone can receive and send messages overseas. He or she can also dictate on the phone to the word processing secretary. In addition, the executive can insert a card into a security card reader to communicate with the computer to retrieve information when necessary. A microfilm reader is available to read stored documents. Each executive has a visual screen ready to display documents from files, other locations, or the word processing secretary for approval, revisions, or information. Messages can be recorded for distribution to as many recipients as necessary to inform them of upcoming meetings or report on trips. The desk may be an off-the-floor desk supported by partitions and accompanied by a large, expandable table to hold large charts and drawings. The partition contains the wiring necessary for the phone and electric outlets for equipment as well as a task lighting lamp with only the appropriate amount of light required for the office, preventing energy waste.

The executive can glance at the phone signal system to see if any messages are waiting, divert calls when not wanting to be interrupted, transmit messages to designated recipients, and phone the information specialist to ask for a file. The information specialist has documents stored by a coding system into the computer. This allows the specialist to act as a librarian in searching computer data base for information, write special programs for record retention systems, or order up printouts of any files desired.

When the executive dictates, the word processing specialist keyboards that information on the intelligent typewriter, which the specialist then has displayed on the executive's visual screen. Copies of the document may be requested for printout on the high-speed, lower-quality printer or on the high-quality ink-jet printer. The executive, when viewing the just typed letter on the screen, may make his or her own minor revisions. If it is a longer document, the executive may want a paper copy. Paper copies are provided by the administrative support unit. In addition, the executive is able to attend more meetings with other executives, since the firm has a video conferencing system where each executive sees the other on the visual screen by means of the computer.

The Computer Center   The word processing secretary may communicate any documents typed on the intelligent typewriter into the large computer center for processing, distribution, storage, or whatever other action is desired. Besides the computer, this center contains shared high-speed printers, an ink-jet printer for high-quality phototypeset documents, and microfilm-producing equipment.

The previous paragraphs contain one description of future offices. Many of the capabilities are already available in some of our nation's government and industry offices. All forecasters predict a widespread growth of the word processing industry. Word processing's tremendous potential for expansion appears to result in offices structured similarly to the work group approach as described in this section.[1]

Creative Strategies forecasts an annual growth rate of 21 percent through 1980 in installed automatic editing typewriters, 10 to 15 percent annual growth in dictation equipment, and 10 percent for office copiers.

Predictions of the **merging** of word processing with data processing are apparent in many firms in which word processing is managed by data processing personnel.[2] One of the major reasons that such merging is being investigated is the continuing trend towards increased office operating costs, causing firms to search for more functional and productive office systems.

[1] Carol Glover and Alan Purchase, "All in a Day's Work," *Word Processing* (March/April 1977), pp. 11–13.
[2] Robert Greenblatt, "Forecast for Data Processing/Word Processing Integration," *Word Processing* (September/October 1976), pp. 10–12.

Word processing applications are expected to center around three types of computing systems:

1. Standalone minicomputer.
2. Shared-logic systems or a minicomputer supporting several devices such as terminals and printers.
3. Time-sharing systems, using a computer which will support large numbers of users and applications.

Applications normally handled by computers already being processed in word processing include basic accounting, time charging (particularly for legal and medical offices), order entry, and inventory control. A shared-logic system can have such devices as additional disk drives, other storage media (some use magnetic tape storage), OCR readers, high-speed printers, and photocomposers.

Time-shared computing systems use communications modems on the word processing terminals for backward and forward communication of information and distribution of information. With **time-sharing**, the simple word processing terminal can become a tool to aid management in a number of functions other than correspondence. The work group structural concept aids in advancing the functions and technologies. Work groups can provide increased support in such services as mail handling, copying, telephone answering, report and document preparation, filing, and record retention. By placing a terminal near the executive, both word processing and data processing are available to provide the executive the tools to process his or her information as desired.

Effects on the People

Merging the two technologies will require additional learning on the part of the administrative support secretaries, particularly more paraprofessional skills so that they can absorb responsibilities delegated by management.

Assignments for correspondence secretaries may vary between word and data processing, and a new job—the word processing systems analyst—may appear on the scene.

OTHER WORD PROCESSING PREDICTIONS[3]

James Forese, IBM vice president, says, "It is getting to be too expensive to operate in the old ways because the basic cost of an office is people. The question is: 'How can we help people to be more productive?' "

Evelyn Berezin, president of Redactron/Burroughs, states,

In 20 years the typewritten document will be a thing of the past. Printing with its inherent economy will be substituted, distributed communications and infor-

[3] Carol Glover and Alan Purchase, "All in a Day's Work," *Word Processing* (March/April 1977), pp. 11–13.

mation processing networks will conserve energy and create new work and work-place structures.

The tremendous drop in the cost of computation and memory functions for data processing has shifted the focus from large central computers to a distributed environment of small computers. The output from small computers will be used locally and not transmitted to a central processing department. And of considerable importance, small computer capability will extend beyond strictly data applications to include text and other kinds of information processing.

The small computer may become the control device for a much larger network of advanced copiers, facsimile equipment, and printers . . .

As communications costs begin to drop due to the widespread deployment of satellites, home roof-top antennae, and optics cables, the full-scale realization of a true information processing network will occur.

The office of the future will have many work stations equipped for text, number, and picture communication. Information will be disseminated electronically and 'reconstituted' at the receiving end. Such a decentralized work environment will not suit today's hierarchical work structures, and these will change.

Howard Anderson, president of The Yankee Group market research firm, predicts, "Not far away, maybe five years or so, a private wire setup with antennae on top of corporate buildings which transmit material to satellites and beam it to antennae in other cities will allow voice, data, and electronic mail transmission all combined into one system."

Mary Jane Ornelas, former manager of secretarial services, Eastern Airlines, suggested, "There will be a person, possibly vice president of information systems, who will coordinate the four big information areas: telecommunications, word processing, data processing, and records management (libraries of information). Each of these four areas will stand on its own. However, they must all be compatible, and the responsibility (equivalent of the vp of marketing today) will be to ensure cost control in these areas and that the equipment all works together. This person will gear the system to the company's individual needs." Like many others, she leaves the traditional mailroom out of her system, explaining, "It just moves what has already been created."

Mr. Forese continues, "Today's users are looking for even more effective solutions to the problem of getting information to the point of need—both faster and at lower cost." This problem requires a solution flexible enough to handle all the information requirements of the office organization.

WORD PROCESSING COMPANY'S VENTURES WITH ELECTRONIC MAIL

At Cook Industries, the nation's largest grain exporter, the Memphis headquarters is tied to all domestic and 14 foreign offices through a computer-based message system. Using a 370/158 computer and store/forward switches, Cook is able to use a single terminal to serve their users for message sending, receiving, time sharing, accessing commodity trading information, inquiry, response, and data entry.

General Electric has over 100 subminute facsimile devices installed throughout the company as a result of deciding in 1976 to implement electronic mail throughout the company.

Growing at a staggering 40 percent per year, Digital Equipment Corporation decided that its needs justified setting up an electronic mail system. Still in implementation stages, the system is being used by a sizable pilot sample with indications of success. Currently users are 21 percent management personnel, 51 percent professional personnel, and 28 percent support personnel.

Travelers Insurance, in Hartford, Connecticut, has an electronic mail system that polls locations every 90 seconds. Today it offers cost-justified electronic mail. Currently Travelers is exploring new, specifically tailored services that include a variety of terminal and facsimile support systems.

NASA combines a traditional electronic mail system with forms of teleconferencing, allowing both increased span of control and more immediate decision-making. NASA, too, is investigating further capabilities in the field.

In the Executive Office of the President of the United States, the Office of Administration, through its Information Systems Division, has been actively investigating sophisticated electronic mail systems with the goal of implementing an advanced communications solution.

Digital Broadcasting Corporation uses an FM subchannel to broadcast messages to retail drug chains, supermarkets, and retail outlets. The cost of these messages can be as low as 7½ cents.

Regulations

The Communications Act of 1978 will have considerable influence on the future of electronic mail systems and their capabilities. Bell Telephone Company's Advanced Communications Service also carries much impact. Regulations from the Postal Rate Commission and the Federal Communications Commission are being watched to determine the dividing line between the two.

The use of intercompany electronic mail is becoming an everyday occurrence, as more and more firms use telecopiers (facsimiles) and communicating word processing typewriters to distribute information from one location to another. Communication between companies and teleconferencing are well on their way, as is public distribution.

What options does the U.S. Postal Service have in relation to electronic mail? What would be the cost to implement electronic mail and what would the effect be? The Postal Service plans to inaugurate electronic mail service internationally via PTT's and Comsat in April 1979 and is actively investigating other domestic forms of electronic mail. A recent survey indicated that the combined forces of electronic mail and its subset, electronic funds transfer, could remove as much as 40 percent of the first-class business volume from the Postal Service. What are the solutions and what hardware does the Postal Service need to develop in its next generation of services?

The three forms of electronic mail—intracompany, intercompany, and public distribution—will grow tremendously in the upcoming years. New products in facsimile, computer based messages services, as well as new carrier offerings, will greatly influence the market and services provided.

Teleconferencing

Many firms have been experimenting with teleconferencing for several years. Technology developments involved include audio conferencing (which is used by many large and medium size firms), freeze-frame video, computer conferencing, all the way through full-frame video conferencing, as mentioned in the introduction to this chapter.

Word Processing Communications

Ever since the first word processing typewriter successfully communicated to another, communications between word processors and computers has been expanding rapidly. Some word processors now can communicate with word processing typewriters manufactured by other companies (through developing compatibility, particularly by means of such technology as OCR), as well as with Telex and TWX. Figure 19-1 shows an OCR reader. Communicating via word processors is becoming so common that it now has its own abbreviation, CWP, meaning communications word processor. Investigations are underway regarding the potential for specific networks of CWP's and the use of intelligent terminals for communications.

Massachusetts Institute of Technology has investigated structuring office procedures so that they can be encoded, furthering the cause of office efficiency and lowering operating costs. In line with this, electronic mail is becoming an important tool to augment office productivity.

TELECOMMUNICATIONS

> With the technical advances of the past decade, a thorough understanding of the industry's offerings is essential to the manager.[4]

The period of 1971 through 1977 saw a dynamic growth in data communications. In order to focus on the specific developments and trends, it is necessary to first divide the participants into four categories: (a) established carriers, (b) specialized common carriers (SCC's), (c) value-added networks, and (d) satellite services.

Established or common carriers are AT&T, comprised of Long Lines and its 23 operating companies, 1641 independent telephone companies, and Western Union.

Specialized common carriers initially were inspired by MCI's application to the Federal Communications Commission in 1963, in which they received a free-entry policy in interstate private line and SCC services in 1971.

Value-added networks (VANS) introduced a truly unique service. This concept utilizes a number of minicomputer nodes established to package data into packets to be transmitted through the network (private line connected) and reassembled at the distant end. Through the use of minicomputer switching capabilities, values such as code, protocol, speed conversion, and error detection and correction are added.

---

[4] Jerry Striplin, Manager of Telecommunications Systems, The Coca Cola Company, Atlanta, Georgia.

The WordCom interfaces word processing with phototypesetting by reading   FIGURE 19-1
data stored on IBM, Redactron, or Vydec floppy disks. (Photo courtesy of
Northwest Microfilm, Inc.)

Satellite companies, inspired by the success of SCC, were granted open-skies opportunity from the FCC in June 1972. Today, the major satellite services are provided by American Satellite Corporation, RCA, SPC (Southern Pacific Communications), and Western Union. With the mainstream of services and carriers defined, we see what the future portends in technology and policies for the industry.

Switched network offerings historically have been dominated by the Bell System and are predicted to remain so for the foreseeable future. Technologically, there may be a graying of the basic distinction between traditional private line services and Message Telephone Service (MTS) as a result of the conversion of the switched network to an all-digital system.

The VANS are expected to become a larger part of the communications industry, inspired by the dissimilarities between leased and MTS rates, low cost of entry, and the growth of interactive on-line data processing.

Satellite services, encouraged by new industry applications, co-located customer earth stations, shared and resale policies, and the introduction of the new high-level data link control procedures (HDLC, SDCC) are expected to decline dramatically in cost.

AT&T is expected to introduce into its existing network a service in which any user with any terminal can interface with any computer or terminal authorized. This service, through nodes, will provide protocol and speed conversions routed over facilities shared in the same principle as the dial voice network.

Optical fibers will be of major interest throughout the industry, providing wider band-widths and lower costs, possibly less than satellites at distances less than 1000 miles. (Optical fiber technology is already being used in office copiers.)

Examples of Current Telecommunications Systems in Use

At 3M headquarters in St. Paul, Minnesota, customer service calls are handled in the Service Center through the network phone system. Each person in the center has a visual screen and routing control. When a service representative calls in for messages, the communications specialist immediately brings the service representative up-to-date through the network system. Copies of reports can be viewed on the display or copied on a copier.

Wang Laboratories, a major manufacturer of computers and word processing typing equipment, uses bisynchronous communications that transmits large blocks and operates at extremely high speeds from disks on word processors to disks on computers (storage to storage). Their second generation word processors, with their more sophisticated capabilities, allow the word processor to be a more equal partner with the computer. As a result, the word processing clusters can operate independently and autonomously while the computer also operates autonomously.

As a result, two subsystems can be combined very easily and offer tremendous expansion through combining the word processor and computer. Integration of information for corporate (or top) management information systems can be accomplished through this combination. Word processors, working with the computer, can become a part of providing management with the necessary tools for management information systems (MIS). Many MIS planners are currently using and incorporating the word processor into their MIS systems. Figure 19-2 illustrates how an integrated information processing system works.

Wang reported that over 50 percent of its word processors shipped in 1978 had communications capabilities (options). Wang executives feel that bisynchronous communication will become standard in the industry.

Applications Merging of word processing with data processing at a processing level, or teleprocessing, can now be accomplished. Word processing communicates jobs into the computer for computer processing (for example, updating lists, processing of calculations by using programs, and editing stored information). Document transfer, or electronic mail, allows the computer to act as a mailbox to move the document on to multiple addressees, people in other companies, as designated. Western Union's Mail-

---

The Components of an Integrated Information Processing System   **FIGURE 19-2**

---

gram system is an excellent example of the computer serving as the mailbox at destinations. A person can phone a message to Western Union from home and it will be delivered in mailgram form the next day or that same day using Western Union's computer located in the center of the country as its central mailbox.

The California Public Employees' Relations Board in Sacramento, with branches in Los Angeles and San Francisco, previously mailed or hand carried documents for board reviews and hearings, from which a review was conducted and documented, and then returned. The cycle could take as long as five months and they experienced a very heavy volume of documents. They changed to using a word processor at one location to communicate to one at the other location. This system has reduced their turn-around time to 20 days. Most of these 20 days are taken up by the review board meetings. Their productivity has increased by 2 to 1 (without use of a computer).

Word Processor-Minicomputer-Word Processor (Teleprocessing)

Harvard Medical School's Admissions Department devised a mated word processing/data processing system, using a Hewlett-Packard 4000 computer, data base management system called "Image," and the Wang word processor. The operator keys in applicable information for a medical school applicant; the computer stores an alphabetic directory from which lists are issued; and personalized letters are mailed out on the word processor to the applicants, indicating that they have or have not been accepted into Harvard Medical School.

What Is Needed in the Industry and Developments

Pipelines are needed to communicate between communicating word processors and facsimiles and would allow a firm to have one piece of equipment instead of two. They are particularly needed in the case of facsimiles, which are dedicated pieces of equipment; that is, they can be used to transmit documents only, while word processors can transmit (or communicate) documents and also produce regular office typing.

Communications vary as do computer languages. AT&T uses analog communications, while IBM uses digital. Data communications require digital codes; as a result, two different computer languages are being spoken in the world of information processing.

Satellite Communications   Pipeline of the future: The amount of information that can be sent down a communication channel that lets terminals talk to each other. Fifty-six million megabits per second can be transmitted by satellite. This is the fastest and cheapest method of transmission. Larger modems are required to meet these speeds. In the future, satellites may allow users to avoid using modems. The important area is smart switch control (a switch containing microprocessors), a no man's land which allows changing the information to transmit it over the pipeline. AT&T and IBM offer switch controls which, in the future, will have code conversion within the network.

Important Government Decisions

In 1956 the United States government's consent decree was an attempt to divest AT&T and keep them out of the computer business, while the 1968 Carterfone Decision affected future communicating systems. Tom Carter had built a device to attach to the telephone, and the government had to decide whether other people or companies could attach devices to AT&T telephones. Today, of course, this is possible. This 1968 decision has greatly affected the communications industry.

In 1977 the FCC decided that other companies could buy chunks of AT&T lines and resell them; this decision eliminated AT&T's monopoly of long-distance phone calls.

Important Aspects

The ability to batch information with bisynchronous communications is important in order to use a word processor to communicate into a computer. Asynchronous communicating cannot be batched because it does not allow high-speed transfer. A word processor needs a front end microprocessor to handle the conversion and make parts of the operation compatible. In the case of incompatible facsimiles, ITT may provide a switch for conversion. The Consulting Committee for ITT (CCITT) is currently attempting to standardize the industry. Presently there are programmable PBX systems to handle conversions. It has been suggested that word processing users should form a user's group to demand that the word processing manufacturers address this incompatibility-conversion problem.

Electronic Document Distribution of Long Documents

Ways to send a long document would be to transmit over the Bell dial-up network and computer data communications networks. Word processors could piggyback onto the system to transmit these long documents. This would require fairly large scale computers with minimum software, but the resource is available.

Distributed Word Processing

Word processing systems utilizing computers for document distribution are called distributive word processing systems and, in addition to using the computer for storage and processing, can interface with microfilm to produce and handle files for document storage and retention. The system looks as shown in Figure 19–3 and uses host computers as their means of data base.

Personnel   Word processing specialists, or secretaries, who create documents for data entry as well as standard office use need to be prepared to learn more highly technical skills. Many secretaries who have no data processing background tend to fear terminals, with or without screens. Since most have had no training in keypunching and other data processing skills, language, and terminology, they frequently are at a complete loss when confronted with data processing operations. People already trained

FIGURE 19-3   IBM's 3031 (background) with its dual operator console in the foreground, the
3705 telecommunications controller in the center background, and a
high-speed 1403-NI printer that prints 1200 lines per minute (right
foreground). (Photo courtesy of International Business Machines, Inc.)

in data processing find it easier to adapt to word processing jobs. The obvious growing
job opportunities may appear more and more challenging to data processing personnel.
Robert Greenblatt, consultant in data processing and word processing, observed that
word processing secretaries, in order to succeed in this merging office system, need to
have the four I's: Insight, Imagination, Ingenuity, and Initiative.

PHOTOTYPESETTING

As organizations recognize the need for typesetting in the word processing
operation, managers are beginning to investigate how it can best be integrated
and utilized.[5]

Charles Cumpston stated that industry top management is beginning to look at
word processing operations with new respect as a result of their proven effectiveness.

[5] Charles Cumpston, managing editor, *Word Processing World*, and editor of *Word Processing
Report* newsletter, both published by Geyer-McAllister Publications, Inc. (*Administrative
Management*).

Therefore, capable word processing managers are being watched to determine whether they can effectively integrate peripheral operations in an efficient manner.

An area currently receiving much attention is typesetting (see Figure 19-4). The first reason is that a page of typeset copy holds up to 40 percent more material than a typewritten one, thereby saving paper, postage, and filing space. Secondly, typesetting is generally seen as a natural extension of the other work being performed in word processing operations.

As a result, once an organization recognizes the convenience and necessity of typesetting in the word processing operation, it usually begins to investigate how it can best be integrated and utilized. In many cases, the material being prepared in word processing is eventually typeset. Therefore, combining these two operations for more efficient coordination makes sense.

The Itek Quadritek 1200 phototypesetter. (Photo courtesy of Itek Graphic Products.)   **FIGURE 19-4**

Problems   The problem which has delayed merging word processing with phototype-setting is that each speaks its own language; the common alphabetic codes on word processors differ from the codes used in phototypesetting. This can be solved by adding a code conversion system, often called *the black box*. This black box, when placed between the word processor and the phototypesetter, converts one system's codes to the other so that word processing input can produce the final phototypeset document.

Any kind of word processor with its own microcomputer input can be used, since it has its own software program. The trend is toward universal terminals, such as word processors. The only difference between word processors (as terminals) and electronic data processing terminals is the software (or programmed instructions written to make the system perform its functions).

In-plant Market   Many firms want better than standard typewritten copy, which increases the demand for phototypeset copy.

Print Shops (Commercial)   Print shops with phototypesetting equipment can take word processing media and have it converted to their language to produce their phototypeset documents. (See Figure 19-5.)

Integrating word processing with phototypesetting frequently turns out to be more difficult than it appears. One approach which may be taken is using present word processing equipment, taking the stored media, and converting it to usable form for the phototypesetter. Some firms are marketing converters that convert information created on word processors ready to print on certain phototypesetters. Another approach is acquiring machines which have the capability of preparing phototypeset storage media built into their software and adding these to the word processing equipment system. In summary, the user may either use the computer and black box converter to the phototypesetter to produce phototypeset copy, or the firm may obtain the dual-purpose equipment.

In our earlier predictions of the office of the future, phototypesetting was pictured as being accomplished in the word processing center where information could be converted from input typed by the word processing specialists in the work groups on their intelligent word processors. This approach can be used, or, as in the case of long documents created by one author, a document may be originally prepared in word processing on the new hybrid text-editing/typesetting machines. The decision depends upon which makes more sense for the particular firm because of the nature of its business.

William Lippold, consultant in word processing and composition, feels that the technology of phototypesetting is ahead of present word processing needs, but this is not apparent to many. Modern and future phototypesetting systems are expected to become lower in price and become easier to operate. Because of this, phototypesetting may be done by secretaries within the organization and sophisticated operators will not be needed. In 1978, a full-page electronic typesetting machine containing software (updatable) programs was marketed for $50,000 and possibly less. Just as in the other office equipment technologies, the equipment costs are expected to continue to decrease while capabilities increase.

The WordCom allows commercial phototypesetters to use word processing media   **FIGURE 19-5**
as input. (Photo courtesy of Compugraphic, Inc.)

OTHER ASPECTS OF CHANGING TECHNOLOGIES

Records Processing

The role of the computer in merging information processing will continue to expand as new products are introduced that will integrate the various phases.

Document origination is presently accomplished from longhand, copy, machine dictation, shorthand, and machine shorthand. Figure 19–6 illustrates Baron Data System's computer-aided transcription. Cassettes created by the stenotypist when taking down machine shorthand are translated on the Baron system which uses a high-speed daisy-wheel printer and 500-page hard disks. OCR can be a source, but it still is keyboarded one time. Equipment is being tested and even used on a limited scale that uses voice origination.

FIGURE 19-6   Baron Data Systems Time Machine features verbal to written information with
Baron computer-aided transcription. Information is recorded onto a cassette
when the stenotype takes notes. The computer-aided transcription system
translates the information, allowing the operator to edit on the display.
The machine prints out the completed transcript on the printer at the left
of the console. (Photo courtesy of Baron Data Systems.)

Document Production

Systems are being improved and simplified to produce typewritten documents. Figure 19-7 illustrates an intelligent typewriter that has a one-line display and offers four sizes of type in addition to many other features, including phrase storage.

Reproduction is changing dramatically, particularly as intelligent copiers and printers become available. IBM's 6670 information distributor, shown in Figure 19-8, combines the technologies of computer processing, electronic communications, text processing, copying, and laser printing into one unit that can enhance printed communications in either a single or multiple-location organization.

Electronic storage of many functions in the information distributor helps provide ease of operation in using its varied communications and text processing functions and its convenience-copying capability.

Two microprocessors use 128,000 characters of random access memory and 12,000 characters of read-only storage. One microprocessor is used in conjunction with logic operations of text processing and communications control. A second microprocessor is used for copier operations.

A single nonremovable diskette provides storage for system operational code, including diagnostics, and variable customer data of up to approximately 100 standard length letters. A microprocessor automatically monitors all functions while the machine is in operation and alerts the operator to malfunctions that may occur.

FIGURE 19-7

Magnetic cards, which can be encoded on an IBM mag card typewriter, Office Systems 6 Information Processor, or via communications from a computer, are used to store specific job instructions called operator control language, along with the text or data to be printed.

Communications Operations

With the ability to link data processing and text processing more closely, the IBM 6670 can print multipage documents that contain intermixed pages in text formats and pages of computer printout in condensed format printing.

Variable data, such as updates to insurance policies or mailing lists, can be entered into the data processing system and merged with a standard letter stored in the IBM 6670, providing personalized, repetitive letters. If window envelopes are used, the

FIGURE 19-8   IBM's 6670, a multipurpose information distributor that prints
documents with a laser in original quality and receives and transmits
electronically over ordinary telephone lines. It can be used with the IBM
mag card II typewriter. (Photo courtesy of International Business Machines, Inc.)

IBM 6670's duplex addressing enables printing of the letter recipient's name and address on the reverse side, eliminating the need to address envelopes.

High-priority documents, if recorded on magnetic cards, can be transmitted rapidly. For example, a 2500-character letter can be sent in 15 seconds over a 4800-bits-per-second switched line. This increases transmission efficiency, offers better quality copy at the receiving station, and reduces line costs.

The IBM 6670 condenses traditional size computer-generated printouts onto letter size paper with a 13.3-pitch typestyle with the same printing quality as that provided from magnetic cards. Each computer report is an original and can be printed in upper- and lowercase letters on both sides and electronically collated. Print speeds are up to 400 characters per second for the first set of pages and up to 1000 lines per minute, or 36 pages per minute on subsequent sets.

Condensed format printing can be achieved without modification to a user's existing computer programs, and computer-based data can also be transferred to magnetic cards on the IBM 6670.

In the communications environment over switched or leased lines with speeds of up to 4800 bits a second, the IBM 6670 information distributor can transmit to and receive information from compatible computers, communicating printers, and communicating keyboards. It can print the first set of pages at up to 400 characters per second. Subsequent sets are printed at up to 1800 characters per second or 36 pages per minute.

Text Processing Operations

In the text processing environment, a magnetic card storage method called operator control language enables unique formats to be created by the user. The customized commands allow a variety of automatic text processing features to be used and permit constant and variable text to be merged in a document where desired.

Micrographics

Along with merged production and communications/distribution, COM systems are beginning to be developed that fit into system integration. Equipment is being developed that will update microfilm (fiche) storage so that a document can be stored and later updated in a centralized store-and-retrieve system. This will save tremendous amounts of storage space and store and retrieve time and at the same time offer a means of control, eliminating duplicated filing within firms.

EXAMPLES OF MERGING TECHNOLOGIES

An example of merging word processing with data processing can be studied by examining systems introduced in 1978 and early 1979: IBM's 3730 and 4300 and

Wang's 100 series. IBM's 3730 text processing system offers office automation data processing with word processing. System 3730 is IBM's way of offering the office executive and the secretary the ability to process information by using computer technology.

This system, consisting of three components, has the ability to interface with 370 computers. It can perform many office functions through the input created on its 3732 work station, processed by its 3790 controller, and printed on its 3736 bidirectional printer (see Figure 19-9).

Input to the controller may be recorded on floppy disks or magnetic cards, offering compatibility to the Office System 6 as well. Each controller can handle up to 12 work stations. The 3791 controller, which stores on hard disks with 10 to 30 megabyte capacity (10 to 30 million characters), sends information to the 3736 bidirectional printers, which print out at a speed of 55 cps on Qume-like printers using plastic print wheels. These printers can justify the right-hand margin but presently do not use **proportional spacing**. Each controller can handle up to eight printers. Maximum mix for each controller is 16 work stations and bidirectional printers.

Work Stations The work stations are simply designed to perform a few word processing functions. These include inserting, deleting, correcting characters, and automatic wraparound in the right-hand margin, which the system calls *wordspill*. In addition, the **cursor** on the CRT keyboard can be moved up, down, left, right, and home (the beginning of the document).

Controller Each controller handles hard disks to store information and process it for printing. It directs input and output communications and provides text processing of

---

FIGURE 19-9   **IBM's System 3730 applies the sophisticated technology of data processing to information processing. (Photo courtesy of International Business Machines, Inc.)**

information from floppy disks from the work stations or from a communicating magnetic card system. All programming for text-handling functions not handled by the work stations is performed by the controller.

Each text display station displays 22 lines containing 80 characters each plus two system control lines.

Capabilities   The 3730 itself cannot perform the following:

* hyphenation algorithm or dictionary
* spelling verification (accuracy)
* easy repetitive letter generation
* easy to use glossary (ability to add often repeated character strings to text by one or two keystrokes)
* report generating routines which are available on Office System 6

Therefore, when not connected to a host 370 mainframe computer, the system has unsophisticated word processing power. Once it is connected to the 370 through the Systems Network Architectore (SNA) at a cost of $1600, these capabilities and more become available.

Capabilities of 3730 System Plus 370 Mainframe Computer

* Communicate (receive) electronic mail (letters and memos), reports, schedules, data base to the secretary or manager or other administrator with the 3832 text display station.
* Use large data bases through the SNA; use the management information system file to produce reports, form letters, schedules.
* Eliminate rekeying data processing reports which, once printed on a line printer, are frequently retyped in word processing or on typewriters.
* Use the computer to automatically hyphenate words, correct and verify spellings, develop large customized glossaries, fill in forms.
* Create input for phototypesetting and multifont output such as the ink-jet printer.
* Maintain and update records, schedules, and monitor production. Use for charge-back billings to customers and calculate production jobs.
* Basic accounting functions combined with paperwork. Produce multicolumn reports and calculate the statistics within them.
* Maintain a simplified MIS on each manager's desk as routine scheduling, provide and maintain notes and information, access files and records.

When the 3730 is connected to the 370 mainframe computer, it will be able to begin to actively process all office paperwork through a distributive information system using the capabilities of these large computers.

COMPUTERS MINIATURIZED

John Fletcher notes that "the Intel microcomputer chip is as powerful as the large computers produced during the 1950s."[6] He goes on to quote Harry Edelson, a research vice president with the brokerage firm of Drexel Burnham Lambert in New York as stating:

> "Some smart home builder is going to start wiring his new houses for a centralized computer to turn on and off lights automatically, to call the police department in case of a break-in... Over the next ten years the computer will have a major influence in the home... Very closely tied... will be the use of communications. Instead of wiring each city for Cable TV, which is very costly, we will leapfrog that and send information via satellite to each home. I expect that each home will have an earth station on its roof or in the yard, which will enable the people to receive programming and to communicate with anyone else in the country."

Other popular predictions are that the television set will become a printing plant: newspapers, magazines, even personal letters will be printed almost instantly and in full color; they will have storage capability equal to today's neighborhood library and be able to rerun favorite television shows.

Until recently, large companies with extensive marketing and software capabilities, such as IBM, Control Data, and Burroughs, built mainframe computers—big, high-speed machines that took three to five years to develop and cost from $100,000 to $5 million or even as much as $25 million. The microprocessor/microcomputer (a computer on a chip), by cutting the size and cost of electronic data processing, has changed all that.

A microprocessor is a computer on a chip that cannot be programmed, whereas the microcomputer is a chip that can be programmed. Both opened new markets and spawned increased competition (see Figure 19-10).

Originally used to control industrial machinery, microcomputers now control home appliances such as microwave ovens and dishwashers and are being used in word processing, accounting, and business inventory, to name but a few applications. The list is endless, and the following is just the beginning:

- An attorney's office can file information on a complex case and retrieve and categorize it within seconds.
- A mail-order house can automatically prepare individually typed letters from basic formats stored in a computer.
- Small contractors can speedily compile bids on the construction jobs.
- A doctor or dentist can maintain up-to-date records.
- A small law office using a computer can have the same data base and the same personnel as a large competitor. Instead of hiring law clerks to search a case file,

[6] John Fletcher, "The Next Computer Revolution," *Mainliner Magazine* (June 1978).

FIGURE 19-10

This tiny microcontroller chip combines high performance and high density to become one of the most advanced logic chips on the market today. It can execute half a million instructions in the time it takes to blink an eye, even though its circuits comprise an area equal to one-tenth the size of a penny. (Photo courtesy of International Business Machines, Inc.)

the attorney can query the computer; or in liability suits, the attorney can use the computer to compute stress and failpoints in machinery.

"People's lifestyles will change," predicts Gordon Bell, vice president of Digital Computer Corporation. "Computers will be in every telephone, in every typewriter, in every copying machine, in every mechanism."

Word processing, which introduced computers in the office in typewriters, is expanding as use of these microcomputers and microprocessors moves into other office equipment: dictation machines, copying and duplicating machines, facsimiles, and phototypesetters.

John Fletcher stated, "The first computer revolution . . . largely unseen, transformed big business. The next one is taking place in the home, the office, and the corner store." The result in the office is the revolution in the way people work and the skills required.

Today's word processing manager may well be tomorrow's management information system manager or may work in direct alignment with the data processing manager, both reporting to the vice president of Management Information System.

The revolution in the office, early envisioned as important only as it related to typing daily correspondence and documents, is emerging into a revolution far more significant to people in business everywhere and companies small and large. It proves to be increasingly provocative and challenging to the people who work there.

"Just as electricity sparked fundamental changes in the office, new technologies are repeating that process at a rapid pace. Today, for example, it is no longer farfetched to discuss the possibilities of combining electronics with earth satellites and facsimile techniques to make worldwide electronic mail practical."

The way we generate, record, process, file, and distribute information is only at the start of a complete transformation. Word processing is a solid foundation, but it is only the beginning.

SUMMARY

What will the office of the future be like? Some predictions are that workers will select their own working hours, many firms will move offices out of the cities nearer the homes of the workers, and the office as we know it today will no longer exist. Instead of the traditional office and desk with drawers standing on the floor, desks may be supported from above; only executives will have movable offices; partitions will be placed around the workers. Work groups may be working in teams of administrative support centers where there will be a supervisor over an administrative support specialist, communication specialist, word processing specialist, information storage and retrieval specialist. These specialists may be provided with a convenience copier, and the word processing specialist will have an intelligent typewriter with a visual display that can direct printout on a high speed or higher quality ink-jet printer.

A word processing center may provide large document revisions and high-quality printing by phototypesetting and duplicating; a computer center will be provided with the ink-jet and high-speed printers as well as microfilm recorder.

The executive will have a visual screen and telephone-directed message center and be able to see by a visual signal whether he or she has any messages waiting, divert undesired phone calls to another extension, signal for documents to be shown on his or her screen, and communicate in conferences with other executives at other locations.

Many firms already have much of this equipment in use; some already have some of their people working in situations somewhat similar to the one just described. Most experts believe secretarial work groups with intelligent typewriters will work near the executives, while a large center will provide the larger document needs of organizations.

The prediction of the merging of word processing with data processing is centered around the ability to use the same terminal or word processor for input to the computer and to perform functions which are important to both.

Word processing applications are expected to center around standalone mini-computers. shared-logic systems, and time-share computer systems. Word processing secretaries will be able to take on work for accounting, including accounts receivable, payable, and inventory control, because of the upgraded sorting capabilities added to these systems.

Workers will be learning more skills, particularly about data processing, including programming and data management.

Many firms have already begun to implement electronic mail systems. Transmission may be from word processing typewriters and their media, from typewritten or graphic copy transmitted by OCR, from remote facsimile scanners, or from the firm's data network.

Future offices may use high-speed printers and higher quality ink-jet printers, communicate to copying and duplicating machines, and have a wide range of peripheral equipment to speed up transmission of their messages.

Work stations with electronic mail capability may serve as input and output to computers and for text and graphics. Increased memory and storage capacity may be provided by links to data networks and information storage systems. Telegram services may be expanded to receive signals from word processing keyboards, media, and data networks. At the same time, senders may select from a wide range of devices the type of output desired.

First users most likely will be large companies that transmit on an intracompany basis data/text/graphics information, with 54 percent of the nation's large and medium size offices using electronic mail by 1985.

Several firms already have expansive electronic mail systems and are investigating further expansion and development of their systems' capabilities. The three forms of electronic mail—intercompany, intracompany, and public distribution—are rapidly improving. Further developments include teleconferencing using audio conference, freeze-frame, and full video conference.

As a result of recent governmental decisions, new entries into the communications business, and the advancement of technology, many changes are occurring in telecommunications. There are four categories of data communications: (a) established carriers such as AT&T, independent phone companies, and Western Union; (b) specialized common carriers with many new companies; (c) Value Added Networks (VANS) that transmit packets from one end to another, and (d) satellite services.

AT&T is expected to continue to dominate the switch network offerings. VANS will grow with new companies offering their capabilities and services, and satellite services should be lower in cost.

Computers now act as mailboxes for electronic mail services. Teleprocessing (using word processors along with computers to communicate information and process information) is being used by universities to process applicants. In the future, intelligent switch control networks will allow code conversion which will open up data communications capabilities and allow improved communications systems.

Recent government decisions have allowed other companies to purchase chunks of AT&T lines for resale and attachment to their systems, opening up opportunities for other companies to interface with the Bell System.

Distributed word processing systems, using computers for document distribution as well as storage and processing, can interface with micrographics for record storage and retention. Word processing secretaries who will be involved in the merging of data processing with word processing need to be prepared to learn more about data processing.

Costs of phototypesetting are coming down, and it is becoming easier to do. A problem that has delayed merging phototypesetting with word processing is that each speaks its own language and conversion of one to the other is required. Phototypesetting is receiving much attention because of the potential cost savings and the fact that phototypesetting is seen as a natural extension of word processing.

Many firms want better quality and see the advantage of the reduced amount of space utilized in phototypesetting which results in cost savings. Print shops are using word processing input more, as it will be easier to locate personnel and they will require less training.

Other aspects of information processing are undergoing changes that result in automatic merging of technologies. Intelligent typewriters, copiers, and printers are interfacing with computers to originate, produce, reproduce, store, retrieve, communicate, and distribute documents.

Development of the microcomputer chip introduced the second computer revolution. In the future, builders may soon wire new homes for centralized computers which can turn lights on and off and tie in with communications. People may be able to use their television sets as printing plants and a library to store documents, as well as rerun favorite shows.

In industry, the chip may be in a microprocessor, where it is not programmed, or a microcomputer, where it can be programmed.

Originally used to control industrial machinery, microcomputers are now being used to store, retrieve, and categorize information rapidly, compile bids, maintain up-to-date billing records, or compute machinery failpoints.

Predictions are being made that computers will be in every mechanical device, revolutionizing the way that offices are run and the way people work. Word processing typing equipment was the first office equipment to use microcomputers and microprocessors. Now they are being used in copying equipment, micrographic equipment, phototypesetting, and all other office equipment.

The word processing manager faces new challenges as microcomputer technology expands. Some may become vice presidents of management information systems. Some may work alongside the data processing managers. Whatever systems and structures implemented by their firms, there is no doubt that word processing managers of today and tomorrow face some very provocative and challenging times ahead.

REVIEW QUESTIONS

1. What are the future predictions for how the telephone will be used by executives?
2. What applications usually done by computers are being adapted into word processing?
3. Why has the focus shifted from large central computers to distributed environments of small computers?
4. Why do telecommunications, word processing, data processing, and records management need to be compatible?
5. Explain the benefits of electronic mail.

6. What peripheral equipment might a firm have with electronic mail systems?
7. Explain how electronic mail can augment a firm's productivity.
8. Explain why telecommunications is experiencing so much change and competition with the Bell System.
9. State how VANS affects the growth of telecommunications.
10. How does the Wang system's capabilities assist top management?
11. Explain how the computer may act as a mailbox.
12. What is needed in the telecommunications industry to reduce the amount of equipment a firm might require to meet its modern business information processing needs?
13. What will IBM and AT&T have available in the future which will allow more information to be communicated? Explain its importance.
14. Explain how distributed word processing works and why it is expected to grow in the future.
15. Why is phototypesetting growing? What are the problems of merging phototypesetting with word processing?
16. Explain how microprocessors and microcomputers affect business and describe the difference between the two.

QUESTIONS FOR DISCUSSION

1. Discuss the key to the changes occurring which bring data and word processing close together. What problems do you foresee for a firm which merges the two?
2. Discuss the use of facsimile units and CWP's as electronic mail devices, including the advantages and disadvantages of each.
3. Discuss why people predicting what future offices will be like have the administrative secretary equipped with an intelligent typewriter while many firms now equip the A/S with no typewriter at all and have all of the typing processed by the correspondence secretary.
4. Discuss why teleconferencing can save a firm money.
5. Discuss how the use of small computers in place of large central computers affects office personnel and procedures.
6. Do you believe that the recent legislation which has opened up the communications industry to more competition and offers opportunities for other firms is good for the national telecommunication effort? Explain your reasoning.
7. Why are many MIS managers incorporating word processors into their system?
8. Discuss what problems companies can have with CWP's which the vendors should address.
9. Discuss why top management in many firms is gaining respect for word processing.
10. Discuss why phototypesetting has not been growing as fast as word processing. What problems need to be resolved? Do you believe that it will replace the typewritten output in some firms? Why?
11. How do the future predictors think people's lifestyles will change as a result of microprocessors and microcomputers?

CASES

Case 19-1 Pharmaceutical Company

Health Systems, Inc. is a large drug and pharmaceutical supply firm which develops, manufactures, and markets its products and services nationwide. At their head-quarters they have had several word processing typewriters for medium to high secretaries for several years. They have decided to take a look at their internal organization at headquarters and modernize it with all appropriate equipment, sys-tems, and procedures which will meet management's objectives of reducing costs, improving employee productivity, and maintaining their highly regarded image. You have been hired to set up the new system to meet these objectives. For this purpose you have been given a free hand to make whatever changes you feel necessary. What systems do you feel you should investigate and what changes do you think you might want to make? You also are responsible for communicating and distributing informa-tion to all of the branch offices throughout the country. How do you plan to go about handling this responsibility?

Case 19-2 Insurance Company

You have been working as word processing manager for Smithers Insurance Company, which has its headquarters in Los Angeles with three other offices in San Diego, San Francisco, and Fresno. Up until now each has had its own word processing operation, and there has been no interfacing. Your boss, the vice president of finance, has put you in charge of all locations and asked that you set up, organize, and manage a system of production, communication, reproduction, and distribution throughout the firm. This means that you are responsible for the phone system, document distribu-tion, and records management, as well as total word processing. Explain what types of systems you believe you should investigate, how you plan to go about handling this responsibility, and your action plans.

Glossary

AM   Administrative management; administrative manager.

AMS   American Management Society.

APS   Alphanumeric photocomposer system.

A/S   Administrative support.

ASK   American simplified keyboard.

ATS   Administrative terminal system. A software package using a typewriter input/output device linked to a computer to process and retrieve information.

Access time   The time taken by a computer to locate data or an instruction word in its memory or storage selection and transfer it. Also, the time taken to transfer information from the input device to the location in the memory where it will be stored.

Accounting   The system of keeping records of financial transactions and of summarizing data in appropriate reports for management, financial institutions, or government agencies.

Acoustic coupler   A device permitting the transmission of information over telephone lines to a computer from input/output equipment, such as the IBM communicating magnetic card selectric typewriter.

Active document   A document requiring original thought. Research, organization, proofreading, and revision are generally required. Error-free copy is often needed.

Activity list   A department's main operations as defined by its manager.

Activity-oriented   Term used to define an administrative support operation in which aides are specialized by task, as distinct from one in which aides are principal-oriented and do many tasks for specific executives.

Address   (1) Name given to a specific location of encoded material on a recording medium. An address could be designated by a line number. (2) The act of finding such a location, usually through machine instruction.

Adjust   A text-editing typewriter feature that automatically breaks each line of revised copy during playback to conform with established margins.

Administer   To manage, especially in a setting that emphasizes the application of fixed procedures and minimal environmental turbulence.

Administrative aide   A job title also sometimes designated as administrative support aide or administrative secretary.

Administrative center   An area where secretarial specialists perform activities other than typing, such as mail handling, filing, telephoning, and special projects.

Administrative hours   The time devoted by a secretary to office activities other than typing.

Administrative manager   A general executive responsible for numerous information and support operations, including word processing, data processing, record-keeping, in-plant reproduction, mail systems, telecommunications, and office furnishings.

Administrative secretary   A secretary who supports a principal(s) with activities other than typing, such as mail handling, filing, telephoning, and special projects.

Administrative supervisor   The person in charge of an administrative center; a supervisor of administrative secretaries.

Administrative support   One of the two broad areas of specialization under word processing (the other being typing). In general, it comprises all the nontyping tasks associated with traditional secretarial work, carried out under administrative supervision.

Administrators   Persons who administer. Also a title used for some managerial positions such as the administrator of a hospital.

Advertising and promotion specialist   A person well versed in the cost and appropriateness of different modes of advertising and promoting a product or service and thereby able to advise on the best means to use in generating interest in that product or service.

Affiliate   A company that works closely with another company in serving a particular market. A subsidiary of a multinational corporation that serves a country other than the larger company's home country is an affiliate.

Align/alignment   Horizontal reference line used when inserting forms.

Allocate   To divide resources among competing interests. Allocating financial resources through a budgetary process is a prime example of such division. Other resources, such as people and time, are allocated by some mechanism if there are varying ways to employ them.

Allocation   A quantity of a resource allocated for a particular item. In speaking about money, a travel allocation would be an amount of money set aside for travel.

Allowances   Time which is computed into a work standard for fatigue, rest time, activity reporting, and other normal delays.

Allowed time   The time fixed as a standard for performing a given task. Also sometimes designated as standard time or standard allowed hours.

Alternate section   Expandable part of an 8000-character memory (mag card II).

Analytical methods   Methods of analysis that use mathematics and logic to resolve managerial problems. Financial ration analysis and operations research analysis are prime examples of analytical methods.

Announcement unit   Answers incoming phone calls and gives a prerecorded message. At end of message, unit usually switches audio from outgoing to incoming permitting callers to leave recorded messages.

Antitrust legislation   Laws that prohibit the formation and operation of business monopolies. The Sherman Antitrust Law is the basis of American antitrust laws.

Applications   Refers to a type of document processed for a particular purpose or in a special way.

Assessment center   A method of evaluating candidates for a managerial position that involves bringing the candidates to a central location for a series of tests, interviews, and exercises. Assessors evaluate the candidates' performance and make recommendations to the person or persons who will make the final choice.

Assets   The items of value owned by a company or person. Also the items fitting this description that appear on the left-hand side of a balance sheet opposite the liabilities.

Asynchronous   A mode of communication that consists of a string of individual characters bracketed by a stop and start bit signal. Therefore, each character is burdened by at least two additional signal bits. This reduces the load factor per character.

Attendant phone   In a central dictation system, a phone which allows the word originator to communicate with an attendant in the word processing center or other remote recorder location.

Augmented mode; augmented system   An administrative support arrangement which introduces some word processing/administrative support principals into a traditional secretarial environment with little or no change in office layout.

Authority   The right to use assigned resources within one's discretion to accomplish an assigned task, including the right to direct people and other resources. Authority is always limited by the organization's policies and procedures and the rules of the larger society.

Automated typewriter   A general term covering all types of word processing keyboard equipment.

Automatic forward reset   A feature of telephone dictation recorders which enables the unit to continue automatically in playback mode to the end of recorded dictation, even though the person who has been reviewing his dictation has disconnected, so that the next dictator will begin recording on an unused part of the belt.

Automatic repeat key   A live typewriter key, such as the underscore, which will continue to operate as long as the key is depressed.

Automatic reverse   The ability of some dictation recorders to reverse at the end of a tape for playback without having to change reels.

Automatic selector   In telephone dictation, a connection method which links the handset to the first free recording unit available for input.

Automatic typewriter   (1) Typewriter with ability to record onto a medium for later playback of recorded words. (2) The simplest of the automated typewriters, used mainly for straight, repetitive output involving little or no text editing. Used for rapid production of form letters and similar documents.

Automatic word recall   An adjustable feature of a transcriber unit which enables the word originator or the transcriptionist to replay a measured portion of the previous dictation by depressing the foot pedal or hand control.

Automation   The system of production that uses self-controlled machines to accomplish the task at hand. When further self-controlled devices are incorporated, one says that there is greater automation in the process.

Autonomy   The ability to operate independently of other units. A manager may have great autonomy in his job, or one can speak of a subsidiary of a conglomerate having limited autonomy.

Availability   The time or the percentage of time in a certain period during which a piece of equipment functions properly.

Average letter   Approximately 92 to 115 words or 18 to 23 lines of twelve-pitch typing. As the standards are hard to define, this method of measurement is generally unsuitable and is not a widely recognized standard.

BPS   Bits per second. Method of measuring machine speed.

BSC   Backspace code. Functional code on magnetic keyboards.

Backlog   A reserve of unprocessed work.

Backspace code   A key-operated instruction which backspaces the carriage or carrier of a word processing typewriter without backspacing the recording medium. It is used, for example, in underscoring.

Backspace strikeover   Correcting method that through magnetic media allows the keyboard technician to immediately correct typographical errors.

Balance of payments   The payments due a country for exports less the payments it owes for imports during a particular time period. The notion can be applied to a single pair of countries or to one country versus all others. The term *balance of trade* is also used.

Bankrupt   A legal or economic term that means insolvency or inability to pay one's debts.

Baseplate   A device attached to the underside of certain nonautomated typewriters, enabling performance of various automated typing functions, including text editing and playback.

Basic strategy objective   A company or organization's central aim in trying to achieve its overall financial or other objectives. For example, Sears and Roebuck's basic strategy objective during its early decades was to merchandise true values to farmers and their families through mail-order merchandising.

Basket   Term applied to the typing mechanism of a standard typewriter in which each character, as an upper- and lowercase pair, is conveyed on a separate typebar—the entire set of typebars being basketed in a curved array in front of the platen. *See also* Single-element; Typing element; and Typing mechanism.

Batch   A collection of similar work which can be processed at one operation.

Batch control   A control device which permits the issuance of predetermined quantities of work to an employee at regular intervals of time.

Batching (Batch processing)   A technique in which a number of similar programs are grouped and processed during the same machine run.

Batch recording   Identical or similar documents which are recorded on magnetic media or into memory in groups whenever possible, such as forms, or form letters.

Beating the shift   A typewriter action in which a very fast or erratic typist causes a character to misprint following or preceding a shift.

Behavioral psychology   The school of psychology that relies exclusively on the analysis of empirically observed behavior in accounting for why people act as they do.

Behavioral science approach to management   The school of thought that gives primary importance to the disciplines of psychology, sociology, and anthropology in explaining management and in trying to improve the practice of management.

Billing   The business function of giving customers or clients formal notice that payment is due on a certain date for goods or services provided.

Bit   (1) A binary digit; loosely, a code representing one digit of information. (2) The smallest unit of information recognized by a computer.

Black box   Refers to the operating unit or brains of an electronic system; slang term for a central processor unit.

Bleeding   (1) A term referring to the splashing or bleeding of carbon material from a carbon ribbon onto the paper or the typewriter mechanism. (2) Intermingling of the differently colored inks in a red/black typewriter ribbon.

Boilerplate   Construction of a document using parts of many other documents or a list of paragraphs.

Brand name product   A product sold with a company's name or other specific name attached to it rather than being sold with only a generic name.

Breakeven point   The level of sales or production that is necessary to break even— that is, to lose no money and to make no money. Analysis whose objective is to determine this level is called breakeven analysis.

Budget   An approved scheme that specifies how much is to be spent on each category of expenditure during a given time period. The scheme is usually compiled in a document referred to as *the budget.*

Budget allocation   The amount to be spent in a particular category as specified in a budget.

Budget-based institution   An organization that receives relatively assured income rather than being subject to an immediately responsive market. Government agencies and nonprofit organizations are examples of such institutions.

Budgeting   The process of developing a budget.

Buffer   (1) A device or system used to make two other devices or systems compatible. (2) An area of storage temporarily reserved for use in performing an input/output operation. (3) An 8000-character solid-state memory in the mag card II.

Buying-in   The process of getting approval to provide a product or service by underestimating the total cost.

By-product   A substance, product, or condition produced by a production process in addition to the primary item produced.

Byte   (1) A sequence of eight adjacent bits that is treated as a unit. (2) A sequence of adjacent binary digits operated upon as a unit and usually shorter than a word.

CMC   Communicating mag card. Magnetic keyboard used for either point-to-point communications or as a computer terminal.

CPI   Characters per inch.

CPS   (1) Certified Professional Secretary. (2) Characters per second.

CPU   Central processing unit. Sometimes used as a synonym for computer.

CR   Carriage return.

CRT   Cathode ray tube. A vacuum tube in which a beam of electrons can be focused to a small point on a luminescent television tube screen and can be varied in position and intensity to form alphanumerical characters.

CT/ST   Cassette tape/selectric typewriter.

Calendar of conversion   A calendar developed to schedule the implementation of a word processing system.

Capital   Wealth that an organization possesses to employ in achieving its aims.

Capital equipment   A company or organization's equipment or building the purchase of which required the expenditure of substantial capital.

Capital formation   The process by which capital is created in an economy.

Capital-intensive industry   An industry that in comparison to other industries requires large investments of capital per dollar of sales or production. Frequently contrasted with labor-intensive industry.

Capital investment   An investment or an employing of a company's capital in a specific project.

Capital investment decisions   Decisions regarding the employment of a firm's capital. Since capital is usually invested in plant or equipment for long periods, it is of utmost importance that decisions be made with as much knowledge as possible about the expected rate of return on the capital. Thus there is a vast body of literature on this kind of analysis and decision-making.

Capstan   The driven shaft in a tape dictation recorder, usually the motor shaft, which rotates against the reel or cassette hub, pulling the tape through the machine during input and playback.

Carbonless (Carbon-coated business forms)   Business forms that permit impressions from copy to copy without the use of carbon. The image is made when special coatings on the back of one sheet and the face of the following sheet are brought together under pressure.

Carbon sets   A multi-ply form manufactured with carbon paper interleaved between the original and tissue copies.

Carbon splash   *See* Bleeding.

Card console   Separate unit attached to the typewriter of a magnetic keyboard that utilizes magnetic cards.

Card folder   Protector folder into which magnetic cards are inserted for storage.

Carrying costs   The costs incurred by holding inventory.

Cartridge   (1) A single reel of magnetic tape in a plastic or metal container designed to feed the tape into an automatic typewriter. (2) A container of magnetic tape, usually associated in word processing with magnetic tape selectric typewriter equipment. Available in 35-,50-, 100-, and 120-foot lengths of 16mm magnetic tape. Magnetic tape selectric typewriter recording density is 20 characters per inch, or approximately 24 characters per 100-foot reel of tape.

Cassette   A container of magnetic tape, two reels of one-eighth inch, used with certain dictation equipment as well as with certain word processing typing equipment. Relatively inexpensive, it is used extensively in portable recording machines. The standard tape drive speed is one and seven-eighths inches per second. Can store approximately 60,000 characters in text-editing typewriter use.

Center   (1) To position typing with a given measurement equidistant from the margins. (2) Command to a word processing typewriter that it automatically center lines during playout. (3) An area where certain work is performed by specialists such as a document center or a word processing center.

Centralization   (1) Having a dedicated area in which personnel specialize in performing particular tasks, for example, a centralized document center. (2) A method of organizing that concentrates decision-making at the top of an organization's hierarchy.

Centrex   A telephone switching system allowing direct dialing to an extension phone without going through a manned switchboard.

Chad   The small pieces of paper tape or punch card removed when a hole is punched.

Clean line   A circuit supplying power to only one unit.

Clerical administrative support   Unit that supports word processing center by providing the following services: batching, logging, dictation, filing, decollating, bursting, signing, mailing, and quality control.

Clerk   An employee responsible for correspondence records, accounts, or the performance of general office work.

Client   A customer for a service-producing enterprise.

Clipping   A condition in dictation where the first part of a word is not recorded because the mechanism does not engage fast enough.

Code   (1) The pattern or system of signals recorded on media which stand for alphanumeric characters or machine actions. (2) Name given to the specified instruction or action required of a typing unit in playback; a command, e.g., center, indent, justify, stop. (3) In telecommunications, the language that translates the bits into identifiable characters. The most common code is ASCII, which stands for American Standard of Code Information Interchange, a seven-bit code. EBCD code, the Binary Code Decimal, was originated by IBM and consists of six bits. EBCDIC is an eight-bit code.

Cold type Composition for offset printing produced by a direct-impression type-writer-like machine, such as the IBM selectric composer or photocomposing equipment. It is distinguished from hot type, which is made up of one-line slugs cast from molten metal by linecasting equipment.

Command An instruction to a machine, such as a word processing typewriter, to perform a certain action.

Command key A key which, when hit, enters a particular command into a system.

Communicating typewriter A word processing typewriter which can send text to and receive text from another communicating typewriter or, in exchange with a computer, over phone lines or via other telecommunications hookups.

Communication The transfer of meaning from one (the sender) to another (the receiver). The sender and receiver may be persons, corporate entities, or other groups of people.

Competition The companies that are alternative sources of supply for a given company's customers or clients.

Computer Electronic device that can perform multiple complex calculations or logic operations.

Computer code A machine language used by a given computer.

Computer program A set of instructions and/or statements used by a computer in accomplishing a specific result.

Computer programmer A person who creates computer programs.

Configuration The layout of a word processing station or center.

Conglomerate A company made up of many other companies in a wide variety of industries. Many such companies were formed in the late 1960s.

Connect time The time during which an input/output terminal is connected to a computer.

Conscience activities The activities directed to giving vision and to setting standards and auditing performance against them.

Console The unit housing the record/playback mechanism and related controls of a text editing typewriter.

Constant Term used to define information that is placed in permanent storage.

Constituencies The various interest groups who vie for the attention of an organization, e.g., faculty, students, parents, foundations, and government agencies each constitute a constituency for a university.

Consumerism The social movement that insists that products and services be of unassailable quality and without any possible hazardous side effects.

Continuous form stationery One set of forms is joined to another in a series of accordion-pleated folds.

Continuous loop A recorder system employing an endless loop of magnetic tape as the recording medium.

Control The management function that aims to keep activities directed in such a way that desired results are achieved. Monitoring of performance is the starting point of all control. In case performance deviates from what is expected, corrective action must be taken to get the process back on the track.

Control clerk Individual responsible for maintaining input equipment, logging, work distribution, and some quality review.

Control point An established performance standard within a system that is continuously or periodically monitored.

Cooperation Joint effort to achieve a desired result.

Copy   Text material in typed or printed form.

Copy file   Mylar sheet with chemically treated ink molecules used to produce high-quality copies while typing (used in place of carbon paper).

Copy revision   Includes console preparation, automatic playback when making corrections due to editorial changes, and actuating of various playback controls. Console adjustments are included, if required.

Corporation   A legal entity formed by persons to enter a business while limiting their liability to the monies they have contributed to the enterprise.

Correctable film ribbon   Polyethylene carbon ribbon used in conjunction with liftoff correction tape.

Correction fluid   A liquid coverup applied over an error that blends into the paper.

Correction paper   A chalk-coated strip of paper, coated on one side. The typist places the coated side against the error and retypes the error so that some of the chalk transfers and covers it.

Correction tape   Includes either lift-off or coverup tape, used on mag card II/memory typewriter or other keyboards with a similar correcting mechanism.

Correspondence center   A word processing center; a secretarial group performing typing activities.

Correspondence secretary   A secretary responsible for typing activities and assigned to a correspondence center; a word processing operator; a typing specialist.

Cost accountant   An accountant whose primary responsibility is to determine the cost of goods or services. The cost figures are to be used in determining profit levels and in meeting other demands for judgments on what the costs are.

Cost center   In a business, costs are either assigned exclusively to the business as a whole, or the business is broken into parts each of which is responsible for certain costs. In the latter event, the parts are the cost centers. In a multidivision company, the divisions may be the cost centers.

Cost effectiveness analysis   The method of analysis that compares the cost of alternative solutions for a problem with the relative benefits provided by each.

Cost of capital   The rate of return that should be used as the minimum acceptable for considering a given capital expenditure; the rental cost of money. Thus, projects must pay more than it would cost to rent the money required, or no financial benefit has been produced.

Credit   Ability to borrow funds, or the funds so borrowed.

Critical path analysis   A method of analyzing the scheduling of a project with multiple subactivities. The method uses network diagrams that represent the component activities. Time required to complete each activity is analyzed, and the earliest and latest beginning date for each activity is specified. Finally the longest path through the sequence of activities (the critical path) is identified, and that path receives special attention so that the project will be completed on time.

Critical path method (CPM)   A procedure for planning the completion of each part of a complex operation or project so that successive steps can be accomplished on schedule.

Cross-training   The switching of personnel among various workstations so that they may learn more than one job.

Cursor   The movable dot on a CRT screen which shows the place on a displayed document for entering new text or making editing changes.

DDRP Dial dictation relay panel.

DE Dictation equipment.

DIS Dial input system.

DP Data processing.

DSK (Dvorak simplified keyboard) An improved typewriter keyboard rearrangement whereby, through scientific key placement, 35 percent average faster production is claimed over the conventional keyboard arrangements. First patented in 1932 by Dr. August Dvorak of the University of Washington in Seattle.

Data entry Creating information for a computer to process, originally by keypunching.

Data processing The function of handling the masses of data involved in the multiple transactions related to a firm's business. Since most large firms use computers in this function, the department in charge of the computing is frequently called the data processing department. Similarly, the function is often referred to as electronic data processing (EDP).

Dead key A typewriter key which does not automatically advance the carrier to the next character position when struck.

Decentralization A method of organizing that disperses decision-making to multiple locations and levels rather than concentrating it at the top of the organization's hierarchy.

Decibel (dB) The unit of measure for the relative loudness of sound.

Decision theory A body of analytical tools including logic, mathematical models (especially models that use probability theory), and diagrams to be used in decision-making.

Decision tree From decision theory, a diagram that looks very much like a tree and that allows alternative decisions to be pictured in an orderly fashion.

Dedicated recorder A recorder devoted exclusively to one type of dictation or specific individual(s).

Deficit The amount by which expenses exceed the funds available (or allocated) to cover them.

Delegation of authority The process of establishing and maintaining effective working arrangements between a word processing manager and the people who report to him/her. Delegation results when the performance of specific work is entrusted to another, and the expected results are mutually understood.

Demand pattern The relative distribution of demand among the various markets served or that could be served.

Departmentalization The process of grouping organizational activities into basic subunits, usually done using a common characteristic such as function, product, or geography.

Depreciate The process by which the worth of equipment or buildings is assigned decreased value due to deterioration, obsolescence, or other considerations.

Diablo Trade name of a typing mechanism employing a high-speed, interchangeable printwheel.

Dial seizure Gaining access and control of a recorder system unit by dialing assigned telephone numbers. In some cases this also includes switching on motors.

Dictation speed Median dictation of 60 words per minute.

Direct impression Term applied to text-production techniques in which each character is struck onto the paper, as in conventional typing.

Direct labor costs   The cost that is attributable to the production process itself and that is so ascribed in accounting for the results of the business. Direct labor costs are frequently contrasted with indirect labor costs, which are costs counted in determining results but are not part of the production payroll.

Discounted cash flow analysis   A method of allowing a stream of fund flows that are to occur over a period of years to be summarized into a single number so that alternative streams can be compared.

Discrete media   Term applied to recording media that are individually distinct—that can be filed, mailed, moved, and otherwise separately handled. In dictation equipment, for example, belt, disk, cartridge, and cassette media are discrete; endless-loop media are not.

Display   (1) Provide a visual picture; the picture. (2) Term applied to the screen of a CRT-equipped word processing typing system, as well as the textual images appearing on that screen. (3) The act of commanding a CRT-equipped word processing system to produce specified text on its screen.

Distortion   The difference between an audio input signal and that played back by the recording device.

Distribution   The function of dispensing the goods manufactured or warehoused to the locations where they will be consumed or received by customers. Choices of modes of transportation to be used and their timeliness and cost are important elements of the distribution function.

Distributive system   The mechanism set up to accomplish the distribution task.

Distributor   A company or business agent who is the middleman between the manufacturer and the end user.

Dividend   The amount of profit for a given period returned to the owner of one share of a company's stock.

Division of labor   The method of dividing a task into specialized subtasks with different people doing different subtasks so that they may become very efficient at performing their subtask and thereby contribute to accomplishing the overall job at least cost.

Document   Copy.

Dolby system   Circuitry used primarily in audio recording equipment to reduce the amount of noise, principally tape hiss introduced during recording.

Dot leader   A word processing typing command which automatically places a series of periods between two items of copy, as in index work.

Double voicing   A condition most commonly found in earlier magnetic belt recording systems where an echo effect was noticeable until the transcriber sound head was tuned to the same place and on the same track where the recording was made.

Downtime   Time when equipment is not in use because of malfunction.

Draft   A rough and unedited outline of a document.

Dropout   During playback, the brief loss of a recorded signal due to tape imperfection.

Dual media typewriter   Automatic typewriter with the capability of using two media—magnetic card and/or cassette.

Dual track recorder   Usually a monophonic recorder with a recording head gap covering less than one-half the width of the tape. This permits recording one track on the tape in one direction and by turning the tape over, a second track in the opposite direction.

Dvorak simplified keyboard   *See* DSK.

EDP   Electronic data processing. In general, computer operations. *See* Data processing.

Econometric methods   Methods used by a branch of economics that makes extensive use of mathematical modeling and simulation.

Editing   (1) Reading back, scanning, deleting, inserting, and reformatting. (2) The act of revising and correcting text or a manuscript prior to its production as a final document or publication. (3) The act of operating the function and alphanumeric keys of a word processing typewriter to alter the recorded text it will eventually play out automatically.

Effective demand   The demand that will be realized if the product or service is made available.

Effectiveness   The extent to which the desired result is realized. Frequently compared with efficiency.

Efficiency   Output divided by input, or the extent to which the result produced was produced at least cost.

Electrostatic printing   A system whereby images or alphanumerics are burned into the paper electrically.

Element   (1) Golf-ball size sphere that holds all type characters on magnetic keyboards. Available in different type styles and pitches. (2) In word processing, usually a reference to the typing component on an automated typewriter, such as the Diablo or Qume printwheel or the selectric "golf ball."

Elite   (1) The smaller of two common typewriter typeface sizes, the larger being pica. (2) A standard of typewriter spacing, twelve characters to the horizontal inch, also called twelve pitch.

Embossed media   In data entry, a vinylite disk or belt recording media whose sound tracks are grooved like a phonograph record by an embossing needle, in contrast to magnetic media.

Endless loop   Term applied to a family of data entry systems which employ sealed, continuous loops of magnetic tape as recording media. The tapes are kept in containers called tanks.

End-of-ribbon shutoff   Standard feature on mag card II that automatically prevents continuing playout when ribbon runs out.

Entrepreneur   A person who starts and develops a business.

Environment   The external setting in which a business operates. Of special importance are the factors that may have a large impact on the business's success, such as competition, labor market conditions, the general economic climate, government regulation.

Error-free   A characteristic of recording on magnetic media which allows correction of errors by recording over unwanted material.

Executive   A manager. Most frequently used to refer to middle and upper levels of the organizational hierarchy.

Exports   Goods and services provided from one country to another. Generally contrasted with imports, goods consumed in a home country but produced abroad.

Extrapolation   A method of forecasting that assumes that the future will continue to reflect already established trends.

Fabric ribbon   Typewriter ribbon made of cotton, nylon, or silk.

Facsimile   The process of transmitting textual and illustrative copy electronically, sometimes by radio but in office operations more typically by telephone.

Documents scanned on a rotating drum at the sending site are recreated on a comparable drum at the receiving site.

Factors of production   The elements necessary in order to produce goods and services in an economy, for example, capital and labor.

Fan fold   Refers to paper tape supplied in convenient flat, folded form.

Fast forward   A tape recorder feature which permits the tape to be rapidly run in normal play direction for search purposes.

Federal decentralization   A mode of organizing a large multidivision company by decentralizing authority and centralizing control.

Feedback mechanism   A mechanism to allow recognition of unexpected deviations in a process and prompt corrective action so that the process will stay at the level needed to obtain the desired results.

Feed code   A no-action code recorded to block out any unwanted character.

Fidelity   The degree of accuracy with which sound is reproduced.

Film ribbon   Usually a mylar carbon typewriter ribbon.

Final copy   A correct finished document.

First-line supervisor   A manager who supervises other employees at the lowest managerial level in the organizational hierarchy. These people are also referred to as first-line management.

Fixed capital   Money invested permanently in buildings, machinery, and equipment.

Fixed costs   Costs that are incurred regardless of the level of production. Frequently contrasted with variable costs, which depend on the amount produced.

Flexible staffing   Use of temporary/casual/part-time employees to meet peak workloads.

Flicking   A term referring to too rapid use of the selectric keyboard whereby random hyphens appear.

Floppy disk (Diskette)   A recording medium used in certain word processing typing systems, called floppy to distinguish it from the rigid version often employed in computer memories.

Flowchart   A graphic representation of the sequence of work from origin to completion in which symbols are used to represent operations and equipment.

Font   An assortment of type of one size and style, including all the letters in the alphabet.

Foot pedal   Activates transcribing machine. By pressing the center of the pedal, the operator can listen to recorded dictation. By operating other parts of the foot pedal the operator can reverse and fast-forward dictation.

Formal organization   The structure that indicates to whom each person in the hierarchy reports, frequently diagrammed in an organization chart.

Format card procedure   Procedure whereby just formatting instructions are recorded on a card (tabs, carrier returns, and stop codes).

Form letters   The same basic letter to be sent out to a number of different people, usually prepared in advance and duplicated.

Four-track recorder   An arrangement whereby four different sound channels can be recorded on audio tape. Conventionally, tracks 1 and 3 are recorded in the forward direction, with tracks 2 and 4 being recorded in the reverse direction.

Free enterprise system   The economic system that has private ownership of property and business units operated with a minimum of governmental interference.

Function   (1) An identifiable operation or segment of ongoing work. (2) The operational unit, line or staff, responsible for such work.

Functional authority   Authority based on a business function whose exercise may require compliance by persons who are not subordinates of the person exercising the authority. For example, a purchasing department may require persons in another department to follow its procedures for ordering equipment.

Function organization A mode of organizing a business that makes the manufacturing, selling, engineering, accounting, and other departments defined by business functions the basic subunits of the organization.

Galley proof A preliminary printout of type in columnar form, for checking purposes.

Gantt chart A chart to be used in planning and coordinating an activity that involves several parallel subactivities. A timeline is depicted horizontally at the top of the chart. Below the timeline are horizontal bars for each activity, with the length of each bar representing its duration and the lefthand border representing the beginning time of the activity.

Gazetteer Portion of dictionary that lists names of places (cities, states, towns, etc.) as well as information on their location and population. Useful to transcribers to check the spelling of names of places to which correspondence is sent.

Generalist A person who performs a combination of general duties rather than one or a few specialized tasks.

Glide time A timekeeping principle where, within limits, the employee sets his/her own starting time.

Global replace A feature on a word processor which allows a particular item or set of items to be changed throughout a document with a single instruction. On a word processor, there may be a key called *global replace* which when depressed instructs the system to replace a word such as *company* with another word such as *firm* throughout the document—or globally.

Goof sheet An interoffice form in which word originators and word processing personnel can note suggestions to one another for improving service and avoiding problems.

Gross documents Number of pages typed including those retyped.

Gross lines Number of lines typed including those retyped.

Gross national product (GNP) The sum of the values of all the products and services produced by a national economy during a single year.

Grouping The combining of secretarial or typing work stations to facilitate supervision and improve support for principals.

Hard copy Written, typed, or printed matter; a document.

Hardware The electrical, electronic, magnetic, and mechanical devices comprising a system.

Headliner A photolettering machine which produces headlines and other large display copy.

Hierarchy of needs A construct in Maslow's theory of motivation. The theory postulates that human needs consist of the hierarchy: physiological, security, affiliation, esteem, and self-actualization needs. The theory suggests that the lower-level needs must be satisfied before higher order needs come into play and that once lower-level needs are satisfied, they lose their motivational importance.

Hot zone The area, adjustable in width, for controlling the right-hand margin of text. When a line of typing is played out under reset margin conditions, the word processing typewriter, having reached the hot zone, will either decide to start a new line, or pause so the operator can make a hyphenation decision.

Human asset accounting   A set of methods for trying to evaluate a firm's human resources.

Human relations approach to management   An approach to management thought and practice that insists on the primacy of the relations among a firm's employees as the determinant of success.

Hunting service   Hunting allows the records to be set up so that if one is in use, the originator is connected to the next one in a number series.

Hybrid   Term applied to certain jobs in a word processing/administrative services system where the worker is a typing specialist for part of the time and an administrative aide the rest of the time.

Hygiene and housekeeping activities   Activities that do not contribute to the basic results of the business but that if done poorly could damage the business, for example keeping the premises clean, the employees fed, reporting to the government.

Hygiene factors   A construct in Herzberg's theory of motivation, factors that do not motivate positively but that could demotivate if handled poorly.

Hyphen drop   The dropping of a hyphen at the end of a line by an automatic typewriter when the hyphenated word appears in the middle of a line in playback.

I/O   Input/output, as in I/O terminal.

I/O unit   Input/output device.

IPN   Information processing network.

IPS (Inches per second)   Usually refers to speed of tape moving past a recorder head. Faster speeds generally produce higher fidelity.

IWP (International Word Processing Association)   A word processing user group affiliate of the Administrative Management Society (AMS). An association concerned with the progress of word processing systems and methods.

Impact   The consequences an action has in addition to those that constitute its raison d'etre, for example an action taken in one department may have consequences far beyond that department, or a production process may have polluting wastes as an impact.

Implementation   The phase following management approval of a word processing system, during which the details of the system are developed and carried out.

Indent   To bring a line or lines of typing in from the margin, as at the start of a paragraph.

Index return code (I/R)   Functional code on a magnetic keyboard.

Index slip   A strip of paper containing information about the contents of the recording (number of items, length of each item, and special corrections).

Individual professional contributors   Managerial personnel who may supervise no one (except possibly a secretary and an assistant) but who make major contributions to the results of the firm by applying their professional competence, for example, an advertising specialist.

Industrial anthropology   The science of man in the workplace. Concepts of sociology, psychology, and physiology are applied to understanding life in an industrial setting.

Industrial engineer   An engineer who applies scientific methods to solving work-related problems, especially in a factory or production setting.

Industrial psychology The branch of psychology that studies human behavior in organizational settings, with special attention being given to behavior in business firms.

Industrial relations An approach to management promoted by some behavioral scientists. The central theme is the relief or prevention of dissatisfaction among employees.

Industrial sociology The study of human institutions and groups and their operating characteristics in an industrial setting.

Inflationary pressures Economic conditions that, if left unchecked, will bring on inflation, for example, continued wage increases unmatched by productivity improvements.

Informal organization The set of relationships that reflect actual interactions within an organization as contrasted with the formal organization structure.

Ink jet A method by which alphanumerics are electronically "squirt printed" onto paper.

Input (1) Information or ideas in raw form. (2) Term used when referring to the submission of work to a word processing center.

Input processing equipment Dictation equipment used to input material to the word processing center.

Input unit A device into which something is placed, e.g., a dictation recorder.

Input word processing equipment New name used by IBM for dictation equipment to better describe its function in a word processing system.

Installment credit Credit extended in exchange for the promise to repay the money with interest in equal payments at specified intervals until the money is repaid.

Institutional investors Investors who represent large organizations and as a consequence buy and sell very large blocks of stocks and bonds, for example, mutual funds, pension funds, university endowment funds. Since the late 1960s, such investors have come to dominate the market, whereas individual investors were once a large part of the market.

Insurance A method of protecting individuals against the effects of a specific kind of loss by having each individual in the insured group pay a fee in exchange for a promise to be compensated in the event the loss occurs.

Integrate A process by which managers mesh their work with that of others (in their own units, in other units, above them, below them, and laterally) in order to pursue a particular objective.

Interactive Term applied to word processing typing systems that communicate with computers or other word processing terminals, in contrast to standalone systems, which are self-contained.

Interface The point at which two systems connect.

Intermediate product A product made to be used in making another product rather than to be used by an end user, for example, a basic chemical product such as carbon dioxide.

Interpersonal relations Relations among people, based on continued face-to-face interactions.

Inventory The supply of goods or resources on hand at one time.

Inventory models Models that may be used to determine when inventories should be resupplied.

Investment An application of a firm's resources (especially money) in a means that is expected to pay off in future results.

Investment decision   A decision about how to employ substantial portions of a firm's resources, especially capital.

Investment instruments   Vehicles that may be used to invest funds, for example, stocks, bonds, mutual funds, certificates of deposit.

Irreversible decision   A decision whose impact cannot be removed or reversed, for example introducing a completely new technology (the secrecy of the technology cannot be reinstated).

Job description   An exposition of the duties and responsibilities that are inherent in a particular job; a definition of what each worker should do. A written statement of the duties, responsibilities, and requirements of a specific job.

Job enlargement   Including more tasks or more kinds of tasks in a given job in order to make the job more satisfying.

Job enrichment   Changing some aspects of a job in order to have it satisfy more of a person's higher order needs.

Job evaluation   The process by which jobs in an organization are appraised to determine their relative value to other jobs in same organization.

Job levels   The steps in a career path from entry level to the highest level.

Joint venture   A business venture that is funded by more than one company. For example, the European supersonic transport was a joint venture of British and French companies.

Justification   The adjustment of spacing in a line of type to produce a flush-right margin to a specified measure.

Key activities   Activities in the most important business areas: marketing, innovation, human organization, financial resources, physical resources, productivity, social responsibility, and profit requirements.

Keybar   Term applied to typewriters having conventional typebar or basket typing mechanisms.

Keyboarding   The act of operating a typewriter.

Knowledge worker   An employee whose major contribution depends on his employing his knowledge rather than his muscle power and coordination, frequently contrasted with production workers who employ muscle power and coordination to operate machines.

LPH (Lines of typing per hour)   Unless specified, this should always refer to net lines of finished typing which is ready for final dispatch or disposition.

LSI   Large scale integration.

Labor economics   The branch or discipline of economics that concentrates its studies on the supply and demand of labor in an economy.

Labor unions   Organizations of workers banded together to promote worker interests, especially high wages and better fringe benefits and working conditions.

Language translator   A routine designed to convert input statements in one language into equivalent statements in another.

Large-scale organizations   Organizations that require huge investments or employ thousands of workers, as contrasted with small businesses, proprietorships, or businesses with limited managerial employees.

Lateral mobility   Ability to move from one area of business to another, as from production to sales. Frequently compared to vertical mobility.

Leading   Amount of space between lines of type, usually referred to in terms of point size. The notation "10/12" or "10 on 12" means ten-point type on a twelve-point space, or, expressed another way, ten-point type with two points of leading between lines.

Lead time   The time that must pass between a decision and its coming to fruition, for example the number of years between the decision to build a new steel mill and the time when it can be placed in operation.

Learning curve   A measure of the rate of learning in relation to length of training and/or experience.

Level   Used in paper tape or magnetic tape jargon, refers to vertical rows of perforations or electronic codes.

Line   A row of typing often used as a unit in work measurement. There is no universal standard, but one common definition fixes a line at six inches of elite type (twelve characters to the inch) or 72 typewritten strokes. Because lines could include rough drafts, etc., such statistics would be meaningless. Therefore, only net lines (those lines of finished typing ready for dispatch) are usually counted. Allowances are made for headings, endings, carbon copies, and envelope addressing.

Linear programming   An operations research technique that can be used to determine the proper mix of products or ingredients to maximize profits or some other dimension of interest to management.

Line count   (1) Function on a mag card II which allows the technician to control a predetermined number of lines to a page. (2) Term given to a line of type when determining keyboard production.

Line management job   A managerial job that includes supervision and one of the central business functions such as selling or production. Frequently contrasted with staff jobs.

Liquidate   To terminate an operation by disposing of all assets and inventory, returning the proceeds to the owners of the operation.

Load transfer   A method of rerecording material from a continuous-loop recorder onto a different medium.

Lockout   A dictation equipment feature which ensures that users will not be able to intrude on, or review, another person's dictation.

Log   Term used for entering workflow information, e.g., in/out, author, amount, technician, and turnaround time.

Logging   A method of recording, cataloging, and filing incoming and outgoing work to assist in monitoring it and controlling its flow.

Logic   The instructions programmed into the system which make it perform all designated functions, such as centering across a page.

Logistics   The function of moving, storing, and distributing resources and goods.

Log sheet   A document prepared and maintained by supervisors of word processing operators to keep track of incoming and outgoing work, turnaround times, and the like.

Longhand   Writing in which words are written out in full by hand.

Long-range planning   Planning with a multiyear time horizon. Contrasted with yearly plans and other shortrange plans.

Lower case   The small letters of type, in contrast to capitals or upper case.

MC/ST   Magnetic card selectric typewriter, an IBM product.

Ms.   (1) An alternative to the use of Miss or Mrs. when neither of these is known or if it is desired. (2) Manuscript.

MT/SC   Magnetic tape selectric composer.

MT/ST (Magnetic tape selectric typewriter)   These units are produced in several models, with a variety of options.

Machine language   A particular language or code that can be directly interpreted by a machine.

Machine shorthand   A silent machine keyboarding system to rapidly record speeches, minutes, etc., at speeds up to 400 words per minute. Uses 23 keys and numeral bar printing in all caps on a continuous paper roll. Entire words can be keyboarded with a single stroke.

Machine transcription   To make a typewritten copy of dictated material using a transcribing machine. The distinctive feature of machine transcription is that the typist works not from visual materials, such as shorthand notes, but directly from sound (from a recording of someone else's voice).

Mag   Short form of the word magnetic.

Mag card   Computer-sized, plastic, magnetized media that are used to record and playback from magnetic keyboards (50 lines, 5000-character capacity).

Mag card exec   Magnetic keyboard that incorporates proportional lettering for quality correspondence.

Mag card/mag tape   Tape or card coated or impregnated with magnetic material on which information may be stored in the form of coded polarized spots.

Mag card II   Magnetic keyboard that incorporates the latest solid state technology.

Magnetic keyboard   (1) A device for recording alphanumeric characters on a magnetic tape or card, such as the IBM magnetic tape selectric typewriter or mag card selectric typewriter. (2) A device, commonly a word processing typewriter, which records keystrokes and editing changes on a magnetic medium.

Magnetic keyboard output   Playback of previously recorded typing from magnetic tape or card initiated by an operator or prerecorded command.

Magnetic media   Any of a wide variety of belts, cards, disks, or tapes coated or impregnated with magnetic material, for use with appropriate word processing equipment and on which dictation or keystrokes are recorded and stored.

Magnetic tape/selectric typewriter   *See* MT/ST.

Make ready, do, put away   The basic components that make up every job, i.e., preparation for the job and putting away materials after completing the job.

Manage   In an organizational setting, to mobilize resources for the achievement of a human purpose.

Manageability   The characteristic inherent in an organization that can be managed, believed to be related to complexity and size. For example, some commentators have questioned the manageability of large cities.

Management   The group of persons who manage an organization. Also the discipline concerned with understanding and improving the knowledge of how to manage.

Management by objective (MBO)   The approach to management that emphasizes the central role of objectives for each unit of an organization and for each individual contributor. The approach emphasizes self-control as a consequence of having clear objectives for each individual.

Management development   The means by which an organization contributes to the development of the managerial abilities of its management group.

Management information system (MIS)   A term created to describe a management's mechanisms for obtaining, processing, storing, retrieving, and using information, frequently suggesting the use of computers.

Management science The approach to management that emphasizes the application of scientific methods for the improved understanding and practice of management.

Managerial accounting The accounting done in a firm to produce reports that will contribute to management decisions. Contrasted with tax accounting or financial accounting.

Managerial economics (1) The subdivision of economics that emphasizes notions of direct relevance to managers. (2) Decisions such as investment and pricing decisions receive special attention.

Managers The people in an organization whose jobs include managing responsibilities.

Manual selector In telephone dictation, a connection method by which the handset is linked to an available recorder. The switching is done manually, in contrast to the automatic selector method.

Manual worker A worker whose primary contribution is a result of his or her muscle power and coordination.

Manufacturing business A business whose central role is to produce an item, the chemical industry for example. Manufacturing is frequently contrasted to retailing or to other service industries.

Marginal cost The cost of producing and selling an additional unit.

Marginal efficiencies Efficiencies that if adopted would make very small change in overall results.

Marginal revenue The revenue that would be produced by producing and selling an additional unit.

Market An area in which buyers and sellers may come together or an area of demand (however defined).

Market analysts Specialists who attempt to define, map, quantify, and develop information about markets.

Market research The research produced by market analysts.

Market standing The relative ranks of various firms in a single market, for example, first, second, etc.

Mass-distribution system A system for distributing goods or services to large numbers of customers who are dispersed within an area.

Mass-production system A system of production that is geared to produce large numbers of units.

Matrix organization A mode of organizing, especially of large technological projects, that includes persons having both task and function assignments and as a consequence being attached to two units of the organization at one time (with the possibility of having two bosses). The matrix is suggested by a diagram that has functional units across the top and task units down the side with entries indicating persons from various functions assigned to a given task.

Measure (1) A line standard usually expressed in terms of character units. (2) The unit value of line length.

Measured backspace In dictation equipment, a transcriber feature which provides a controlled repeat of recorded dictation each time the foot pedal is depressed.

Measured review Measured backspace.

Media (1) In general, the recording supplies, commonly magnetic-coated or of paper, used with word processing equipment (*see* Magnetic media). Common forms include paper tape; and magnetic belts, cards, disks, and tapes in cassettes or cartridges. (2) Vehicles for communication, for example television, radio, newspapers.

Medium (1) Singular form of the word media. (2) A paper or magnetic entity for recording used with a word processing device.

Memory Refers to a solid state computer buffer.

Merge (1) To combine, as in the automatic combination of information recorded on two tapes on the IBM magnetic tape selectric typewriter. (2) To combine in an arrangement according to some rule.

Microcassette Miniature cassette smaller than a minicassette.

Microfiche (Fiche) A sheet of film containing multiple microimages in a grid pattern. It usually contains identification information which can be read without magnification.

Microfilm (1) A fine-grained, high-resolution film containing an image greatly reduced in size from the original. (2) The recording of microphotographs on film. (3) Raw film with characteristics as in (1).

Micrographics Combines the science, the art, and the technology by which information can be quickly reduced to the medium of microfilm, stored conveniently, and then easily retrived for reference and use.

Middle managers Managers who occupy positions in the formal organization above first-line supervisors and below top management.

Minicassette Miniature cassette. Smaller than standard cassette but larger than microcassette.

Minimum profitability The least level of profitability a particular industry should accept in order to take the risk inherent in that industry.

Mode (1) The operating state of an automated unit. In word processing typewriters, modes include record and playback. (2) In telecommunications, the mode of transmission expresses the method of assembling and propagating digital pulses on a telephone line. The two major modes are asynchronous and synchronous. It directly influences the data transfer speed—the amount of information that can be pushed along the electronic pipeline.

Model A simplified replication of a problem situation that can be manipulated to explore the range and quality of solutions to the problem.

Modem Modulator-demodulator. A device that varies the characteristics of signals transmitted via communications facilities.

Module An interchangeable plug-in item or other building block for expanding capacity.

Moonlighters A slang term referring to members of the workforce who hold two different jobs.

Multifunction Ability to perform more than one function.

Multinational corporation A corporation that has significant production, markets, and operations in many countries.

Multiplier impact An impact that prompts multiple other impacts, as the multiplier impact of the building of infrastructure in a developing nation.

Multiproduct, multimarket, or multitechnology company A company that produces multiple products, operates in many markets, or employs a wide variety of technologies in its operations.

NWPM Net words per minute.

Net documents Number of pages typed excluding retypes.

Net lines Refers to finished lines of typing which are ready for dispatch or final disposition. Includes author corrections, also called net output.

Network analysis Analysis used in planning and scheduling, for example, critical path analysis.

Nonmanufacturing business A business whose primary function is selling or some business function.

Nonprofit organization An organization such as a university whose mission is other than to create a profit from its operations.

Nonselector In telephone dictation, a connection method which links various handsets to only one recorder. Thus, only one handset may access the recorder at any one time.

OCP Optical character printing.

OCR (Optical character recognition) A form of data input employing optical scanning equipment.

Objectives The levels of results to be sought within a specific time period.

Office environment Refers to physical furniture, furnishings, and design of office.

Office landscape A form of open-plan layout in which desks, files, screens, and plants are arrayed in nonrectilinear, free-standing clusters, for reasons of better communication and easier rearrangement.

Off-line Operating a peripheral device independent of a central processor.

One-for-one structure An office structure in which the secretary performs both administrative tasks and production tasks for a single boss.

One-to-one The traditional office staffing concept of one secretary to one executive.

Onion skin paper Lightweight stationery used to make carbon copies.

On-line Connected directly to a main processor through or by cable.

Open landscape Refers to office design in which there are no walls and partitions separating work areas.

Operations The activities associated with the production of current results. Frequently contrasted with the preparations for future business opportunities.

Operations manager A manager whose prime responsibility is in operations.

Operations research The discipline that studies the application of mathematical tools and logic to the solution of industrial problems.

Optimal solution A solution to a problem, usually using an operations research model.

Optimization The process of finding the optimal solution to a management problem, usually using an operations research model.

Organization chart Shows graphically the line of authority, span of control, and responsibility for work in each function or department.

Organization design The design principles incorporated in the formal organization of a company or the discipline that studies alternative ways to design organizations.

Organizational psychology The branch of psychology that studies human behavior in organizations, includes industrial psychology.

Original dictation Communications that are machine dictatable and original in content. In a word processing system, one of three forms in which work reaches a typing station.

Output (1) The final results after recorded input is processed, revised, and printed out. (2) The final documents or other information produced by an automated system. (3) That which results from a production process.

Output unit   A device such as a transcriber for producing material.
Output word processing equipment   Automated typing systems.

PABX, PBX   A central input word processing (dictation) system using telephone wiring and dial or Touch-Tone telephones. PABX (Private automatic branch exchange) is machinery which switches calls between the public telephone network and inside extensions. PBX (Private branch exchange) is, loosely, a switchboard with a human operator.
PERT (Project evaluation and review technique)   A method of planning and controlling complex projects.
Page   Messenger.
Page control   A word processing typewriter feature that causes pages to be numbered and ejected automatically during playout, thus reducing the need for human monitoring.
Paper tape   A recording medium used by certain word processing typewriters and photocomposition systems. Punched perforations carry the coding. Normally codes are recorded at ten to the inch at a cost of approximately three cents per thousand characters.
Paragraph indent   Standard measure of indention used to mark paragraphs or other indented material.
Participative management   An approach to improving management practice that emphasizes participation of all impacted parties in decisions.
Partnership   A mode of legally structuring a business that includes specifications of each partner's role and responsibility.
Patch cord   A wire or cable for connecting two pieces of audio equipment.
Patching   A method of transferring previously recorded material onto another medium.
Pause control   A control feature on some dictation recorders which enables the tape to be stopped temporarily without switching from the play or record settings.
Payback period   The period required for the proceeds from an investment to equal the amount invested.
Payroll   The business function that calculates the amount due each employee and conveys those funds to the employee by check or alternative means.
Pension   A regular amount received by a retired employee based on certain payments made by employer and/or employee during the employee's working years.
Pension fund   The invested proceeds of the funds contributed by an employer and/or employees for the purpose of paying pensions.
Performance   Actual results obtained. Sometimes used to denote the achievement of positive results.
Peripheral equipment   (1) In data processing and word processing, accessory units which work in conjunction with a large central unit but are not part of it. (2) Units, such as input/output terminals, which work in conjunction with a major systems component such as a CPU.
Personal income   Wages and salaries paid to individuals. Frequently contrasted with investment income.
Personnel administration   The management role concerned with the hiring and training of employees and with keeping employee records.
Personnel appraisal   The evaluation of employees' performance and interaction between a boss and subordinate to discuss the subordinate's performance and

future objectives, a process frequently discussed in conjunction with management by objectives.

Personnel department   The unit of an organization that performs the personnel administration role.

Personnel management   The management of the firm's human resources. Sometimes called human resources management.

Photocomposition   A form of text production in which each character is exposed photographically on light-sensitive paper, which is then developed to become a reproduction-quality proof.

Photoelectric reader   A light-sensitive reader device used on tape-driven power typewriters.

Pica   (1) The larger of two common typewriter typeface sizes, the smaller being elite. (2) A standard of typewriter spacing, ten characters to the horizontal inch, also called ten pitch.

Pilot-plant   A plant built to test a new process, usually on a scale much less than that proposed for subsequent implementation. Frequently a pilot-plant test of a process, if successful, will suggest ways to improve the larger facility to be built later.

Pin feed   Term applied to typewriter platens having sprocketlike end pieces which help convey continuous forms through the unit.

Pin-feed platen   A typewriter platen having sprocket-like pins for feeding continuous forms through a typewriter.

Planned obsolescence   An approach to design that utilizes the expectation that the product design will become out of vogue before the product itself is physically unuseable; the approach includes subsequent designs that are intended to make previous designs unfashionable. Also, the design of products to become obsolete earlier than necessary in order to be able to introduce new designs.

Planning assumptions or hypotheses   Assumptions or hypotheses used in plans.

Planning-programming-budgeting system (PPBS)   A comprehensive planning methodology utilized by some public agencies.

Plant   The facilities that a firm can use for production.

Playback   (1) The process of listening to recorded dictation. (2) The automatic typing out of recorded text.

Policy   A definite course of action based on a principle or procedure.

Power keyboard   A term referring to the family of automatic or text editing typewriter equipment.

Power typing   (1) An application of magnetic media typewriters which increases productivity by allowing a typist to type at maximum or rough-draft speed without concern for errors. These are corrected by backspacing and retyping over the errors to produce a perfect recording on a magnetic tape cartridge from which an error-free document is automatically printed out. (2) Automatic typing that is essentially repetitive and involving only minimal text editing.

Precon tape   Two-program tape with standard instructions to condition composer and other systems to accept and obey keyboard or tape codes to achieve desired playback of final copy.

Prefix   A coded signal to a word processing typewriter console to accept a subsequent coded signal.

Preparation   Includes handling paper, loading the recording media, console preparation, and typewriter preparation (tabs, margins, margin resets) prior to typing.

Prerecorded   Material stored on magnetic media for repetitive use, such as standard paragraphs or form letters. In a word processing system, it is one of the forms in which work is kept at a typing station.

Principal   An individual within an organization who originates paperwork and requires secretarial support. An executive; a word originator.

Principal-oriented   Term applied to administrative support operations in which aides perform many tasks for a few specific individuals, as distinct from an activity-oriented arrangement in which aides handle a few specific tasks for many individuals.

Principal-to-secretary ratio   A numerical expression of the number of principals served by one secretary. A four-to-one ratio means one secretary serves four principals.

Printer   That unit which types out the page—a typewriter or a line printer.

Printwheel   A typing element, daisy-like or cylindrical in shape, used on certain word processing typewriters and printer units.

Probability mathematics   A subdivision of mathematics that is concerned with modeling situations with outcomes that have relative likelihoods of occurence.

Procedures manual   Guide used by users of and technicians in a word processing center setting forth a step-by-step process for completing a particular job.

Process industry   An industry that neither manufactures nor provides an intangible service; rather it subjects certain resources to a process, for example, the oil-refining industry.

Process technician   Title used for person involved in typing production on a magnetic keyboard in a word processing center.

Producing capital   Capital invested in the land, buildings, and equipment used to produce the product or service.

Productivity   The relative output for given levels of input, especially the production per production employee. The continuing challenge is to improve productivity.

Product lines   The various basic categories and subcategories of products produced or provided.

Product manager   A managerial role that has responsibility for coordinating all of the activities that affect the results produced from the assigned product. Such a manager might coordinate all of production, advertising, selling, and distributing.

Product mix   The variety of products offered by one company.

Profit centers   In large multidivision companies, profits may be calculated in various subdivisions of the company to add up to the overall profit; compare with cost centers. A manager in charge of a profit center (one of the subdivisions) has profit and loss responsibility.

Program   A set of machine instructions for the operation of automated equipment such as computers and word processing typing systems.

Programmed search   The automatic finding of various segments of prerecorded material, or media, for playout in some predetermined sequence.

Programmer   A person who creates computer programs.

Project evaluation and review technique   *See* PERT.

Proofreading   Reading copy to detect and mark errors to be corrected.

Proportional spacing   A typewriter feature whereby alphanumeric characters are given horizontal spacing proportionate to their natural space requirements.

Proprietor   The sole owner and manager of a small business.

Protocol   A procedure or predetermined sequence of signal exchanges that control the transmission between different devices. Protocols are frequently named after the devices most commonly associated with them such as the 2741 protocol originated with the IBM 2741 terminal, while TTY protocol refers to teletype equipment.

Prototype   A model of a potential new product, used to evaluate the product's prospects.

Public-service institutions   Institutions such as government and nonprofit institutions which exist to provide a service in a nonprofit manner.

Punch   A device which punches holes into paper tape or cards in accord with a program. These holes are then usually sensed electronically with wire brushes, metal fingers, or photocells and converted into signals that represent alphanumerics.

Punched paper tape   A strip of paper on which characters are represented by combinations of holes punched across the strip.

Purchasing power   The ability a person or a group of people has to purchase goods and services because of its income.

Qualitative factors   Factors to be incorporated in decisions that cannot be quantified, such as values and beliefs.

Quality control   (1) A check on work to keep a uniform quality and appearance, always striving to standardize where possible. (2) The production function that sets quality standards and monitors the production process to insure that the process yields goods meeting the established standards.

Quality of life   The qualitative assessment of the relative quality of living conditions, including attention to pollutants, noise, aesthetics, complexity.

Queueing theory   The branch of management science that uses models of waiting-lines to approximate certain industrial problem situations.

Qwerty keyboard   The current typewriter keyboard which remains unchanged since produced by Christopher Lathan Sholes in 1873. So named after the top lefthand row of alphabetic keys. This keyboard arrangement was specially designed to deliberately impede typing.

RAM   Random access memory.

RCR   Required carrier return.

RMN   Abbreviation for remote microphone network.

ROM   Read-only memory.

Random access   In data processing and word processing, a storage technique in which the time required to obtain information in memory is relatively independent of the location of the information most recently obtained. Disks are generally regarded as randomly accessible media, in contrast to tape, which is serial.

Random assembly   A word processing typewriter feature which eases the production of documents by automatically putting together parts from separately recorded material. Also called *Programmed search.*

Reader   A projection device for viewing an enlarged microimage with the unaided eye.

Ready tone (Talk-down tone)   The talk-down or subjective telephone tone which indicates to the user that he or she has seized a recorder and it is ready to accept his or her dictation.

Receivables   An accounting term denoting the amounts owed the company.

Record   (1) To capture on a medium such things as the speech of dictation or the keystrokes entered into a word processing typing system. (2) To log data or other notation on a document, such as a business form, for purposes of control and evaluation. (3) That which is written to perpetuate a knowledge of events. (4) A document, form, or other paper containing information for the control of business operations. (5) In general, any of the encoded media used in word processing, such as belts, cards, and cassettes.

Recorder   In a dictation system, the unit which transfers the dictation onto a medium.

Reference code   (1) An electronically recorded magnetic tape indexing point. (2) Loosely, any indexing signal, regardless of medium.

Regulation   Governmental action sanctioned by law to control business behavior.

Repeat code   Functional code that allows repetition of material previously played out.

Repetitive typing   Documents, such as form letters, that are typed over and over again usually for mass distribution.

Reprographics   Refers to the reproduction and duplication of documents, written materials, drawings, designs by photocopy, offset printing, microfilming, office duplicating.

Reserves   Monies held out of use by a company to meet certain demands or serve designated purposes, for example reserves for the replacement of worn out equipment.

Response time   The time a system takes to react to a given input.

Result-producing activities   Activities that produce measurable results that can be related, directly or indirectly, to the results and performance of the entire enterprise. Among result-producing activities are revenue-producing activities such as selling, nonrevenue activities such as manufacturing (result contributing activities), and information activities.

Return on investment (ROI)   The ratio of the amount earned per year to the amount invested in a particular project or business (stated as a percentage).

Reverse index   Optional feature that allows indexing one-half line up or one-half line down. Used for superscripts or subscripts.

Reverse search   Electronic searching in either direction for reference points on magnetic-tape text-editing typewriters.

Revision cycle   Path of a typed document from initial keyboarding to final output.

Revision work   (1) The typing of corrections and editing changes at some point after the original keyboarding of a document. (2) The final playout of a document.

Ripple   Term used to describe the ability of mag card II and the memory typewriter to playout at a predetermined automatic line length.

Robot typer   A unit which usually operates an electric typewriter from a piano roll device.

Rough draft speed   Term used to describe the fastest speed that a center technician can type.

SAH   (1) Standard average hour. (2) Standard allowed hours.

SP   One typewriter space.

Scanning   (1) The rapid listening to recorded dictation to locate a specific part. (2) Optical scanning; OCR; a form of data input in which an electronic device reads the marks or characters on a document. (3) Function of mag card II that allows movement through total memory without printing until a stop code, page end code, or a line count is read.

Scientific management   The approach to management fathered by Frederick W. Taylor. Its core is the organized study of work, the analysis of work into its simplest elements, and the systematic improvement of the worker's performance of each of these elements, resulting in higher levels of output per worker.

Sealed system   Usually used in reference to a continuous loop dictation recorder system.

Search   The function of a word processing typewriter in which specific material is located on a magnetic tape, (*See* Global search.)

Secretarial support center   (1) A secretarial group performing all secretarial activities, including typing. (2) In some contexts, an administrative center.

Secretary   (1) One entrusted with the secrets or confidences of a superior; one employed to handle correspondence and manage routine and detail work for a superior. (2) In word processing/administrative services systems, a title sometimes assigned, along with prefixes such as word processing or administrative, to the typists as specialists within the system.

Secretary, Administrative   A specialist who supports principals with activities other than typing, such as mail handling, filing, phoning, and special projects. An administrative support aide; the individual who provides administrative support for management or professional personnel.

Secretary, Correspondence   An individual primarily responsible for transcribing dictation and producing documents on a word processing typewriter; a word processing operator.

Seize   To electronically connect with a dictation recorder.

Selector   In private-wire data entry systems, a device which connects the user's handset to the centralized recording equipment. *See also* Automatic selectors; Manual selector; and Nonselector.

Selectric   A typewriter that uses an interchangeable golf-ball typing element that spins and rotates when typing.

Self-logging   A worker's record of his or her own tasks and the time required to do them.

Service industries   Industries whose primary output is not the provision of a manufactured product. Such industries are generally contrasted with manufacturing industries.

Service institutions   Organizations constituted to perform a public task not involving the production of a product. The service is provided in a nonprofit mode. Examples include the postal service, educational institutions, and utility districts.

Shared logic   Term applied to a type of text-editing system in which several keyboard terminals simultaneously use the memory and processing powers of a single central processing unit.

Shield   A piece of plastic or cardboard used to prevent smudges when erasing on original copies.

Shift   A typewriter key which activates the typing mechanism to print either in capitals or lower-case characters.

Shift key   A typewriter key which activates lowering or raising the type case to print in capitals or otherwise.

Shutdown   After the originator has completed his or her dictation and hangs up, it takes anywhere from one minute to three and a half minutes for the connector to disconnect from the telephone line. The telephone company can adjust the length of shutdown time by installing a special feature called calling party disconnect, which will significantly reduce the disconnect time. Shutdown can be a very important facet, depending upon the application for the recording and the volume of dictation.

Simplified letter   Letter style created by the Administrative Management Society characterized by (a) extreme block form with date at the top at the extreme lefthand margin, (b) name and address in block form for use with window envelope, (c) omission of formal salutation and complimentary close, and (d) simplified language and content of letter.

Simulated decentralization   A mode of organizing large companies that are too big to remain functionally organized and too integrated to be genuinely decentralized. One function or segment is treated as if it were an autonomous business relating to other units as if in an actual marketplace. The mode is typical in the materials, computer, chemical, and pharmaceutical industries.

Simulation   (1) A management assessment technique in which mathematical models or formulas are used as test substitutes for real-life situations. (2) In the testing of data processing programs, a technique in which specific software substitutes for the actual use of terminals and lines.

Single element   Term applied to a typing mechanism in which all print characters are contained on a single unit, such as a printwheel or selectric golf ball.

Skip   A text-editing feature used in playback mode to skip or delete printout of a specific character, word, line.

Slave   An output unit operating in parallel with and controlled by the coded tape or electronic signal of a master unit.

Social impacts   The societal consequences of actions that go beyond the consequences that are the action's reason for being.

Social psychology   The branch of psychology concerned with human behavior in groups. The behavior of the individual in the group and the behavior of the group as a group are studied with the expectation that the results may be applied to improve individual and group performance.

Social responsibility   An institution's obligations to the society in which it resides. Recent discussions have highlighted differing points of view about what these obligations are.

Software   All materials needed to control and operate the hardware of an automated system, such as flowcharts, manuals, programs, routines. Any of the specially prepared programs or routines designed to optimize the operation of a computer.

Sound-on-sound   A method by which previously recorded material may be rerecorded while at the same time adding new material to it.

Sound sheets   A flat, magnetic vinyl dictation recording medium.

Span of control   Refers to the number of employees who are directly supervised by one person.

Specialist   A person who performs one specific task.

Special request   A category of communications in a word processing system which is original in content and whose format, content, or design precludes machine dictation; synonymous with hard copy input.

Speculations   Investments that have high likelihoods of failure but promise huge returns if successful.

Speed   In telecommunications, speed is the number of bits per second. Common phone lines can handle up to 4800 bits per second.

Split keyboarding   Keyboarding and editing on one unit and playing back on another.

Squeal   Noise caused by sticking and release of tape.

Staff   Individual contributors who advise or counsel rather than directly manage a group of people. Such persons are often contrasted with line managers.

Staffing   The management function that recruits, places, and trains the firm's resources.

Standalone   Term applied to a word processing typewriter or typing system that is self-contained, i.e., not connected to other systems or system components.

Standard   The time allowed an individual to satisfactorily complete an activity.

Station   (1) The receptacle of a magnetic tape word processing typewriter in which cartridges or cassettes are placed for recording and playback. More precisely, the record/playback drive mechanism of an editing typewriter; the MT/ST Model 4 has two stations. (2) In telecommunications, any of the input/output points in a system, such as an individual telephone extension or a teletypewriter terminal.

Stat typing   Priority typing.

Stenographer   A writer of shorthand; one employed chiefly to take and transcribe dictation.

Stenotype   A silent machine keyboarding system to rapidly record speeches, minutes, etc., at speeds up to 400 words per minute. Uses 23 keys and numeral bar printing in all caps, on a continuous paper roll. Entire words can be keyboarded with a single stroke.

Stop   (1) A code recorded on a medium which instructs a word processing typewriter to halt at some point during playback. (2) A word processing typewriter key which, when hit, encodes stop instructions or halts action directly.

Stop code (SC)   Functional code on magnetic keyboards that when read will stop playback at that point to enable insertion of variable material.

Storable   The portion of a prerecorded document that is not subject to change. Examples are the format of a will or the body of form letters.

Strategic planning   The planning for a company's long-term future that includes the setting of major overall objectives, the determination of the basic approaches to be used in pursuing these objectives, and the means to be used in obtaining the necessary resources to be employed.

Strategy   A company's basic approach to achieving its overall objectives. For example, Sears' early strategy was to become a major supplier of products to the rural population by means of mail-order sales utilizing attractive catalogues and efficient mail-order factories (order processing and shipping facilities).

Stroke counter   A device fitted on the typewriter that counts every key depression that is made. While this method is useful as a supplement to other methods, complete reliance on it demands very strict staff supervision for it is obviously easy to falsify results.

Structure   The arrangement of processes and functions within the company as regards their relationships to each other. The methods used vary including the functional approach, decentralization, simulated decentralization, and matrix forms.

Subjective tone   A telephone talkdown tone signal which indicates to the user that he or she has seized a recorder and it is waiting to accept dictation.

Subordinate   A person who reports to a particular manager is said to be one of that manager's subordinates. Thus each line manager except the chief executive both has subordinates and is a subordinate.

Successor   The person who is appointed to a managerial position immediately after another person leaves the position is called the departing person's successor. The question of who the successors for top positions are to be frequently has great impact on a company's chances of success.

Supervisor   A person who has responsibility for directing the activities of a group of employees.

Supervisor's console   Usually refers to a panel from which tank recorder dictation can be manually or automatically distributed.

Support activities   Support activities include conscience activities (staff), and such functions as legal counsel, labor-relations activities. They are compared to result-producing activities, hygiene and housekeeping activities, and top-management activities.

Supporting capital   Working capital, that is, capital used to bring goods and services to market or to finance the time between their production and the time the buyer pays. Frequently contrasted with producing capital.

Support requirements   The secretarial assistance required by a principal.

Surplus   Profits and other savings that successful performance can produce.

Switch (Switch code)   An instruction to a two-station word processing typewriter console to selectively play material from one medium and then switch to the second one and play.

Synchronous   A mode of transmitting communications that is a stream of many characters, or a block. This block is sent along telephone lines with single stop and start characters bracketing the entire block of information. This increases the load factor and efficiency of data transmission. It is used for higher speed data transfer.

System   An assembly of components united by some form of regulated interaction to form an organized whole. The operations and procedures, personnel and equipment through which a business activity is carried on.

Systems approach   The examination of an overall situation or problem with the aim of devising a total solution, as opposed to dealing with the separate functions which comprise the whole.

System thinking   Analysis that uses systems and their dynamics to examine problems and possible solutions.

TIS (Tone input system)   Telephone input processing system that utilizes either a Touch-Tone phone or a dial phone with a Touch-Tone pad or an individual input device to a central recording system.

TMC (Telephone message coupler)   Interface equipment connecting recorders to telephone lines. Allows recording from any telephone in the world.

T/S   Time sharing.

T/W   Typewriter.

TWX   Teletypewriter exchange service.

TAB   (1) Short for tabulator, the typewriter key which controls space indentation. (2) The act of operating the tab key. (3) Predetermined indention. (4) Term applied to typing work involving heavy tabulation, such as statistical work or multicolumned text. (5) In dictating equipment, sometimes a reference to the indexing slip on a recorder.

Tab grid   Preset series of indentions (e.g., every five spaces).

Talkdown tone   In telephone dictation, whistlelike tone which tells the user that he/she has seized a recorder and that it is ready to take his/her dictation; also reminds users to speak up when dictating. A subjective tone.

Tank recorder   An endless-loop dictation system.

Task data sheet   A record of jobs by time period during a single work day.

Task force   A group assigned to accomplish a task. Committees may limit their attentions to making recommendations, while task forces are expected to perform a job.

Task list   A detailed record of each type of work performed by each worker and the average number of hours spent performing it per week.

Team organization   A mode of organization that creates and disbands teams for a succession of projects that constitute the majority of a firm's business.

Tech III ribbon   Advanced carbon film ribbon developed by IBM that reduces ribbon changes on the magnetic keyboard used in conjunction with a coverup tape.

Technology   A way or means to accomplish a task. The technology may or may not include the use of machines.

Technology assessment   The function of trying to determine the impacts of utilizing a particular technology in advance of its introduction. Proponents argue that technology assessment is possible, and Congress has established an office to do technology assessment. Opponents argue that it is impossible to assess technology in advance of its introduction.

Technology monitoring   Following the impacts of a technology as it is introduced in order to identify and combat the harmful impacts, if any. This process is recommended by some who think that technology assessment is difficult if not impossible.

Telecommunications   The transmission of information between widely separated locations by means of electrical or electromagnetic systems such as telephone or telegraph.

Telephone message coupler   Interface equipment which connects data entry to telephone lines and allows recording from any telephone in the world. The term is loosely interchangeable with recorder coupler and trunk link.

Teleprocessing   A form of information handling in which a word processing or data processing system utilizes communication facilities.

Teletype   Trademark of Teletype Corporation, usually applied to a series of different teleprinter units such as tape punches, reperforators, page printers, and keyboard terminals used in hard-copy communication systems.

Teletypewriter   Generic term for teleprinters and keyboard terminals used in hard-copy communication systems, but distinct from communicating word processing typewriters, which possess a wide range of text-editing capabilities not found in teletypewriters.

Teletypewriter exchange service (TWX)   A public switched service of Western Union in which suitably arranged teletypewriter stations are provided with lines to a central office for access to other such stations throughout the United States, Canada, and Mexico.

Telex   A dial-up teleprinter service of Western Union comparable to TWX, but with separate rates and certain operating differences, which enables subscribers to communicate directly and temporarily among themselves, and also with TWX users, throughout the United States, Canada, and Mexico.

Ten pitch   Term applied to typewriter spacing of ten characters per horizontal inch. Also known as pica spacing.

Terminal   (1) Any device capable of sending and/or receiving information over a communications channel. (2) In data processing and word processing, an input/output device. (3) In word processing, often a reference to a communicating typewriter.

Text   (1) The actual matter of an author's work. (2) The main body of matter on a typed or printed page, as distinct from illustrations and marginal matter. (3) Broadly, the output of a word processing system.

Text editing   An application of magnetic media typewriters which speeds retyping of revised texts. The typist keyboards only new material and instructs the machine to skip unwanted text already recorded. The revised document is then played out automatically from the magnetic tape cartridge or other medium.

Text editor   A word processing typewriter; one that records or captures keystrokes on a medium and that has the ability to make additions, deletions, corrections, and format changes in the recorded text prior to automatic playout of finished documents. Text-editing typewriters may be either interactive or standalone.

Theory X and Theory Y   Theories about human behavior formulated by Douglas McGregor. Theory X assumes that people are lazy, dislike and shun work, and have to be driven. It assumes that most people are incapable of taking responsibility for themselves and have to be looked after. Theory Y assumes that people have a psychological need to work and that they desire achievement and responsibility and will find them under the right conditions.

Thesaurus   A dictionary of synonyms and antonyms.

Throughput   The complicated cycle of a document from thought origination through typing and distribution.

Time and motion studies   Methods first promoted by the scientific management school. They include the study of physical work using stopwatches in order to break a task into segments that are redesigned in order to be performed more readily so that the productivity of the job is improved.

Time-sharing   (1) Splitting personnel or equipment, according to need, in two or more areas. (2) A method of arranging the operating characteristics of a computer so that several users can be working on it at the same time. The term also refers to computing that a person does while the computer is set up in this way.

Time sharing service bureau   An organization which sells the use of its computers, i.e., sells data processing time.

Tone control   A dictation equipment feature used to vary treble and bass response during playback.

Top-management activity   Activity that is to accomplish the top management tasks, which include thinking through the mission of the business, setting of standards, building and maintenance of the human organization, major relations that only the people at the top of a business can establish and maintain, ceremonial functions, and the provision of an organ to respond to major crises.

Touch control   A device which adjusts the pressure of a typewriter keyboard to suit the operator.

Touch-Tone   A Bell System trademark applied to the ten-key panel on a pushbutton phone.

Touch typing   The skill of typing without looking at the keys.

Track   The path of magnetic tape or card along which a single channel of sound or codes is recorded.

Trade associations   Organizations that bring the companies of an industry together for the purpose of exchanging information and jointly promoting the interests of the industry.

Traditional secretary   A pre-word processing secretary; one employed as a general-purpose assistant to an executive, to handle correspondence, phone calls, errands, and other random tasks, in contrast to an administrative or correspondence secretary.

Transcribe   To convert recorded dictation into a typed document or other form of hard copy.

Transcription   Conversion by a secretary of recorded dictation to hard copy.

Transcriptionist   One who transcribes dictated or recorded material; a correspondence secretary or word processing operator.

Transfer   To copy material from one medium to another.

Transport   The mechanism that moves or drives a recording medium in data entry or word processing equipment.

Trunk   Telephone line.

Trunk link   A type of interface system which permits phone company telephones to give instruction to centralized dictation equipment by converting rotary (dial) or Touch-Tone signals into commands such as record and play back.

Tuning   Alignment of a sound head with the track on the recording medium.

Turnaround   Time consumed from origination to completion.

Turnaround time   Elapsed time between dispatch and receipt of material back at the starting point.

Turnover   Refers to the frequency of replacing employees.

Twelve pitch   Term applied to typewriter spacing of twelve characters per horizontal inch. Also known as elite spacing.

Typebar   (1) Term applied to typewriters having a conventional basket typing mechanism, with one capital and lower-case character pair per keybar. (2) An individual typing element in the basketed set.

Typewriter button   Mode button on mag card II or memory typewriter that allows activation or deactivation of the memory.

Typewriter spacing   Term used to describe the vertical format of six lines to an inch on a standard spacing keyboard.

Typing element   The unit which produces a character or characters of typing by striking on paper through an inked ribbon. Individual typebars, printwheels, and selectric "golf balls" are all typing elements.

Typing mechanism   Generally the subassembly within a typewriter that includes both the typing element (or elements) and the linkages which position and power its (their) strike.

Typing station   An individual work station at which documents are typed.

Unaffected correspondence   Correspondence expressed in hours of work, which will not be completed on magnetic keyboard equipment for word processing/administrative services record-keeping purposes.

Underscoring   In word processing typewriters, the automatic underlining of designated words and phrases.

Understaffing   Providing fewer employees than necessary to handle a given workload.

Union   An organization that brings workers in a trade or industry together for the purpose of bargaining collectively for improved wages, benefits, and working conditions.

Union relations   The business function of conducting interactions with the unions to which a company's employees belong.

Unit   In proportionally spaced typing, an arbitrary size value assigned to every character.

Unit sets   Preassembled packets with interleaved one-time carbons or carbonless paper.

Unity of command   A management notion emphasized by early thinkers. The concept states that each employee should have one and only one boss.

Unloading   The act of rewinding a magnetic tape into its cartridge and removing it from an automatic typewriter.

Upper case   (1) The capital letters of type, in contrast to small letters or lower case. (2) Typing done all in capital letters.

User's manual   A book of instructions issued to work originators outlining procedures for proper dictation and setting forth other document, style, and word processing standards used in the organization.

Utility   The usefulness or inherent value of something as perceived by an individual or an organization. A branch of economics tries to empirically measure and compare utilities.

Utility specialist   Title used for person totally trained on all functions performed in a word processing center and designated as supervisory backup.

Utility typing   Short, out-of-the-ordinary typing tasks not sent to the word processing center, but handled more or less informally by administrative services personnel.

VSC (Variable speed control)   Used in voice compression machines.

VU meter   Volume unit meter used in recorders. Indicates audio-frequency levels. Generally used to monitor recording levels to maintain them within the distortion limits of the tape.

Variable   A segment of a prerecorded document that is subject to change. Examples would be the name and address listings that are merged with form letters, or the specificic information that is merged to produce a complete will or other legal document.

Variable costs   Costs of a production process that vary with the level of production.

Varityper   A direct impression composition device. Type sizes generally range from six to twelve points.

Velocity   Speed and force at which the typing element strikes the platen.

Voice bank   A recorder system whereby spoken material can be stored and easily accessed for reference.

Voice compression   A device that compresses speech into a shorter time interval than the original recording.

Voice guard   A dictation equipment feature which sends a loud, steady tone over the phone if the recording medium is not moving.

Voice-operated relay   A device in central dictation systems which activates the recorder when it senses that voice sounds are coming over the line, and stops the process when only silence fills the line. The VOR thus eliminates long pauses during playback and transcription.

WATS (Wide Area Telephone Service)   A United States telephone company service which permits a customer to dial an unlimited number of calls in a specific area for a flat monthly charge.

WP/AS   Word processing and administrative support.

WPC   Word processing center.

WPM   Words per minute.

Wage and salary administration   The business function that determines wage and salary rates and adjusts them in response to market conditions and changed assignments.

Window envelopes   Envelopes designed so that the inside address of the letter appears through the window and the envelope does not need to be addressed.

Word count   A count of the volume of work of an employee.

Word originator   (1) A principal; an executive. (2) A person who dictates copy for transcription into final documents. (3) In general, an individual within an organization who originates paperwork and requires secretarial support.

Word processing   (1) The combination of people, procedures and equipment that transforms ideas into printed communications and helps facilitate the flow of related office work; design, implementation, and management of an organization's resource to achieve clerical and administrative productivity objectives. (2) Word processing is a method of producing written communication at top speed, with the greatest accuracy, the least effort, and the lowest possible cost through the combined use of proper procedures, automated business equipment, and trained personnel.

Word processing center   (1) The room or area housing equipment and personnel for the production of typed documents. (2) The centralized location in which word processing operations take place.

Word processing system (WPS)   The combination of specific procedures, methods, equipment, and people designed to accomplish the transition of a written, verbal, or recorded work and distribution to its ultimate user.

Word processing systems manager   The individual who has responsibility for conducting a word processing study and implementing and managing the word processing system.

Word processor   A text-editing typewriter; one that records or captures keystrokes on a medium, and that has the ability to make additions, deletions, corrections, and format changes in the recorded text prior to automatic playout of finished documents. Word processing typewriters may be either interactive or standalone.

Words   Commercial schools usually express typing speeds in words, a word being five strokes (periods and spaces), so that a person typing 40 words per minute is considered to have struck 200 characters in one minute. It is not considered a suitable measurement.

Work distribution   The manner in which the work is distributed among those who perform that work.

Work distribution chart   A consolidation of task and activity lists to show what a department does and how each employee fits into the department's activities.

Workflow   Path from start to finish of a task.

Work group   A cluster of personnel who work together to perform certain work.

Working capital   Supporting capital.

Work measurement   A process of determining how much time is required to do a given amount of work.

Work sampling   A work measurement technique which determines the amount of time spent performing various activities by random sampling.

Work simplification   A planned approach to simplifying tasks and thus increasing production per workhour.

Work station   (1) An identifiable work area for one person. (2) In an office, a desk and the associated furnishings required for a worker to accomplish assigned responsibilities.

Wow   In dictation equipment, a relatively slow, periodic variation in tape speed affecting pitch.

Writing line   The maximum horizontal space within which a typewriter will print.

Index